ONCE, WHEN I WAS TREE

and other true stories

MAYA WYLD

(MAYA MELISSA "THE BOBCAT" WYLD)

To all my Relations.

To the Spirits of the Land,
the Trees, the Plants,
the Two-Leggeds, the Four-Leggeds,
the Winged Ones, the Finned,
the Crawlers, and the Allies
in this Realm and Others.

To Aya, La Abuela
for opening the door.

To Jaguar
for walking me home.

To Cacao and Hongos
for financing this literary adventure.

To Pachamama,
for trusting me
with her stories.

Thank you,
Thank you,
Thank you.

Aho.

TABLE OF CONTENTS

NOTE TO THE READER

Heads up:

 This is a book of true stories. As true as stories can be, having passed through the filters of memory, time, and the shape-shifting nature of reflection.

Although it begins with a girl talking to trees, *Once, When I Was Tree* is not for sensitive or young audiences.

Some stories move through trauma, grief, and loss—both personal and ecological. Others challenge accepted paradigms, explore altered states of consciousness, and dive into psychedelic journeys.

Some of these journeys were supported by sacred medicines—in particular *Pcylocybe cubensis* (magic mushrooms) and *Banisteriopsis caapi* (Ayahuasca)—used with intention, reverence, and respect.

If you're ready to walk through both beauty and darkness, speak with plants and allies, and remember what it means to listen deeply—then this book is for you.

Welcome!

The shape of this book is not linear—it builds like a spider web mandala, spun from the edges inward. Each story is a thread, pulled from different times and places in my life and woven through common themes.

Once Jaguar joins the dance, the weave tightens. The web gives way to a current, forward-moving, with no turning back. From that point on, the stories unfold sequentially in linear time.

So take your time. Or dive in. But know this: nothing here is fiction. And nothing is here by accident—not even you.

Part 1

TREES

Chapter 1
Mimosa

Houaïlou, New Caledonia - 1977 to 1980

When did it all begin—this business of talking to trees and plants? Maybe I was born with it, a gift from another life. Or maybe it began right there, with the buffalo grass tickling my belly, waiting for the school bus to rattle down the gravel road to my dad's gas station.

"Hi, Mimosa. Good morning." Mimosa was my best friend—maybe my only true friend, aside from Dad, but that suited me just fine. On school days, I always left the house early and ran down, legs pumping, to greet her. I tossed my school bag aside and plopped down onto the patch of grass by the road, right next to her.

Have you ever spoken with Mimosa? If you lean in close and speak to her, your breath will brush over her tiny leaves, and she'll close, just like that. She's a sensitive plant. And if you're a seven-year-old, that's proof enough that she's smart, and listening.

But the greeting was only the beginning. Mimosa and I had a whole morning ritual.

I trailed my fingers slowly, lightly caressing each leaf along her stem. One breath of anticipation and, just as slowly,

Mimosa closed her leaves in the exact order I'd touched them. Closed but not forgotten. If I waited just a moment, she reopened, patient and ready to play again.

This time, I touched only the leaf at the very tip, testing her. What would she do?

She brought the two nearest leaves together, paused, then closed the next two, gradually and elegantly. She didn't close the third row though; she waited for me. And I waited for her. When she reopened, I touched her leaves in random bursts, like a chaotic child. Ha, but Mimosa was too wise to fall for my silly games. With her quiet grace, she closed the whole branch at once, as if to say "That's enough now." She reopened much more slowly this time, and I knew that whether I tickled, caressed, or tapped her, she wouldn't close again.

That's how she was. She humored me, but she was a plant after all—a poised being deserving of respect, not a toy planted in the grass for my entertainment.

I brought my hands under me and just watched her sway in the breeze. She was resting now. But I knew the next day, after the sun had revived her, we'd play again.

Mimosa wasn't my only plant friend. New Caledonia, jutting out in the middle of the Pacific Ocean, far from all other lands, sure grew strange creatures and plants in the folds of her thick forest.

Up the hill from my parents' house, in the red nickel dirt where my bare feet knew every rock, lived the strange and wondrous creatures of my childhood. Long-antennaed beetles, glistening with colors like jewels, stick-like insects that moved like living twigs, furry jumping spiders, giant flying cockroaches, deafeningly loud cicadas—and the fierce carnivorous plants that feasted on them.

Sundew, with her sticky, glutinous red hairs, was more of an acquaintance; I personally never fed her. I watched too many flies and beetles drawn by her deceptive nectar only to get trapped as her leaves curled tightly around them. Their frantic buzzing and flailing was in vain. Sundew was fatal. My heart always ached a little watching insects die such a slow, horrible death. Thank God I was tall, and she was small.

If I'd been a fly, I'd much rather have died in a pitcher plant. Unlike the sundew, the pitcher plant simply sat and waited like a shapely vase, delicately tucked under her own lid, glistening with sweet nectar.

But she wouldn't need to lure insects today. A lost fly, confused by the solid glass of my bedroom window, had buzzed in vain, trying to get out. She barely twitched now and would die soon anyway. I pressed my hands to the pane, carefully closing in, and trapped the fly within my palms. I ran up the hill, awkwardly cradling the fly toward one of the patient vases I knew. I dropped to my knees beside the pitcher plant and hesitated. I'd never seen her move but wasn't convinced she couldn't. What if, one day, she snapped her lid shut and caught my finger, digesting it along with her meal?

I approached the plant's lid slowly. The trick with feeding her was in the precision of the opening—just a fly-sized gap between my palms. Too wide, and the prey would escape; too tight, and perhaps I risked a finger. And if she ever got me, it would almost have seemed fair, given how many meals I'd teased her with while perfecting my feeding technique.

I nudged my hands against her lid and lips and opened just a fly-sized exit. The fly buzzed straight to the bottom of her vase, and that was it. No struggle, no desperate buzzing or frantic fight. The fly simply slipped into the digestive pool at the bottom. A silent, instant death.

I waited until I felt her smile, stood back up, dusted off my hands, and grinned with satisfaction.

Mimosa didn't need to be fed. She thrived all by herself in the red soil, and her feathery leaflets sprawled all around our house, down the hill by the gas station, and even at school, along the banks of the little creek behind the schoolyard.

I often slipped away to find her during lunch break, after I returned my empty aluminum plate of rice and fish to the cafeteria's attendants. There, by the trickling creek, we sat together, Mimosa and I—two beings who didn't need words. She enjoyed dappled shade, as I did, and she didn't mind the color of my skin.

Nédivin was a private Protestant missionary school built and run by the Charlemagne family. Though my parents were neither religious nor Protestant, they moved me to Nédivin after less than a year at the public school in Houaïlou at the recommendation of my teacher. I was bored in class, she said, and had become restless and unruly.

The teachers at Nédivin were members of the Charlemagne family and a few young, vivacious French expatriates who brought passion and a spirit of discovery to their teaching, finally a match for my curious mind. And they understood wildlings' need to move; recess at Nédivin was much longer than at the public school.

The entire campus was nestled between forested hills and the tranquil Houaïlou River. The kindergarten house stood at the edge of a coffee plantation—which we unofficially used as the children's toilet. Farther up the hill, the older students, up to 4th grade, studied in long, doorless concrete classrooms with tin roofs that thundered in the rain. The pounding could get so deafening that teachers abandoned their lessons, leaving us to work quietly on homework under the downpour's metallic roar.

Students at Nédivin came from all the neighboring tribes—about three hundred in total, almost all of them Melanesian. Only a few of us, including the Charlemagne children, were of European descent.

I was the only white child in my grade.

And really, I wasn't *that* white. My sun-toasted, chocolate-toned skin was only a shade or two lighter than some of my schoolmates'. But, I was different. My nose was long rather than wide, my eyes almond-shaped rather than round, and while we all had short brown curls, mine were big, wild, and bouncy, while theirs were tightly trimmed afro-coils. My family lived in a cinder-block house, not a thatched-roof hut, and my dad owned the gas station—the only gas station on the east coast of the island.

Everyone knew me. Everywhere my parents drove, children from the tribes waved from the side of the road, their shouts trailing in our wake. If they liked me, they called my name, the syllables bouncing with pride—as though knowing me added something to their own stature. If they didn't, they called "capitalist," a word they hurled like a stone, though it always missed its mark, as I didn't know what it meant.

They all knew my name; I knew few of theirs. And if I knew their names, it didn't make us friends. As much as knowing me conferred a certain status, being friends with the white girl would have been social quicksand, a sure way to be ridiculed. Not that I minded; I never looked for friends on the playground anyway. When recess came, the boys kicked makeshift soccer balls between planted sticks or chased girls with lizards in their hands, laughing as they ran across the yard. The girls, in their cotton missionary dresses, gathered for volleyball or cricket, huddling together in games that kept the boys at bay. Sometimes, out of kindness or compassion, one of the older girls would invite me to join, but I always declined. Ball games didn't interest me—not when Mimosa and Niaouli waited for me by the creek.

Niaouli was another great love of my childhood. His branches seemed to grow thoughtfully, as though he knew a child might need a ladder to climb him. Every higher branch was just within reach of a lower one, though never too easily—where would the fun be in that? Each recess, I'd try to climb a little higher. At each stage, I'd look up to my goal, heart pounding, waiting for a burst of courage to jump onto the next level. Although I felt niaouli's kind encouragements, often, I didn't take the leap but sat on the tallest branch yet and dangled my feet. Sometimes, it could take me months to reach the top of a particular niaouli tree.

I only fell once, when I was seven. It wasn't the tree's fault, and I never held it against him. Even with my arm in a cast, I kept climbing. It was worth it to finally sit in the Y-seat at the top, completely within the canopy, surrounded by fragrant leaves. Up there, I could hide in peace and solitude, far away from the grunts and shouts of ball games in the schoolyard.

Once there, I'd pluck a leaf and crumple it between my fingers, breathing in the sharp, almost-minty scent. It smelled like the Vicks my mother rubbed on my chest when I was sick—cooling, bracing, and comforting all at once. The fragrance tickled my nose, almost like the tree was laughing at me for smelling it too hard.

Niaouli never let me leave without gifts. I'd climb down with pocketfuls of leaves and peel off his papery bark—very slowly, to get the biggest sheets I could get. These were perfect for writing down secrets, drawing treasure maps, or simply for rubbing against the skin—they were the softest. I'd roll them like ancient scrolls and run back to the schoolyard.

More than once, I arrived late for class. It was hard to hear the school bell from the top of a tree.

In 1977, my little sister was born. I was already prone to disappearing in the woods, but with the arrival of a baby in the house, I vanished even more. She was a quiet and calm baby, but the weight of the expectation that I would play with her made me feel restless. I had no interest in being a big sister.

On weekends, I slipped out of the house even before dawn. In the fresh morning light, before the heat baked the hills dry, the air still carried the tang of damp earth and rust, and the red nickel dirt clung to my bare feet as I climbed the hills. I walked through low shrubs, heavy with fog and morning dew. They brushed against my legs, their cool touch like a gentle greeting. Then, all day, I carved stairs into the dirt leading to my favorite trees or built forts with reeds along the creek behind the house. I only returned when hunger pulled me home or when Dad's voice echoed from the yard, calling me for a day out on the ocean in the boat or on a rescue mission with the tow truck.

That is how wildlings grew up in the Bush. And it fit my untamed spirit perfectly—but even the wildest are uprooted eventually, cast out to find their way in new landscapes. Landscapes of a radically different kind.

ॐ · ८३

Nouméa, New Caledonia - 1980

My mother's shoes echoed sharply as she climbed the tiled stairs to the second floor. I followed with muffled clacks, my flip-flops dragging reluctantly against my heels. Clutching my backpack to my chest, I held tight to the only things I'd brought: two weeks' worth of clothes and a couple of my favorite books. My parents had promised they'd pick me up in two weeks—plenty of time, they'd said, for me to settle in and gather stories. Two weeks in the big city and one whole week at a new school, where shoes were mandatory and going barefoot wasn't even an option.

Knock knock. A turn of a key and the door swung open to a woman and a girl about my age. The woman smiled, but it barely reached her eyes. Madame Carpentier was large, with fat fingers and beady eyes. Her daughter had much the same look, though spared from ugliness by the grace of youth.

"Bonjour, Madame Carpentier," I knew good manners and polite greetings, even though I'd grown up in La Brousse (The Bush)—what they called any wild part of the island that wasn't Nouméa.

"Bonjour, entrez, s'il vous plait." Madame Carpentier invited us with one of her fat hands, and we both stepped into what was to be my new home.

In 1980, the year I finished 4th grade—the highest grade Nédivin offered—the Col des Rousettes, the mountain pass linking New Caledonia's east and west coasts, was still unpaved. The road to Nouméa stretched for five long hours of twists and bumps and loose rocks from Houaïlou.

And because the big city's schools were so far, after 4th grade, many of the Melanesian children either went to a local trade school or stayed in their tribes, working the fields of taro and yams and helping build the huts. The ones who moved to the big city joined boarding schools. But boarding school wasn't an option for me. I was always the youngest in my grade and, at not even ten years old, I was too young to qualify. Besides, my parents believed boarding school wouldn't suit me and my solitary ways. They thought I'd be cozier with a private family while I adjusted to my new life without them.

So, they placed an ad in the paper.

And that's how they found the Carpentiers.

The Carpentiers' apartment was small and tiled white like the stairs, with only two bedrooms: one for the parents and one for us, girls. The only plant in the whole place was a spindly dragon tree growing out of a parched flower pot in a corner. Her skinny trunk grew long and straight, and her sparse leaves pressed flat against the window as though she were desperate for a glimpse of sun and fresh air.

"Clemence? Why don't you show our new friend her room?"

The daughter led me down a short hallway to the room we'd share. It had two single beds, each neatly made, and one small window that overlooked a steep, smelly street. Across the road stretched a long, yellowish building with barred windows—something between a factory and a prison. I peeked outside, to the right and left—just concrete, asphalt, cars, and people in a hurry.

Before the Carpentiers, my only experience of Nouméa was of drive-in movie theaters, hotels, and ice cream on the beach, when Dad brought me along on his monthly resupply run to the city. But to live here? The thoughts weighed on my heart, yet I knew I had no choice.

I dropped my bag on the bed farthest from the window and sat on the mattress, knees together, hands clamped tightly in my lap. The mattress felt stiff under me.

From the living room came the steady hum of voices. "Oui oui, bien sûr. Oui oui." Whatever directives my mother was giving Madame Carpentier, which I couldn't quite hear, were met with quick and automatic agreement. After a time, we were summoned back to the living room for the moment I had dreaded most: the goodbyes.

The door clicked shut, and the echo of my mother's shoes faded down the stairs. I stood still, pinching my lips and squeezing my eyes shut. I didn't want to start my stay at the Carpentiers with a cry. I swallowed hard, forcing the lump in my throat down. When I finally opened my eyes and turned, Clemence was sitting on the foam sofa, smiling at me.

She led me back to our room, where I began unpacking my clothes and arranging them on the narrow shelf by my bed.

"I leave you two girls to get acquainted." Madame Carpentier leaned into the bedroom doorway while patting the pocket where I'd seen her slip my mother's check. "I'm off to the grocery store. I'll be back in a bit."

As soon as the front door closed, the gentle, pig-tailed girl who had been sitting quietly on her bed sprang up and peeked down the corridor. "She's gone... come on! I want to show you something." She led me into her parents' bedroom with a sly smile, pushed back the foam mattress, and revealed her treasure: stacks of hidden magazines.

Between the bed frame and the mattress, lay dozens of magazines. On their glossy covers, blondes and brunettes bit their fingers coyly or looked away from the camera with arched backs. Some were open, their hinge frozen to a centerfold. My eyes fell on one blonde reclining with her legs spread wide, revealing parts of a woman's anatomy I had never seen before. I felt a wave of nausea—not just from the images, but from the fear of being caught, and a deeper dread I couldn't name.

"Ni vu, ni connu." The girl giggled, dropping the mattress back in place and readjusting the fitted sheet. (Neither seen, nor known). She ran back to our room, leaving me standing there with the clenched feeling that strange things—things I wanted no part in—took place in this household.

And I was right.

A few days later, when Madame Carpentier had left us alone to run errands, Clemence turned to me and said, "We should practice kissing." She lifted the back of her hand to her mouth and, with exaggerated motions, rubbed her lips all over it. "Like this."

I shook my head. "No way."

"Don't worry, we won't touch each other." She grabbed her sheet and lifted it between us. "Like this. Kiss me across the sheet."

I hesitated, then leaned in. My lips found hers, the warmth passing through the soft fabric of the sheet. She began moving her mouth, her tongue pressing against the sheet and poking me where it stretched.

At first, I sat stiffly, the corners of my eyes darting from the door to her wriggling shape, but slowly, I eased into the game. I'd never kissed anyone before. It was not unpleasant, and the barrier between us made it feel safe—like it wasn't real.

12

That night, she woke me up. "Hey," she whispered, shaking my bed with her foot. "Let's kiss again. It's even more fun in the dark."

Still half asleep, I sat up, and there she was, holding the sheet up again, her puckered lips pressing against it. In the dim light, I saw the outline of her face so close to mine, and just then, the bedroom door swung open.

"What on Earth are you two doing?" Madame Carpentier's voice cut through the room like a whip.

It was me. It was all me. I was the wild weed dropped in the perfect tiled garden, corrupting their sweet, innocent daughter. I was banned from the bedroom that instant and forbidden to be alone with Clemence ever again.

Under Madame Carpentier's vigilant eye, I gathered my few things hastily and slid my small backpack under the foam sofa in the living room, which was to be my new bed. She shut the light, and I brought the thin blanket to my chin with a sigh of relief. This arrangement actually worked better for me; I much preferred the company of the dragon tree to that of the kissing girl.

But there were other repercussions. As part of my punishment—"so you'll truly learn your lesson," Madame Carpentier had said—I was banned from the family table. Instead, for every meal, she handed me a skinny sandwich on square white bread: a thin smear of butter and jam for breakfast and a single slice each of ham and cheese with no other condiment for dinner. All the same—small, dry, and so bland I could hardly tell one bite from the next.

And I couldn't tell my parents. Although the telephone sat in the living room, just a few feet from where I slept, I wasn't allowed to use it unless Madame Carpentier was present. I *could* call my parents, but with her hovering there, what could I say? So I just swallowed my words and my skinny sandwiches. Silence, sometimes, is the best way to stay safe.

I spent the next three days locked in the house, eager for school to start—at least then I'd eat lunch at the cafeteria and be out of their sight. I just read during the day and looked out the window at night. I couldn't see the stars because of the streetlights below, but at least I saw the sky.

Monsieur Carpentier left early for work and came home late. He ate his meals in the kitchen, and I don't remember him ever addressing me. I often wondered if he spent so much time away because she also fed him skinny ham and cheese sandwiches.

Clemence kept her eyes low, avoiding mine whenever we crossed paths in the hallway on my way to the bathroom. It might have been obedience to her mother's directives. I imagined she might have felt bad, but she couldn't say anything—not with punishments like these.

Thank God for the dragon tree. I would have felt so alone without her. At night after the family was asleep, I cleaned her leaves with my shirts and gave her water from my glass. In return, she made me feel safe. She sat with me, kind and friend-like.

ॐ · ੪

A girl stepped out of the yellowish factory-prison building across the road. She looked about my age, maybe a little older. With her bouncing blonde curls, her gigantic blue eyes, and her fluttery pretty dress about her, she looked like a doll. She glanced left, then right, and crossed the road with a confident gait. She walked straight to the step where I sat, plopped herself down beside me, and began scanning the street.

I didn't move. This was my first time waiting for a bus in the big city. Madame Carpentier had given me strict instructions: "Walk up the road, find the step in front of house number 36, and sit there until the bus arrives."

Was this girl also waiting for the bus? Before I could ask, she turned to me.

"Is the fucking bus late?" I blinked. Her voice was so deep—at least a few octaves lower than you'd expect from such a young, sweet face.

"Wh—Why did you say that?" I came from a Protestant missionary school; I knew words like that were a straight ticket to disappointing God.

"Say what?"

"The Big Word." I couldn't even repeat it.

"What Big Word?" She answered with such wide-eyed innocence that I began to giggle, and she giggled with me, though I wasn't sure she knew why.

"How long have you been waiting?" Not only was her voice deep, but she spoke funny, with an accent halfway between the heavy-potato-in-the-mouth local French (called "Caldoche") and a crisp not-quite British English.

"About ten minutes."

"Have you seen the people yet? I took this bus last week, if you lay flat on the step, you can see their shoes."

Before I could answer, she lay flat on her belly, her pretty dress pressed against the dusty step. She aligned her face to the crack beneath the door, closing one eye as though she were looking through a spyglass. "Here's one…" she whispered.

I dropped down beside her, our heads so close they touched. The pointy tips of a pair of high heels clicked across the corridor inside. Behind them, a pair of black business shoes followed. We held our breath and stifled our giggles until the business shoes turned and started heading toward us.

"The bus!" she sprang to her feet.

We scrambled up just as the door opened and a man walked out. The bus pulled in. The girl flashed me a smile, and we climbed aboard. *Ni vu, ni connu.*

I followed her down the rows of students in crisp first-day outfits. When she picked an empty seat and moved near the window, I understood that the other half of the seat was for me.

I dropped next to her, and we burst out laughing.

15

"What's your name?" I asked.

"Amanda," she said, pronouncing it in English. "But here they call me 'Aah-muh-duh,' (in French) which is just awful."

We laughed again.

My strange life at the Carpentiers became almost irrelevant, just a waiting zone between my times with Amanda. We weren't in the same classes, but we'd find each other at recess and always took the bus to and from school together.

Amanda's parents lived in Ouinné, a village even more remote than Houaïlou, so remote that it could only be accessed by plane or helicopter. Amanda's Dad was the bush pilot for the village. All the people in Ouinné worked for the same company: the nickel mine. And most of them were from New Zealand, like Amanda and her family. She'd learned French in the mines, from the sharp tongue of miners. She sure swore a lot, but this was normal French to her. And she didn't mind that it made me giggle.

The first week of school passed in a blink with my new friend. Finally, Friday evening came, and with it a knock at the door. Madame Carpentier opened it, exchanged a few pleasantries, and stepped aside. I stayed quiet, keeping my head down, and followed my mother out the door, down the steps, and into the car.

"Mom," I began as soon as the car door shut. "These people are not nice."

She glanced at me as she turned the key in the ignition. "What do you mean? How are they not nice?"

"They don't talk to me, I can only eat tiny ham and cheese sandwiches, and I have to sleep on the sofa in the living room."

"What nonsense are you saying?"

I couldn't bring myself to tell her about the kissing, about how it all started. I had been involved, after all, and I wasn't proud of it. Neither could I speak about the uncomfortable dirty magazines without admitting to snooping in the parents' room.

"Just what I said, about the sandwiches and sleeping in the living room."

"Come on now. I know you'd rather be home with us, and I'm sure this is hard for you, but there's no need to invent stories about the Carpentiers."

And that was that. I knew from her tone she wouldn't believe me, no matter what else I said. When I was five, there had been ghosts in my room that no one else could see. My parents had sent me to a psychologist whose diagnosis was that I had "too much imagination." Then, when I was eight, I'd lied about my homework, and my mother had caught me. Since then, she'd doubted anything I said. Why would this time be any different? Dad might've believed me, but he had stayed home to run the mechanic shop and care for my baby sister.

I stared out the window, forehead pressed against the glass.

"I met a girl named Amanda," I said after a while. "I really like her. She lives at the Institut Jeanne d'Albret, across the road. It's a boarding school for girls. Could I maybe stay there with her?"

Even if she didn't believe me, maybe she'd be open to something else—anything else.

"You're too young for boarding school." She continued looking to the road, her voice even and definitive. "And besides, I've already paid the Carpentiers for the upcoming month. So no more nonsense, okay?"

Her words landed like a door slammed shut. I leaned back in my seat and swallowed my reply.

We didn't return to Houaïlou that weekend. My mother had opened a boutique of clothes and toys in the heart of the village, and she took the opportunity to be in the big city to meet with vendors. I trailed behind her from store to store, quiet and gloomy. Not even ice cream on the beach could lighten my mood. Sunday evening came all too quickly, and there I was, back at the Carpentiers, and there was nothing I could do about it. This time, when the door clicked shut, I did cry.

"What the… She didn't believe you?" Amanda's big blue eyes fixed on mine.

I shook my head while tears slowly rose.

"But… you can't stay there."

I shook my head again and began to cry.

"Okay, okay. Let me think." She leaned back against the door of house number 36, her brow furrowed, two fingers pressed to her lips in deep thought.

"Maybe I could escape…"

Amanda spun toward me, her curls bouncing in excitement. "Yes! That's it. On Wednesday. That's when a lot of girls who don't stay at Jeanne d'Albret come for lunch after school. I can sneak you in. Nobody would know, and then…"

"…and then I can hide under your bed, and by the time they find me, I'd already be at the Institut, and I'll just say I don't want to leave, and they'll have to let me stay, won't they? You think it could work?"

Amanda shrugged, a mischievous smile creeping across her face. "It's worth a shot."

And so the plan was set. On Wednesday morning, our half-day at school, I'd discreetly pack my clothes and books into my small backpack, leaving nothing behind at the Carpentiers. I'd take the bus as I did every morning. I just wouldn't return, ever.

I sat on the sofa, a skinny sandwich untouched on a plate next to me, and pretended to read, but my heart beat so loudly in my chest that I feared the Carpentiers might hear it. I just needed to lay low for one more day, one more evening, then I'd pack everything and be ready for the great escape plan.

Knock knock.

Madame Carpentier shuffled to the door, dragging her slippers with each step, and peered through the peephole. Her back stiffened as though a rod had just shot up her spine. But still, she opened the door. And there, looming taller than her actual height, stood my mother. My jaw dropped. She had believed me enough to come back and check my fantastical story after all.

She stepped through the door. Her eyes flicked to the sandwich then to me on the sofa.

"Is this all you had for dinner?" she simply asked.

"Yes." I was safe to speak now. She nodded.

"Get your things and wait for me in the car." Her tone was flat and measured, her words almost whistled through thin lips. She didn't need to say it twice. I crammed everything into my backpack, spared one last glance for the dragon tree, and bolted down the stairs. I jumped into the car, slammed the door, and hit the lock button—just in case.

I waited and almost— *almost*— felt bad for Madame Carpentier. My mother was not a woman to be trifled with.

I never learned what was said at the entrance of the Carpentiers' apartment. I wasn't even curious, too happy to turn the page. Nor did I ever learn why my mother decided on a surprise visit. But how glad I was that she did!

That night, we stayed in a small hotel by the beach and the next day, Wednesday, we visited the Institut. She explained my situation, and, despite my being only nine and a half years old, I was welcomed at the Institut Jeanne d'Albret.

ଞ · ଔ

There were seventeen girls in my dorm, all from the Bush, like me—girls of all ages up to seventeen, and of all shades and colors. They were all so kind, especially the older girls who circled around me like mama bears. Amanda had told them the tale of the girl down the street with the mean

19

captors. Without being asked, the girls rearranged their beds to give me the one right next to Amanda's.

"Did you see the courtyard yet?" Amanda pulled me by the hand.

"There is a courtyard?"

"Of course. There are swings and even trees we can climb."

Down past the dining hall, there was indeed a magical courtyard with two flamboyant trees. Their branches were a bit harder to reach than those of a niouli, but I had a friend now, and we could lift each other. And at the base of the wall—the same wall I'd stared at from Clemence's window— was a patch of mimosa, her delicate leaves basking in the sun. Some even climbed the cracks in the wall, waiting for little fingers to tickle them.

೮ · ೮

My life at Jeanne d'Albret quickly settled into a new rhythm. Amanda and I became inseparable. One weekend, she'd come to my parents' house in Houaïlou—where her foul language appalled my mother but never failed to amuse me. The next, we'd fly to her home in Ouinné in her dad's Cessna. That's where I began learning English—except for the words "thistle" and "photosynthesis" (thithle, photosynsesis)—I could never get these right, and Amanda would roll with laughter every time I tried. We'd sprawl on the carpet in her parents' living room, reading books and snacking on her mom's famous carrot cakes. No matter which house we visited, as soon as we dropped our bags, we'd escape to the red nickel hills and spend our weekends playing in the dirt, in rivers, and under waterfalls. Then we'd return to boarding school, to our side-by-side beds, plates, and homework chairs.

On Wednesdays, after our homework was done, Amanda and I would cross the dining hall to the courtyard. She always raced to the swings first, and sometimes, I went with her. But other times, I sat quietly by the wall with Mimosa, brushing her leaflets with my fingertips and watching them close and reopen.

In the end, we weren't so different, Mimosa and I. We opened and closed depending on how we were touched—by people, by places, by life itself. We were resilient, growing where planted, even in the cracks, even in the shadows. And eventually, when the sun returned, we unfurled, ready to play again.

Mimosa felt like home and still does to this day. There is a patch right outside my cabina as I type this. Although she has closed her leaflets because of the heavy raindrops, I sense she's enjoying this Costa Rican downpour.

Chapter 2
The Secret Room

Institut Jeanne d'Albret for Girls, Nouméa, New Caledonia, 1981

The Institut Jeanne d'Albret was as much my home as it was a whole new world to explore. With sixty girls housed in private rooms upstairs and two bustling dormitories on the main floor, there was always something happening—whispers of gossip, bursts of laughter, impromptu fashion shows, heartbreaks soothed with snuggles, card games with and without wagers, and even late-night Ouija board séances.

There were rules, of course. Meals were served at precise times in the dining hall. Latecomers were turned away. We lined up to show clean hands, sang Grace together, and only then could fill our plates.

After dinner, the courtyard was off-limits. The younger girls in the dorms were not allowed upstairs, and while the older girls could study in their rooms, we had to do our homework in one of two dedicated study rooms near the entrance on the main floor.

Naturally, over the years, Amanda and I broke every single rule. We sneaked up the forbidden stairs to see what was there and out to the courtyard after dark to count the stars. We even belly-crawled through the administration office once to spy on Madame Martin, the night guardian, in her private quarters. We explored every corner of the Institut, until only one room remained—the Secret Room.

The Secret Room, as Amanda and I called it, was always locked and off-limits, perhaps even to the night guardian. A small window with overlapping glass slats linked the Secret Room to one of the study rooms. But the slats were locked in place by small metal retainers, and the window couldn't be opened without serious tinkering.

This mysterious space belonged solely to Mademoiselle, the owner of the Institut.

Mademoiselle, a 63-year-old spinster, lived in a house somewhere else and only occasionally visited the Institut. When she did, she disappeared into the Secret Room for about an hour, shutting the door behind her. Then she reemerged, quickly visited the rest of the building, and left.

What, oh, what was in that room? Amanda and I drove ourselves silly with curiosity. We asked the older girls; no one knew.

So, eventually, we had to slip out into the night and find out.

"Hurry! You're heavy." Amanda held my foot in her hands, as a ladder, while I carefully bent the side metal retainer.

"I got it. I got it." I carefully slid the first glass slat to the side and peered into the darkness of the Secret Room.

"What do you see?"

"I don't see anything. It's dark."

"Well, hold on, I'll go turn the lights on," she said with a straight face. We both stifled our giggles.

"My eyes are adjusting… I can almost see."

And suddenly, "Whoa!" I could see, but I couldn't believe it.

"What do you mean, 'Whoa'? What do you see?"

"Plants! I see plants. The whole room is filled with plants."

A noise down the corridor and we both froze. Madame Martin was doing her rounds early. I silently replaced the slat in place, and Amanda lowered me back to the floor. We both crouched under a desk and held our breaths. Madame Martin turned the lights on, then off again. This time, we were lucky.

"Plants?" Amanda whispered, incredulous.

I shrugged. "I promise you. Plants."

And with that, we quietly slithered back to the dorms with an even larger mystery.

℘ · ℭ

It always happened in the middle of the night. All sixteen other girls in the dorms slept soundly. The varied rhythms of their breathing mingled and harmonized. Annette, near the window in my row, snored slightly. Maeva, across the room, on the other side of our individual small lockers, moaned and tossed. I thought she might be having a nightmare. Amanda, in the bed closest to mine, breathed slowly and fully. I listened carefully to each one then attempted to match Amanda's restful breaths to calm mine. But the subtle tightening in my chest that had woken me up only intensified.

I knew what happened next.

My chest would become pressed then crushed under an invisible weight, leaving me gasping for air like a fish flailing on a dock.

Asthma, that familiar foe, was upon me. It seized my throat and strangled my breath. Wheezes constricted to gasps. "I'm okay. I'm gonna be okay," I comforted myself, but my body didn't believe me. My heart pounded against my ribs. The more I tried to slow my breathing, the shallower it became.

I sat up on my bed. I was alone in this.

Amanda couldn't help. I had woken her once; the worry on her face had only tightened the vise on my chest. And Madame Martin? Oh, no. I feared our night guardian too much to wake her. Amanda and I were always under her close scrutiny. Just that day, we'd been grounded twice—once for bending spoons (with our hands) and once for jumping in the corridor with mattress springs we had found in the mines in Ouinné tied under our shoes.

No, it was best I let Madame Martin sleep. Besides, what could she do?

Oxygen.
What I needed was oxygen.
Plants exhaled oxygen.
My eyes grew wide with the excitement of a solution found. Our biology teacher had just introduced us to plant photosynthesis: plants released oxygen when exposed to light. And I knew just where to find them.

Still in the grasp of laborious gasps, I took to the corridor at full speed, through the entrance and into the study room. I turned the lights on, dragged one of the heavy desks under the window, and climbed on it. My life hung in the balance; it didn't matter if I was caught. I quickly dismantled the side metal retainers of two window slats. This made a three-slat opening, including the one Amanda and I had dismantled and never bent back. It was tight but sufficient. Without thinking, I slid my head and shoulders through the opening and pushed off from the table. There I was—suspended, feet on one side and head and hands rushing toward the floor on the other side—when, by the grace of the God to whom we sang before meals, a shelf appeared under my hands. I wiggled my hips through the window and landed fully on the shelf. From there, I jumped down among the plants.

I landed softly and sat in the center of the room, hands on knees, lungs still wheezing. The air suddenly shifted. It felt sweeter, richer, lighter. I could have sworn the plants exhaled deliberately in my direction. Not just oxygen, but warmth, presence, and the quiet reassurance that I wasn't alone after all.

My mind unclenched. My lungs expanded. A deep inhale. At last, I breathed.

I straightened and looked around for the first time. A deep peace hummed in the space. The plants sat in neat rows along the walls, housed in pots of various shapes and sizes. Some stretched upward, their leaves brushing the ceiling, while others—mere seedlings—sprouted in ice cube trays, fragile but determined. Beneath the window I'd slipped through, gardening tools and potting soil lay orderly on the bottom shelf. The top shelf, fortunately, was empty. Mademoiselle was short—perhaps she couldn't reach that shelf.

I stayed in the room for several hours, though it felt like minutes. For a while, I lay on my back against the cool tile floor, eyes closed, simply breathing in the space. Then I visited each plant, trailing my fingers over their leaves, pressing my fingertips into their soil, whispering soft hellos. I stretched out on my belly in front of the seedlings. One of the smaller ones was Mimosa—my childhood friend. It only had a few small, sensitive leaves, which closed at my touch, though much slower than the adult plants I had known. Or perhaps it was just shy and playful. I giggled.

Eventually, I had to return to my bed. I climbed back up, crawled back out, landed on the desk, replaced the table and chairs, and slipped silently down the corridor to the dorms.

Annette had turned over and no longer snored. Maeva also slept quietly. Amanda mumbled a few words in response to the creaking of springs in my bed frame as I lay down. It sounded like a muffled, "Where have you been?" We normally woke each other to go to the bathroom during the night—because of the ghosts—so where could I have gone without her?

Luckily, she neither woke up nor remembered. And I, who told her *everything*, never told Amanda—never told anyone until now—about my night in the Plant Room.

ಹಿ · ೞ

When my mother picked me up from the Institut that weekend, I told her about the asthma attack, but not about the plants. The night attacks had become more frequent, and the homeopathic treatment I was on wasn't working.

That same week, my mother found a kind and skilled acupuncturist. Ten sessions was all it took. My asthma vanished, never to return.

I never sneaked back into the plant room, though the metal retainers remained bent, and therefore easy to bypass.

Was the risk of being caught too great? Yes—but not for fear of punishment. If they discovered me, they'd discover the plants. And I felt a duty to protect my secret friends.

Each time I passed the locked door, I felt more peaceful just knowing they were there.

But why were they there?

Why were there plants in a locked room at the Institut Jeanne d'Albret? Why were they so luxuriant in a locked space with no obvious light? And why did Mademoiselle keep them there, instead of in her own home?

As of the writing of this book, this part of the mystery remains intact.

Chapter 3
Whittaker Woods

North Conway, New Hampshire - September 2016

I carefully twisted the capsule open. *Tap, tap, tap*—a tiny mound of powder spilled onto my square of chocolate, no more than a dusting of grains, too light to weigh.

I closed my eyes and whispered over the tiny offering.

"Hello, Mushrooms. My intent today, as it is every day, is to learn how to speak with trees. Thank you for helping me."

Then, quickly, I ate it. That was all the ceremony I had time for—I was already late for work.

I slung my pack over my shoulder and slipped out the back of the Catmobile, ducking under the maple leaves that had first spoken to me. They brushed against my hair, and a few became tangled.

I always parked against the woods on purpose, to feel closer. On warm nights, I left the back hatch open and slept with my head toward the tailgate. Small branches always followed me in, so when I opened my eyes in the morning, there they were, grazing the fiberglass shell, their leaves dangling like small green charms above my pillow.

Sometimes, from my warm sleeping bag, I reached up and traced their edges or caressed their smooth surface. Immediately, the leaves' aroma filled the shell—not the sweet almondish fragrance you'd imagine from a maple tree, but simply the smell of leaves, a fresh green scent, earthy, and unpretentious.

It was our quiet way of communicating, but I wanted more. Not just whispers in rustling branches and real or imagined surges of aroma. I wanted real conversations.

Did trees have memories? Secret wisdom buried in their roots? Opinions about us?

I closed the back carefully, making sure no maple leaf was caught in the door.

"Bye, Love."

A loving warmth spread in my chest. It felt like, *Have a good day!* I tapped the shell and replied out loud, "Thanks. You too." Then, with a skip in my steps, I headed down Mechanic Street, past Oak Road, and to the edge of Whittaker Woods.

That was it—I wanted to talk with trees the way I talked with the Catmobile.

By 2016, the Catmobile and I had been together for sixteen years, four of those on the road. We roamed freely, through scorched deserts, lush forests, snowy mountain passes, north to south, east to west, nowhere and everywhere in between. More than a truck, it was my companion and my full-time home.

"Do you need an oil change yet?" I would ask.

The answer always came. Not in words, but in *knowing*. A flicker of certainty beyond logic or my mechanical abilities. I never missed a repair or wondered if something was wrong. The truck always told me before anything broke.

If I could talk with my truck, surely I could talk with trees.

I used to. When I was little, the whole world was alive. Every red rock, tree, leaf, and blade of buffalo grass had a personality as real as mine.

But the more I traveled, read, and learned, the more facts took root, replacing magic with logic, presence with classification. Science had answers—beautiful, fascinating answers. Mimosa folded its leaves when touched because pressure sensors triggered a pulse; motor cells reacted, and the leaflets closed. A marvel of biological evolution, but no longer a conversation.

Life, however, moves in spirals. As I left the world of science behind to roam freely, something forgotten began to stir—something beyond reason. Away from humans and their constructs, I began to remember: beyond their intricate mechanisms, all things are alive. Aware.

Science had given me the *how*, but I had lost the *who*.

Until, in early September 2016, I met Jim.

Jim was a carpenter, and he spoke with trees.

"They don't just let me cut'em, they're like 'Ooooh, pick me, I want to be a deck, I want to frame a house'. And they get to stay on their land, in their same neck of the woods with all their friends. Better that than buying mass-cut boards from stranger trees in a giant warehouse. That's just sad wood. They don't know what's up. These here, I give them all the love. I trim and sand and stain them all artsy-like. Makes them feel pampered and admired, you know?"

"Really? They don't mind dying?"

"Some do… I don't cut those."

"But how do you know which ones are okay with dying?"

Jim opened his palms up as though stating the obvious. "I ask them. You can tell some are excited and willing, if you listen." He placed a hand on my chest. "You have to listen from here though." Then he burrowed a finger into my ear canal. "Not from here. Ears are for the songs of the birds."

I recoiled from the invasive finger and slapped his hand out of my ear. He laughed and reclined back in his chair.

"Who *are* you? What planet are you from?" I shook my head and laughed.

That was all he said about it. He pulled out a joint from his chest pocket and lit it. He reclined farther, as far as the chair would go without falling over, and gazed quietly at the forest canopy. A smile appeared at the corner of his eyes.

Was he speaking with the forest right then? How did he do that?

The magic mushrooms I microdosed on four consecutive days each week before crossing Whittaker Woods on my way to work also came from Jim.

Shortly after our first meeting, Jim and I invested in a pound of *Psilocybe cubensis*. By then, I'd only tried a microscopic dose once before, and I used no other substance. I was new to all of it.

The day we received the paper bag filled with our investment, Jim invited several of my friends and co-workers to sample the gnarled, desiccated fungi friends.

I ate one gram—my first macrodose, my first real psychedelic journey.

I rested a hand on Jim's chest, but my eyes drifted from the maple tree just outside the Catmobile to the leaves hanging over our heads. I knew this tree and its leaves; I lived and slept with them. Yet never before had I noticed the intricate, scaly texture of its bark or the meticulous fractal design of its branches and leaves.

Through the awe, a peculiar feeling appeared in my heart. It was unlike any feeling I had ever felt. Was it a mushroom feeling? Or maybe one of Jim's? His eyes were closed, lost in his own journey, or maybe just napping. I didn't want to disturb him to ask, so I decided to test it.

With eyes and attention still on the tree, I lifted my hand off Jim's chest. The new feeling remained. I placed my hand back and focused all my attention on Jim, staring at the rise and fall of his chest under my hand. The new feeling vanished, replaced by a host of familiar human feelings—a mischievous gladness at first, then a thick heaviness or darkness I didn't understand, then in the center Love, pure Love. These feelings weren't mine; I was perceiving Jim's. And so that meant… I focused my attention back on the tree. The peculiar new feeling returned. *A tree feeling!* I was feeling a tree feeling. I sat up and concentrated even harder. What was the tree saying?

[Curiosity] The tree was exploring me. "Curiosity" was the closest human feeling equivalent, yet the term was inadequate. Tree curiosity was thinner, curlier, like an energetic tendril unfurling through my chest with slow, deliberate intent. It didn't press or pull but coiled itself around my heart. And it tasted like wood, earthy and tingly. I had never *tasted* a feeling before.

Jim had said this might happen. "Synesthesia," he'd called it. All senses open, cross-wired, unbound. Seeing sounds, tasting emotions, feeling presence's texture like a touch against the skin. That was the mushroom's gift.

"Hi." I gathered the essence of a greeting in my heart and sent it toward the tree.

A pulse. A ripple. The tendril curled tighter for a fraction of a second. It had *heard* me.

"Hi." I offered again.

Another pulse, and… one single leaf began swinging wildly on its stem. It was an inside canopy leaf, and I couldn't imagine how a rogue wind could catch it. There was neither logical nor biological reason for this leaf's behavior. But it was swinging on a plane parallel to my uplifted hand, so I waved back.

We were communicating, and gladness filled my heart—a general gladness, probably a mixture of mine and the tree's.

"I should microdose mushrooms every day. Trees communicate with each other through the mycelium; probably I can too." The thought appeared with complete confidence and clarity in my mind. Was it mine? Were the mushrooms downloading instructions through my neurons?

Or was I so immersed in Jim's energy that I was picking up on his secret method? Perhaps all of the above.

Regardless, I was sure. And conveniently, a whole pound of cubensis lived with me—with us—in the Catmobile.

ಬ · ಣ

North Conway, New Hampshire - 2016

I microdosed four days on, three days off. Just a few taps, a hint of powder. At that small a dose, the effects were subtle—perhaps nothing at all, perhaps a heightening of awareness, or perhaps, as skeptics might argue, a placebo trick of the mind.

Whether I microdosed or not, and no matter how late I thought I was for work, I always stopped at the end of Oak Road, right before the portal.

At the end of Oak Road, the soft mat of pine needles and previous years' leaves stretched over the road, subtly yet continuously reclaiming their domain. There, a path opened through the forest. At the junction of these two worlds, towering sentinel trees extended their branches over the entrance. They overlapped and intertwined, weaving a low arch that slightly hid the path. This was the portal. I stood beneath it and again spoke my wish.

"Hello Woods. I would like the ability to speak with you in a two-way conversation. Would you please teach me?"

A pause. A bow. And I stepped through the portal into Whittaker Woods.

I listened first with my ears. The crunching of leaves under my steps, the chirps, trills, and whistles of the birds—that's what ears are for—and in the background, the faint hum of the human world—the cars, trains, and occasional planes. Still, for being right in town, Whittaker Woods was an unexpected oasis of nature and calm.

In the winter, it was a different story. These trails were part of a criss-crossing network of cross-country ski trails. Humans bought passes to enter these woods, and the whole forest echoed with the swish-swish of skis, the chatter of small talk, the yips and yaps of excitable dogs. But the rest of the year, it was quiet. Only a few dog owners, the same ones every day, and I, on my way to work, strolled the dappled path.

When I listened to the woods, my heart slowed, my thoughts quieted and my senses sharpened. The forest felt more alive. Each tree, mushroom, squirrel—even each pine cone scattered on the path—became an individual being. My senses shifted from the forest to the trees.

"Hi, tree." "Hello, Amanita." "Oooh, hi there, squirrel."

I greeted each one as I passed, wanting to linger but knowing I couldn't. Past the portal, time seemed to condense, and always, I arrived at the power lines too soon.

The trail continued straight, but I turned, following the power lines to a residential street that descended to the main road, depositing me right across from The Local Grocer Café.

I slipped through the back, past the kitchen, donned my official barista apron, and clocked in. Another inexplicable time warp—no matter how late I thought I was, I always clocked in on time. This was one of Whittaker Woods' little magic gifts.

I also walked through Whittaker Woods after my shift at the Café, but the forest felt sleepier in the afternoon, unless it was just past sunset.

In that shifting time, *entre chien et loup* (between dog and wolf), when the sun had dipped below the horizon but darkness had yet to fully settle, the woods felt more alert, more alive. Perhaps trees rested during the day and woke at sunset. Did they? Did trees sleep at all? Would I have progressed faster if I walked the woods in the moonlight?

I had so many questions, but for now, I only gathered and collected them like fallen leaves, waiting for the day when I could finally ask.

The trees I had first met in spring's tender green deepened to summer's lush shades, then darkened further before bursting into the warm, fiery hues for which the Northeast is known.

With each passing day, gradually, almost as imperceptibly as the shifting hues, my relationship with the woods evolved.

Some trees began to stand out. I greeted each one equally as I walked by, but with some, I felt extra trepidation. Some were becoming friends, while others remained acquaintances, or strangers. Some I hugged frequently, especially the fragrant pines right on the trail and the two sentinels at the entrance. And then, there was the oak.

Oh, I was in love with that oak.

It stood outside of Whittaker Woods in a patch of well-groomed grass at the corner of Oak Road and Mechanic Street. Once its leaves turned red, I stopped and gaped at it in astonishment, every day, twice a day.

"You are *so* beautiful!"

[Recognition] The majestic oak was the first, aside from the maple above my truck, from whom I sensed a response. Its energy shifted when I approached, like a subtle acknowledgment rather than an overt greeting—steady, knowing, sovereign. I never trampled the private lawn to approach it. It wasn't the kind of tree one hugged; it was much too regal for that. No, when I sensed its recognition, I bowed from the sidewalk with a hand on my heart, and it seemed to like it.

Whether the oak spoke to the trees of Whittaker Woods, I never knew. But once *it* recognized me, the others began to as well. Not in movement, but in energy—subtle shifts and turning of attention toward me when I greeted them. One by one, they responded, as if the oak had vouched for me, granting me passage into their world. After that, my progress was exponential, like roots spreading underground in fast-forward—until winter cut it short.

A dusting of frost and snow, like a silent end-of-school bell, told me it was time to consult maps and give my notice to the Café.

On December 1st, the first heavy snow blanketed Whittaker Woods. Jim packed his belongings and the paper bag of magic mushrooms into my Catmobile, and together, we fled the cold for the sunlit deserts of the Southwest.

Life carried on, unfolding in adventures, twists, and detours. A few months later, Jim and I parted ways—whether as a pause or an ending, I wasn't sure. He flew back to Maine, and I drove north to Alaska for the summer—Alaska, the land of short, stoic trees.

Two full cycles of seasons passed before the White Mountains called me back.

I was working as a hiking guide in Sedona, Arizona, with a flexible schedule that allowed me to shift with the wind whenever a sudden longing struck—like the need to jump in the Saco River, climb the Whites, and wrap my arms around the trees of Whittaker Woods.

By the next dawn, the Catmobile pointed northeast. Three days later, unannounced and unexpected, I arrived in North Conway.

"Perfect timing, Bobcat, as always. We need help. Can you start tomorrow morning?"

That night, I pulled into Micah's driveway and backed against my maple tree. The Catmobile settled in like it had never left, and so did I.

Road-weary but happy, I crawled into my shell, into my sleeping bag, into the familiar embrace of home. A few branches slipped through the open hatch to welcome me back. I let my eyes close, the scent of leaves and earth filling my breath.

Sleep took me before I had the chance to say goodnight.

৪০ · ৫৪

North Conway, New Hampshire - 2018

I quickened my steps down Mechanic Street, heart pounding with anticipation. It came into view, and I ran the last few feet to the corner.

My oak! My, it was even more magnificent than I remembered—taller, wider, wiser, greener. I laughed with delight and bowed, as I used to, with a hand pressed on my chest.

"Hello Oak! I've missed you."

I sensed its recognition. It felt like gladness in my direction. It remembered me. And— how wonderful!—I could perceive its attention without magic mushrooms.

"I'll see you again tonight. And I'll see you a lot. I'm here for a few months." I promised out loud. I always wondered if the people of the house could hear me. "Hmm. That weirdo who speaks to our tree is back," they might have said, peeking through the blinds, but I was already gone. I half-jogged half-skipped to the end of the road and stopped at the portal.

Oh, they knew I was coming. Whether the oak had warned them or we were simply connected and always aware of each other's whereabouts—they knew.

Before I even spoke a wish, I could feel their excitement. There was my excitement—pounding heart and a physical sensation of vibration in my entire body—and there was the trees' excitement—an energetic rumbling of joy, imperceptible to the five senses yet all pervasive.

Forgetting to wish, I stepped under the archway, the portal's entrance, and felt a shock wave of this rumbling. I felt dizzy and stopped to stabilize myself. I took a deep inhale of scented forest air and cried and laughed all at once.

Have you ever walked into a room where everyone loves you? Where they turn at your arrival with bright eyes, open arms, and a chorus of "Yay!"? If you have, then you know how I felt that day as I entered Whittaker Woods.

I danced down the trail, weaving from side to side, embracing trunks, pressing my hands to bark. "Hi, friend." "It's so good to see you." "Look at you—My, you've grown." "Thank you."

I arrived at the Café high on love, still buzzing from my reunion with the trees. I pushed through the back door into the kitchen and...

"The Bobcat is back!"

Jeff the Chef flung a spoon into the air in celebration, catching it with a flourish. Before I could laugh, Micah and Lilly were on me, arms wrapping tight, squeezing the breath from my lungs in a tangle of warmth and friendship. And for the second time that day, I laughed and cried at all once, all before I even donned my apron.

Some new faces had joined the Café while I was away. One of them—a bright-eyed girl with a gangsta' hat and flour-dusted hands—nodded in my direction.

"So, you're The Bobcat. I've heard a lot about you and your adventures."

"Ah! Don't believe everything you hear." I laughed and winked at her.

"I'm Caleen, I want to hear more about—" *Ding!* An order was up, and a dozen more lined the cooks' rail as hikers, yogis, and locals poured into the Café. A typical summer day, the peak of high season. No time for chit-chat.

"Woooo! Let the Games begin!" Jeff snapped his gloves on, and the whole team dispersed to their respective stations.

I dedicated the summer of 2018 to replenishing my adventure funds and refining my energetic felt sense. By day, the bustling pace of the Café kept my hands moving, my mind engaged, and my wallet steadily filling. The rest of the time, I was a student in the woods.

Whittaker Woods had welcomed me back with open branches. The trees recognized me, responding with subtle shifts when I reached for them. I could feel their presence, their awareness, their curiosity curling toward me like unseen tendrils. But a real conversation required a different attunement, a finer calibration of perception.

If I could sense a tree's feelings in contrast to my own, as I had during my mushroom journey, then first, I needed to know mine intimately. Only by recognizing the particular shape and taste of my own feelings could I distinguish which were mine and which weren't. But how?

As luck had it, every Tuesday evening, a meditation class gathered in the quiet, dimly lit basement of the Local Grocer. And—because fate has a sense of humor—it was free for employees.

The very next Tuesday, I stepped hesitantly into the cool, windowless space. Flickering candles cast golden pools of light onto the stone floor. Two other people already sat in silence, their bodies draped in stillness atop small cushions. I chose a cushion by the door. Fidgeted. Shifted. Crossed my legs, uncrossed them, crossed them again. Why was I even here instead of in the woods? I was about to get up and leave when in walked a petite, spunky, curly-purple-haired grandma, her arms wrapped around a basketful of oracle cards.

She moved like a wind-blown seed, light and playful. She smiled at each of us and sat down. I let out a breath I hadn't realized I was holding and stayed.

Before that summer, I thought of meditation as mild torture. I sat cross-legged, attempting to follow my breath and quiet my mind, but my breath was so shallow that I quickly lost interest. Then, inevitably, my mind bemoaned its own lack of quiet, then bemoaned its bemoaning, until an inside voice I called The Storyteller began recounting the whole cascading set of events. Then, usually, I just listened to The

Storyteller's stories until the bell or gong rang and I was set free.

Leah, our meditation guide, laughed, her eyes crinkling with knowing amusement—she'd heard this before.

"Your mind doesn't need to be quiet. You just need to notice what disturbs the quiet and observe it."

That single shift was the key.

No, I couldn't silence my thoughts, but I could stare. Staring—focusing my attention—I was good at. So I stared. At my thoughts. At feelings as they arose. I followed each one to where it lived in my body, then stared at that body part until it revealed yet more secrets. Curiosity took over, and effortlessly, the meditation hours flew by.

After a few sessions, once I felt satisfied that I could stare at myself, I turned my energetic attention to Leah and the other participants in the room, but mostly Leah. When I placed my attention on her, I instantly felt more peaceful, joyful, powerful, and expanded—a sharp contrast to when my attention was only on myself. Was this what it felt like to be Leah from within?

[Peace] A sapling by the trail. I felt peaceful when I stared at it. Did Leah feel peaceful the way a tree did? I softened my gaze and focused harder. If my eyes lingered on the bark's intricate patterns, sight eclipsed the other senses. If my ears caught a songbird's melody, that song filled my mind. To sense a tree's energy, all inputs—eyes, ears, nose, tongue, skin—had to be blurry. Only then did the feelings—mine and others'—emerge clearly.

The peace I felt from Leah was closer to my own than to the sapling's, yet I labeled them both *Peace*. I knew these labels I assigned to body sensations were just mind-constructs, loose translations to help me understand my process until I could further refine it. True communication wasn't in words—it flowed from and through the heart, effortlessly, without the need for labels.

The more I stared, the subtler I perceived.

[Joy] Mischievous, amused, masculine energy from that thick pine. What tickled it? Maybe that my arms were too short to fully encircle it, even though I climbed on tip-toes to reach a thinner cross-section and pressed my chest into its trunk until I couldn't breathe. And still, my fingertips—oh, so close—couldn't touch.

[Joy] Serenity of simple tactile pleasure as I caressed the bright green tips at the end of a spruce's branches.

"Would you allow me to eat one, please?" I looked up to the trunk.

[Yes, you may.] A tree nod equivalent.

I pinched the tip, right at the junction between last year's dark green and this year's fresh green and, respectfully—like Communion—placed it on my tongue. Oh, the citrus intensity! I giggled and felt the tree giggle with me.

And there were the power lines, always too soon.

Summer surreptitiously turned into fall. The majestic oak dazzled leaf-peeping pedestrians with its rich dark reds, fresh spruce tips became respectable dark green chlorophyll gatherers, and *Amanita muscaria*'s white-dotted red caps popped all along the trail.

Like a lover desperate to stretch every moment with their beloved, I left the Catmobile for the woods earlier and earlier. I sat with families of Amanitas by the trail, zipped my jacket fully, and watched my breath rise and expand in the shafts of golden light through the thinning canopy.

All the diligent staring and intense focusing had honed my felt sense. Now, it was effortless. At last, the trees and I, we could chat.

But there wasn't much time left for conversations. Already, the leaves were turning brown, curling, and surrendering to the forest floor. When the first frost glittered on naked branches, I pressed my hands to the trunks of my tree friends in farewell, turned in my apron, hugged my human friends, and pointed the Catmobile west.

41

A farm job had opened near Portland, Oregon. The winters were milder there, kinder to truck-dwellers. The road was calling.

"Take me with you!" Little Caleen leaned through the food ordering window, eyes wide, brimming with certitude. "Please. I've never even been out of this tiny town. If I don't go with you now, I'll be an old hag, still standing here making sandwiches when I'm eighty years old."

And so, this time, it was Caleen who packed her bags, loaded them into my Catmobile, and drove out west with me.

Life unfolded, as it always did, with twists, turns, and adventures. With the money she earned in Oregon, Caleen bought a truck and returned to New Hampshire. With mine, I spent a whole year walking in wilderness, speaking with desert plants from Anza-Borrego to Death Valley, with ponderosas from Montana to Washington. Then I flew to Costa Rica, where every tree is a towering metropolis, where vines spill from the canopy like green waterfalls, and where I met a jaguar.

A year and a half had passed when again my heart stirred to the call of the Whites.

Except, the year was 2020, and the whole world was quarantined. I heard the call, unmistakable and insistent, but I had to wait a few months for travel restrictions to be lifted.

When finally the world reopened, I drove for seventeen hours, straight from the southern woods of Hendersonville, North Carolina—where I had spent the long, strange pause—to North Conway.

I pulled into Micah's driveway, backed fully against the maple leaves, and crawled into my shell for a much-needed rest.

Right before I fell asleep, I heard the creak of wooden steps. Micah's familiar gait descending. His steps stopped and, with a chuckle, he said:

"Ha! The Bobcat's here. I guess it must be summer."

৪৩ · ৫৪

North Conway, New Hampshire - 2020

I stood in the middle of Whittaker Woods on my first full day back, turning slowly, taking it all in—the familiar pine scent, the soft stir of leaves, the wide trunks I remembered, and the saplings I didn't. The thrill of our reunion was as potent as in years prior, yet different. Rather than a rush of excitement, my body *landed*—a settling that grounded my bones.

I had been away, and yet, had I really? What was this feeling? *Dod yn ôl at Fy Nghoed*—a memory of a painted wooden sign I'd once seen in the green woods of Snowdonia, in Wales, appeared in my mind. The translation below read "Returning to my trees," but the deeper meaning carried the energy of "returning to a balanced state of mind."

These, here, were my trees.

[Yes] The trees nodded with a felt sense of "Yes, you will always be welcome here."

After a few much-needed weeks of backpacking in the White Mountains, I returned to North Conway and slipped back into the familiar rhythm of my daily walks through Whittaker Woods to the Café.

Every morning, I greeted each tree with love as I passed, but I no longer stared or listened as intently as in previous years. These were my trees, my family. And as one does when returning to family, I filled the woods with stories of my travels.

"...and in Death Valley, they have Joshua trees—and they're not even trees, they're giant herbs and they..." Unconcerned about being overheard, I spoke aloud, lifting my hands to mimic the towering height of Joshua trees. In my mind, I pictured the dried dusty earth, the scented sage wind, and the wide open landscape. I broadcast the image of spiky,

43

praying Joshua trees—unlike anything a New Hampshire oak or pine had ever seen.

[Awe. Curiosity.]

"…and in Montana, they have ponderosa pines. Their sap smells like vanilla. And they're nonflammable. They can exfoliate their bark, so even if they're hit by lightning, they don't fully catch on fire.

[Incredible.]

"Oh, and you should see the grandmother trees in the jungle." I recalled the thick, moist air alive with the flutter of Morpho butterflies and the thunder of howler monkeys, the sinuous vines, and the dense green canopies. I recalled it vividly, then sent the memory to the trees.

[More. What else?] The trees' energy followed me—eager, invested in every word I spoke aloud or image I sent telepathically. Branches swayed in the warm summer breeze, and the sharp sweetness of pine tickled my nose. I imagined these were tokens of gratitude for the stories I shared.

Despite my human form, I felt like an integral part of Whittaker Woods. I was the traveler of the family, the one with legs and a Catmobile. My gift was to gather stories from distant lands and spill them, like treasures, into the waiting felt sense of the trees.

My heart felt full that summer. The trees and I laughed and exchanged stories every day. I worked with close friends, cherished my morning rituals, and loved my new position in the bakery of the Café. Life flowed harmoniously. All the pieces fit perfectly.

Until August 4th, when everything changed.

On the evening of August 4th, 2020, a swift but intense windstorm swept through North Conway.

On a residential street at the northern edge of Whittaker Woods, the wind tangled itself in the branches and needles of an isolated white pine. No other tree stood by its side to shield or uphold it. Its trunk splintered near the base. With a deafening crack, the mass of the trunk left the vertical plane. It reached the roof of a house, caved it in half, destroyed the walls, and landed squarely, exactly, on top of Micah's mother standing in the kitchen, killing her instantly.

At that same moment, Leah and I stood at her kitchen window, the Catmobile safely tucked in her driveway. The trees along the road leaned, bending wildly, their interlocked canopy straining against the wind's fury. Together, they held. The storm was swift, and the woods community strong. These trees survived.

Branches and leaves littered the parking lot I called home when I returned from Leah's after the storm. I cleared the debris to reach my spot under the maple tree. The house was eerily quiet, but I thought nothing of it. I crawled into my shell, leaving the back hatch open. The leaves I knew so well seemed intact. They followed me in and hung over my pillow, as they always did. I fell asleep peacefully, completely unaware that three of my closest friends, including Micah, had just lost their mother.

"Why? Why? Ohhh, ohhh, ohhh."

I was awakened a few hours later by the sound of someone sobbing. I listened closely—several people sobbing. I got dressed quickly and found the Café family gathered in the dark at the base of the house's wooden steps.

I understood the words, the recounting of the event, yet stood in shock, wondering if I was still asleep, caught in a surreal nightmare. Mouth agape, I sat next to Micah and wrapped my arm around his hunched shoulders, pulling him close.

He looked up at me with swollen, red eyes. "Ask me, Bobcat, ask me… 'How did your mom die?'" He brought his hands up parallel to each other. "Splat!" He clapped his hands together. "Like this! Like a pancake." Then a wave of sobs.

Nobody moved. "I hate trees. I hate all trees. Why, Bobcat? Why? Why did it do it?"

My heart sank twice as I held my friend's trembling body in my arms. Once for his grief, and another for his sudden hatred for trees. His hatred wasn't just for this one tree, but all trees, all plants, everywhere, and it was retroactive.

"I've always disliked plants. They've always made me uncomfortable, and now I know why."

Several hours later, long after Micah, exhausted from grief, had retired to his room, I lay in my shell under the leaves listening to his repeated "Why" still echoing in my mind. I knew grief and anger had spoken through him and distorted his perception. Yet I too began to wonder... Why? Why would a tree purposely kill such a lovely woman?

Some, of course, would argue that it was just an accident. These things happen. But there was a precision to the death that was difficult to dismiss. If the tree had fallen just a couple of feet to the left or to the right, his mom would still be alive. If she had been in the bathroom, or the bedroom, or anywhere else, she would still be alive. But no, the tree had fallen exactly—exactly—on top of her.

I looked up at my leaves. Normally, I would have caressed one of their spines and delighted in the burst of green fragrance in my space. But not that night. I rolled to my side, buried my face in my pillow, and cried.

I didn't stop to bow to the magnificent oak tree at the intersection, though I did notice, with a sigh of relief, that it had survived the storm. I didn't stop at the entrance before the archway over the portal either. I sped through with a stomp in my step and planted myself in the middle of the trail, hands on hips, facing the forest.

"Why? Why exactly on her? Was there a greater purpose to this death? Why did you do it?"

I let my heart grow quiet, exhaling the lingering anger I realized wasn't even mine. I closed my eyes and waited for a felt answer.

[Grief.] Tree grief, like a somber, stoic silence. And there was more. I felt a wave of wordless energy through my heart. My hands dropped from my hips. And I understood—"We are sorry for your loss, Human. We also have lost many companions in the storm."

I opened my eyes and suddenly noticed the devastation through the woods I had missed, so engrossed was I in my own feelings and questions until that moment. There were downed trees all throughout the forest—young and old, saplings and grandmothers, piled in jumbled heaps, some even across the trail.

A second wave of grief hit me then. I had felt tree grief in lumber areas before, but had never considered that natural deaths could send ripples of grief through the woods.

I placed my hand on one of the fallen trees, and let the pain I felt in my heart for all my friends—three siblings and an entire forest—roll out as tears across my face.

Tree grief had a quality of deep acceptance, an understanding of life's natural cycles. Human grief, at its peak, turned inward, enclosed within the self. Yet beneath both was [Gratitude.] I had felt my friend's gratitude for my presence as I held his sobbing body. I felt a similar sense of gratitude and friendship from the trees as I rested my hand on the fallen wood.

Then I wondered again...

"So it was the wind. Why did the wind do it?"

[Melancholy. Amusement.] The feeling settled in my heart as: "No, Little One, the wind just blows. That's what it does. It's not personal. It's not malicious. Death is just part of life. Death is not the end. We get recycled."

"But, you're sad."

[Family.] "We honor fallen family, as you do. We are a collective of energies with mutual care and reverence."

The simplicity of the answer belied the wise and ancient felt sense behind and beyond it. The trees spoke to me with the kindness of grandparents humoring a child who asks strange questions with obvious answers.

I sat in the leaves at the foot of a stately pine and pressed my back against its bark. In that moment, in our shared grief, I felt closer to the Whitaker Woods than I had ever before.

I never told Micah about the grief of trees. I don't think he would have heard it then, and he never fully trusted plants again.

I didn't tell anyone at the Café either. We all felt the weight of what had happened. The team stepped up without hesitation, covering Micah's shifts so he could grieve. We started earlier, stayed later, worked harder. I began driving to work rather than crossing the woods to steal just a few more minutes of sleep from each night.

Summer turned into fall, the air crisping at the edges, the cold settling into the mornings and stretching deeper into the nights. I switched to my winter sleeping bag.

Even after Micah rejoined us, I kept driving for the heated cab as much as the extra rest.

Then, one morning, I woke up to a frozen-solid mug of tea *inside* the Catmobile's shell. Ice crusted the rim, the liquid locked in time. That was my cue to finally accept Leah's offer of her warm upstairs spare bedroom.

I knew I wouldn't stay long. I never did. But I enjoyed Leah's company while I waited for my next destination to reveal itself.

"Bobcat, come work for me," Aaron's message began. "I'm setting up canvas tents in Tampa to sell fireworks over Christmas and New Year. Guaranteed two grand minimum. I'll give you the best tent. Just come on down. Isn't it cold where you are anyway?"

Selling fireworks in Tampa? I could trade frostbitten days for shorts and tank tops *and* earn travel money?

Why not?

On my last day in North Conway, I returned to my trees for goodbyes. They felt sleepy, almost groggy, already sinking into winter's sleep, but I still felt their gentle love as I embraced the bigger ones by the trail.

"Take care! I love you, Woods."

I left again, and this time, I took *them* with me.

Here is my secret: At the height of that summer, I filmed my entire walk through Whittaker Woods. The sun-dappled leaves. Flickers of movement in the understory. The familiar bends I could have walked blindfolded. The twin sentinels at the portal. The trees where my palm always lingered, their bark warm even on cool mornings. The wind weaving through the canopy, and those single leaves that shouldn't sway yet frantically waved hello.

I wanted to remember it all—the way the woods breathed, the way they held me.

The unedited footage sits on my laptop, always ready for a stroll. No music, just the hush of the trail—the wind, the birdsongs, and the rhythmic crunch of leaves under my steps.

Sometimes, when I press play, I can almost catch a whiff of pine in the air.

Chapter 4
They all talk to me

North Conway, New Hampshire - 2018

The sweet, earthy scent of green moss, the sparkles of mica in the schist, the gentle flutter of the wind through the ready-to-depart leaves, the golden streams of late afternoon light dancing on the trail as the canopy breathed open and closed. My trusty poles by my side, resting on the moss and extending across the trail, my pack against a tree, a smooth round rock by the side of the trail on which to sit, rest, listen, and absorb.

This was my perfect moment in the Whites.

I had climbed two mountains that day—up the exposed granite to the first summit of Baldface, then across the link-up trail of sparkly sand and soft moss to the second summit, where I ate a handful of nuts and gazed out at distant peaks. But I waited until I had returned below the alpine zone and into the woods before eating the one magic mushroom I had brought.

I had spent much of the fall of 2016, two years prior, and all summer that year learning how to communicate with the trees in Whittaker Woods, right in town. I was pleased with my progress, but had not yet taken my new skills to the hills or tested my felt sense in wild woods.

I held the fun friend in my hand and spun its dry stem. Its umbrella formed almost a perfect circle, so that it appeared stationary even as it spun. I felt into the mushroom to see if it was ready, as I was. I felt a [yes.]

"Hi!" I pressed the mushroom to my heart. "My wish today, if you're willing to help, is to hear the trees, listen to their secrets, and learn from their wisdom."

I chewed the dried mushroom, chased it with a piece of chocolate, then knelt by the nearby stream and washed both down with fresh mountain spring water.

"Thank you, Mushrooms. Thank you, Stream."

I continued hiking, joyously planting poles and soles on the path, weaving through roots and rocks.

A few miles later, the mushroom announced its arrival with a subtle somersault in my stomach. A warm, spreading sensation tingled in my limbs, loosening the tension in my shoulders. My jaw felt… fuzzy—like it had been clenched and now, at last, could let go.

I stopped and leaned my pack against a tree. Wrapping my arms around its sturdy trunk, I hugged it tightly and pressed my cheek to its rough bark. My love poured into the tree, but it remained energetically silent.

I settled back on a smooth round rock by the trail and opened my senses to the woods—the moss, the sparkly mica, the golden light, and of course, the trees. All that was left to do was wait for the shift in perception I knew was imminent.

A thought drifted in:

"So… since trees have feelings, they must feel when we hug them…"

I looked back at the tree that held my pack and placed my hand on its bark, listening.

Still nothing.

"I wonder if the other trees are aware when one gets hugged. Do trees feel jealousy?"

[Connection.] An unmistakably tree feeling appeared in my heart, and through it, a silent response unfurled, which my mind translated into words as "We are connected energetically and physically through the mycelium in the soil. So it makes no difference. When you hug one, you hug us all."

By 2018, I had not yet, ever, received such a detailed answer from the trees in Whittaker Woods.

"Well," I muttered, "that sounds like something *I* would think. Maybe I can't actually communicate with trees, maybe I just imagine I do." I shook my head in agreement with my own skepticism as though someone else had just pointed out an obvious truth.

I placed my hands in a cone shape in front of my mouth. "Can you hear me?"

There was no answer, but my attention was suddenly drawn to one particular tree across the trail, slightly down the hill toward the river. That could have been an answer—the tree pulling my attention—but I couldn't prove it. Conversing with trees still felt so murky then.

I focused on the one tree. I thought it might be a birch, or maybe a beech, or a fir, or…

"I'm sorry, tree. I don't know what you are. I only recognize oaks, maples, and pines. I've tried to learn the names of other trees, but no matter how many times I've tried, I've forgotten even faster."

[Good.]

The response thrummed through my chest—subtle yet certain, like a pulse of knowing that wasn't mine.

By then, the mushroom was dancing a nauseating jig in my stomach. It was worth it. My perception was shifting. The woods separated in layers by distance, like a diorama, with front trees, middle trees, and background trees. I moved my head side to side to explore this new version of reality and noticed that when I did, the layers moved in relation to each other—front trees swinging in my field of view, middle trees a little less, background trees holding steady.

"Why is it good?" I asked the one tree.

The gold light filtering through the canopy illuminated swirling suspended particles, maybe bugs, pollen, or seeds, transforming each ray of light into a fairy world. A sense of pure joy welled up within me—the pure joy of sitting in the woods with fairy lights and trees. Was this joy mine? Was I sensing the baseline feeling of a forest?

Focus!—I tilted my head and stared at the bark of just the one tree.

"Why is it good?" I repeated, sending the energetic feeling of "why" from my heart to the tree.

[Because…]

A sudden, complex feeling, and all at once I understood the relationship structure of trees. This birch—if it was a birch—shared a closer bond with the nearby pine sapling than with the birch down by the river, in the background zone. A family of trees wasn't defined by common physical characteristics but by bonds of familiarity. The trees in my immediate circle all knew each other, had grown up together, relied on each other, and *felt* similar—a common energetic signature, almost like a last name.

[Family…]

The tree feeling morphed and expanded on the same topic. [Good.] Because had I known the names of trees, my mind would have classified them by default. I might not have been open to a different classification.

My Geology training had led me to organize rocks by the classification I had learned at the university. The schist I first met in the Washington Cascades had similar characteristics to the schist of New Hampshire—same foliation, same sparkly micas, etc. That is how I had recognized it. But in that moment on the trail in the Whites, I felt and knew beyond a doubt that this schist was more closely related energetically to the moss and trees that surrounded it than schist anywhere else in the world. Freed from learned taxonomy, the natural world revealed itself as a network of friendly, interconnected neighborhoods.

I smiled and bowed in gratitude to the tree for sharing this new perspective.

[Friendship...]

I felt the tree's kind gaze upon me, a feeling similar to sensing someone—a human—staring at one's back. With a hand on my heart, I returned the friendly attention.

That first tree had a youthful, masculine energy, while its nearest neighboring plant felt feminine and older, although she was smaller and potentially younger in human linear years. The tree next to them, a pine I think, felt calm. I returned to the first tree. It felt... [Patiently eager.]

Many years prior, in a remote Yemeni village, I had met a man who truly wished to communicate. He and I had stubbornly drawn in the sand with sticks, made gestures, sounds and pantomimes until a spark of mutual understanding lit our faces and whole phrases were shared without common words. [Patiently eager] was similar to that feeling.

[Benevolent witness] was the feminine plant's energy. I had once observed a woman on a subway. The man across from her had stood up and offered his seat to an elder. I watched her watch them and smile without intervening. The feminine plant watched us, the tree and me, communicate in the same spirit, [Benevolent witness.]

[A human who can hear us.]

My gaze swept the forest, sensing the personality of each tree and plant more clearly than ever before. Each one I touched with awareness turned toward me, slow at first, like a ripple spreading outward, until a critical point was reached. Then, all at once, they all turned. Every tree. Every plant. Every root and leaf, every unseen tendril beneath the earth, the mycelium, the rhizomes—everyone. They turned and stared. Friendly. Curious.

I wasn't prepared for the overwhelming flood of connection. A wave of probably unjustified panic and claustrophobia swept through my body. I stood up from the rock. I was a tiny human in a land of giants leaning down to stare at me, albeit kindly. Even the moss was curious. The berry bushes perked up. The trees rubbed their canopies together, conferring, deciding. I felt all their feelings at once in a deafening silent cacophony.

"Thank you!" I spoke aloud to the forest in general and the first tree in particular. It was a dismissive thank you, with the energy of "I have enough now." But the feeling of engulfment only intensified.

"I'm sorry. I'm new at this. This is a bit much." I could hear growing panic in my trembling voice.

I quickly shouldered my pack, slipped my poles' straps around my wrists, and hurried down the trail. But it was too late. Even down the trail, trees and plants seemed to call out to me.

[Are you the human who speaks with trees?] [Can you hear us?] [Can we talk to you?][Wait. Human. Wait!]

I quickened my steps, but the wave of the news of my being able to hear tree feelings outpaced me. I was submerged as if a dam had broken and all the opinions and wisdom, complaints and curiosities the forest held poured in my direction. Because I had opened the door. Because I said I wanted to hear. Because I ate the mushroom with specific intention.

And so, I will admit, not proudly, that I began to run.

With legs pumping and heart racing, I ran down the trail, using my poles to vault over rocks and roots. I felt the trail closing in energetically, each plant to the side leaning to watch my swift passage. I could have sworn they even leaned physically as I seemed to hit many more branches and leaves than I had on the hike up.

I was alone, but if someone had seen me, they'd probably have thought a bear was on my heels. I ran to the Catmobile, fumbled for the key, unlocked the door, flung my pack in the passenger seat, jumped in, and slammed the door shut.

Only then did I catch my breath.

The truck's attention turned toward me, but this was a familiar, welcome energy. I sensed a curiosity, an inquiring tone to its attention.

"Pphew. Hi, Love. I sure am happy to see you. You won't believe what just happened..."

I told the truck the whole story, and then I laughed and laughed at myself. And the truck held me in its love and filled my heart with kind words: "It's okay. You're just human. You're just learning. It's okay."

Chapter 5
The Pacific Northwest Trail

Pacific Northwest Trail (Montana to Washington) - July to September 2019

Something happens to the human psyche when steeped in Nature for a prolonged time. Far from other humans or their constructs, whether physical or mental, doors crack open in the mind and our younger self reawakens. Once again, we can hear the humming of the world, perceive creatures across the veil, attune to the language of trees, and inhale air thick with knowings. But do we choose to believe it? And if we do, can we handle it?

For several months, on the Pacific Northwest Trail (PNT), my only tie to the human world was my backpack, its contents, and a map on my phone.

I began the trail on the eastern side of Glacier National Park, in Montana, with what I would consider "normal hiker insanity." I narrated my own hike aloud, sang songs to birds and bears, hugged trees and blessed my drinking water with trust and gratitude rather than filtering it—nothing unusual for me.

But Glacier still had obvious trails, clear signage, and the safety of other people and park rangers. Once past Polebridge, Montana was as wild as I had dreamed: hundreds of miles of pristine forests in the sole company of wolves, grizzlies, and other forest dwellers.

The PNT was unlike any trail I'd walked. Sometimes, there was a clear ribbon of dirt through the forest, but more often, it was a game of bushwhacking, navigation, and survival. I spoke aloud almost constantly. "Is this the trail?" "Are you the trail?" "Hey, Tree, do you know where the trail is?" And called through the woods, "Hey, Bear. I see your scat. It's fresh. Never mind me, I'm just passing through."

At the time, these seemed like normal navigational and safety monologues. In truth, the loosening of my mind was so subtly gradual, it was imperceptible, except in hindsight.

By Western Montana, after several stretches of trail with no other humans in sight for weeks, I began to see and hear *things*.

They always lurked right at the edge of my field of vision. They wore green, gold, and brown garments, stealthy outfits with pointy sleeves and curly hoods. They were tall, slender, and swift. I only caught glimpses of their movement as they ran through the woods parallel to the trail and kept in step with my progress. But if I stopped or turned to find them, there was only the forest—only trees and the undeniable sense that something had just been there. I heard their giggles and strange whispered language that rose and fell with singing tones. Yet, if I paused to listen, the giggles tumbled down with the sound of bubbling brooks, and the whispers hid in the buzz of insects and rustle of wind through the trees. Still, I was sure they were there.

I was completely alone though, and when I'm alone, what I fear most is fear itself. So I asked them, "I feel you. I hear you. Someday, I'd love to meet you and speak with you. But please, don't show yourself now. If you're something unnatural, I'll get scared, and I have nowhere to hide and a long hike to go."

Although the Woodlings, Elementals, Tree Spirits—or whatever they were—respected my wish, I still felt uneasy, so I began speaking more intently with the trees.

Before the Woodlings, I'd simply greeted trees and plants in passing, but now I made a point to engage them in longer conversations. I felt safer and less alone that way, and I learned a lot from the forest.

[Curiosity.] Some of the trees I met in Western Montana had only encountered a few humans before. And some I met when I was lost and completely off-trail—which happened more than I'll admit—felt surprised, as though they'd never seen a human before. Their focused curiosity followed me as I walked by.

Even in Whittaker Woods, where I considered the trees personal friends, almost family, there was always a certain... *restraint* to the energy of the trees. But the pristine forests in Montana buzzed unabashedly, like a bustling village where all members supported each other, vibrant and filled with joy. They observed me with brief curiosity, but their attention quickly returned to their endlessly interconnected lives, too busy thriving together to linger on my presence.

Wild plants didn't compete for sunlight or nutrients as some humans believe—they thrived together. That is what one ponderosa who took the time to speak with me taught me.

One afternoon, the trail dipped into a shady glade, where an inviting bed of ponderosa needles called my name and spoke of a nap. As I rested on the ground, looking up at the light filtering through its branches, I asked the tree, "Do you grow taller because, in this glade, you don't compete with other plants?"

[Ppppfuf.] The closest I could equate the energy of the ponderosa's answer was a mixture of a scoff and a chuckle. As the branches swayed in the wind, I imagined the tree was shaking its head.

[Growing slowly; growing wisely.] I felt the energy of the answer, but I wasn't sure what the tree meant, so I leaned my back against the trunk and closed my eyes.

"Explain, please."

The thoughts that flooded my mind felt like my own, yet they carried new understanding. Small trees growing in the shade of large trees weren't struggling but thriving in safety—just as children grow under the protection of their mother's care. Rather than compete, members of the forest preferred being in close proximity. When an Elder died, the Young reached the sunshine having learned all the lessons of the shade. Even when sap no longer flowed under their bark, the wisdom essence of the Resting Elders remained, offering peace and protection to the saplings. [Cycles. Life.] There was no death as humans understand it in the forest's worldview. New plants grew on the Resting Elders, and the cycle continued.

I thought about how humans often intervene in forests, thinning trees, claiming that this helps the forest breathe and prevents forest fires. There had been so many forest fires lately, and their number seemed to increase every year.

As though it had been following my thoughts, the ponderosa's energy shifted—a subtle, layered feeling I couldn't quite decipher. It wasn't anger or judgment. There was a calm patience about it, perhaps even a tinge of bittersweetness.

[Thinning. Not for us. For you.]

Yes, of course. How arrogant of us humans to even dream we could improve upon the forest's ancient and self-sustaining system. The forest didn't need help breathing; we did.

The ponderosa's energy softened, wrapping me in amused compassion. Humans. We were so young, yet we too were part of the cycle—flawed, but learning.

I stood up and pressed my heart against the ponderosa's bark, arms almost reaching around its girth for an embrace.

"Thank you." I sent it love from my heart and felt [Love, gratitude] in return.

By Eastern Washington, the Woodlings' half-glimpses and the giggles in the woods had become daily occurrences, as familiar as the fresh bear tracks and scat. They no longer worried me; they were simply part of my journey. By then, my legs were also stronger, and I hiked with ease and joy, singing songs and greeting trees and plants with a nod or a "Hello." I kept my felt sense wide open, receiving the trees' and plants' energetic messages as I walked by.

[Joy. Happiness. Curiosity] were the main energies of saplings by the trail.

[Motherly protection] was the most common feeling among short berry bushes. I'd ask and thank them for their bursts of sweetness, and their energy would shift to [You're welcome. Smile.]

If I asked, and they felt [no,] I kept going, even if my food bag was down to its last drags of peanut butter and crackers.

On one such occasion, I turned around when I reached the ridge to take in the view of the berry-lined trail. A bear had just arrived and was eating berries. If I had not asked, listened, or obeyed, I would have been right there with the bear. The berry bush had known and kindly urged me onward. It was a marionberry bush, I believe. I bowed to it in gratitude from the ridge and hiked on.

With the passing miles, I grew more and more attuned to the trees' feelings. Either my senses sharpened, or the news of my approach preceded me and I was allowed deeper sharing. Yet I grew frustrated. The trees were sharing freely, but all I could sense were vague feelings—tree feelings, very different from mine—I then had to interpret based on my limited human understanding. Nuances were lost. I longed to sit with a tree and ask questions out loud and hear undeniable answers—preferably in English—with my ears.

One late morning, the trail sloped gently down into a valley with winding switchbacks. I had spent most of that day in the woods and was grateful for a small patch of sun with views of the forest canopy below. I dropped my pack on the trail to enjoy one last snack in the sun before returning to the shaded woods. Hawks soared overhead, leaves rustled, and the forest canopy swayed in the breeze. I noticed one leaf waving, its pendulum motion more pronounced and faster than the surrounding leaves.

"Hi, Leaf! I see you." I waved back.

As the rest of the canopy swayed, two trunks brushed against each other, creaking back and forth.

"Maybe you too are trying to get my attention." I chuckled, but just then, the creaking stopped. The hawks still soared, the canopy still swayed, and the leaf still waved, so why had the creaking trees stopped?

When they finally resumed, I listened closely. The sound formed a pattern:

"Iiiinnn. Iiin. Silence. Iiiiiinnn. Iin. Silence."

"Can you hear me?" I asked the rubbing trees.

"Iiiiinnnn. Iin."

"If you hear me, speak twice."

"Iiiiinnn. Iin." Well... that didn't help. It was the normal pattern.

"Okay. If you hear me, say something else."

"Iiiiinnn." My jaw dropped. It had to be a coincidence. So I tested it.

"Okay. Speak twice."

"Iiiinnnn. Iiin."

"And something else?"

"Iiin."

I know. At first, I didn't believe it either. I sat right on that trail and conversed with the rubbing trees for over an hour, collecting as much data as my inner scientist required. There wasn't an exact correlation, but it exceeded the probability of random chance, and I was sufficiently convinced to begin asking real rather than test questions.

We established that two rubs meant "yes" and anything else meant "no," and we were talking. I can't recall all the questions I asked, but one stood out:

"As a forest, are you happy?"

There was no answer.

"Can you still hear me?"

"Iiiinnn. Iin."

"Are you happy?"

It remained silent. I repeated the question several times. This was the most consistent set of data yet. This forest was not happy. But how to ask "why" with only "yes" or "no" questions? Besides, the sun was getting low and I still had many miles to the next river, where I hoped to refill my water bladder and camp.

I stood back up, shouldered my pack, and sent love to the rubbing trees, thanking them for the conversation. As I entered the forest, I felt an immediate shift. The air felt... heavier. The trees stood still, but not in peace—something was missing. Joy? Connection? It was true. This forest wasn't happy, but why? I had been walking among happy trees for so long—what was different about this place?

The trail descended into the sad forest, contouring the mountain until it met a T-intersection with a dirt road. For weeks, I had hiked on narrow, rugged trails deep in the wilderness, surrounded by the hum of pristine forests. At first, the open sky and wide road felt like a reprieve—space to stretch my stride and soak in some sun. But as the road curved and my trail runners crunched loose gravel, a cold sense of unease curled in my stomach.

A logging road. Of course.

It was so obvious in hindsight, I just hadn't thought about it. As I turned the next bend, a pile of cut trees came into view, all jumbled with stripped branches and torn bark. The sharp, sour smell of decaying wood filled the air, mingling with the faint iron tang of sap bleeding from raw stumps onto the dark, ravaged earth. In my mind's eye, the image flashed of piled bodies in Auschwitz. The silence of the forest seemed to echo the same [Agony. Death.] Nausea churned in my gut and rose toward my throat.

I quickened my steps, clinging to logic as if it could shield me. They're not human bodies. They're trees. My thoughts stumbled forward, frantic to make sense of so much death. "These trees are likely grown specifically to be cut, to fulfill human needs. I use wood. I use paper and tissue, don't I? Well… This is where they come from. Let's not be a hypocrite here."

Suddenly, my body lurched, heart in my throat. Still within view of the lumber pile, I doubled over off the side of the road, hands pressed on my knees for support, and rode wave after wave of dry retching. Finally, I forced myself upright and wiped my mouth with the back of my hand.

I didn't cry that day. I just walked on, my vision blurred with the sting of tears I refused to let fall. I kept my eyes fixed on the ground, one hand pressed against my sternum to hold myself together. I didn't look back at the pile of severed lives behind me.

But this was just the first pile. For the next few days, the official PNT followed logging roads, forcing me to confront one mound of carnage after another. Each pile of lumber, each torn forest, felt like a fresh wound on the earth. The Auschwitz image kept flashing through my mind—piles of lifeless forms that had once been living families, their silence now louder than any chainsaw.

I tried to make peace with the devastation, sending apologies to the woods as I walked. "I'm sorry. I'm sorry." But the words felt hollow. Logic crept in, eager to console: "Humanity needs this. We need the lumber for homes, for paper, for everything." But, underneath, a bitter rage grew. The anger was toward myself for my helplessness, the world for its endless hunger, and God, Spirit, or whoever had designed this cruel and broken system.

The trail became my private little Hell. The "Road of the Dead," as I called it, was muggy and buggy, incessantly uphill, and lined with sorrow. Old pickup trucks rumbled past, kicking up dust that stuck to my sweat-drenched skin. None of them stopped or offered a ride out of Hell.

Only one stopped, a man on a horse, his boots caked with mud and hat pulled low to his eyebrows.

"What are you doing here?" he snarled in a deep voice.

"Hi! I'm walking a long trail called the PNT," I forced a smile and a cheery, light tone. "It goes from Montana to the Pacific Ocean."

"Walking? Well, that's *stupid*. The Good Lord gave us horses for a reason." He pulled on the reins and spat to the side. "Just don't bother my cows."

I assured him I wouldn't bother no cows and hurried on, eager to leave his property behind.

I was just past the river, past the edge of his property, when the dam holding back my anger and frustration finally broke. I think the cowboy was the last drop. Out of nowhere, a raw, primal roar erupted from my core, ripping through my throat like wildfire. My head snapped back and shook with rage as my fists clenched toward the sky.

The roar echoed off the surrounding hills, reverberating through the empty air, crashing back down on me and the forest. My whole body shook with the force of it.

Then, silence.

The forest paused, holding its breath. No birdsong, no crunching of leaves underfoot, no creak of tree trunks rubbing in the wind. Even the insects seemed to halt. I blinked, inhaled deeply, and felt the quiet settle around me. For a fleeting moment, the entire forest had heard my pain. I nodded to it. It understood. It knew.

Then, as a paused movie resumes, the forest came back to life. A bird chirped, leaves rustled in the breeze, and the faint hum of insects once again circled me. I took another deep breath, readjusted my pack's straps on my shoulders, and walked on, uphill in the muggy, buggy air.

The trail is like that. No matter what happens, one must keep walking, at least to the next town; survival depends on it.

I lost my voice for a couple of days after that roar. A silent ache lingered in my throat. But strangely, I felt lighter, as though something dark and heavy had been released and left behind on that hillside. Eventually, the trail veered away from the logging roads and returned to single-track ribbons of dirt. The weight didn't return until I was almost within sight of the next town—the town of Republic.

According to the map, only one more hill, a plateau, and a long descent into Republic separated me from my next food resupply. My food bag was near empty, my heels rubbed raw and blistered, and my thoughts laser-focused on the promise of reprieve. A warm, hearty meal and a couple of nights in a real bed—that would no doubt lift my spirit and reignite my love for the trail. That was how it usually worked.

The trail climbed steadily through a young forest, its trees thin and evenly spaced, with underbrush so sparse it barely clung to the ground. But I hardly noticed. My mind was elsewhere, ticking through logistics: food resupply, recharge electronics, find a trail angel's house for a couple of nights. The rhythm of my steps and poles lulled me into a kind of waking trance, the trees barely at the edge of my awareness.

Until I popped up onto the plateau, and stopped.

A wildfire had swept through recently and the forest was burnt to skeletons. Blackened trunks jutted skyward like jagged spears, their gnarled branches clawing at nothing. The uniformity of the charred remains betrayed the truth: this had been a planted forest. It was not born wild but sown by human hands for human purposes.

The ground was littered with charred pieces of bark. From their patterns, texture, and faint vanilla scent, I recognized my friend Ponderosa. But these were not like the Resting Elders of old-growth forests, whose spirits lingered to guide the living. Nor were they like the sap-bleeding stumps of logged forests, where sorrow and pain hung heavy in the air.

No, these felt different.

Here, there was nothing. No life, no energy, no trace of wisdom or stories to be shared. Not even the faint echo of pain. The trees weren't just burnt; they were absent, utterly energetically *gone*.

"Wow. You guys must have gotten caught in a wildfire." I stepped off trail, trail runners sinking into ashes. "But… aren't you ponderosas? I thought ponderosas' bark was fire-resistant. How did you all get so burnt and… gone?"

The trees felt so absent, I didn't expect an answer, yet one came—a sudden download of understanding in the tree-equivalent of a young male voice in my mind:

"We left on purpose. All over the world, we are letting ourselves burn. That is why there are more and more forest fires each year. We have no Elders to guide us. We are all the same age here. There is no life, no joy, in such a forest. We live on in the Spirit world. But, down on Earth, we will no longer do humans' bidding."

The words carried no anger, only a stern resolution. Then came the images—wordless yet vivid. I saw the burnt forests I had crossed on the Pacific Crest Trail. One of the pioneer plants, first to emerge from the ashes, was a tall grass with purple flowers called Poodle Dog Bush. I remembered its painful lesson. The rash it gave me had been worse than Poison Oak. Now I understood—Poodle Dog Bush wasn't merely a pioneer species, it kept humans at bay with its poison-laden hairs, preventing them from returning to the scene and exploiting the newly enriched soil. The plant world was setting boundaries.

I nodded slowly, the pieces falling into place. Another memory surfaced: the forest I had walked through near Yaak in western Montana, blackened and still smoldering. Right along the trail, through the ashes, I had found the most delicious morels I had ever tasted. The mushrooms had been abundant, almost otherworldly in their generosity, and many roamed the ashes in search of them.

"But what about the mushrooms?" I asked the tree spirit. "They're not setting boundaries or keeping humans away. If anything, they draw us in."

Again, a young male voice answered. "Mycelium has chosen another path. They believe humanity can be saved, and so they produce fruit—the mushrooms—that humans ingest. All mushrooms have the power to alter human consciousness, not just the hallucinogenic ones."

Then, the voice left, and I was once again alone in the forest of hollow shells.

I walked through and out of the dead forest to a ridge from which I could see Republic in the distance, the angularity of its roofs obvious along the river. In spite of the good news about the mushrooms, I couldn't help a sense of deep loss for all the trees that had chosen to leave Earth. I sat on a rock and sobbed—deep, unrelenting sobs. With no one to witness, I let my sadness flow freely, as many tears as it needed.

Through the blur of my crying, a small, dark shape caught my eye. A black feather lay on the ground, delicate and sharp against the barren earth. I picked it up and twirled it between my fingers. It felt significant. I tucked it into my hair, imagining it as a chimney to funnel the dark thoughts from my mind, to let them rise and dissolve into the sky.

When I looked up, an eagle soared overhead, its wings outstretched, gliding with effortless grace. This also felt significant, another symbolic message to soothe me. Perhaps Eagle, from his higher vantage point, could see what I couldn't—a way out of this sorrow, a solution to the human needs predicament.

But before I could dwell on the thought, thunder rumbled in the distance and a flash of lightning lit the underbelly of dark clouds on the horizon. I suddenly remembered I was standing on an exposed plateau. I wiped the tears out of my eyes, quickly shouldered my pack, and hurried down the ridge before the storm could reach me.

I wasn't fast enough. I almost died in that lightning storm, but that's a story for another book.

By some classic trail magic, the lightning missed, and shortly after, I found a ride into town and to a trail angel's house. There, I spent the next few days soothing my hoarse throat with tea and honey and my heavy heart with the soft purrs of a house cat curled on my lap.

ℝ · ℞

I quit the trail shortly after, not because of the miles ahead, but because of the weight within. I had opened myself wide to hear the trees' truth and feel the forest's grief, and found I wasn't ready to bear it.

So I stood by the road outside Republic to hitchhike back to Bellingham—back to civilization, ice cream, movies, and the comfort of my bed in the Catmobile.

It took five rides.

The third ride came from a man about my age in a battered pick-up truck. He was soft-spoken, with gentle eyes and strong callused hands. As I climbed into the passenger seat, he glanced at me. "I figured I'd give you a ride. A woman alone could get herself in trouble in these parts. At least I'll know you're safe until the next town."

His voice was calm and kind, but I felt a slight unease.

We filled the silence with small talk: "Where are you from?" "What do you do?" The safe, shallow waters of conversation. Then it slipped out—he was a logger.

I wanted to ask him the tree-hugging, aching questions burning in my heart: "How do you do it?" "Don't you see you're killing conscious beings?" "Don't you feel them?" But of course, I didn't. He wouldn't have understood the sadness, anger, and judgment simmering just beneath my tongue, not when he had so kindly offered me a safe ride.

Instead, I started cautiously.

"So... how long have you been a logger?"

"Pretty much my whole life. My dad was a logger, and now my youngest works alongside me. It's hard work, but I like being out in the forest, working with the team."

His tone was steady, matter-of-fact, but there was something underneath—a flicker of pride, maybe even love.

As the ride neared its end, one of the questions I'd been holding finally escaped.

"Do you ever feel sad when cutting trees?" I almost said "killing."

He paused, his eyes fixed on the road ahead.

"You know," he said slowly, "... yeah, I do, sometimes. They're beautiful. I mean, forests are beautiful. Mostly, I guess I'm thankful. Logging has put a roof over my head and food on my family's table my whole life. You know?"

He turned to me with a smile. Simple words, but I sensed in them his quiet reverence.

His love for the forest wasn't like mine—connective and spiritual—it was rooted in gratitude, self-consistent with his accepted worldview, and just as genuine.

As I stepped out of the truck, I turned to thank him, and he wished me good luck. The tires spun against loose rocks as he sped away, the truck's metal bed creaking and groaning with each bump. I stood for a moment, watching the dust settle, then stuck my thumb out again, my thoughts swirling.

How could I be so certain my perspective was the right one? How could I judge what was right or wrong, vile or necessary? Perhaps trees truly spoke to me; perhaps I imagined their voices to validate what I already believed. Had I become so attuned to the trees that subtler truths were shared with me, or had I walked alone in the woods for too long and lost my mind a little?

Lost it, found it? Who knew?

Chapter 6
The Joshua trees of Death Valley

Death Valley National Park, California - April 2019

I felt it in my sleep. Something or someone was moving near my body in the physical world. Yet this was impossible. My body was on a sleeping pad on a small tarp in a rocky wash at the edge of an alluvial fan below the Cottonwood Mountains in the middle of Death Valley National Park—as far away from any humans as a sleeping pad could be.

"You can't cross Death Valley solo. It's just too remote. It's too dangerous," my friend Hippie Long Stockings had warned me. And Hippie had hiked over thirty-five thousand miles alone on various wilderness trails, so she would know. But I had left the Catmobile at the Tecopa hot springs, traversed the Amargosa Range, braved the twelve-mile expanse of the Badwater salt flats—in the dark, chased by a lightning storm—and sunk in mud pits along the deserted West Side road. Somehow, by 50% miracle and 50% grit, I had emerged alive into the civilization oasis of Furnace Creek. The Park ranger there had warned me about impending hundred-degree days and possible flash floods. I had rested, resupplied, and begun hiking again, this time from the Eureka Sand Dunes toward Ubehebe Crater.

And that was how I found myself miles and miles from any logical human presence.

The presence felt male. A man was near me. Instinctively, my breathing quickened in my sleep. This was a technique I used often in my years of solitary living in the Catmobile, to quickly wake myself up in case of danger. As my breathing quickened, so did my heart rate. My body wriggled and twisted on my sleeping pad until, at last, my eyes snapped open.

There, in the rocky wash, by my sleeping pad, stood a tall, thin man in mustard-colored pants. He didn't look like a hiker, tourist, park ranger, Native American, or even like the ghost of a long-dead pioneer. His face was young, framed by auburn curls and a well-groomed beard that rested over the collar of a light-colored shirt.

A surge of fear shot through my body like an icy fluid from my fingertips to my toes. Our eyes locked. Suddenly, I was wide awake. I caught a flash of surprise on his face, but immediately, his expression softened.

"It's okay. I'm a friend." He extended a soothing hand toward me, palm open and fingers wide. His voice was soft and kind. And I think I believed him, until I caught his furtive glance up the wash toward... I tilted my head back to follow his gaze. Two men and one woman, slightly older than the mustard pants man, knelt ten or so feet away from me. Between them sat a box, like a small white cooler.

"The human..." the mustard pants man began. The woman looked up and lifted a white device toward me.

I woke up at dawn the next morning with a certitude in my heart about the visit, but no physical evidence to back it up. Rocks do not betray visitors' footsteps.

℘ · ℭ

The previous afternoon

"You're just too good to be true. I can't take my eyes off of you..."

I sang at full volume to the canyon around me—the incredibly colorful canyon. The iron yellows and pinks, the manganese purple, and the weathered mica greens painted the walls of the narrow canyon as it slowly rose and opened to a plateau. In any other location closer to a drivable road, this canyon would have been one of the highlights of Death Valley's tourist attractions. And yet, this dry, dusty floor held no footsteps but mine.

I was still singing when I reached the plateau and exited the painted canyon, scrambling on hands and knees to clear the last of the climb.

"But if you feel like I—" My song cut short. Suddenly, I felt a presence behind me. I spun around and looked down into the canyon I'd just left. Something inexplicably mustard yellow flashed by. Mustard yellow was not the color of any minerals in the canyon, nor was it a shade found in the dirt on the plateau. I listened intently. Nothing moved. There was nothing there, except the canyon, the plateau, and right below me, a lone Joshua tree, arms outstretched to the cloudless sky, with nothing mustard yellow about it.

Still feeling uneasy, I knelt down, unfolded the map on the dirt, and aligned my compass to the GPS. I knew where I was; I just needed to orient myself toward a safe exit canyon on the other side of the plateau, one I hoped would lead me safely to the skirt of rocky alluvial fans in the valley below. From there, it would be a straight walk to Ubehebe Crater and my water cache the next morning.

But as I was studying the map, there it was again—this presence.

"Hello? Anybody here?" I heard the slight trembling in my voice. Somewhere down the canyon, something moved. I stood up and saw the tail of a lizard as it disappeared behind a small pile of rocks at the foot of the Joshua tree.

I took a deep breath and shook off my unease, letting it flow out through my arms and fingers. I then lined the compass to the horizon. My exit was due north. I slipped the GPS and compass into my pack's side pocket and set off across the plateau with long strides.

The plateau was a stark, pristine landscape, a vast expanse of beige sand and pebbles glinting under the desert sun. The barren world held its breath, motionless under the piercing sun, no breeze to stir the dust, no vegetation, no shelter, not even a shadow—only at the horizon, heat waves rising and falling in slow, endless shimmers where earth met sky. Nothing could survive here—only flies, lizards, and me, for the length of one precious crossing.

I licked my cracked lips and began humming to the rhythmic crunching of my steps. How I loved this solitude. How special I felt to be the sole witness of this raw, unyielding beauty.

My heart lightened, and a little skip joined the cadence of my steps. Soon, I was singing again.

"…I love you Baby, and if it's quite alright…"

I was still singing when I reached the northern edge of the plateau, where the packed beige dirt met reddish-black cinder sand and pebbles, remnants of an ancient volcanic eruption. They didn't mix, though; instead, the sharp boundary of their contrast traced a sinuous line on the ground. I left the GPS track to follow this yin/yang line as it seemed to coincide with my compass heading. The moonscape, now split in half by the striking line, gradually began to slope downward. Small shrubs reappeared on each side of the line, and with them Life—spiders, beetles, butterflies. The line contoured the cinder cone, then faded back into beige, revealing a field of Joshua trees surrounding the mouth of my exit canyon.

I stopped abruptly and wiped the sweat from my brow with a sigh. I pulled out the map and compass and traced my journey with a finger, across the featureless plateau, around the cinder cone, and to this point. I tapped on my location on the map and shook my head.

No doubt about it, this *was* my exit. And to reach it, I had to cross the field of Joshua trees.

It is not difficult to walk through a field of Joshua trees as they tend to cherish their personal space and grow far apart from each other. Just a day prior, I would have jumped for joy at the opportunity to walk among them. I would have greeted them as friends, fellow lovers of stark landscapes and solitude. I would not have tapped on the map while nervously biting my lip.

Because, a day prior, I hadn't yet seen them for what they truly were.

೮ · ೮ଽ

The morning before that afternoon

"Joshua!"

I had been hiking up rocky washes since I had left the cracked mud flats at the foot of the Eureka dunes. The landscape was barren except for occasional black cryptobiotic patches and sparse ankle-height sagebrush and mesquite. I had been, by far, the tallest living thing around, until I spied the first Joshua tree.

The magnificent being stood about eight feet tall, solitary and resilient among the rocks.

"Hi, Joshua! It's so good to see you." I approached it for a hug, but my shade umbrella, tied to my pack to shield me from the scorching hundred-degree day, prevented me from a full embrace. I bounced back and suddenly saw it—a white flower the size of a small pineapple. In all my years being in love with Joshua trees, I had never known they produced such blooms.

"Woah. Look at your flower. May I please touch it?"

I received no answer, so I respectfully plucked just one petal and left the rest of the flower undisturbed. The white petal felt unexpectedly supple and moist. I gazed up at the Joshua tree in wonder.

"How incredible! You have a watery flower, and there's no water here anywhere!"

I carefully placed the petal into my pocket to study it later and hiked on up the hill.

Slowly and gradually, the concentration of Joshua trees increased as I gained elevation. Some were over ten feet tall, others shorter than me. Some stood solitary; others grew in small groups, with saplings tugging at their skirts. A few had flowers, but most didn't. Some had decaying fallen Elders at their feet. And one, about a foot taller than me, had fallen over and was bent just a few inches above the dried dirt. It was still alive, just bent and fallen over, for no reason I could see.

"What happened to you? How did you fall? Here, hold on." With a heart full of compassion for this fallen friend, I dropped my pack and approached its trunk. I checked in with my felt sense and asked, "Can I help you?"

The tree had a male energy. That is all I could perceive. It neither reacted nor responded to my presence or question. Determined, I wrapped my arms around its trunk, about the width of a young man's waist, and tried to lift it. It was much heavier than I had expected. It didn't move at all. I repositioned myself, using a bent knee for leverage, and tried pushing it up.

In my younger years, I had taken a Wilderness First Responder class, during which I had helped carry a pretend injured man to safety. Lifting this Joshua tree felt exactly like lifting a man—same height, width, and weight. But, beyond that, *it felt like lifting a man.* Maybe not exactly human, but not vegetal either—something else.

[Annoyance] was the first feeling I felt from the Joshua tree. It didn't want my help. I frowned, slowly lowered it to the ground, and stepped back, confused.

"Let me help. I'm strong enough to lift you. I can prop you up. I think if you stay bent like this, you could die because your circulation is cut off," I explained to the Joshua tree, aloud and with clarifying gestures. I spoke as I would to a reluctant, injured human clearly in need of assistance but too stubborn or in shock to accept it. I wasn't certain that being bent meant death for a Joshua tree, but it seemed likely based on what I knew about other trees and human limbs.

[No.]

At least, that answer was crystal clear.

I shouldered my backpack and reluctantly left the Joshua tree as it wished, bent, with its arms dragging on the ground.

Still puzzled by the unwilling Joshua tree, I began checking each one I passed by energetically staring at their trunk, the same way I had greeted the trees in Whittaker Woods. But none responded, and I sensed their silence was deliberate. But why? Were they shy? There were no other footsteps, maybe they had no prior experience with humans.

I only knew one way to find out. I planted myself in front of a particularly tall and wide Joshua tree and focused all my attention on it. I placed a hand on my heart, bowed slightly, and spoke to the Joshua tree, respectfully, as I would have to an oak or pine in an old-growth forest.

"Hello, Joshua. I'm The Bobcat. I have loved your kind for many years. I know you might not have seen any humans before but…"

[We have.]

A felt answer interrupted my introductions. The closest human words were "We have," but the simple words carried the weight of an ancient history I couldn't perceive and nuances I couldn't decipher.

[Annoyance. Contempt.] There—those were the feelings behind the words. I focused even harder, emptying my mind to perceive more of its answer. What ancient history? Why the contempt?

Although she shared nothing more, I felt her energy was female, old, wise and regal—like an ancient empress, older than the Earth itself. I shifted my focus to the Joshua tree next to her. He felt male, also regal, but slightly younger. Her energy turned away in contempt, but he answered me.

His answer came in the form of an instant knowledge download. A wave of complex feelings hit me, and it took my mind a minute to sort and translate the download into concepts I could understand. I stared blankly at his trunk as the realizations trickled into my conscious mind. Then, with eyes wide and mouth agape, I took a step back.

Joshua trees were not of this world. They came from another galaxy long before most life appeared on Earth. Their sense of time was different from ours. By my human reckoning of time, they felt almost immortal. They arrived as a seed, possibly on an asteroid. Their regal, contemptuous energy and the longing for their home world was passed from tree to flower to seed, or directly to offspring, as Joshua trees could reproduce in both ways. They saw themselves as vastly superior to humans and other life forms but held contempt for humans the most. We were a nuisance—not because of our careless or dangerous ways, but because of our insufferable primitiveness. They had interacted with early humanoids, then later modern humans. They saw little difference and had consequently chosen high-altitude deserts as their habitat to minimize interactions with other life forms.

"If you came as a seed on an asteroid, does that mean all Joshua trees are descendants from the one same seed? Or just this family here?" I pointed to the Joshua trees in the rocky wash where we stood. "You know, I have spoken with Joshua

Trees in Anza Borrego before. They were much friendlier. Are they also descendants from the same seed?"

[Move along, human.] I felt energetically shushed, as a king might wave away a filthy peasant by wiggling bejeweled fingers. The feeling bordered on animosity, but I stayed planted in front of it. There was something else... something the Joshua tree was not saying, yet relevant... And suddenly, I got it.

"Oh!" I took another step back and looked around. "You are not the only representative of your planet currently on Earth, are you?"

༄ · ༄

Ubehebe Crater, after the mustard yellow pants man visit

I left the alluvial fans' rocky ridges and washes, where no alien footsteps could be seen, and headed toward the rolling hills of black cinder leading to Ubehebe Crater. The morning sun still hung low near the horizon, yet the fierce wind that blew over the crater and threatened to topple me was already hot.

GPS in hand, I followed the geocache arrow down the hill from the Ubehebe parking lot and to the creosote bush where I had hidden a two-gallon water cache.
"Yay! Water!"
There was never any guarantee that my water caches would be intact when I reached them. With a sigh of relief, I dropped my pack and slid it into the shade under the creosote bush. The events of the night, which had felt completely real to me, still swirled in my mind. I lifted the low creosote branches, crawled into its shade, and reclined on my pack.

"Hi, Creosote." I caressed a few of the small leaves on the spindly branches right above me. "Thank you for the shade. Thank you for keeping my water safe."

I pulled out a bag of almonds from my pack and took a large gulp of lukewarm water from one of the jugs.

"Okay," I thought. "So let's say I really had aliens visit me, and I didn't dream or imagine the whole thing. Why? What were they doing?"

[Collecting DNA sample.] The creosote answered the question I had not spoken aloud. I don't know how it knew, but the felt sense was unmistakable.

"Were they aliens?"

[Mustard Yellow.] I shook my head in agreement. Mustard yellow indeed.

"But why were they collecting samples of my DNA?"

[Woman hiking alone in the desert. Aberrant human behavior. Data point needed to be collected and studied.]

I opened both palms to the sky and gazed up at the branches.

"What's aberrant about my behavior?"

The creosote remained silent.

Chapter 7
Witnesses

Cocles Beach, Puerto Viejo, Costa Rica - March 2022

The island was a turtle, or maybe a whale—a turtle-whale—and she seemed to be looking right at me. She must have sensed that I could see beyond her physical form to her primal, animalistic essence. That's why she smiled.

The coral shelf had always been there, as had the small, round cave streaked with pelican droppings. But never before had I noticed the shelf was a smile and the cave a curious eye, scanning the beach, finding me there, breathless with wonder. With her green foliage hair and rocky arms folded by her sides, she exuded the patient wisdom of one who had watched the world shift, one who had seen it all.

Before that moment, the island had always intimidated me. Since I first saw her, I wanted to swim to her and climb on her back, but her jagged cliffs, jutting straight out of the sea, seemed unreachable and unscalable. Violent waves battered her sides constantly. And the resident hawks and pelicans guarded their sanctuary with fierce cries and sharp swooping maneuvers.

Yet, I'd heard stories. People did swim to the island— past the breaking waves, the sharks, and whatever else lurked below. They climbed on her sharp back, jumped off, and returned alive. So it could be done, but how?

And there she was now, smiling and winking her one eye invitingly. She wasn't a dangerous island; she was a gentle grandmother turtle-whale with opinions about whom she let climb on her back. And it seemed she was beckoning, inviting, calling me to her.

Oh, how different the world looked through psilocybin eyes.

It was my third day in a row on magic mushrooms— strictly for business research, of course. The Golden Teachers were my latest experiment, one of four strains of *Psilocybe cubensis* stashed in my backpack, soon to be the magic in my upcoming mushroom chocolate business. And really, how could I sell mushrooms without trying them myself first?

So each day, my friend Sky and I ate a gram each of a different strain, letting the mushrooms choose the time and place. The Wollabas had asked for sunset on Playa Negra, the Cambodians had preferred midday deep in the jungle, and the Golden Teachers had chosen mid-afternoon at Cocles Beach, right across from Cocles Island.

Cocles Island, who was now smiling, beckoning.

"Sky, I think…" I began, meaning to say, "…I'm gonna swim to the island." But in that instant, the island's energy shifted. Her coral smile twisted, and her winking eye glanced past me toward the jungle. A wave struck her rocky face, rolling back to the sea like tears.

What had just happened? What was this new energy? A message, perhaps? I closed my eyes, inhaled deeply, and focused all my altered attention on the island.

[Red Flag. Not safe. Leave.] A chill crawled up my arms and prickled my neck. Her energy was a kind warning, with an undertone of concern.

"Sky, I think… we need to go. It's not safe here."

I sprang up from our shared sarong, startling Sky from her reverie. She turned to me, her eyes still soft and distant—the look of someone lost in their love of the sea. Slowly, she tilted her head, bringing herself back to land.

I scanned the jungle behind us for whatever hidden threat the island had sensed. Sky's gaze followed mine. Trees, plants, birds—nothing seemed unusual in the jungle.

"If you feel it, Maya, I trust you." She swept the view with an open palm, "But… it feels so safe here. Look."

I looked, and yes, she was right. The sun was warm, the sea crystal clear. Tourists lounged, melting in the sun like scoops of vanilla ice cream. Children and dogs buzzed around them, giggling, tracing spirals in the sand, building and wrecking castles, then surrendering back to the sea. Just a postcard-perfect afternoon on a Caribbean beach.

Sky looked back to me, her brow a gentle question mark.

I knew what I had felt, but—alright, I was on mushrooms. Maybe the Golden Teachers had stirred some latent paranoia in me that had nothing to do with the beach or jungle. I sat back down on the sarong and scooted closer to Sky. She smiled and placed her hand on mine.

"Besides…" Her gaze drifted back to the sea. "We're divinely protected. Always."

And to further anchor her unwavering faith, she began to sing.

"I release control, and surrender to the flow of Love, that will heal me…"

Each word settled peace back into my heart. She watched the ocean; I watched her.

Through the Golden Teachers' lens, I saw Sky as she truly was—an Elf Princess, timeless and ethereal. It wasn't just her long, graceful neck, her wide Caribbean-blue eyes, or her naturally pointed ears. Rather, it was the sense of primordial wisdom she carried, a regal calm beyond her young Earth years, and the magic forest melodies she shared wherever we went. Everyone fell in love with Sky when she sang.

[You need to go. This is not a safe place.] The island's energy broke even through Sky's medicine song. The message was clear, pressing, and I couldn't ignore it.

"Sky. We—we need to go. I don't know why; we just do."

She nodded. No further questions asked. We stood, shook sand from the sarong, shouldered our beach bags, and walked toward an opening in the trees along the beach. As we walked, Sky continued singing, "… release control and surrender to the sea…" over and over.

When we reached the jungle's edge, Sky stopped abruptly. At that same instant, something slammed into my stomach, like an energetic punch.

"Did you feel that? What was it?" Sky's voice held a rare edge of worry as she glanced at me. Now she felt it too.

In front of us, a clearing opened through the trees, accessible by a muddy path from the main road. A fallen tree lay across the entrance, like a purposeful barrier between the beach and the clearing. To our left and right, almond trees stood like guardians, their roots sprawling out like draperies bridging the two worlds. All around, smaller bushes clustered around the edge, ambassadors of the dark tangle of the jungle behind them.

As I scanned the trees around the clearing, a shiver ran through me, lifting every hair on my arms and neck.

"It's the trees." My voice was low and solemn.

"What do you feel from them?"

"It's… heavy, whatever it is. I don't know yet."

Without a word, we both climbed onto the fallen tree, as if it had been placed there just for us, a raft of safety between worlds.

Sky pressed her hand gently on my upper back. "Ask them. Ask the trees," she whispered. "I'll watch your back and keep you safe."

I chose the tree to our right—a tall, steadfast almond tree with a grounded presence. I stared at its trunk, then let my eyes defocus and my inner sense unfurl in its direction, as I'd learned in the woods of New Hampshire.

"I will hear you, Tree," I called to it. "Whatever it is."

Slowly, the tree turned its awareness toward me—heavy, raw, pulsing

[Disgust. Heartbreak. Pain.] I shivered. Sky pressed a little harder on my back.

"Why?"

[Fear. Terror. Pain. Despair.] The energetic answers uncoiled in my mind, and nausea rose inside me, thick and insistent. I fought to steady myself as my mind scrambled for reasons. What had humans done to this tree? Was its trunk carved, cut, burnt? But no—I checked; the bark looked intact, the tree's trunk was whole and unscarred.

[Terror. Despair. Disgust.] The tree continued, and each of its energetic waves struck like blows. I opened myself wider, calling on the mushrooms to take me deeper, to the root of the tree's angst. I would hear it, as I had promised.

And the images came, shadowed and jagged, more feeling than form. Sounds. Screams. Glimpses. Fragments... A small motorized vehicle, rumbling in the dark. A girl, standing alone. Men circling. Her confusion curdled to fear, then to terror beyond words. Violation worse than death. Repeatedly. Nausea reached my throat. I felt her despair pouring from the tree. The force of it lurched me forward, and I gagged, retching the weight of what I felt. Sky's arm wrapped around me as I doubled over.

"Maya!" Her voice pulled me back, and I opened my eyes, tears now streaming down my face.

The girl was long gone. The act was long done. But the trees—those silent witnesses who'd heard her screams, felt her terror—still held her anguish as a dark imprint into their bark and roots. Now the weight was in my heart too, pressing into my chest, thickening the air in my lungs with anger. These trees were suffocating under the memory, unable to shed it, and there was nothing I could do to ease the grip of that dark energy.

I couldn't... but Sky was with me. I shared the vision, sights, sounds, horror, and despair with her.

When I finished, we stood together, side by side on the fallen log, hands clasped tight. In silence, we looked at the trees, bearing witness to the witnesses, our eyes damp with tears.

Sky finally spoke, her voice soft but sure, "We can't change what's passed. But maybe we can help ease the weight they carry."

"How could we do that?"

She smiled, even through the tears. "With song medicine. I can sing to the trees, and we can let the love flow through us and to them."

From Sky's heart, throat, and lips rose a melody so pure, so sorrowful, it felt drawn from the ocean's deepest currents. No words—only sounds, high and low, like waves lapping softly against the shore. She sang as though time had melted away, as though we had stepped into another realm—the trees' world.

The sun dipped to the west, casting long shadows across the forest canopy. Tourists folded their towels, gathered their children, whistled for their dogs, and left the beach. And still, Sky sang. The last glow faded, and dusk engulfed the jungle. At last, her song slowed to a hum, then fell into silence.

[Thank you.] The felt words came, not from one tree but from the whole community in the clearing. Their presence softened, a peaceful gratitude settling around us. And my own heart eased, finding rest in the quiet that followed her song.

We placed our hands on a few trunks, wishing them well and promising to return to visit sometime.

I turned back toward the island and waved goodbye. There she was—smiling once more, her rocky shelf mouth a quiet, sad smile, but a smile nonetheless. I felt her nod, a small but unmistakable gesture of kinship and gratitude. Had she warned me of a danger because she felt the heavy energy along the shore, or had she sized us up with her little cave eye and thought, "These two have songs and love in their hearts. Let's see if I can push them toward the trees."

Either way, my relationship with the island was never the same after that day. I have since swum to her and climbed on her back dozens of times. She is Home, that sweet turtle-whale floating in the sea.

ꕤ · ꕤ

I hesitated to ask. Did I really want to know? What if knowing made it worse? But the weight in my chest didn't lift, so after a week, I asked. I knew Joe would know; he devoured news for breakfast daily.

"Hey… was there ever an attack at Punta Cocles?"

Joe's expression darkened. "Yeah." He set his coffee down.

Not only did he know, he'd been part of the search party that night. His voice dropped as he recounted:

Two young German girls—they'd done everything right. They'd called a Tuk-Tuk, a local taxi, to take them home safely. But instead, the driver had veered off onto the beach path, delivering them to a group of his male friends. One girl escaped and raised the alarm. The other… was violated and discarded in the jungle. Yet she survived. She played dead, hid in the darkness, and walked out of the trees at dawn.

Sky and I had known none of this before the trees showed us.

The scene of the horror lay just around the bend at Punta Cocles, about 500 feet from where we'd stood. It was a place I'd always avoided without knowing why. Such was the reach of human violence that, even months later, hundreds of feet away, the trees still trembled from the memory of that night.

I was grateful we spoke to trees at a reasonable distance. I don't know that I could have withstood, within my own body, the energy carried by the trees at the epicenter of the tragedy.

Two weeks later, Sky flew home to the United States, and for several months, I kept my distance from the clearing across from Cocles Island. But, eventually, my love for the turtle-whale drew me back.

[Hola!] The almond tree in the clearing recognized me.

[Song. Thank you.] All the trees remembered Sky's song.

I believe that without Sky's song, I would have carried the trauma of the images the trees showed me, but her magic melody sheltered me. I kept enough of the memory to recount it here, but the jagged edges do not pierce me as they did that day on the log.

I don't know if the trees will ever fully heal. Perhaps they chose to keep some of the energy, holding it as silent vigils. I haven't asked them, but if we're all connected, I'd like to believe that somewhere in Germany, a girl feels the strength of the Cocles trees in her bones, a quiet support that lessens her pain. And perhaps Sky's song reached her too, a thread of grace and love woven through the distance. I hope so.

<u>Part 2</u>

THE ANCIENT ONES

Chapter 8
Spiders

Houaïlou, New Caledonia - 1977

The strong water flow hit the center of the spoon and immediately cascaded around in an extended spray like a skirt of water diamonds. Spoon waterfalls, as I called them, were the main reason I loved doing the dishes as a child. The game wasn't water efficient, but our water came from a stream up the mountain behind the house. It was always running, and always with strong pressure.

The pipe to the house ran from the stream to our yard, disappearing beneath the red dirt past the banana trees, plumeria trees, hibiscus bushes, and the ubiquitous bougainvillea.

These plants marked a sharp boundary between the untamed Bush—a blend of shrubland and dry tropical forest endemic to New Caledonia—and our carefully tended yard.

My mother worked ceaselessly to tame the Bush's advance. She meticulously manicured the buffalo grass and planted fruit and flower trees in the yard. Around the papaya, lychee, and fragrant frangipane trees, she arranged river rocks into circular gardens and filled them with rich soil from the river bank to grow daisies of all colors. The prettiest of the jungle plants, she invited into our home and on the covered patio in front of the house. She wove intricate macramé hangers to suspend planters and pots, showcasing their natural beauty.

On the weekend, my parents loved hosting friends on the patio for leisurely afternoons of coffee and cookies to the tunes of the phonograph—Bombastic or lyrical classical pieces, soulful old American blues, rhythmic Cuban melodies, or the dramatic French *chanteurs* and *chanteuses* of their childhood.

As I remember it, my parents' house was an oasis of sophistication, a haven of civilization in the midst of the wild Bush.

Only two incontrollables vexed this sophistication. The first problem was my feet—as a barefoot wildling in a land of red iron-nickel dirt, I stained anything I touched. My mother's rule was: "Always hose yourself outside before you enter the house." But the Houaïlou red dirt wasn't so easily tamed. I scrubbed and scrubbed, and still, it followed me onto floors, sofas, linens, even walls. And the rule only applied to me; my mother's cat was free to follow his whims in and out of the house. In the end, she painted the cement floors iron-nickel red, adding colorful confetti in the paint for flair. This partially fixed the first problem.

The second problem was the creepy crawlies—crawlies were the dominant lifeform in the Bush, and no amount of spraying, cleaning, or sealing could prevent their intrusion. Cockroaches crawled in our beds, centipedes dwelt in the sofa, ants ate our bread, and long-legged hairy spiders and short legged bug-eyed ones vied for prime ceiling corners all around the house. There was no solution to the second problem, but still, my mother upheld us to a tight cleaning code. All potential hiding places, like clothes and toys, were to be diligently stowed and stored in their proper places. The kitchen in particular, the focal hub for most crawlies, was to be kept impeccable. And as part of this protocol, it was one of my duties to clean the dishes promptly once meals were over.

And so it was, on one sunny Sunday afternoon, as my parents and their guests relaxed on the patio, phonograph tunes mingling with the aroma of little post-meal coffees, that I stood at the sink with a sizable stack of dishes, ready to play.

I moved the spoon in and out of the water flow, shifting the waterfall of little diamonds to one side then the other, and giggled. This was the last of the spoons. I climbed on tiptoes on my stool to reach the drying rack and placed it with its siblings. It was time for my next game: spin-the plates. I lifted the first one, fingers ready to spin, when suddenly, I froze.

Mrs. Spider herself, as big as my seven-year-old's palm, sat in the middle of the next plate. I had seen many spiders in and around the house, but never this close. I leaned in, pushing my hands on the sink to lift myself off the stool and move closer. Her body was in two sections, the rear about twice the size of her torso. Her hairy legs were spread evenly as though she were about to jump on me. But she didn't jump, she just rested on a strange white cushion and didn't move at all.

"What are you sitting on? What did we eat that was white?"

No sooner had I asked her than the egg sack—because it was an egg sack—broke open. A swarm of a hundred tiny black copies scurried out from under the spider, raced up the sink on all sides, and crawled on my fingers before I could understand what I was seeing.

"Haaaaa!" I screamed, jumped off the stool, and flailed, hands brushing frantically at my skin. But there were too many. They climbed higher, tiny legs pricking my neck. Panic erupted, and with one continuous screech, I bolted for the outside hose, cranked the spigot to full force, and stood under its salvation.

My dad rounded the corner, fists clenched, eyes wide— ready to fight to protect me. But instead of danger, he found me, drenched and stomping, fully clothed under the hose.

I dropped the hose and ran to his arms, tears now flushing the fear.

"What... What's going on? What happened?"

"Dad! They were crawling all over me." With my face hiding in his shirt, I pointed to the last of my nemeses swirling in the water siphoned down the concrete drain.

"What was?"

"Spiders!" Dad leaned over the drain just in time to catch the last of the baby spiders as it spun in the water's pull and vanished down the drain.

"I see..." He chuckled and engulfed me in his arms. "What we have here is a case of the Big Beast afraid of the Little Beasts."

Big Beasts or Little Beasts, no matter—that was the day I became afraid of spiders, *dreadfully* afraid of spiders.

After that day, my eyes became spider radars. All throughout the immaculate house, I found them, lurking in corners and crawling along walls when my mother was not looking. They even hung right above my bed on the top bunk, close enough to touch. We watched each other, the spiders and I. But I didn't make a move against them until after the incident at Nédivin, a few weeks later.

ഇ · ന

"Yaaaaaah." The boy screamed as he ran across the schoolyard toward me, one loosely closed fist forward. "I'm gonna throw it on you."

"I'm not afraid of lizards. Leave me alone. And let it go, you're gonna hurt it." I shook my head and squarely waited for the boy. Not only was I not afraid of lizards, but they were some of my favorite creatures, and I considered it my duty to protect them. The boy stopped right in front of me and brought his fist inches from my face. I grabbed his hand with both of mine to open his fingers and release the prisoner.

"Let it go. Don't be mean. It's a living creature, you know." We wrestled back and forth, but he was stronger, and I couldn't open his hand.

"Only…" A smirk appeared on his face, "… it's not a lizard."

He pulled the collar of my dress and flicked his fingers as though he were dropping something. Something black remained in his hand. Lizards did detach their tails when in danger. In my mind's eye, I saw the piece of lizard tail still moving in his hand. I was sure of it.

"Leave me alone. Now because of you the poor lizard has no tail."

He brought his pinched index and thumb closer to my face. One large black, hairy leg dangled between them. He cocked his head to the side, pointed to my chest with his other hand, and calmly said, "I told you. It's not a lizard. And the rest of it is in your dress."

I didn't understand right away, but followed the finger pointing at my chest. I lowered my eyes and saw the bump. I pulled the collar and looked inside the dress.

An even larger spider than the one I had found in the sink clung to my breast bone, all seven legs spread wide, beady eyes looking up at me.

I shrieked. My hands pulled on my dress and shook it. My feet stomped on the ground in terror. The boy laughed. The spider didn't fall, so I grabbed the bottom hem and threw the whole dress and spider package over my head and as far from me on the ground as possible.

Yes. That middle school nightmare where one stands in front of the whole school in their underwear? As though I didn't stand out enough—I did that.

80 · 03

97

After that day, it became personal. I was ruthless. If I saw a spider, it was a dead spider. My hands shook and my heart pounded every time, but still, I smashed, sprayed, and swatted with a fear-fueled rage. And the more I killed, the more of them there seemed to be, skittering in corners, lurking just out of reach. I sought them out and destroyed those too.

It was war, and I didn't win every battle.

One afternoon, I came home to find a *monster* spider perched right at eye level on the front door. For something that size, I knew my flip-flops were inadequate killing tools, and all chemical weapons were inside the house. Besides, I wouldn't have been brave enough to approach this one even armed. I backed away slowly, heart pounding, then circled to the back door, only to find another spider, smaller but decidedly crouched on the exact rock where the back door key was hidden, and looking at me.

I didn't even try to scare it away or kill it. Instead, I slumped under the banana tree behind the house. So much smaller than me, yet they had effectively locked me out of my own home. I looked down the hill and sighed. From the banana tree, I could see my dad's gas station and his mechanic shop. Dad had a very short commute home. Sometimes he came up just to change his shirt, if he worked on a greasy engine, or to grab a snack between jobs. I pulled out my notebook and pens from my little backpack and began doing my homework. My only chance now was to wait for Dad. He'd know what to do. He always did.

Finally, a joyous whistle drifted up the hill. Dad always whistled, all day, wherever he went. He whistled the happy tunes of a man who lived his best life.

"Dad!" I jumped up, waving both arms. He waved back, but his eyebrows rose with question marks when he saw my notebooks and pens scattered on the grass.

"But? Why are you here?"

"Dad, there's a huuuuuge spider on the door. And there's another one guarding that door." I pointed emphatically.

He laughed. "Two of them! Ha, so, they got you cornered." He continued up the path. "Come on, let's go have a little chat with these spiders and see if maybe they'll let us in." He gestured for me to follow, still laughing. "Come on, Big Beast afraid of the Little Beasts."

୧୦ · ୧୫

My spider-killing spree lasted a few months, until summer vacation, right before Christmas. It was senseless. I spared mosquitoes, rescued injured birds, beetles, and grasshoppers, shed tears for tailless lizards and wingless butterflies. I carefully stepped around stripped-shirt snakes—some of the world's deadliest—and followed my dad in shark-infested waters. The only other creature I feared, besides spiders, was the rooster in the pen at the edge of our yard—a proud, ankle-pecking tyrant furious at my daily theft of his offspring. I avoided him, but spiders, I feared and killed by the dozens.

I still vividly remember the spider that ended the hostilities. She had a round body and long, skinny legs covered in short brown hair. She ran down the white cinder block wall toward the drain and hose by the side of the house where I was scrubbing my red feet so that I could enter the house.

Why did she run toward me? Didn't she know who I was and what I did to spiders?

She leapt off the wall and landed on the concrete, mere inches from my feet. I jumped back, hose still in hand, heart pounding, but she followed me. So I pointed the high-pressure flow straight at her and blasted her back toward the drain. She swirled with the water until she caught one leg on an edge and clung there, above the abyss. I slowly moved a foot closer and leaned to see what she was doing. She was so precarious, all I'd have to do was point the hose again, and she'd be done for.

But I didn't. She was looking at me, and she felt like a gentle spider. *A gentle spider*—what a novel concept. I pointed the hose away, toward the grass. We continued staring at each other. She felt gentle... and sad. She just hung there and wasn't even scared—or so my seven-year-old imagination told me.

And, in this interminable standstill, I suddenly had a vision:

What if this spider were ten feet tall—maybe a sentient spider from another planet. What if she landed on Earth to find us, these hideous creatures standing upright with two dangling useless legs up in the air. And although she had come to Earth with kind intentions, because the sight of us caused her such fright, she killed us all—just so she wouldn't be scared anymore—the Big Beast afraid of the Little Beasts. Like me.

I turned the spigot off, dropped to my knees in front of the drain, and began to cry. Through blurry eyes, I found a stick and handed the other end to the spider—a long stick, because I was still very much afraid of her. She climbed onto the end of the stick in full trust, and I dropped her back on safe ground. She scurried off through the grass, but I remained on my knees. I had killed so many spiders—I hid my face in my hands and continued crying. So many... I had been so mean.

I wished my dad would come home early and find me. I would have explained that I didn't mean to kill them all; I was just scared.

But Dad didn't come home early that day, and I carried the shame and guilt for all my killings well into my adult years. I never killed a spider again, even though I remained dreadfully afraid of them.

It would take two more notable spiders to heal the fear.

The first of these, I met on the Pacific Crest Trail.

෨ · ෫

Pacific Crest Trail, Sierra Foothills - June 2012

Only about eight miles from the resupply store at
Kennedy Meadows, the trail descended to follow the Kern
River. It was still early in the afternoon, but I had seen on the
map the 10,000-foot climb that awaited me. My pack was
heavy with about eight pounds of food for the next ten-day
stretch in the High Sierras, and I was weary from the bustling
hiker scene at Kennedy Meadows.

Down by the Kern, a small, human-sized patch of flat
and level sand caught my eye. I ducked under the vegetation
separating the trail from the river and sat in the spot. I was
mostly out of sight, near running water, and had ample
snacks. This was a perfect home for the night.

I dropped my pack and spread out the worn piece of
Tyvek I used as a ground cloth. I refused to carry a tent, not
only because of the weight but because I had fallen so deeply
in love with the trail that even a thin layer of silnylon or
mosquito mesh was too much separation from my beloved.

So I slept on the ground every night—rain, snow, or
shine. In the desert, scorpions had skittered across my
journal. I had cohabited with ants and snakes and never once
regretted it. But I had yet to face a spider. Other hikers had
told stories of tarantulas, black widows, and brown recluses—
some had been bitten, some had gotten ill. So far, I had been
spared both sight and bite.

"Mile 710 - by the Kern River," I began writing in my
trail journal. I had a lot to share. I had met two men in
Kennedy Meadows. How to describe them and my feelings
toward them? With the pen in my mouth, I lifted my eyes to
find the right words just in time to see her. She was typical—
brown hairy legs with orange knuckles, a fur coat on her chest

and a big elevated butt. A tarantula was decidedly running straight toward me.

The younger version of myself would have screeched, jumped up, quickly packed, and hiked on to sleep somewhere else. But after 710 miles of wilderness, the trail had already changed me.

I raised my palm like a stop sign. "Stop right there!" I commanded her.

And the spider stopped.

"Do you understand me?"

She lifted one leg but didn't approach any closer.

"Okay." I traced an imaginary circle around my sleeping space. "This is my space for just tonight. I will not hurt you as long as you respect my space. You can go now." I pointed a finger to a far place upriver.

And the spider actually turned around and ran in that direction.

"Mile 710 - by the Kern River. I just met a spider that seems to understand me."

Forgetting all about the Kennedy Meadows men, I described the spider instead. I felt a kinship with that spider as I increasingly did with all creatures on the trail. I let my mind muse about the interconnectedness of all living and non-living things. I wrote several pages on the topic, then closed my journal, rolled to my side, and reached to tuck it into my pack's side pocket.

There she was again, perched on top of my pack, a mere foot from my body, completely still, all eyes fixed on me.

"Hey, no." I shook a finger in front of her. She didn't move.

"The pack is part of my territory. It's also off-limits to you for the night. You understand?"

And the spider immediately turned around and ran off the pack, back to the grass by the trail.

She honored my rules. I never saw her again, yet I kept looking. Even as night fell, I scanned the rocks and bushes around me, until I had to admit I almost wished she would visit again.

That spider understood me. What if I had given her a chance to communicate rather than immediately cast her away? What could I have learned? What could have been forgiven? I guess I'll never know. I just wasn't ready yet.

It would be another six months before I had another opportunity to speak with a spider.

ৎ৩ · ৩

Happy Valley, Fairhaven, Washington, December 2012

She ran across my bare foot under the desk. My knee jerked up and hit the table—an involuntary reflex. With the blow to my knee, my swivel office chair tilted back past the point of balance and down to the floor.

Somehow, I still landed on my feet, legs wide on each side of the fallen chair.

"What the *fuck* are you doing?" Logan turned around from his own desk, a mere ten feet from mine, and glared.

This is what we had become after twenty days of living together, both unemployed in a tiny studio in a town where rain never stopped—intolerant. We had loved each other once—the way moths loved all-consuming flames. Now we glared, wings burnt to cinders.

"There's a spider. It ran across my foot, and I got startled, that's all."

"Well, just kill it. I'm trying to work here."

"I'm not going to kill her. She's a living thing, you know."

He sprang from his chair. In two steps, he crossed the space between our desks. He lifted my chair by its sidearm and tossed it to the side. Once again, I jumped out of the way. I knew this mood. When Logan lost his mind, nothing rational was safe. He leaned to locate the spider under the desk, and I watched in horror as his large foot sped toward the frozen creature.

"Nooooooo!" I threw my small frame against his body to deflect the blow. He lost his footing. "It is *my* spider. I will deal with it! Back off!"

He clenched both fists and lifted them up in attack position. I walked into the danger zone, chest high, jaw clenched and repeated in a controlled, calm voice, "It is *my* spider. Not your concern."

"What is wrong with you? It's a fucking spider. Just kill it."

I held up one hand to keep him away and, with the other, ripped a page from the journal on my desk. Then, with my protective hand still up, I scooted under the desk and offered the corner of the page to the spider.

The truth is, against all physical evidence, I was much more scared of the spider than of the man. Yet, I had to rescue her. A lifelong history with spiders compelled me to rescue her. If I didn't, he would kill her.

She seemed to understand what was at stake because she immediately ran up the page.

By the time I stood back up, she had reached the boundary between the page and my fingers. I silently shuddered as eight tickling feet scudded across my forearm. The hair on the back of my neck stood on end. I wanted to scream, run, flail, brush her off, but Logan stood watching me.

So, with apparent calm, I let the spider run up my arm. With measured steps, I walked to the sliding door. She reached my shoulder. I slid the door open. She crawled back down the front of my chest, past my pounding heart. I was in the grass. I lifted the paper, and she once again understood. She climbed back on the paper, and I deposited her gently in the grass.

"Thank you for your visit, Miss Spider. I hope you have a happy and long life."

Logan snorted. That was unnecessary sass, and we both knew it. But as I spoke these words, the spider stopped and turned toward me. She seemed to lift herself by straightening her two front legs, as though angling herself in my direction. And I imagined she was saying, "Thank you!"

All the fear drained out of me in that moment. Something shifted. That was the day I resolved my fear of spiders. That cycle was complete. And I have lived in harmony with these gentle creatures ever since.

If you're wondering, I did leave Logan shortly after. The spider incident was not the main reason, but it was the cap on the final ember.

That was when I finally left my old life behind.

I drove to Arizona, found a corner of peaceful desert near Sedona, and officially began my full-time life in the Catmobile.

ᘓ · ᘔ

Puerto Viejo, Costa Rica, February 2021

"When you live in Costa Rica, you must accept that you will be sharing your space and body with insects."

I wasn't part of the conversation, and I know neither the context nor the author of this sentence. I was simply crossing the Envision festival grounds when it floated to me through the crowd and somehow became imprinted in my mind.

I often thought about this sentence—this *truth*—when later I moved to Costa Rica, but especially in my first Costa Rican room, an open-air cabina called "the Bird House".

At the Bird House, the only barriers between the jungle and me were a wooden deck, mesh walls, and a mosquito net around my bed. During the day, I rolled the net back to feel closer to the jungle, to feel part of it. But at night, I slept better in my cocoon of mesh.

My closest neighbors, Annie and Nancy, lived above my bed, at the apex of the thatched ceiling.

They might have been sisters. They looked alike—large black-silvery backs, hairy golden knuckles and ballerina-like pointy feet—and they seemed to share the ceiling space peacefully.

Nancy was colossal, larger than my palm, including her legs. She had woven her golden web higher than Annie's, closer to the ceiling.

Annie's web was wider, spanning about six feet right above my bed. My hair and forehead often got tangled in her peripheral net. Golden orb spiders' silk didn't break, though. Whenever we met this way, I carefully peeled the threads off my body and watched them spring back to their rightful place in the balanced symmetry of her web masterpiece.

"Sorry, Annie."

"You can clear the spiders out with the broom, if you want. They're not poisonous, but they do take over. I don't know why newcomers never push back against the spiders. It's okay to claim your space. They just recreate their web in the jungle in no time. It doesn't actually hurt them."

The man had pointed to the compost toilet under the cacao trees, to the Bird House near the artificial pond, and had handed me a broom, thus concluding the ten minute orientation to my new life at the farm.

I had walked to my cabina, broom in hand, backpack ready to be dropped for a few months, determined to clear my living space of crawlies. But when I entered the room and saw them, my jaw dropped. The sisters' superimposed golden webs were a lustrous, seemingly floating mandala with a clever poke-an-wheel design of tight parallel lines, a testament to patience and precision.

I leaned the broom against one of the entrance post. I couldn't destroy such a feat of weaving. When you live in

Costa Rica, you must accept that you will be sharing your space with the most fascinating spiders you've ever met.

"Your web, wow!" I told the spiders. "Are you two deities in the arachnid world? Maybe you're daughters of Anansi—Anansi, the trickster spider God, weaver of tales and fate. Are you? I have a history with Coyote too. Another trickster. Well, I'll assume you are, and it will be an honor to live with you. Just, you stay up there, and I'll mind your web."

I then addressed each spider in turn, "I'll call you Ann, or Annie, and you can be Nancy. Annie and Nancy, daughters of Anansi."

At first, I was a little wary of sharing my space with Annie and Nancy. A lifelong journey of fear, hate, guilt, sorrow and redemption still lingered in corners of my memory.

I often glanced to the ceiling to reassure myself they remained in their own half of the Bird House. But with the passing days, I relaxed. Their territory was above mine, and we each knew where not to trespass. They never left their webs.

Annie and Nancy were not gentle pets but great huntresses, rulers of the ceiling.

Motionless, they waited patiently until an unfortunate insect brushed the sticky spiraling threads. A leg, a wing, a body part got caught, and the struggle began. Whenever this happened, I always put my book down and watched in morbid fascination, learning the intricacies of their hunt.

First, the prey naturally tried to escape, but the elastic thread bounced back and only tangled it further with each attempt. The struggle intensified until the whole web swung back and forth, with flaps and clicks and sometimes deafening shrieks, if the insect was a cicada. Parts of the web sometimes tore, but in the month and a half I lived with them, only once did I witness a successful escape—when a full-size bird got caught in the web.

But they did not engage. They waited until the prey surrendered to exhaustion. Only then—some twenty to thirty minutes later—did they approach strategically from the periphery. Strengthening the web in a concentric pattern, they moved closer and closer to the prey. When the struggle finally stilled, they struck with a precision bite. A few final shudders, then death. With their back legs on the guide threads and front legs moving rapidly, they wrapped the prey in its final resting silk cocoon.

I never witnessed the feast; it happened at night, after I turned off my reading light. By morning, the prey was always gone and the web rebuild to exact mandala specifications.

Did they really eat the entire prey—sometimes their own size—or did they have a secret pantry in the ceiling?

Regardless, I gave thanks daily that I was the Big Beast, as Dad used to call me, and not prey-size to these not-so-little Beasts.

I didn't leave the Bird House and the farm because of the spiders but because of the birds.

About a dozen ducks, seven roosters, twenty-two hens, two geese, and daily new batches of chicks and ducklings converged daily on the artificial pond ten or so feet from my bed.

The ducks and geese, I didn't mind. They followed a civilized schedule, sleeping at night and clucking during the day. But the roosters and hens—oh, those chickens —they brought me to a level of hatred of which I had not known myself capable.

Cluck cluck, cockadoodledoo, at all hours of day and night— but especially in the wee hours, when the sleep-deprived human mind turns to murderous thoughts. I tossed and turned like a prey in a web, clenching teeth and fists, burying my plugged ears further under the pillow. Sometimes, I yelled, "Shut UP!" They only clucked in return. Sometimes, I sat on the bed in the dark and meditated on the hatred. "Here is a new feeling, let's get to know it." But in the end, I was going mad and I had to leave.

"Annie, Nancy, this is my last night. I'm moving out tomorrow. I've loved living with you. Thanks for your company and for letting me watch you hunt. You are fierce beyond reckoning." I gave them both a small, respectful bow.

"Also, I heard someone else will be moving in shortly. I don't know who yet, but they might come here with a broom and clear out your web, so if you understand me at all, I recommend you move out too, just in case." I then repeated it in Spanish, just in case.

I tucked the mosquito net under the side of the bed, careful not to trap my giant green grasshopper friend in its folds. Green Grasshopper had lived with me for about a week. I assumed if the spiders understood me, he probably did as well and would act accordingly to save himself from any potential jungle-weary newcomer.

The next morning, I opened my eyes, smiled, and stretched my arms against the mosquito net. Oh, glory, this was my last morning in the Bird House. At last, the rooster nightmare would end. With a joy I hadn't felt in weeks, I flung open the mosquito net and sat on the edge of the bed. My toe touched something, and I quickly retreated both legs and looked.

Right at my feet was the back half of Green Grasshopper. I knelt next to him and brought my head closer for a forensic inspection. The severed part looked gooey.

"Oh no, Green Grasshopper, you got half digested." I looked up to the most likely culprits, but the ceiling was empty. Annie and Nancy were gone, and their webs partially torn down.

I stared at the empty space where their webs had been.

Why hadn't the grasshopper been wrapped in silk, consumed or stashed? Had the spiders left me a parting gift— half of a prey, as cats do? Had the struggle with Green

Grasshopper been so great that the webs were destroyed beyond repair, prompting them to leave?

Or had they abandoned their webs and moved away because they had understood perfectly well my warning?

I stepped outside and scanned the jungle around me.

Dozens of golden orbs dangled from webs. Were any of them my spiders? How could I know?

I waved to the jungle, just in case they were watching, then turned back to the Bird House. Time to pack—on to the next adventure.

Chapter 9
Mosquitoes

Nouméa, New Caledonia - 1985

Now, I know what you're thinking. It's all well and good to love and speak with trees and smart lifeforms like jaguars, coyotes, even spiders, but... mosquitoes? Really?

Well. Let me tell you how my love of mosquitoes began.
The year was 1985, and to be fair, before that, I didn't hate them. As a member of a family of four, I was by far the one with the least delectable blood. They didn't just choose others to bite; they actively avoided me. I could plunge my hand into a swarm and part them like Moses at the Red Sea, then retract my hand and watch the cloud reform at the tips of my fingers—such a cool trick for a tenth grader.

In 1985, I was fifteen years old and moved into a little shack in the corner of my parents' yard. It wasn't much more than a hollow concrete block with a wooden door and one small window—the kind with glass slats that could be removed quietly by bending the metal that holds them on each side, and then, just as quietly, be replaced from the outside. I'd learned how to dismantle windows like these at the Institut Jeanne d'Albret, when I was only eleven years old.

Sometimes, I still missed boarding school. But in 1984, global political unrest on the island had forced my parents to leave Houaïlou behind—the house, the gas station, my mother's store, and their beloved Bush—and start again from scratch in the "big city." With the whole family in Nouméa, it no longer made sense for me to stay at the Institut. By then, though, I'd been sneakily independent for far too long to simply adjust to being under my parents' roof again.

My official excuse for moving into the shack was that my parents bought an air conditioning unit and kept it on "Antarctica" at night. I shuffled into the kitchen in sweaters and long pants, grumbling and shivering. Sometimes, I even turned the oven on and left the door open until tropicality was restored. But in the end, the rest of the family loved the cooler nights, and I was outvoted when the decision to install the AC unit was proposed.

The other—*real*—reason I wished to live in the shack was that I was fifteen years old, and the window slats could be removed and replaced quietly.

Every Saturday night, after the rest of the family had huddled in their frozen world, I slipped on my striped leg-warmers and shoulder-padded silk shirt and slithered out. I landed softly among the bougainvillea, tiptoed across the buffalo grass, ducked under the AC unit in my parents' window, and slowly, carefully, climbed up and over the metal fence.

From there, it was only a five-minute walk to the intersection where three roads converged: the one that continued straight—which I walked every day to my high school—the one that climbed the hill to my best friend's house, and the one that turned at the post office and continued down to the beach and nightclubs.

These first five minutes were crucial. Until I turned the corner at the post office, I could still be seen from the house. My heartbeat pounded. It was so loud, louder than my thoughts. I always feared they might hear it from the house.

But I couldn't run. What if a neighbor was watching? Running would have looked suspicious. No, I walked, steadily and casually, soaking up the buzz of adrenaline coursing through my veins, every step a victory. Finally, the corner. I'd made it. Freedom! I exhaled the stress of the last few minutes and set my mind on the night ahead. Now, the whole town was my playground. Dark alleys didn't matter—nothing did— I had survived the first five minutes.

I wasn't actually a "bad kid." I didn't take drugs, didn't drink alcohol, didn't fool around with boys. All I wanted was to dance, but I was too young to go to nightclubs according to the law. So I did what any fifteen-year-old with five years of shenanigans experience would do: I made myself a fake ID—a laminated school card with an embossed seal over the photo.

Alexandra Dickens, unlike me, was old enough to dance. She was born on November 7, 1967, because I thought she'd enjoy being a Scorpio. At fifteen, I already had the body and the steady gaze of someone older, someone who could bluff her way past the bouncer's half-hearted questions. I walked into those clubs with confidence and casual detachment, and no one looked twice.

If anyone had paid attention, they might have found it odd when I stepped up to the bar to order a plain glass of milk. The first few times, it raised eyebrows, but after a couple of months, the bartenders knew me. Before I even asked, they'd pour me a glass of milk, and that was all I needed. One glass and I was off. Reggae, soca, calypso, Michael Jackson, Madonna, Kool & the Gang—I danced until sweat ran down my back, soaking my clothes in the moist tropical heat. I danced until two in the morning, until the last song—a slow one, usually—when I let a boy take me by the hand and melt with me, his arms circling my drenched body.

Then I walked home, heart thumping again as I approached the house, starting with that moment of truth when I turned the corner at the post office. Would the lights be on, and I'd been caught, or off, and I lived to see another Saturday night on the dance floor? Either way, it was worth the risk. With the lights out, I moved like a shadow: over the fence, through the dismantled window, glass slats quickly back in place, and finally to bed, my body tired, but my heart filled.

With the night light low, I rolled onto my belly and opened my journal.

What would have been the point of having adventures if I didn't record them?

Every week, I recounted every detail of my escapades—where I'd been, what I'd worn, new dance moves I'd learned, friends I'd met, and whether Jean Claude had danced with me—ooooh, Jean Claude, with that smile and the way he moved through the crowd like a cat on the prowl, straight to my heart. He always had at least a paragraph. And all this highly classified top-secret information was kept in a simple school notebook. My entire covert operation was at the mercy of one curious look from my naturally (and apparently justifiably) suspicious mother.

The thing about my mother, though, is that she had the most delectable blood in the family and was allergic to mosquito bites. If the four of us were gathered in a mosquito-infested area, they'd pass over my dad and sister, completely ignore me, and specifically swarm her.

So I devised a plan. All around the shack, I placed all kinds of empty container, as subtly as I could, and let them fill with rainwater. Some I even tucked under my bed. I grew my own mosquitoes, and lots of them.

It worked. My family, but especially my mother, avoided my room, as it was known as a "bad room for mosquitoes." If anyone broke through my first line of tiny winged defense, I knew right away by the smell of chemicals or citronella. Sometimes, I even found anti-mosquito coils left behind.

If snooping had happened, I checked my second line of defense: a single hair tucked between the first and last pages of my journal. If that hair had ever been gone, I would have known my secrets had been breached and would have braced myself for impact.

In the end, it wasn't the secret journal but the striped leg-warmers that gave me away near the end of 1987. One of my dad's friends thought he'd recognized me at the club, and I owned the only pair of striped leg-warmers on the entire island—nothing the mosquitoes could have done about that loss of plausible deniability.

I was on the hot seat and under my mother's magnifying glass for a while after that. My dad simply shook his head, his eyes squinting halfway between amusement and disapproval.

"Well, I probably did worse when I was your age, but that doesn't make it right. You've really upset your mother this time," was all he said. Still, as he looked over my fake ID—front and back, and front again—I caught, or imagined I did, just a hint of secret pride.

I only lived a few more months in my parents' home after my escapades were discovered. Although I could no longer escape at night, I continued growing mosquitoes in my room, as I still had secrets in need of guarding and had grown quite fond of their reassuring buzzing. I didn't specifically talk to them then, not like I did in later years, but always, when I got home, opened the door to my room, and was greeted by a swarm, I smiled and whispered, "Thanks, guys."

My mother and I didn't recover from the violation of her already thin trust right away. In search of a peace solution, it was agreed I would return to the Institut Jeanne d'Albret for a few months, then off to Tahiti, to live with my aunt and uncle and finish high school.

By the time I returned to New Caledonia, diploma in hand, the house in Nouméa no longer felt like home. I had outgrown it, outgrown the shack, outgrown even my own need for rebellion. I found my own apartment, took a job teaching Writing at a trade school in Houaïlou, then eventually moved back to Nouméa to sell computers. I worked hard, saved every franc, and set my sights on the wide world beyond the small island.

The day my bank account hit one million Pacific francs— about $10,000—I knew it was time. In mid-March 1992, I bought a one-way ticket to the USA. My parents bought me a large suitcase and wished me grand adventures.

I flew away, giddy with excitement, and into the unknown.

ᛒꝋ · ᚳᚷ

Long Pine Key Campground, Everglades, Florida - January 2021

"Bobcat
I love you!
~ Puck"

I plucked the note from under the Catmobile's windshield wiper and looked across the field. The gray Cuben Fiber tent was gone. I likely would never see Puck again, but I knew that our deal had worked. That had to be why he wrote me this love note.

Twelve hours prior

I guessed the man across the field from where I parked the Catmobile was a thru-hiker from the scene in his campsite. A simple ultra-light Cuben Fiber tent was held up by two hiking poles. On the picnic table next to the tent, a small stove made from a cat food can and fueled by the antifreeze Heet was boiling water in a titanium pot. I smiled. These were classic thru-hiker telltale signs. His gear looked just like mine—except mine was still soaked from four days of slogging through the swamps of Big Cypress Preserve.

I pulled a cord between a tall pine and the Catmobile's side mirror and began sorting my wet gear on the campground lawn. I hung my pack and tent across the line first, then shook my down sleeping bag to break down its wet clumps of feathers. I turned around to hang it and stopped, startled. The young man from across the field was standing right in front of me, smiling and staring, an expectant hand extended.

"Hi, I'm Puck. You're a thru-hiker?" He nodded his bearded chin toward my soggy silnylon pack and tent hanging on the line—these were also telltale signs.

"Hi. I'm The bobcat." I shook his hand. "Well, technically, I'm a thru-hiker, but I'm not currently thru-hiking. Are you on the Florida Trail?"

"I will be. That's the plan. But I haven't started yet. So what are you doing here?"

"Oh, I just crossed the Big Cypress Preserve. I needed to rest and dry for a day, you know? I saw this campground on the map, and I liked the name."

Puck's eyes widened. "Wait, what? You walked across Big Cypress? I thought the whole trail was knee-deep in water right now."

"It is. Sometimes shins, sometimes knees, sometimes mid-thighs, and a few sections up to the bottom of my pack. Swamp walking the whole way." I lifted one of my bare feet, still pruned, to prove the deed.

Puck's head suddenly rolled back with laughter. I had not expected *this* reaction.

"Oh, my God, you're crazy! Where did you even sleep at night?"

"There are actually islands in the swamps. Well, sort of. There are places with slightly higher ground. Sometimes, it's just enough room for a tent or two. The problem is the alligators also sleep on dry ground…"

"Woah. You saw alligators?"

"I did. One hissed at me. I didn't even know alligators hissed. And I almost stepped on a cottonmouth but I…"

"Oh, my God! Sleeping in the swamps. That's insane! What about the mosquitoes? I can't even… The mosquitoes must have been out of control."

"Maybe? I don't know. Mosquitoes don't really bite me. But the mice—ooooh, the mice!" I clenched my fists and mockingly shook them toward the sky so that the whole Micedom would be apprised of my disapproval of their ways. "I have a history with mice!"

"I have a history with mosquitoes. I swear, if there's one within a mile radius, it bypasses everyone and finds me. I don't mind mice, but mosquitoes, they're the worst."

"Well. I'll tell you what we're gonna do, Puck. I'll take all your mosquitoes tonight if you take all the mice."

"Deal!" Puck extended his hand again, and we shook on it. I then placed the palm of my hands like an amplifier by the side of my mouth and theatrically called:

"Oh, winged ones, tiny, blood-thirsty denizens of the night, rising from your watery homes, I summon thee! I stand here, beneath the southern canopy, and pledge to open my home and to seek harmony and coexistence with you. I acknowledge your ancient role in the Web of Life and your place of honor in my own life, with eternal gratitude, I thank you!"

I bowed and continued, "I only ask in return that you please spare this kind man, here, your painful stings, your maddening buzz, and your relentless torment. Bring them all to me, I will have them, as this brave man, here, has vowed to rid my night of mice." I trailed off the sibilance of "mice" until it faded.

Puck's amused eyes remained fixed on mine.

"And so it is. It is done." I clapped my hands to seal the deal.

"Yep. As I said… you are crazy!" Puck laughed then turned abruptly, called back to his camp by a puttering hiss—an end-of-fuel signal we both recognized.

"Good night, Lady Bobcat," Puck called over his shoulder as he strode back to his camp. "It's been weird meeting you. Enjoy the mosquitoes. Ha."

"Good night to you, Sir Puck. Enjoy the mice." I curtsied playfully.

Puck had already been in his tent for several hours by the time I crawled into the back of the Catmobile. I lay with my head near the opened back hatch, staring at the night sky and enjoying the melody of southern nights—the chirping of crickets, the rustling of needles and leaves, the hoot of a lone owl in nearby woods, and that buzz…

Oh, that buzz! I had been so focused on the delights of the night, I hadn't noticed how many mosquitoes had entered the Catmobile.

I closed the hatch and turned my headlamp on. Oh, my! Hundreds of them swarmed and flocked, flying so thick. They gathered on windows and the carpeted sides of the truck's cap. They circled my body with their high-pitched hum, yet hardly stung me. Maybe one lone proboscis on the shoulder blade, right where I couldn't reach, and a few on my exposed arms. I leaned down to see Puck's tent through the window. His light was still off. Could it mean he was sleeping soundly? Had they heard me? Had they actually come as summoned?

"Well, if they have…" I lay back down, resolved. "I have to uphold my end of the deal."

I lay still and listened. They landed and flew off again, and again. They buzzed and buzzed, around and sometimes inside my ears. Occasionally, a tiny pinprick of pain informed me of a successful feast. I killed none. That was the deal—harmony and coexistence. If they landed, I brushed them off gently with the back of my hand. If they flew too close to my face, I blew them away with a puff of breath. And eventually, it became clear: I wasn't going to get a wink of sleep that night.

"Unless…" a thought formed. "If these mosquitoes really have responded to my call and spared Puck, then I must assume a level of intelligent communication is possible, so…"

I continued out loud: "I would like to renegotiate the terms of our agreement."

And with far less ceremony than my original plea, I revised the deal and laid out the new terms to my many, many roommates:

"Dear winged ones who have entered my home, I do not wish to kill you, and I promise to do my best not to. But I need to sleep. I would like to offer you these options:

1. If you fly to the back window, I will open it and set you free.

2. If you fly into my hands or let me catch you, I will carry you safely to the back and set you free.

3. If you wish to remain in the truck, you can, but only silently. I will even allow you to feed on my blood for a short window of time, then you must tuck yourself away quietly and under no circumstance disturb my sleep.

4. If you refuse all three options, I will, unfortunately, have to kill you. I will take no joy in it, but you will have left me no choice.

This amendment still upholds that Puck shall remain free of mosquitoes and I free of mice.

And so it is. And it is done." I clapped my hands twice to seal the deal.

I waited quietly for something to shift, but the buzzing and probing continued as before. I shook my head and smiled.

"Maybe Puck is right. I *am* insane. I mean, I can speak with trees, but trees want to speak. Why would these guys listen to me? I'm so clearly outnumbered here."

I sighed, resigning myself to a long night. I wasn't about to sleep—not with wings brushing my face and proboscises probing my skin—but I could at least close my eyes and pretend. If I didn't move, if I let my body sink into the warmth of the truck, maybe I'd get some rest. I focused on the sound of the night beyond the swarm: the rustle of palm fronds, the distant croak of a frog, the sigh of the wind in the canopy.

Minutes passed. Maybe an hour. I wasn't quite awake, but not asleep either—drifting somewhere between surrender and irritation.

Then something shifted. The hum seemed to have moved. I turned my headlamp on and pointed it toward the back hatch. My jaw dropped. Pressed against the back window was a dense cluster of mosquitoes, far more than anywhere else. Had they feasted enough and were ready to fly onward, or had they agreed to the new terms?

Option 1. I pushed the hatch ajar and, with a swift but careful brush, accompanied all ready to exit to the outside world. Then I sat up on the mattress, legs crossed, ready to engage option 2.

I followed their wings' flutter with the halo of the headlamp, offering a friendly open palm if they wished to land. None landed directly in my hand, but I observed a slowing in their flight, allowing my open hand to catch them. I softly closed my fingers around their fragile bodies, leaving ample space to ensure their safety, then pushed the back hatch ajar, slid my closed fist through the opening, and opened it to release the winged friends.

The more I did this, the easier it became. I imagined within the indistinct buzz as I perceived it, entire codes and messages were shared among them, and perhaps one of those was: "Hey, this woman's legit—let her catch you, she'll actually take you outside."

And so it was, for an hour or so, that I patiently shuttled mosquitoes to the outside world. Finally, only a few remained, buzzing against the windows, yet refusing to comply. These I assumed had opted for option 3.

Of these last renegades, only five woke me up. Two were finally escorted out. Three were killed. I felt a lump in my throat with each death sentence, but I had to uphold the deal; otherwise, how could they take me seriously?

Finally, whether from exhaustion or by agreement, I slept a peaceful night until the sun found me.

I never saw Puck again. And as we didn't exchange contact information, I had no way of asking him about his night—though I did try to find him through hiker forums, unsuccessfully. But I did hear from RV and tent campers that almost everyone at the Long Pine Key Campground, except for me, had mice incidents in the night.

℘ · ℘

Pacific Northwest Trail (PNT), Glacier National Park Section - 2019

A grizzly bear had taken down an adult moose and was feasting on the carcass right on the official PNT. A bright orange sign and red-and-white danger tape blocked the way: TRAIL CLOSED.

I pulled out the map from my hip belt and studied the terrain. I'm no trail purist and had no intention of testing a grizzly's mealtime boundaries. I traced several lines with my finger until I found some I could connect. A faint line climbed up a narrow valley to a small summit. From there, with careful navigation, I could follow the river back to the main trail, thirteen miles past the grizzly, and still reach Polebridge, my next resupply point within three days. Perfect.

I slipped my pole straps back on their respective hands, and turned away from the main trail to follow my new route.

I pressed my hands to my knees to catch my breath and turned to take in the valley I'd just climbed. My legs burned from the push, but the view… What a reroute! The river closely followed the trail, tumbling down in successive crystalline waterfalls. And right where the trail veered, before the final switchbacks, a lake the color of a cut sapphire stretched beneath the afternoon sky, so blue it looked unreal. I straightened back. Almost there. Just a short scramble away, the summit waited.

I huffed up the last few feet and emerged into a sea of wildflowers rippling across the rounded summit. White, yellow, blue, purple petals—they swayed and danced in the warm, playful breeze. Butterflies drifted from bloom to bloom, bees hummed, the whole meadow felt alive, shifting and rippling like a slow-moving tide. And right in the middle of this wild heaven sat a perfect boulder—wide, round, and throne-like, just for me.

I carefully stepped through the flowers to my throne and leaned my pack against its side.

"Well. It looks like I'll be having lunch in paradise!"

I extracted my bear-proof food bag from my backpack and, with an expert toe-to-heel tug, dropped my dusty trail runners in the grass. Oh, the bliss of freed toes.

Before enjoying a well-deserved lunch, I unfolded the map to ensure I was still on track. With one hand, I traced a line down the topographic lines, while my other hand automatically, repeatedly, traveled between the zip-lock of nuts, dried fruit, and seeds, and my mouth.

But that hand's path wasn't linear. It flapped left and right, dispersing the summit mosquitoes slowly amassing around my exposed skin.

Now usually, mosquitoes ignored me, but out there, I was the only warm body on the menu. There had been a marmot when I arrived, but it had whistled its disapproval and vanished in the flowers. And there was a bear and a dead moose, but two miles away as the crow flies. So it was just me, a yummy furless human. Lucky them.

I flicked my wrist, sending a few stragglers spinning off into the air, still unwilling to kill them. But they kept coming—first a handful, then a cloud. The hum thickened around me, rising in pitch like a warning. Needle-pricks punctured my arms, face, and toes. And yes—even the upper buttock delicacy, where my thinning pants gave them just enough access.

"Ow! C'mon, you guys, let me look at the map in peace." I shook the map with a fanning motion. All in vain.

This had happened once before, in 2012, in the High Sierra section of the PCT. I had walked through clouds of mosquitoes for days and almost lost my mind. In fact, I probably *had* lost my mind, because my solution had been to sit on a boulder by the side of the trail and roll up my sleeves. "Have at it!" I'd called to them, deciding that if I could neither fight nor avoid them, then I would experience them. I had observed with full attention the tickle of their legs, the puncture through my skin, and the filling of their bellies with my blood. I had turned the mosquito experience into a meditation, and it had worked then.

If it had worked once…

I forced myself still and watched as their spindly legs danced over my arm. They landed, flexed, then drove their needle-fine proboscis into my skin. I opened all my senses to receive the gift of this experience, but…

"Ahhhh. Quit it!" Apparently, it was no longer 2012, and I had run out of zen. I kicked my legs, shook my head, flailed my arms. They didn't care. They swarmed closer, relentless. I tried to outlast them. I really did. But then, one landed on my eyelid and another flew straight into my ear.

That did it.

"Rrrraahhhhhhhh!" I roared. "This was paradise, with all the sunshine and the flowers, and you little… *suckers* are ruining it! You're ruining paradise!"

I took a deep breath. The outburst had helped. My shoulders loosened, my breath settled. The mosquitoes still swarmed, but in the aftermath, I remembered all they had done for me.

"Yeah, seriously, you guys are ruining paradise," I said more calmly, pulling my raincoat out of my pack. "Why don't you go bite that bear or that marmot and give me a break?"

I wasn't expecting an answer, but in my mind, or imagination, I clearly heard, "We have. It's part of our contribution."

"Part of your contribution?" I repeated out loud while cinching the hood of my raincoat so that only the minimum breathing hole remained. *Contribution?* The word rolled in my mind. Mosquitoes were part of the ecosystem, sure—they fed birds, bats, frogs—but what else did they do? If everything was interconnected, as I believed, then mosquitoes couldn't be just mindless bloodsuckers. They had to serve a bigger purpose, right?

I brushed another one away. Its tiny body tumbled into the wind. It had taken a bite of me, a small part of me was with it, on its proboscis. A grin slowly spread in the tiny opening of my hood.

"Oh! What if…"

Darwin's theory of evolution, which I had studied, posited that species changed over time because different genetic traits arose through random genetic mutations. If these traits were advantageous in survival in the current environment, the mutated individuals had a greater chance to survive and reproduce, thereby passing on the new DNA variation.

Random genetic mutations? Just, like that, for no reason? What if this was the missing piece, the mosquitoes' contribution to the world? As they bit the grizzly over yonder, the marmot hiding in the flowers, the deer, the wolves, and me, didn't I get a little bit of all these DNA left over on the proboscis? And didn't this DNA get incorporated and osmosed into my being?

I opened the hood a little wider. "Woah! I am part-bear, part-marmot, and part-everything that has blood, thanks to you!"

And I spoke the words, I knew it was true. I felt strong like a bear, adaptable like a marmot, woven into the great web of warm-blooded life by nothing more than a mosquito's kiss. And that felt wonderful.

Several months later, sitting at a friend's house in Bellingham, resting and recovering from the PNT, I used her access to a library of peer-reviewed scientific research papers to investigate whether others had revealed the true contribution of mosquitoes to the world, and if, and how, they had studied it. Surprisingly, no one had. The current consensus about mosquitoes was that the saliva they inject can transmit viruses and parasites but not DNA from previous hosts.

Maybe they were right. Maybe it was impossible. But then again, how many times had science rewritten its own rules? Hadn't Copernicus been initially ridiculed when he claimed the Earth circled the Sun? Or Wegener when he proposed continental drift?

I closed the screen of my laptop. Some things couldn't be measured in a lab. Not yet, anyway. And when faced with competing interpretations, I always leaned toward the one that presupposed all things were alive, connected, and conspiring—the one that kept the world magical.

A year later, in 2020, with ample time to read during the pandemic, I came across a paragraph in *Plant Intelligence and the Imaginal Realm* by Stephen Buhner. He had been bitten by the same belief that mosquitoes were the agent of random mutations that allowed species to evolve.

Ha! So there were other Copernica out there.

Chapter 10
Bees

In my early years living in the Catmobile, life in the Sedona desert tasted like a thick, sweet nectar of pure freedom and solitude.

Eventually, the wide open spaces and full sovereignty over my time became my new normal. And, as happens with all routines, I started craving a bit more excitement. I even called on Coyote—though that's a story for later.

In the pre-Coyote era, the sharp contrast between my life in the desert and the one I'd just left behind imbued each moment with the sweetness of unexpected gifts.

In some parallel reality, there was a version of me who hadn't quit her PhD in Geophysics. I didn't think about her very often, but when I did, I pictured her still in that small room—neon lights buzzing, stacks of academic papers piling up, sitting in a chair too short to dangle her feet. She might even have thought herself happy. I hope she did. As for me, I was pleased with my own life choices.

Eventually, van-life would explode into the mainstream, reshaping the American Dream and spawning a generation of digital nomads. But this story takes place before all that, when I still had the desert to myself, before the overcrowded designated parking lots and police-enforced fourteen-day maximum stays. Back then, you could camp anywhere along any dirt road, as long as you were two miles off any pavement. Pure freedom! No crowds. No rules. Just me, the Catmobile, and an endless network of dirt roads.

I picked up a backcountry map, and the truck and I explored every inch of it. No matter how remote, we went there. The truck was still young back then, its joints didn't creak and groan over rocks and across washes like they do now. I trusted that truck with my life, knowing it would always carry me back to civilization whenever—and *if* ever—I decided to return.

After months of roaming, I finally found it—home. My own little corner of desert was a slightly elevated mound with a seven-mile radius of complete privacy. The red dirt at the summit was perfectly flat and level, and the view? A full, unobstructed 360-degree panorama of Sedona's iconic red rocks. The truck and I were by far the tallest things on the mound.

The third tallest was a spindly little catclaw plant bravely growing out of the dry, parched dirt. I loved that catclaw. We often talked, and sometimes I danced around it, barefoot in the dirt. It also marked my spot. When I returned in the evening, if I lined the truck's back bumper even with the catclaw, I was guaranteed a level bed.

Life was simple in my desert home, and mornings filled with peaceful rituals.

I'd wake up at sunrise—that glorious moment when the sun, huge and orange, slowly peeked out from behind the silhouette of Sedona's rocks. I'd push my bedding out of reach of the red dirt and sit on the tailgate, inhaling it all in—until hunger found me.

Then, I'd warm up some hot cocoa sweetened with authentic Vermont maple syrup on a tiny alcohol stove I'd made myself by punching holes in a cat food can. From the small cooler in the cab, I'd get the bananas and yogurt, then settle back on the tailgate, dangle my feet and enjoy a peaceful breakfast in perfect silence and solitude.

"Wait... is today Monday?" A random thought. If it was Monday, somewhere out there, people were probably stuck in traffic jams, inching their way to work. Some might even already be in their cubicles, heads down to make deadlines.

"Cubic lives." Another thought. Sure, I worked only occasionally and my wallet was mostly empty, while they had the advantage of a steady paycheck, but... did they have a bee?

Sedona, Arizona - May 2015

One peaceful morning, as I enjoyed my breakfast on the tailgate, a bee flew in from the desert for a little visit. She first investigated the Vermont maple syrup, but finding the lid closed, she quickly lost interest. Next she considered my cup of cocoa, circling it a few times as though she was debating about it, when, suddenly, she veered off and dove straight into my cup of yogurt. A full-body immersion.

She twisted and turned in the sticky cream, trapped and slipping deeper and deeper toward certain death.

"Oh no! Hold on, Bee." I lunged for a spoon and carefully extracted the bee, placing her on my leg.

I was wearing nearly translucent, worn-thin yoga pants that day, and even in her glutinous state, the bee's stinger pointed free of yogurt straight toward my skin. I accepted I might get stung and forced myself to remain still. Stinging me would be suicide for her, and I cared more about her life than any potential pain.

"Are you okay?"

She began shaking violently side to side, twisting her stripped yellow body like a dog shaking off water. Her stinger hovered less than a millimeter away from my leg while the rest of her body was a frantic blur of motion. She shook for almost a minute, until she stood at the center of a ring of splattered yogurt. Finally, her wings were freed.

But she didn't fly off; instead, she flapped her wings with the same desperate fervor she had used to shake her body.

And soon, she had completely shed her yogurt coat. As though nothing had happened, she calmly lifted off and flew back to the desert.

The next day, as I again enjoyed my breakfast in blissful silence and solitude, a single bee flew in from the desert. I immediately covered the yogurt, thinking, "Surely, if she's the same bee, she's not going to make the same mistake twice, but just in case." Instead, she landed on the bottle of maple syrup, and finding the lid open, slipped her tiny body inside. Her buzzing became muffled as she descended toward the bottom.

"Seriously, Bee?" I brought the bottle to my eye and peered inside. She clung to one side, not yet caught in the sticky syrup, but I wasn't sure she could get out on her own. I reached again for the spoon and carefully lowered the handle into the bottle. She seemed to understand; she stepped onto the spoon handle, and I slowly extracted her.

Unperturbed by her second close brush with death, she lingered on the handle, rubbing her front legs in delight and eagerly plunging her proboscis into the syrup.

When she had her fill, she flew up, and hovered right in front of my face. She buzzed there for a bit then flew back to the desert.

The next day, the same bee (I assumed) flew in again from the desert. This time, I was prepared. I had covered the yogurt, poured some maple syrup into a flat dish, and securely closed the syrup bottle. The bee stepped carefully around the puddle of syrup, extending her proboscis to drink her fill, and didn't get herself in any predicament.

Once satisfied, she lifted off, and as she had done the day prior, hovered then buzzed in front of my face, then back to the desert.

The next day, for the first time, I noticed her flight pattern. Before, I simply saw a bee buzzing in front of my face, but now, I wondered. Was she flying in a set pattern every day?

The following day, I watched her closely and mentally traced her flight pattern—a loop, a figure eight, and back across. The day after that—a loop, a figure eight, and back across. Yes! The bee flew the same pattern every day.

I knew bees used flight patterns to communicate with each other. I just hadn't expected she would use it to communicate with me. What was she saying? I shrugged. There was no way to know, but I hoped, maybe, a loop, figure eight, and back across simply meant, "Thank you."

That bee—*my* bee—became my favorite part of my daily morning ritual. Before, I simply dangled my feet without a care in the world, but now, I felt anxious if she was late. I scrutinized the horizon over the hill from where she seemed to arrive and listened through the silence for her buzz. She always came, eventually. And if one day—God forbid—I forgot to place the maple syrup out in the dish, she flew into the truck and buzzed in the food crates until she either found it, or I corrected my mistake with apologies. She always traced "Thank you" right in front of my face. I traced a similar pattern with my finger in response, then she flew off again. We were communicating, and I fell in love with that bee.

As the wheel of idle days turned and those of opportunities arose, I learned of a fire-spinning festival in Joshua Tree. I'd always wanted to learn how to spin fire, so I signed up online, and early the next morning, I bid the catclaw goodbye, inspected my corner of desert for micro-trash, and drove off.

I drove the rough dirt track, down the road I called Slick-Corner, past the two cattle guards, around the junipers and mesquite, onto the main dirt road, which became the paved road. Just as I was past the Bear Mountain parking lot, a hot air balloon glowing in the pink morning light appeared over Doe Mountain. Its silhouette was framed by the red rocks, and it was illuminated from within by the flame that kept it aloft. It was a once-in-a-lifetime photo opportunity, and I just had to stop.

I reached for my camera in the center console. That's when I heard her—"bbbzz bzz". The buzzing came from the food crate, specifically the one with the maple syrup.

"Oh no. Bee, you're in here?" She'd never visited this early before. Did she know I was leaving? Unfazed by the stunning scene outside, she buzzed around in the crate, searching for her maple syrup fix.

"I'm going to Joshua Tree. You can't come." I lifted the crate, opened the door, and gently coaxed her out with my hand. She flew out of the truck without a thank you.

I took the magic photo and continued on, but with a slightly heavy heart. She was so far from where we usually met. I knew bees could find their way home, but that's if they flew the path. She hadn't even looked out the window as I drove her far from her home—wherever that was.

And also, I realized, bees only lived a few weeks. I had known mine for two weeks and was leaving for another two.

Honestly, I didn't think I'd ever see her again.

Two weeks later, I was back dancing by the catclaw under a scorching late spring sun, a brand new fire staff—a gift from a stranger—spinning from hand to hand, when a bee landed on my tailgate. Now, I can't say for sure that it was the same bee, but this bee had a purpose. She was searching for something she either personally knew about or something she'd heard about in the hive. Maybe it was the Legend of the Syrup—a story danced by a bee I once knew, to pass on her legacy before her final breath.

Sedona, Arizona - June 2015 to May 2016

Once the summer heat had fully settled, as measured by my successfully frying an egg on the Catmobile's hood—which subsequently peeled the paint. Oops.—I pointed the truck north to the four-corners, Utah, and beyond. For two months, I drove from town to town on a West Coast book tour and quest to climb mountains. Then, on the way back south, I spent a week at Burning Man—my third time—and soaked for another week in the Saline Valley hot springs.

Finally, on September 27th, at four in the morning, in the reddish light of a blood moon supermoon lunar eclipse, I lined the Catmobile's back bumper precisely in line with my favorite catclaw and crawled in my bed, home again.

A message from my friend Benny, owner of Earth Tours, woke me a few hours later.

"Bobcat, would you happen to be in town? I sense you might be. I'm running a retreat on Navajo land for a group of Russian billionaires and really could use your help."

I laughed, and immediately was employed again.

Fall passed quickly and abundantly, and soon, the chill of desert winter nights chased me to the recess of my zero-degree sleeping bag. I endured it, unwilling to leave, until a thick coat of white covered all the red. Still, I resisted leaving, but Slick Corner lived up to its name, and no amount of four-wheel-drive, rear differential lock, or finesse off-road driving availed me in getting home. So I drove to the Salton Sea instead, and began hiking the much warmer San Diego Trans County Trail (SDTCT). On the SDTCT, I met a man named Kyle, who asked if I wanted to go to Cuba with him for a week.

"For a week? Sure, but only if we go now. I don't want to wait for you to finish this trail."

We landed in Havana four days later, me and this stranger named Kyle. From white sand beaches to cigar shops, we quickly ran out of money. We slept on sidewalks, sneaked into parks and resorts, ate rice and coconuts, then finally bribed our way onto a sailboat back to Florida. It took another month to hitchhike from Fort Myers back to the Catmobile waiting in San Diego.

Truck to truck, Kyle and I were gone five months.

I dropped him off at the airport in Phoenix, with love and tears of gratitude, then I drove home, at last.

On the morning of May 29th—a day I've come to call "Coyote Day"—the Catmobile and I bumped up Slick Corner, forded deep mud puddles, and finally crested the mound. I pulled up and stopped, a wide grin spreading across my face.

My favorite catclaw had grown by almost a foot and was covered in fragrant yellow flowers like clusters of small brushes, each covered in bees. There were hundreds—maybe even thousands—of bees. These bees were rounder and fuzzier than my bee had been. And while my bee had been solitary, these crawled over each other like one bustling, unified community.

I gently sat at the foot of the catclaw, directly on the warm red dirt, and watched their swift and precise movements with glee. I then closed my eyes to delight in the harmonies of their hundreds of superimposed buzzes. They flew all around me, sometimes landing on my arms and stomping for a few steps before rejoining the flowers and the joyous fray.

My heart swelled, overflowing with love for these lively new companions. After their busy harvest, I suspected they might be thirsty, so I filled the tailgate's cup holders with water, and immediately, several bees gathered around the new watering hole.

They visited for several days, filling their saddle bags with pollen and dropping in for a quick drink on the tailgate, before flying off.

Yet, none of those bees ever flew an air "Thank you" like my bee.

I've always loved bees. I think as we grow up, we form beliefs about which creatures are our allies and which are foes, shaping our delights and fears as adults. I grew up watching a cartoon about the adventures of Maya the Bee and her boyfriend, Willie. Maya the Bee was a smart girl adventurer, always curious, always exploring, and afraid of nothing. I admired her. I followed her adventures, and they inspired my own.

My first name, Melissa, means honeybee in Greek. And in Costa Rica, I am known as Maya. And that name was bestowed upon me by the King Bee himself.

Black Rock City, Nevada - 2013

The second time I went to Burning Man, I discovered the free classes. My first time, two years prior, I had wandered wide-eyed through the swirling dust, neon lights, and fire-breathing art cars, never imagining this chaotic playground could also be a place for conscious classes. But on my second visit, curiosity landed me in a classroom tent. Before I knew it, I sat cross-legged on a cushion in a circle of strangers, ready for my first Gamma Breath class.

When that class ended, I picked up a program in Center Camp and circled, out of thousands, as many classes as my bicycle could carry me to.

From "Naked Yoga" to "Poi for Beginners" and "Welding for Art," I spent all day in Burning Man school, and eventually found myself sitting on the dirt floor of a tent, waiting for "Sacred Masculine, Sacred Feminine" to begin. I was early and alone simply because "Increase Your Libido with Truth Telling," had just finished, and I had stayed to catch a moment alone.

I breathed in the dust-scented air, closed my eyes, and enjoyed a moment of peace before the class. A brief moment—within a few seconds, a man flipped the tent flap open and ducked in, antennas and bejeweled crown leading the way. He straightened to his full stature and smiled, his rounded belly stretching the striped fabric of a full-body bee suit. He looked at me, lifted his scepter as a form of greeting, and, without hesitation, walked straight toward me, making a perfect beeline.

"Maya!" He threw his hands in the air, brandishing his scepter in the excitement of our reunion, except… I shook my head.

"I'm not Maya. But I've always loved that name; I wish I was Maya." I thought about Maya the Bee and smiled.

"Are you sure?" He leaned forward until his face was mere inches from mine. "You look like Maya."

"Well, not in this life anyway, not that I know of."

He tapped two fingers on his lips pensively while straightening back to his full height.

"Mmmh. I'm rarely wrong. I'm the King Bee." He pointed to the crown on his head.

"I see that." I giggled, growing more fond of this strange man by the second.

"Do you have a Playa name yet?"

I shook my head slowly. I didn't.

Playa names are like trail names—they must be gifted to you, and from then on, they carry the memory of who you were on that particular adventure. Those who call you by that name always hold a piece of your personal legend from those moments and places. "The Bobcat" was my trail name, but the Playa had not yet claimed me.

"No, not yet," I said with a hint of sadness.

"Well then." The King Bee raised his scepter with flair, then slowly and carefully, placed it on my right shoulder and, in a loud voice, declared, "By the power vested in me by my own self as King Bee..."

He placed the scepter on my left shoulder. "...I hereby name this bee, Maya. May she carry it well, and make the hive proud."

With a grand gesture, he pulled me to my feet and into his arms, then kept me there for an embrace that would've felt far too long if this weren't Burning Man.

"I am Maya of the Playa." I rolled the words on my tongue proudly as I sat back down, my new name settling in as if it had always been mine. The King Bee plopped down beside me, and eventually, others entered the tent and filled the circle from our two positions.

The class was exquisite, and as the Sacred Masculine, the King Bee held space with grace and strength, honoring me and my sisters in the circle. Afterward, the winds of the Playa blew me elsewhere, and I never saw the King Bee again. But from that day forward, I remained Maya of the Playa. And I made sure to live up to it—to be the best adventure bee I could be, always curious, always exploring, and almost afraid of nothing.

Almost a decade later, I moved to Costa Rica. Maya seemed like the kind of bee who would live in the jungle and make chocolate for a living, more so than Melissa. So I began introducing myself as Maya, and eventually, it became my official name. Melissa Maya Wyld: Melissa, the honeybee. Maya, the Bee. Wyld, like the best honey.

Denmark, Maine - November 2016

"You know you got a bee on your nose, right?" Jim asked from the corner of his mouth while the other held tight onto a couple of nails.

Tiny legs tickled my nose, and occasionally, a pinprick of pain made me wince, but I didn't move. If I crossed my eyes, I could see her fuzzy body stomping in place. She bent down and grabbed a bit of dead skin left from a sunburn. She was cleaning me. I smiled and nodded in slow motion, careful not to disturb her.

"You're fun!" Jim chuckled then continued hammering the planks in place for the new deck.

In the fall of 2016, Jim and I lived in a cabin deep in the woods of Maine. He had struck a trade with the owner: He would build a deck and, in exchange, we could live in the cabin until we decided to drive out west together.

There was no running water, electricity, or neighbors, only the spectacular forest dressed in her most vibrant autumn wardrobe.

Our life in the woods was simple. Each morning, Jim hiked to a well deep in the forest to fetch water, then assembled planks salvaged from a decommissioned dock like a puzzle, crafting an art deck that overlooked the forest's majesty.

At night, he built fires in the metal stove with the remnant wood, and we huddled together on the worn sofa, soaking up their warmth. The cabin's walls were patched with particle board, and many windows were missing. The cold slipped through the cracks, but we didn't mind snuggling; we were newly in love.

At the time, I still worked as a barista at The Local Grocer Café a couple of days a week, so the Catmobile and I only spent half the week at the cabin. And most of that half, I spent reading and napping.

The creaking of the wood floor roused me from my nap. I blinked just in time to see Jim tiptoeing into the room.

"Hi! What time is it?" I yawned and stretched.

"Almost sunset. You've been snoring for hours," he said with a straight face.

I laughed. "No, I didn't. I don't snore." —and if I did, I wouldn't have admitted it. I didn't believe it was sunset either, but when I turned to the glass window. "Oh!" I really had slept until sunset. And what a sight! The sun was just kissing the tops of the tallest trees, making the leaves glow as though they each had little spotlights.

I sat up and pressed my forehead to the glass for a wider view. I was taking it all in, when, right above my face, I heard, "Bzzz... bzzzz." I smiled, thinking, "Aww, the bees found me! Even up here."

Still smiling, I looked up—and immediately jumped back with a squeak.

They weren't bees; they were wasps. Three wasps buzzed in circles on the glass, and occasionally tried to fly through it to return to the woods.

The window didn't open, but they couldn't stay here. One, because I wouldn't sleep knowing they were buzzing around, and also, because it would have been rude to leave them trapped.

I grabbed a tee-shirt and cringed as I approached the one most isolated on the window sill. With a quick toss, I threw the shirt over her, and—success! I scooped up the edges, forming a loose pocket around her.

"Ow!" I dropped the bundle. The wasp, now agitated, flew out and back to the window. A small red mound on my thumb suddenly burned and throbbed.

"She stung me." I held out my pulsating thumb to Jim for sympathy.

"Come on now, for real? You just threw a shirt on her. Sorry, Lovey, but I gotta side with the wasp on this one."

In one agile jump, Jim climbed over the bed and extended a finger against the window above the now agitated wasp. He left it there until she was calmer.

"Get on, I'm getting you outta here," he told the wasp.

And she got on as though she had understood him perfectly. Wearing her like a ring, he carried her down the stairs, across the living room, and out to freedom. I followed him to see if she'd sting him too, or fly away, but she waited until the sky was in sight, and only then did she fly to freedom.

"Okay, let me try it."

We were back for the second wasp. I extended my finger, inching slowly closer, but I didn't reach the window. My teeth clenched, my shoulders turned away. I might even have closed my eyes.

"It's not gonna work if you're scared of her. She's feeling your vibe. You're gonna freak her out."

"I know." I tucked my finger back into the safety of my other hand, "It's just... wasps." My face scrunched again.

"What's the deal? This morning you had a friggin' bee on your nose. What's with you and wasps? Same number of legs and wings, same size. Is it because they don't make honey?"

"No, it's because I... had seventeen wasp stingers in my butt when I was seven years old," I said in one breath.

Jim laughed and winced simultaneously, and the memory of the wasp incident suddenly surged back with startling clarity.

The place was Nesson, a black sand beach near Houaïlou. My mother was pregnant with my sister, resting her big belly in the shade of a coconut tree. My dad was leaning against another, and counting. "Eight... Seven..."

I didn't have much time to find a place to hide. The beach was wide open, and the grass offered only skinny coconut trees and a few Cook pines. I wasn't so young to think I could hide behind those. "Four… Three…" Running frantically, I suddenly spotted a fallen, decaying pine. Its trunk was hollow and sufficiently wide for me to slip in.

"Ready or not, here I come!" I committed to the hollow pine.

The pine was an excellent hiding spot. It was such an excellent hiding spot that after a while, I began to wonder if Dad was still looking for me. I didn't want to be found, but I really needed to pee. I held it as long as I could, then I figured I was already in a crouched position and barefoot. I could just drop my shorts and pee right there, then wash my feet in the ocean later.

How was there a wasp's nest between my feet? How did I not hear the wasps before my pants were down? And how did I extract myself so fast, shorts down, from the pine, as the wasps swarmed my naked buttocks? I have no idea. It happened in a blur and with a screech of death.

My shorts were still down, and tears streamed from my eyes when Dad reached me. I don't remember what happened next. I just remember laying on our doctor's table, face down, shorts down, a large ice pack covering my buttocks. He handed a cream to my parents. "Poor kiddo. Seventeen stings! She'll probably still have the fever and swelling tonight. Just keep an eye on it, and let me know if it worsens."

I hadn't thought about that story in decades. I looked up at the two remaining wasps on the window sill. I had loved bees and gleefully let them climb and crawl all over me, yet for forty years, I'd mistrusted wasps. I had loved one and feared the other, life sentences set in stone. But, I mean, I had peed on them; maybe it wasn't entirely their fault.

I took a deep breath and extended my finger right above the wasp, as Jim had done.

"I'm sorry, I forgive you, and I come in peace," I told the wasp. She stomped in place and seemed to hesitate—perhaps my change of heart was too quick to be trustworthy—but I kept my finger against the window, approaching her ever so slowly. I touched her. One leg, two legs. She was up.

Jim nonchalantly extended his index and picked up the last wasp. He led the way down the stairs, both wasps riding our fingers like royalty on carriages until we were outside. They flew up into the golden light and back to their home.

Jim wrapped his arm around my shoulders and pulled me against him.

"You did good. Nice work, Lovey!"

It seemed like an important day.

On October 28th, 2015, while sorting through photos from my summer book tour and mountain climbs, I came across a picture of my bee—the one who had traced "Thank you" and shared the sweetness of life and maple syrup with me for a few weeks.

I posted that photo on Facebook.

On October 28th, 2022, I finished writing the first draft of this *Bees* chapter, up until "It seemed like an important day."

Pleased with my progress, I closed my writing program and opened Facebook.

"7 years ago today—See your memories," it said. And there was my bee. What were the chances? Awed by the serendipity, I reposted the memory with the following caption:

"I've always been blown away by these coincidences. I'm in the middle of writing a book called *Once, When I Was Tree*. It's a collection of short stories, and I *just* finished writing the story about the bee in the desert addicted to Vermont maple syrup. I didn't even remember I had taken a photo of my bee, yet here it is. Facebook knows..."

A few likes, a few hearts, and then this comment: "Looks more like the bee's asshole cousin, 'the wasp,' to me." And another: "Yeah, I think it's a wasp too, but that doesn't make the coincidence any less magical."

No, it didn't make the coincidence any less magical, but it did spin my world upside down for a moment.

Had I spent forty years loving bees and fearing wasps, only to fall in love with a wasp simply because I believed it was a bee? I felt there was some greater life lesson in this, maybe something about appearances, perception, and prejudice. Maybe something about my love life, falling for wasps with addictive personalities I believed were honeybees. Or maybe simply a reminder that kindness attracts kindness regardless of the species.

Once I recovered from the shock, I studied the picture of my wasp closer.

"Look at you." I chuckled fondly. "Even with the lid closed, you always tried to get inside that bottle." I shook my head at her long-past antics. I remembered how she had shaken so frantically after her yogurt plunge. She could have stung me, but she didn't. Good thing I thought she was a bee. If I had recognized her, I would still have rescued her, but I wouldn't have trusted her. I might even have shooed her away and missed out on a very special connection.

At the risk of feeling cheesy, I placed a finger on the image on the screen, drew a circle, then a figure eight, and back across.

Exhibit A: My "bee"

Chapter 11
The Jack

Hyeres, France - 2004

The peculiar piece of cardboard sat in the middle of the kitchen floor. It was a regular piece of cardboard, square and with jagged edges as though someone had cut it quickly with a kitchen knife. And that someone must have been Jack, my husband at the time, as we were the only two people living in the small apartment below that of Madame Ennebique.

What was peculiar about it was the gooey puddle in the middle of it—probably honey. Ever since Jack and I had discovered Hyeres's Saturday market, I had been obsessed with the exquisite honey of a particular beekeeper. I bought a jar every Saturday, and we hardly could keep up with eating it all. Around the puddle of honey, dispersed evenly and all facing the center of the treat, was a ring of ants.

Oh, those French ants—since our first day in Madame Ennebique's apartment, they had taken up residence in the kitchen as though they, too, were paying tenants. They descended in neat files from a large pipe through the ceiling and down at a forty-five-degree angle to the sink. Once at the bottom of the pipe, the ants crossed the sink to the wall, down the wall to the tiled floor, and from there, everywhere.

Until that day, when not one ant could be seen outside of the honey ring.

Jack entered the kitchen. In his hand was another piece of square cardboard with a puddle of honey. I didn't know what to ask. The puzzled, amused look on my face made him laugh. He leaned in and kissed my cheek.

"This is my gift to you." He pointed to the ants.

"Thank you?" I answered hesitantly.

"You know how Madame Ennebique hates insects. I figured it's just a matter of time before our ants spill over to her apartment. Then she'll fumigate them and us. I know how sad you get when small creatures get hurt, so I created this ant elevator. Look! They climb on this one; I take them safely to the garden…" He shook the cardboard to demonstrate the dismount technique. "Meanwhile, they climb on the other one, and so forth. So far, I've done only three trips, and there's already no ants left except on the ant elevator."

If it is possible to have one's heart explode with love and gratitude, I experienced it in that moment. Jack was known in the software industry as a crafty engineer, but to date, I believe the ant escalator was his kindest creation.

We lived with the ant elevator for only two days. I was awed by its efficacy. Down the pipe the ants came in a neat file, straight to the honey, and out to the garden.

But my engineer husband was not yet fully satisfied.

On the third day, when I entered the kitchen for a cup of tea, I found the floor, sink, and pipe completely cleared of ants. For an instant, I feared the worst. Had Madame Ennebique committed some nefarious crime in spite of of our best efforts to save the ants?

No. If she had, I would have smelled it. No chemicals had been sprayed.

"I improved the system," Jack yelled from the living room, expecting my puzzlement.

He joined me in the kitchen and pointed to the top of the pipe, right where it exited the ceiling.

"Do you see it?"

"No. What am I looking at?"

"Up there. I put a piece of French stinky cheese with a bit of honey on it. There's enough of it to last them a while, so they don't need to come down anymore."

"But... won't it attract more of them into Madame Ennebique's apartment above?"

"No, as a matter of fact, I have studied the building's structure."—of course, he had—"There is a gap between her floor and our ceiling. That's where they come through. So, if she has not seen them before—and we would have known if she had—she won't see them now."

And so it was that the ants, Jack, and I lived peacefully for several months. Occasionally, Jack climbed on a chair to feed the ants a new cheese with a fresh few drops of honey. They never came down the pipe, and we never heard of a problem in the apartment above.

Our time in Hyeres, however, eventually came to an end. Jack's French language school session was over, and an opportunity to live in a small studio on a peaceful vineyard west of Marseilles had come our way.

On the last day, our suitcases already packed and ready, I stood at the sink washing the last tea mugs we had used. Behind me, Jack climbed on a chair and cleaned the ant buffet from the top of the pipe. We had our methods but doubted they would be recognized as brilliant by other tenants, and most certainly not by Madame Ennebique.

"We enjoyed living with you. Thank you for your company. *Merci de votre companie.*" I called to the ants in the ceiling. "You need to go now though, or you'll get killed. Find a natural place. Stay in the ground."

"You think they understand you?" Jack asked.

"I don't know, but it's still worth saying, in case they do."

No sooner had I warned them, than one ant—only one—came down the pipe. So small it was, that I didn't see it until it came across the sink. This was notable because not one ant had graced us with its presence since Jack had lodged the cheese up the pipe. The ant climbed on the sponge and stood roughly in the middle.

"Look at this guy!"

Jack came down from the chair and approached the sink. As he did, the ant stood on its four hind legs and extended its two front legs like arms reaching to the sky in Jack's direction.

"What's it doing?" I leaned in closer to the strange ant. It didn't move; it stayed upright and reaching.

"It looks like it's praying." Jack raised his hands to the ceiling, imitating the ant. "The Jaaaack," he said in an adoring voice. "He saaaaves us. He feeeeeds us. Thaaaank you, The Jaaaaack."

We both erupted in laughter, but the ant remained in rapture position. Then, after a minute, it lowered its body back to the sponge, down and across the sink, and back up the pipe. We followed it with our eyes until it slipped through the ceiling. We then both took turns climbing onto the chair to witness the miracle.

This had been the last ant. Not one remained on the pipe or around the hole in the ceiling. And we never heard anything from Madame Ennebique about ants in our ex-apartment.

<u>Part 3</u>

THE WILD ONES

Chapter 12
Bob

Oregon - February 2010

Mike and I were far from any city or town when the snow began. I had explicitly said before we left that although I'd ride my motorcycle alongside his from Washington to California and back, I would *not* ride in the snow.

Yet here we were. In the snow. But the prospect of stopping on the mountain pass to set up a cold bivy bag by the side of the road for hours or possibly days made even less sense than doing the one thing I feared the most on a moto. So, having no choice in the matter, I relaxed my shoulders and took a deep breath, calming my pounding heart. With eyes locked on the slick road ahead, we rode on.

By the time we finally rolled into the gas station on the other side of the pass, I had a solid sheet of ice on my front shock and fender, and my face prickled with cold needles, even inside the helmet.

We refueled and parked the motos by the side of the gas station.

"Let's see if they have warm soup," Mike said, his voice full of excitement. He was a brand new rider; everything was an adventure to him. But me? I'd been riding for years and had memories of many wreckages to compound my fears.

Yes. Hot soup was exactly what my nerves needed.

As I walked into the gas station, a man passed me and nodded toward my moto. "That yours out there?"

"It is."

"You're fucking nuts." He shook his head and kept walking.

Another man approached as I fumbled to remove my helmet with frozen gloves. "Are you riding in this weather?"

"Ugh. Not another one," I thought. But instead of questioning my sanity, he pointed to a house barely visible through the woods.

"I live right next door. You're welcome to come over to check the weather ahead. I'm a rider too. I always have Weather Underground running on one of my screens."

Just then, Mike returned with two steaming cups of soup. We exchanged a glance and, without a word, agreed to follow the man home.

Except it wasn't so much a home, more like a castle of the kind you wouldn't expect to find in the middle of the woods in Eastern Oregon. The front double doors opened into a vast circular room, with leather sofas, dark wood furniture, and fancy throws draped just so.

We stepped inside, stripped out of our frozen riding gear, then followed the man to a small room just off the grand living room. Five wide computer screens fanned out in a semi-circle, displaying a single continuous image. The Doppler radar and extended forecast occupied most of the room.

I winced. The storm was right on us, and the forecast predicted the worst was yet to come—snow and storm on the extended forecast for at least four more days.

"Well, that's… unfortunate." Mike glanced to me, his mouth halfway between an amused grin and a worried grimace.

"You're welcome to stay with us," the man offered in a jovial voice. "My wife and I, we'd be delighted to have the company of fellow riders. Come on, I'll show you around."

Two long hallways extended from either side of the circular living room, each lined with bedrooms named after big cats—Jaguar, Ocelot, Tiger, Lion, Puma, Cougar, Leopard, Cheetah. All guest rooms, perfectly made up yet oddly untouched, as though they'd been empty for ages. At the end of one hallway was the Bobcat room, converted to a bar—the Bobcat bar.

Mike and I perched on tall stools while our host, with slow movements and eyes shifting from Mike to me, uncorked a bottle of his special Bobcat whiskey, which I was almost certain he'd distilled himself. The walls were covered with large paintings of wild cats and, in the back corner, a sleek, pristine, cheetah-patterned motorcycle with long handlebars sat on display, a shiny bobcat-themed helmet hanging off the throttle.

With a grin, our host placed the Bobcat helmet on my head and reached under my chin to fasten the strap. I felt his breath on my face and uncomfortably shifted closer to Mike. He then poured three glasses of whiskey, even though I said I didn't drink, and offered us both cigars from a polished, temperature-controlled wooden box, even though I said I didn't smoke.

Mike gladly held up his glass and cigar, then turned toward the Cheetah motorcycle.

"How many CCs does she have?… Ha, custom handlebars… What an incredible paint job!"

I sipped the whiskey and slowly puffed on the cigar quietly until the man's wife appeared in the entrance of the bar. Dinner was ready.

Four plates awaited us at one end of a long table, each with an even balance of seared salmon, asparagus, and arugula. Mike and I sat side by side across from our host, but his wife sat some distance from us. She smiled graciously if we addressed her directly but ate quietly, eyes on her plate, when we didn't. Our host did most of the talking—motorcycles, adventures, and finally, music. He'd played backup guitar with some of jazz's greats. I wasn't a jazz fiend and knew none of the names he so proudly dropped on the dinner table.

As his wife gathered our empty plates, our host suddenly stood up, plugged in the wooden guitar on display into the large speaker near the dining table and, with one grand motion, strummed the guitar alive. His fingers ran up the chords, and a sharp and fast rhythm soon filled the room. While his wife's hands gently slid a platter of cheese and grapes in front of us, a series of bebop licks with blues undertones kept us captive, the notes rising and falling in unpredictable yet masterful bursts. This melody wasn't meant to soothe; it was meant to impress.

I reached for a grape, and the music tumbled to an abrupt end. Mike and I applauded with the severity the situation required, then thanked both our hosts profusely for the delicious meal, the impressive music, and the shelter from the snowstorm that now raged outside.

The man smiled as he replaced the guitar on the display stand.

"Well. I think it's time you meet Bob."

We followed the man down the other hallway, which ended in the kitchen. The marble counters were shiny and clean and the appliances of professional quality. The room was slightly colder than the rest of the house, and eerily quiet. This could have been a kitchen in any wealthy house, except that all entrances were barred by wide grid metal bars. As we stepped into the kitchen, the man closed the cage behind us.

I glanced to Mike with an uncomfortable lump in my throat. His worry was marked only by a subtle rise at the corner of his lips, only detectable by a friend of many years.

The man stepped to the counter, where a bowl of cubed raw meat was waiting. He placed the bowl in my hands and said, "Wait here." He crossed the kitchen to the back door, opened that side of the cage, and called.

"Bob!"

The sound of rattling metal grew nearer, and the man stepped back from the door. A large, spotted paw landed on the kitchen floor, and my jaw dropped. With amber eyes, a white-bearded chin, and tufted ears, Bob the bobcat walked in.

"You should sit down; he won't eat if you're taller than him. And place the meat on your open palm. That's how he prefers it."

Mike stepped back, and I dropped to the ground. I placed a few cubes of raw meat as instructed and extended a steady hand in spite of my pounding heart. With slow, fluid muscles, Bob crossed the space from the door to my hand, his eyes fixed on the meat. I resisted the urge to lean away and kept my hand steady as an offering. His fangs flashed as he opened his mouth, but they were superfluous for the tiny cubes. Instead, he tilted his head. A raspy tongue scraped against my skin, and the meat was gone, now rolling between his crushing molars. He closed one eye as he chewed, then reopened it and looked at my hand.

He waited as I placed more meat on my palm. Not once did he look at me, but I drank it all in, eyes wide and mouth agape. I inhaled his musty smell, felt the tickle of his whiskers on my wrist, and smiled at the men behind me when small groans and grunts escaped his jaw as he chewed the meat.

When the last of the meat was gone, the man approached. He scratched Bob behind the ears as though he were just a very large house cat, then walked to the back door, followed by the fluid cat.

"We only close the cage when we have guests." He closed the gate and the door to the outside cold. "Normally, Bob has free range in the house."

"And the cage extends outside?" Mike asked while I stood up off the floor, inspecting my palm with fascination.

"Now it does," the man said with a heavy tone. He opened the hallway side of the cage, and we followed him back to the leather sofas in the living room. "Until about a month ago, there were no cages, no fences, and there were... " The man sank into the sofa as his voice trailed off. Mike and I sat in opposite chairs. I noticed the man had tears in the corners of his eyes.

"The fuckers!" he suddenly mumbled, then he wiped his eyes, sighed, and picked up the previous sentence where it had dropped, "...there were two cats."

Mike and I kept silent as our host's shoulders trembled. He was crying.

"I'm sorry. I still get very emotional about it." We wiped his eyes with the back of his index finger. "It happened right there." With the same finger, he pointed to a location across the road without looking. "Some hicks on ATVs. It was a straight hit. I heard the crash and ran out..." He shook his head, tears starting again. "She died in my arms." He paused, head bowed, then his voice rose. "And I can't prove anything, but I'm pretty sure they did it on purpose." He clenched a fist and hit the sofa. I looked to Mike with raised eyebrows. I didn't dare move.

"So, anyway." He shook his head and recomposed himself. "I can't lose Bob too, so I built the cage. It extends to the front of the house, by the entrance, and all the way to the back of the property. It's not right; Bob should be wild and free, but it's what I gotta do for now."

My head whipped around to look through the small window on the side of the entrance doors. There indeed was a cage there. I had been so cold and frazzled earlier that I hadn't even noticed.

"And how does Bob feel about being in the cage?" Mike asked. I looked back, surprised by Mike's question. I didn't expect our host to know how a cat would feel.

But he nodded. "He's grieving now, as we all are, but he understands. I actually work with a professional animal communicator. She doesn't even charge us. She gets so excited to talk to the cats." He caught himself, "... the cat."

"Brandy?" he asked suddenly, startling both of us.

Mike glanced at me as the man stood to retrieve the brandy. I shook my head no.

"No, thank you. It's been quite a day, what with riding in the snow and all. I think we'll call it a day and get some solid rest. But thanks again, for everything."

Our host had an odd twitch in his neck, but he smiled. "Yes, yes, of course." Then with a tired gesture he pointed to the first hallway. "Pick any room you'd like."

I dropped my bag onto the double bed while Mike locked the door of the Ocelot room. Then he sat on the other bed, facing me. The Ocelot room was the furthest from our hosts' and the only room with two beds.

"Mike, I got to feed a bobcat!" I said in a full voice, in case they were listening, then I leaned in and whispered, "But man, is their energy weird or what? His wife is so tense, and he's... I don't know... "

"Agreed. So far, I'd say it's pretty textbook horror flick. We get murdered in the night and fed to Bob, and no one knows we're here. I bet those meat cubes were from the last stranded riders on the pass."

Mike grinned, but we both knew he was only half kidding. With one mind, we both reached for our bags and found our phones.

"You have reception at all? I've got nothing."

"Yeah, I've got one bar. Let me send Kate a message. At least if we disappear, she'll know who done it."

How Mike asked his wife to fact-check our host's stories and take note of our location without worrying her? I have no idea. But half an hour later, a ding-notification confirmed our host had indeed played with all the notable jazz players he had mentioned.

I was already under the covers, hidden up to my chin. "Just because he's not a liar doesn't mean we won't get murdered."

Mike looked up. "I know you said you didn't want to ride in the snow, but…"

"Uuugh!" I brought my fists to my eyes. "I really, really don't. But honestly, I'd rather risk the snow than stay here."

"Alright then," Mike said in an exaggerated, deep voice as he slipped under his covers. "We ride at dawn."

It was snowing lightly on the already white roads when Mike and I walked out the entrance double doors in full riding gear early the next morning. The air was sharp, biting, and the snow crunched under our riding boots. Mike met our host by the idling motos and once again thanked him for the hospitality. We had come up with a story about why we needed to press on urgently. I don't remember the details, but it was enough to get us out of there.

I stood back, taking deep breaths of the crisp air and gathering my courage for the ride ahead, when Bob rounded the corner of the house. He stopped just a few feet from me, inside the portion of the cage by the door.

I removed my right glove slowly and took a step toward him, my heart picking up speed.

"Good morning, Bob. May I pet you?"

But Bob wasn't looking at me. His gaze was fixed across the road—past the bikes and the two men chatting. He was so close, only four or five inches from the bars. His fur rose and fell with each breath, and condensation fog escaped his slightly opened jaw.

I waited for a sign of an answer, but he stayed still. So I extended my hand.

"I'll take that as a yes." I slid my hand through the metal bars.

I didn't reach his fur. Didn't see him move. One second, my hand was inches from his fur, the next it was locked in his jaw. Pain shot through my body as his amber eyes met mine, calm, but unmistakably clear: *I could crush you.*

I understood—his fang just breaking my skin was a warning. I didn't move. I didn't try to pull my hand out or modify the situation in any way. Instead, I filled my heart with love and respect and bowed my head.

"I see now I've made a mistake." I kept my voice steady and calm. "I apologize. I meant no disrespect. If you let me go unharmed, I promise I will never do it again."

His stare remained fixed on my eyes as he opened his jaw. I carefully pulled my hand out until it was clear out of the cage.

"Oh, my God, I just got bit by a bobcat!" I held up my hand to admire the thin line of slowly dripping blood, then turned to Mike with the broadest grin.

Bob had already lost interest. His gaze had returned to the mystery focal point across the road. He slowly looked away, then walked back around the house, utterly unfazed by my excitement.

"Did he bite you?" Our host appeared at my side and grabbed my hand to inspect it. "Ha," he sighed, shaking his head. "Alright, listen. Go to the little bathroom by the entrance and wash it well—very well—or it'll get infected. Cat bites just never heal. And use the alcohol in the cabinet to clean the wound."

I went to the little bathroom, closed the door, and turned on the faucet. The water ran, but I didn't put my hand under it. I didn't touch the alcohol either. I wiped off the blood and wrapped my hand as it was. Oh yes—I wanted that scar. Who gets bitten by a bobcat? This was a story I wanted to wear.

໒ · ໖

Mike and I rode in snow until nightfall. We didn't fall, and we didn't die. We kept riding until the light of a motel sign came into focus in our foggy goggles, like a mirage of sweet salvation. We parked the motos and covered them with plastic bags and jackets as best we could, then disappeared into the warmth of the room, its bathtub, and seventeen TV channels. There was nothing else to do but wait for the sun to melt the snow off the road.

It took four days for the storm to pass and the sun to return. Two days later, we were roasting on a deserted Nevada county road, heading into Death Valley.

The small line on my hand still throbbed inside my riding glove. And with each pulse, I smiled.

໒ · ໖

My skin is older now, and the scar is faint, but I can still make a tight fist and point out the straight line. Of all the scars this body of mine has accumulated over the years, it remains one of my favorites. And I use it often.

"How did you get your trail name, The Bobcat?"

"I was bitten by one." I extend my hand and curl my fingers in a tight fist to accentuate and showcase the scar. "I tried to pet him." I shrug and leave at that.

It's truly not a fair story. I rarely disclose that the bobcat's name was Bob and that he bit me because I stuck my hand through the bars of his cage. And I definitely don't share that I was already called "The Bobcat" long before that bite— thanks to a group of wild geologists who thought it'd be funny, because my boyfriend was nine and a half years younger and I was thirty-nine. So, not quite a cougar... just a bobcat.

But, as we are responsible for the spreading of our own legend, when people ask, I don't lie, I just smile and say, "I tried to pet him." I show them the scar and let their imagination fill in the rest.

Chapter 13
Coyote

Sedona, Arizona - January 2015

In French, the time of day right after the sun has set but while its afterglow still illuminates the land is called *entre chien et loup* (between dog and wolf). It is in this transition that the fingers of two worlds can touch and sometimes interlace—the seen and unseen, light and dark, wild and tame, awake and asleep, real and imaginary, sane and insane. In this liminal space, the world feels hushed and mysterious, as if poised on the edge of a dream.

This is where this story begins—at the edge of a dream, halfway between a bed and a forest. The bed was in this reality but not in my home, the Catmobile. Winter's chill, even in Sedona, had driven me out of the snow-covered desert. A friend needed a house-sitter, and in exchange, I could stay in a warm house with a kitchen and a bathtub for a few days, until the snow melted. I lay on her bed to feel the energy of the room but hadn't expected to fall asleep so early in the afternoon. The sun had just set, and I hadn't even had dinner yet. But as soon as my body sank into the softness of my friend's sheets, the room faded, and I found myself standing in a meadow at the edge of a forest.

The forest was dense and dark, but the meadow where I stood still held the golden glow of the last vestiges of sunset. I felt him before I saw him. Slowly, one by one, as if not to disturb my sleep, the hairs on the back of my neck stood on end. I turned toward the wall of black trees and saw his glowing red eyes. There was Wolf, directly across from me, exactly at the same distance from the forest's edge as where I stood in the meadow. He wasn't looking at me, though. His black, massive body pointed to my right with full attention. This was no ordinary wolf. He was Brother Wolf, maybe even Father Wolf—an ancient, regal, and wise being, attentive yet undisturbed by what lurked in the forest.

The hair on my neck didn't relent, and I understood that Wolf was not the danger my body sensed. I followed his gaze and collided with its object of focus as it erupted from the forest's edge, charging toward me—a pack of javelinas! My breath caught as tingles of adrenaline rushed to my toes and fingertips. A large male spearheaded the group, closely followed by a triangular formation of females and a few youth. There were neither bared teeth nor any other signs of aggression, but I knew I was in their path and about to be trampled to death—if I was lucky—or eaten a strand of flesh at a time. It wasn't personal; I was just a meal opportunity.

I took one step back to brace myself and clenched my fists. My heart beat so hard that its vibrations crossed the dog-wolf boundary and shook the mattress springs in that other world, of which I was aware, where my body rested. A long, piercing howl from Wolf sent birds flying out of the forest canopy and into the night sky. A howl like a beacon— Wolf was calling someone or something.

And they came.

A band of coyotes emerged from the forest behind me at a much faster pace than the javelinas. They reached me first: two elders, a younger male, two females, and two pups. The adult coyotes encircled me while the pups stood by each of my legs, facing outward.

The triangle point of javelinas crashed onto my protective coyote fortress. Rounded backs, flashes of fangs, and snarls surrounded me. In the deepening darkness, I could still see their shapes sharply in shades of gray and follow their movements by their scent—pungent canine fur rolled in pine needles, decaying flesh, and wet earth.

The coyotes protected me as one of their own, so I glanced down at my palms, half-expecting to find paws, but I was still human—just with greatly heightened senses.

Meanwhile, the javelinas had regrouped and now slowly backed away, overwhelmed by the fierceness of the coyotes if not by their numbers. A mama coyote turned her head toward me, her eyes locked onto mine. She gave a subtle yet unmistakable glance toward the two pups at my feet, and I understood: I was to guard them. She then quickly rejoined the others.

Yapping and snapping at the air, the coyotes chased the javelinas away, down the meadow, across the brook, and to the other side of the forest. The "other side"—which hadn't existed before, and which I still couldn't perceive.

I looked up toward the forest. Wolf lingered for a moment, eyes sweeping the scene, then turned away and dissolved into the forest's shadows.

I returned to the mattress, the bedroom, Sedona, with the smell of fur still lingering in my nose. I wrote the dream—if it was a dream—in my journal. By then, night had fallen in this world too. I cooked a quick dinner and ate, but my mind kept replaying the vivid dream. What did it all mean? And why did Javelina keep attacking me? This was the second time in three weeks. The first time had been in this world.

છ · ૭૪

Three weeks prior

It had been so cold in the desert that I had eaten my meals on my mattress with the truck's back hatch closed. Despite my best efforts to keep my space free of food, groceries, pots, and spoons had found their way onto my nightstand, which doubled as a kitchen counter and office desk. Finally, after two weeks of winter, the first wave of snow melted, and the sun thawed the desert and my frozen bones.

I pulled the four crates of food out of the truck and placed them on the desert floor. I slid the wooden board from under the mattress and carefully placed it next to the crates on the red dirt. It would be a clean platform for my mattress, bedding, and clothes. I had white bedding at the time. Sleeping in white sheets made me feel sophisticated in spite of my feral life. Keeping white sheets white in a red desert was a challenge, but I enjoyed the mindful practice of cleaning at least my dirty feet before entering my home.

I placed the sheets on the mattress on the platform, next to the stove, computer, and bin of electronics, next to the hula hoop. I had just climbed back into the truck to sweep out any remaining crumbs when a sound halfway between an old man's snore and an excited pig snapped me back around. Trotting on pointy toes, huffing, snorting, and grunting, a small herd of javelinas was vying for my food.

I jumped out of the truck and ran for the crates. I grabbed the closest two and threw them onto the elevated open tailgate, but the javelinas and I reached the third crate at the same time. The lead male was the size of a wild boar, but it wasn't his size that troubled me. I swore I could see hatred in his squinted, tightly angled eyes. He stared me down defiantly. I understood he had a family to feed, but this was *my* food, and even if I had been willing to share—which I wasn't—what then? Feed them every day? And then their friends? This was unacceptable.

I left his gaze briefly to scan for a weapon—anything, a stick, a branch, or even a large rock—but only found pebbles and packed red dirt. "Grrraaaaahhhh. Ahhhhhhhh." I flailed my arms, pretending to growl and yell. He continued staring, unperturbed. I kicked the air in his direction to scare him away, but he moved faster. Two tusks sank right through my sneaker and into the top of my foot. "Aaaahhhhh!" Pain shot up my leg, and a real scream this time echoed throughout the desert. I kicked my foot again, inside his mouth. He let go but did not back off.

In the corner of my eye, I caught sight of the hula hoop and launched for it. Extending one hand under the protection of the hula hoop, I reached the edge of the food crate and retreated with it. The female javelinas joined the male, flanking me from both sides. I walked backward, holding the herd at arm's plus hula hoop's length, until I felt the tailgate. I threw the crate into the truck bed and jumped in after it. The javelinas grunted and sniffed the area where the food had been, but with the crates out of reach, they regrouped and continued their search through the desert.

My mistrust of javelinas and the painful wound on my foot lingered for weeks. Both were still present on that night when I first became part of a coyote pack in the wolf-dog space-time.

❧ · ❧

On the opposite side of the night when I met the coyotes, just before the sun rose above the red rocks but with already sufficient light to illuminate the land, I had another dream.

I walked downhill on a hiking trail through a forest. My gait and heart felt as light as the morning sun streaming through the branches, catching dew drops like facets of little diamonds. Soon, I reached a clearing, a wide meadow with a split in the trail and a signpost. I expected a classic direction post as you find on hiking trails in this world, but instead, the white sign instructed, "Wait here."

I waited for... a few moments—time didn't flow with any measurable rhythm in that world—when suddenly, out of the forest, a coyote came running at full speed straight toward me. He didn't slow down but leaped and flew the last ten feet into my arms.

He was Coyote—my brother! I remembered how we first met. We met that day when the javelinas attacked me in the meadow. He was one of the pups by my feet. We grew up together, raised in the desert like true siblings. We ate sitting on the dirt under the moonlight every night, and we sang songs. I remembered. I jumped for joy as he bounded around me, leaping high, twisting, landing, and darting through my legs, and then again. We danced for endless moments until, finally, I rested my hands on my knees, laughing and catching my breath.

Then he collapsed.

Joy instantly left my face as worry took its place. My friend was hurt. I knelt next to him and heaved his body into my arms. Why? What was happening? I turned him over in my arms and saw a metal tube, like a barrel, protruding from his stomach.

I yelled, "Help, my friend is hurt!" But the echo was only my voice. There was no one else in that dream who could help. He looked up at me, mischief and friendship still shining in his eyes until the very last moment, when he closed them.

I sobbed. I sobbed so much that it carried into this world, shaking the bed and waking me up. I opened my eyes to find the pillow drenched in tears and my shoulders and back trembling from the grief. I gathered my knees in my arms and continued crying.

I cried on and off for the rest of that day.

ༀ · ༀ

Sedona, Arizona - May 2015

Days, weeks, and months flew by, and eventually, the dreams and the memory of Coyote's death faded into the background. They were just dreams, after all—archetypes and stories woven into my psyche. Besides, Coyote wasn't dead; I saw him every day.

As the cold retreated to its northern home, my life in the desert entered a peaceful, blissful phase. Mornings began with breakfast on the tailgate, basking in the warm sun, followed by full days of work, hikes, and book editing at the library. In the evenings, I danced barefoot in the dirt around the truck. Then I cooked and ate dinner on the tailgate by headlamp before crawling into my sleeping bag, resting my head toward the tailgate to enjoy the nightly show. The Milky Way, sharply defined, crossed the sky right above my pillow while the songs of coyotes disrupted the impeccable desert silence.

They sang every night and with a full repertoire. I listened attentively, sometimes even holding my breath to catch all the nuances. Short howls rising and falling in pitch from various directions—were they calling each other? Staccato yips and yaps—perhaps they had caught a meal. And then, the long, soulful "Aooohhhhh,". Only coyotes could sing such joy and plaintive sorrow in the same breath, delivered to the moon.

I was their biggest fan, though I doubted they cared. They completely ignored me. Sometimes, one would walk within feet of the Catmobile, minding me as much as a creosote bush, cactus, or rock. I had seen coyotes avoid humans and vehicles, so I took this familiar disregard as a rare compliment. They treated me as an integral part of the landscape—neither threat no prey, but an equal of sorts.

My coyotes. I counted five of them—at least two males and several females, judging by their size. The largest male often roamed solo. I'd see him by the little brook just down the hill from where I parked the truck at night—my "desert home," as I thought of it. Sometimes I'd call to him. "You are beautiful!" He'd briefly look my way, unfazed, then continue on.

Two were inseparable. I'd read that coyotes mate for life, and indeed, these two always explored side by side, sharing secrets with eye gazes. They, too, also completely ignore me.

Regardless, I thought of them collectively as *my* coyotes, and their presence and songs added an immense joy to my desert routine life.

In those days, I worked as a guide for Earth Tours, a small company comprised of only my boss, Benny, and me. I led people on hikes among the majestic red rocks of Sedona, weaving tales of the famous vortexes, but mostly, I shared stories of my life and my beloved desert.

The adults were usually curious about numbers: How long had I lived this way? How old was I? How big was my truck? And so on. The kids, however, had more practical concerns:

Did I sleep with lizards, bats, and scorpions? How did I poop, if I didn't live in a house? And I explained—much to the parents' dismay—how one dealt with such matters in the wild, then swiftly redirected the kids to a more exciting scavenger hunt for tracks and scat.

"See the narrow toes?" I pointed to the distinct paw prints. "Definitely coyote. And here—this is cryptosoil. Step around, carefully. Look up—a red-tail hawk is soaring above us!"

Their eyes widened with excitement. In those moments, we were all explorers, discovering the secrets of the desert together.

And so it was that on May 29th, I woke up in my desert home to a glorious sunrise over red rocks. It was already too hot to sleep in, and I had a tour that day anyway—7:30 am pickup, just one client for a Sedona hike.

I hula hooped to a few songs, read emails in the shade of my truck's shell, and ate breakfast with my feet dangling off the tailgate while my favorite bee buzzed around the maple syrup.

When it was time, I packed the truck and bid the catclaw a good day.

I drove the rough dirt track while balancing a mug of tea in one hand—a no-spill game I played daily. I maneuvered down Slick-Corner, around the ancient, spiraling juniper, and past the thorny mesquite thickets.

Just beyond the mesquite was an orange rusty flatbed truck.

Time slowed to a trickle.

In that trickle, I saw blood on the bed of the truck, a gray mass at the end of the blood, a gun in one hand, a look of surprise on a bearded face—why was there a woman alone out here this early? In one swift move, the hand that didn't have the gun grabbed the gray mass and tossed it into the thorn thicket. Something limp and heavy hit the ground. The man had blood on his hands. A coyote! The gray mass was a tailless coyote.

Both men stood by the truck as I drove past. One waved "Hello." I waved back—my brain hadn't processed what had just entered it yet. The larger of the two men climbed into the truck. "The fucker bled all over the truck. Let's get outta here." Two doors slammed. Time resumed its normal speed.

I swallowed hard, put my tea down, held back tears, and sped out of the desert. Their engine roared, but I trusted the Catmobile could outmaneuver them, and I knew these roads like the back of my hand. When I reached the fork, past the cattle guard, I continued straight where the main road turned. I knew I'd find a tree there where I could hide. I stopped under the tree to let the dirt and my wildly beating heart settle. They turned and rejoined the paved road.

My brain then fully caught up, and I gasped. They had killed one of my coyotes. For a tail? My fists clenched. My body trembled. For a tail! If only I'd had a gun, I'd have shot them—shot them dead and taken their shoes. Oh, I was seething. So that's how it felt. That's how men kill men, families kill families (by whichever large definition), massacres feel righteous and justified. These coyotes were my family— innocent and free. Suddenly, I understood how wars began. Sometimes, the injustices were too great to forgive, the shame of one's powerlessness too great to bear. I had never before understood the act of killing, except with respect, to feed oneself, but that day, my heart screamed "Revenge!", and yet, I let them pass. I had to.

It was seven in the morning, miles from any help. I was an unarmed woman alone, and these two had just shot a coyote for a trophy tail. Self-preservation had to prevail over retribution.

Once the last of their truck had disappeared, I curled over the steering wheel and wept, a fist pressed hard against my aching heart.

I allowed myself a moment, but the world lived on, and somewhere down the paved road, my client waited. So, I blew trumpets with my nose, splashed water on my puffy eyes, and drove on.

My client that day was a woman about my age. She lived in Manhattan, New York, had manicured nails, and had never been on a dirt road. She smiled and waved as I pulled up, her bright white sneakers bouncing slightly with excitement for the adventure ahead.

I smiled as she reached for the passenger door. "Hi! Nice to meet you. Come on in."

She settled into the truck and smiled as she pulled and clicked the seatbelt. Then she looked up at me, and her smile faded instantly. My cheerful, professional guide voice did not match the clench in my jaw or the wetness in my eyes.

This violated all the rules in the book of good guiding, but I realized I wouldn't be able to hold back tears for the length of a full-day tour, so I turned the key off in the ignition and turned toward her.

"Something just happened," I told her, my voice wavering. "And I'm going to share it with you so that if I cry today, at least you'll know why…"

I told her everything. We sat in silence for a moment, caught in the wake of my story.

"A week ago," she began in a solemn voice. "I watched two black men gunned down in the subway." She nodded. "And I got off at the next station." Different background, different actors, same story. "Thank you for sharing about the coyote. Strangely, it makes me feel less alone." I felt the same. Shared grief, somehow, was lighter.

I didn't lead a fluffy tour that day. We discussed heavy subjects—senseless killing, protecting one's own, and other plagues of humankind—as we hiked through breathtaking red and white canyons. We must have both needed it—she later told the concierge at the resort that my tour had been the highlight of her trip.

The sun was just setting when I returned to the desert, straight to the dead coyotes under the thicket. I thought the hunters might have returned to remove the evidence, but they hadn't even bothered. There, in the shade, lay not one but two tailless coyotes, one slightly larger than the other. It was the pair I always saw together. They were still intact. If it weren't for the missing tails, I would've thought they were peacefully napping. I knelt by the paws of the larger one, shoulders rounded and head bowed. A few tears hit the dry dirt. I didn't cry for them. They were gone—no lingering Coyote spirit moaning its abrupt life exit. No, I cried for myself, for my inability to protect my desert kin, and for the loss of their distinct voices in my nightly serenade.

Because of my upbringing, I felt it would be disrespectful to just leave them there. I thought I should bury them and bless their place of rest with a cross or other symbol of protection. But the Sedona dirt is packed tight and hard.

Digging a hole large enough for two coyotes would have taken hours. Yet, I would have done it.

I called Benny, my boss and dear friend, seeking counsel and a shovel.

Benny had been a guide in Sedona for over twenty-five years, walking the same lands the Hopi call *Palatkwapi*—the land of the sacred red rocks

"Oh, Bobcat, I'm so sorry." He sighed "But no, don't bury them. In the old ways, the desert itself guides the spirits home. Let their death be part of the life cycle."

I spoke a small prayer of gratitude up toward the sky, where I assumed the coyote's spirit had gone. I'd hoped to feel their presence as I thanked them for their company and songs. Just a small sign that I had mattered to them as much as they had mattered to me, a sign of forgiveness for my wrongdoings—not protecting them—or at least a confirmation of a bond between us. Any bond.

They gave me nothing. There were no songs in the desert that night.

In the following days, I made several phone calls. It turned out killing coyotes was legal in Arizona, along with other predatory and fur-bearing mammals, but only with a valid hunting license. The kind lady at the Arizona Game and Fish Department pointed out that these two hunters did not sound like legal shooters. If only I had taken their license plate number, we could have confirmed the infringement, and I could have petitioned the county to press charges. The fines were hefty, and some hunters even landed in jail. But in the ten seconds it took to indelibly etch the crime scene into my memory, that particular detail had not been recorded.

"It sounds like you kept yourself safe. I hear you're upset, but I'm a mom, and I'm glad you didn't do anything stupid. If you ever see that truck again, just take the license plate number, safely, okay?"

I never saw that truck or those hunters again.

175

I stayed with the coyotes throughout the entire decomposition process. Every evening, I sat for a few minutes on the packed red dirt under the junipers and observed. Not in a morbid way, but just because, at the age of forty-four, I had never truly been around death. If I came across a dead animal, I sped away lest I became too sad. I'd never seen a dead human, and my parents had buried our departed pets. I didn't fear death, but neither did I understand it. This was one of the gifts of the coyotes' death—a rare special-guest experience for the curious child in Earth School that I was, and still am.

So I sat silently next to their bones, and I learned.

In the desert, death was not broadcast by the putrid smell of rotting flesh. The coyote's empty shells simply and slowly deflated and dried, an ephemeral buffet for vultures, flies, and maggots. They sunk ever flatter, as though they were relaxing more fully into the earth. The fur, cracked yet still intact, draped loosely around the mummified remains. Necks eventually disconnected, and the less fleshy parts, like the legs, elongated as each bone separated from its neighbor. Each day, there were fewer bones. The skulls were some of the first to disappear. I would have liked to keep them, but I never found them, though I searched the desert for long, meandering hours.

ஐ · ஐ

Sedona, Arizona - late June 2015

By the time tourist season ended, halted by the approaching summer heat, the sun had baked the coyotes' exposed bones into clean, white specimens. The fur had slid off or been picked off the spine, exposing the entire disconnected series of vertebrae—delicate little pieces of bone jewelry.

"Goodbye, friends." I slowly approached and caressed the fur. This was the first time I'd touched them. The fur was still soft, but its once pungent canine aroma had been replaced by the scent of the desert itself—dusty, earthy, with a hint of wild sage. That was all that remained: two small empty fur coats and a pile of pretty bones.

I selected the most elegant vertebra from each spine and cradled them in my hands as the most precious of treasures as I returned to the Catmobile. I strung them on a leather string, which I hung from the rear-view mirror.

I wouldn't have taken the bones as long as I lived there and could visit whenever I wished. But tourist season was over, and my first book was published. It was time to get on the road for a West Coast book tour and to climb a few mountains. So, I took the coyotes with me.

My friend Mikhael, who is part Choctaw and well-versed in the lore of spirit animals, saw this new truck ornament and raised an eyebrow with a sideways questioning glance.

"Are you sure you want to invite Coyote medicine into your life like this? You know Coyote is the Trickster. It will put your life upside-down, shake things up, and rattle your peace. Unless you're ready for a wild ride, I'd leave these bones be, if I were you."

"Isn't Coyote a reminder to laugh more, to not take life so seriously?" I remembered researching the spiritual meaning of Coyote when I had that first dream.

"Oh, there is laughing… it's just at your expense."

I smiled but took my bones anyway.

The Catmobile rode the straight desert highways north, then gradually transitioned to the twisty Utah mountain roads. All the while, from the rear-view mirror, the white vertebrae of my two coyote companions danced back and forth, sometimes even grazing my driving hand on the steering wheel.

"Are you sure you want to invite Coyote medicine into your life like this?" My friend's words of caution still echoes in my mind.

I understood Coyote medicine was that twist in the plot when everything was flowing smoothly, that shove off the path when the destination was finally in sight, but still, I nodded, "Yeah."

I looked to the snow-covered mountains in the distance, gateways to unforeseen potential adventures and repeated louder, "Yes!"

"Coyote, my Love. With these bones in my home, I invite you into my life from this point forward."

Inspired by the setting sun's golden light speckling my dusty windshield, I lifted the two bones in one hand. A mischievous gladness filled my heart as I declared to the empty desert, the Catmobile, and anyone else listening in the Spirit realm:

"I invite you, Coyote, and I thank you. Because you, my Trickster, make life worth living. Without you, Chaos Master, life would be but a drab, endless, calm bliss." I giggled, then continued, on a roll, "Without you, Great Disrupter of Plans, my wild fire would get snuffed in mundane happy-enough routines. So, *COME ON*, Plot Twister. Here's my life. Take me on a grand adventure. I receive your medicine with an open, willing heart. Aho!"

And with these words, the last of the sun dipped behind the mountain, but its afterglow lingered for a while—right there, between Coyote and Wolf.

The truck kept going. The bones kept dancing. I remained silent for a moment in the wake of my invocation. Then I cringed slightly and giggled.

"Oh, Man! What have I just done?"

80 · 03

Coyote's back was barely taller than the flowers. He moved in short leaps across the field, his head looking through the tall grass and flowers, searching for prey. Suddenly, he stopped and extended his muzzle toward one of the yellow flowers. A bee darted out, and Coyote let out a small yelp of surprise as his body arched and sprang back, landing on all fours amidst the flowers. As soon as he touched down, he quickly recomposed himself and glanced around to ensure no one had witnessed his embarrassing moment.

- Lakota story, as told by my friend Grey Wolf, Curator of the Sacred, before singing the Coyote Traveling Song.

I love you, Coyote.
And I love you, Brother Wolf

Chapter 14
The Conscious Hunter

Nelson, British Columbia, August 2013

"I forgot my towel. You two kids hang out. I'll be right back."

She wasn't coming back. That much was obvious. The whole day was one long setup.

"I think you should meet my friend Hunter." All week, Sari had repeated this sentence in various disguises. "Oooooh," she cooed, "You two are the same age, and you have so much in common. He's a geologist too. He's bright, conscious, handsome… and single! If I were in your shoes…"

I shook my head. "Do not set me up. I'm a free bird. The Catmobile and I, we have places to go. We can't be slowed down by romance."

I laughed, and she laughed with me, then promptly organized a vegan picnic with a few guests, including Hunter. Then, somewhere between the potato salad and the fresh strawberries, she suggested the three of us climb down to the Kootenay River. It was such a hot day, and she had a private beach, we didn't even need clothes, she insisted. But as soon as the man and I had formed neat piles of dry clothes on the rocky beach and entered the cold river water, she had left to fetch her forgotten towel.

I carefully kept the water level at my neck and moved my arms in swimming motion to create a blur in the clear water. The man, slightly turned away, some ten or so feet from me, mimicked my awkward movements.

"So, your name is Hunter?"

"It is."

"Are you a hunter?"

"I am."

"Oh!" I turned toward him, surprised. "I'd assumed you were vegan. All of Sari's friends seem to be vegan."

"I'm not vegan," he laughed, "but I am a conscious hunter. I only eat what the forest gifts me. So I don't technically hunt; I ask."

"You ask? How do you ask?"

"Out loud." He flipped his long blond braid to his back and faced me for the first time. "I always ask the same way. I say, 'Please, Forest, gift me a beast that I might eat. I promise to use all parts with reverence and gratitude. Thank you.' Then I sit and wait until an animal comes. And an animal always comes." He closed his blue eyes and crunched his brow as though remembering a painful memory. "Well... except once..."

⁐ · ⁓

Hunter's story - The Kootenay forest, in the autumn

Hunter knelt on the grass at the edge of the clearing and placed his bow on his lap, then dropped his head and closed his eyes.

"Please, Forest, gift me a beast..." He spoke his request—his prayer—in a soft voice, as he knew the forest always listens to whomever steps in her midst. Then he opened his eyes but remained completely still and silent. The key was to keep the mind in a state of gratitude for the animal to come. His blue eyes followed the edge of the forest,

181

finding beauty in the golden autumn light, the delicate falling of leaves, and the peacefulness of waiting.

A young doe entered the clearing. Her neck stretched upward, her ears twitched, and her eye fixed on Hunter. She continued chewing the fresh grass, then reached her neck back to the ground for more. Hunter waited. If she was the gift for which he had asked, she would place herself directly in front of his bow. Until then, he would not move.

Slowly, safely, she ate and advanced, until, finally, she was directly in front of him. He slowly reached his hand over his head and, with two fingers, extracted an arrow from the quiver on his back. She watched him in full trust. He lifted the bow, nocked the arrow, and pulled the string to his face.

An animal always came if he was alone. He had gone with other hunters, both bowhunters and riflehunters. But they didn't ask the forest. They thought it silly to ask. And so they meandered through the woods for hours. And if they were lucky enough to find an animal, that animal ran away from them as soon it sensed, saw or smelled them. But not him.

The doe blinked, and her ears swiveled, but she didn't move. She seemed to say, "I know what you're doing. It's okay." Normally, at this stage, the string sprung, the arrow traversed the flesh, and the animal fell. Then, normally, Hunter knelt with a hand on the animal and again gave thanks to the forest.

Once home, he carved the animal himself. The hide he tanned. The antlers, he carved into tools and art. The bones he ate in marrow soups and carved into arrowheads. The meat he cut, separated, and froze. Not until every last part was eaten and used would he return to the forest to ask for the next gift.

That is what normally happened. But that day, as the string pressed the corner of his mouth and his eye locked onto the doe, a simple thought crossed his mind.

"Mmh. I would have preferred a bigger buck."

No sooner had the thought crossed his mind, than the doe, as though released from a trance, suddenly jumped up, ears back, tail up, and bolted through the trees.

His heart sank. He felt her, the Forest. She was offended. He dropped his bow and brought his hand to his face. "I'm sorry," he cried, but it was too late.

For the next two years, every week, Hunter asked the forest for forgiveness. He sat in various clearings, bow on his lap and head bowed, for hours. But no animal was offered.

৪০ · ০৪

"I was greedy. The truth is that doe was exactly the amount of meat I needed, but my ego got in the way. I wanted a big buck. I was arrogant, thinking I was special because the forest gifted me what I needed when other hunters worked so hard for so little results."

"Did the forest forgive you eventually?"

"She did. After two years, finally, a large buck came right in front of my arrow. He was majestic. He was like the king of the forest. And I cried when I killed him. I cried in gratitude that I was forgiven, but also in grief that he was dead and would no longer grace the woods."

We walked out of the river and slipped quickly into our warm, dry clothes. We climbed back up the hill without a word and rejoined the group on the lawn. Sari and some of her older friends immediately offered Hunter fresh strawberries and pressed him for stories of his latest adventures—his mountain climbs, his long-distance kayak journeys, his organic garden, the camping cap he built for the back of his Toyota Tacoma.

I sometimes looked up from the picnic dishes in his direction, but as soon as his blue eyes meandered my way, I casually looked away. I studied the trees or turned to admire the sunset glow in the clouds. If I looked back, he quickly lowered his eyes and reached for a strawberry.

As night fell, I stayed on the lawn and folded the blankets; he followed Sari to the kitchen and helped with the dishes. Our tasks ended at the same time. We walked up the hill to the parking lot next to each other but without a word except for…

"Goodnight then."

"Yes, Goodnight."

We each climbed in the back of our Toyota Tacomas. On the roof of his were two kayaks. One of those could have been for me. I peeked out the truck's window and thought, "Yes, it does seem that we would be a very good match indeed. But he's got a home and organic garden here. And I… I need to roam."

When I woke up the next morning, he was gone. I never saw him again.

I often thought about Hunter as the Catmobile and I gobbled miles from Florida to Alaska and everywhere in between. With time, I forgot his face but always recalled his long blond braid flipping to his back, the reverence in his voice when he spoke about the forest, and the respect he held for the beasts.

I thought about him when my coyotes were shot. It soothed my heart and gave me hope to know that conscious hunters do exist, and that with each loosed arrow, each volunteer animal, they honor the sacred bond that should tie a thinking predator to his prey. Wherever Hunter is, I hope he passes on his ways to the younger generation, spreading harmonious coexistence as a dominant paradigm.

It was another three years before I met another man who spoke with trees. That one was a conscious carpenter. You've already met him—he was Jim of the mushrooms, woods and wasps.

ONCE, WHEN I WAS TREE

Part 4

MOSTLY CATS, SOME DOGS, AND ONE BIRD

Chapter 15
Minou and the Dying Dog

"Hello. Is this Sarah? My name is Melissa. I won your free psychic reading at the fair last week. The thing is, I don't need or want a psychic reading. I have my own guidance system and it's working great for me. But I hear you're also a professional animal communicator. Could I trade the reading for a quick lesson? I'd love a few tips on animal communication. I have a gig coming up, and I feel it could be useful."

"You mean the gig with the dying black-and-white dog?"

My jaw dropped. I didn't know the dog was dying, just that he was very, very old. But Toinette had said that he was black-and-white. How did Sarah know that?

"Mmmh. The dog won't listen to you," she continued before I could ask. "It's the cat you need to convince." The cat? I didn't know there was a cat.

"Of what am convincing the cat?"

"To let the dog die."

৪১ · ৫৪

North Conway, New Hampshire - September 2014

The summer of 2014 was one of the happiest in my life. I lived in the Catmobile but earned enough from teaching yoga and selling hiking gear to splurge on renting a room to use as an office.

Though I didn't sleep there, the room became my sanctuary for writing *Crazy Free*. It smelled faintly of old wood, had soft carpet and two small windows overlooking dense woods—the perfect backdrop to conjure up stories. The hot shower and spacious kitchen were luxuries, but the true treasure of the house was the company. Sharing meals and spirited conversations with my two adventurous roommates—one a climbing guide, the other a thru-hiker—filled the space with stories and laughter.

At the end of each day, I closed my laptop, bid my roommates goodnight, and drove up Crawford Notch, where fields of fireflies sparkled like fallen constellations. Waking up above the trees, writing at a desk—I had it all.

But, eventually, summer slipped away, taking its fireflies and green canopy with it. Our lease expired, my roommates moved on, and the rhythm of life shifted. By then, I'd left the more sensible of my two jobs to write full-time. With my income dwindled to bare minimum, the Catmobile once again was my everything—home, office, companion.

Each morning, I woke up to a mosaic of fiery fall leaves, blurred and softened by the condensation on the truck's windows. Even as the air turned crisp and biting, I adored these days of freedom. I hiked, climbed, wrote, and dangled my feet from the tailgate, overlooking the ever-changing vista of the White Mountains. Life was spacious, and words flowed onto my keyboard.

But fall also left, and in a blink, winter was upon me, frosting the Catmobile's windows with hexagonal crystal beauties. As the cold seeped into my fingers, stiffening them with every keystroke, they began to protest. Yet I had to write. Writing was like that—it came when it wanted—relentless. It didn't care if I lived in a truck or a palace.

So it was, on a frosty morning, that I came down the mountain to teach my yoga class and first met Toinette. At the end of class, she approached me and asked if I'd be interested in house- and dog-sitting for her.

How did she know I needed a warm place? Did I look homeless? Maybe I smelled of leaves—or worse. I had tried washing myself in the frigid Saco River that morning but had only managed a half plunge. I resisted the urge to check by lifting my arm.

And also, how did she know she could trust me?

In truth, I don't think she trusted me until Dawa did.

Toinette was leaving for France to care for a dying parent and would be gone for a month and a half—just the time I needed to finish the section of my book I was writing. In her absence, I would care for Dawa, her very old dog. She warned me that it would be a lot of work. Dawa had dementia. He might wander outside and forget how to come home or forget he was inside and relieve himself on expensive carpets. He couldn't be left alone, not for a moment, day or night. If I needed to teach yoga or run errands, I'd have to find someone to watch him. Dawa was too frail to ride in the truck. In exchange, she would pay me, and I could live in her warm mansion. I could sleep in her soft bed and write at her dark wood antique desk. And I wouldn't lose the views. One side of the house was lined with large bay windows, overlooking golden fields, forests, and, in the distance, the snow-dusted summit of Mt. Washington.

Dawa was lying on his own carpet next to Toinette's bed when I first met him. He was a shaggy black-and-white Himalayan sheepdog, born in Nepal over seventeen years prior. He had been a gift from Toinette's ex-husband, and since the moment she had first held the tiny fur ball in her hands, the two had been inseparable.

I knelt beside him and sent an energetic "Hello" from my heart to his, as Sarah had taught me. He lifted heavy eyelids, studying me for a moment before rolling onto his side, legs crossed and head sinking heavily into the carpet. Toinette left the room quietly so that Dawa and I could get acquainted alone. I rubbed his belly, trying to feel into his energy. I felt his exhaustion, but it didn't take special animal communication skills to see how tired this old dog was. I felt further into his energy. There was a quiet peace about him but also a hint of dread and a deep sadness. He knew Toinette was leaving, and I imagined, or sensed, that he knew exactly why I was there.

"The owner is very attached to the dog, and the dog to the owner," Sarah had said. "He's ready to pass on, but he won't let himself die because of the pain it will cause her. I sense another death in her field also, maybe a parent…"

Sarah was good—uncannily so. I hadn't mentioned a word about the situation.

"Are you saying this dog is going to die on my watch?"

She was silent for a moment, perhaps tapping into her psychic intuition before answering.

"Well," she finally replied in a measured tone, "as I said before, there's the problem with the cat…"

I first saw Minou from a distance as I walked through Toinette's house toward the bedroom where Dawa rested. He prowled through the tall golden grass at the edge of the hay field, crouching low in search of mice, lizards, or other unseen prey. His muscles undulated as he placed each paw with deliberate, silent precision.

"Dis, dere, is Minou," she pointed out in a thick French accent. "He's a fierce 'unter. He leeves inside and outside, but he likes to sleep in ze bed."

I smiled. There was the cat! At the time, my love for cats far outweighed my affection for dogs. I was hired to care for Dawa, but for sure, Minou would be my companion and one of the best perks of this gig. I could already picture myself at the antique desk, Minou curled on my lap, his purrs vibrating softly as the words flowed onto my keyboard.

Minou didn't take long to come investigate the new sitter. As soon as Toinette left the room, he appeared in the bedroom doorway. He sat like a sentinel, back straight and regal, paws neatly together, his green eyes fixed on me. He stared with a knowing look—not a curious or judging look, just a knowing look, as though he could see through me.

"Hi, Minou." He closed his eye slightly, as if answering me, and I fell in love, right then.

Minou was gorgeous—a tall gray tabby with long legs and striking green eyes like emeralds. He was young, vigorous, and muscular, and I had no doubt he was the alpha of the house, the fields, and likely the entire neighborhood.

"I see a gray tabby," Sarah had said, her voice as steady as if the cat had been sitting in front of her. "He's a sweetheart, all lovey, but don't be fooled—you won't charm him into anything. He's taken on the owner's energy, and while she's away, he'll carry her will to keep the dog alive. I sense that the dog might've called you in, energetically, to help him. He's ready to go. He wants to die…"

"Wait—So the dog called me in energetically as a dog-sitter specifically to convince the cat to let him die while his owner is away?" That sentence sounded like pure lunacy, even though my own mouth had pronounced it.

"Yeah, pretty much," she replied casually.

I couldn't deny Sarah's psychic abilities—she had accurately described the dog and knew of the cat and the owner with a death in the family. But the rest of it? It was too strange to believe yet too precise to dismiss. I didn't know what to make of it.

"Well," I said finally, "since we're here, and I won this reading, could you help me with this? How do I make the dog comfortable? And… convince the cat?"

On my first night in Toinette's bed, Minou jumped up and walked across my resting body. He curled up against my face, purring loudly, with no concern for whether I could breathe or not through his fur. I gently cradled him in my arms and moved him to a more comfortable snuggle position against my heart. Dawa had eaten well that evening and now rested peacefully on his carpet beside the bed, his breaths slow and steady.

Around two in the morning, Dawa came to the bed, panting heavily. I figured he had woken up wondering where Toinette was, his breath ragged with what I assumed was anxiety. I stroked his head gently. "Go back to sleep, Dawa. All is well." He went back to the carpet as I had asked but continued panting heavily. Half an hour later, he returned and placed his head on the bed next to my pillow. Minou had slipped away while I slept. Dawa's droopy eyes searched the bed. His labored breathing was even louder than before. I tried to tune into his energy, but I was still so new to this that I felt nothing unusual.

"I'm sorry. I think you want something, but I don't know what it is." Perhaps he wanted to sleep in the bed with me, but he smelled like… well, a very, very old dog.

"I'm sorry, Dawa, you can't sleep here. But you can sleep there." I pointed to his carpet and again stroked his head. He returned to lie down.

This cycle continued for a few hours, and I began to seriously question my decision to take on this dog-sitting gig.

"Come on, Dawa, go lie down on your carpet now and let me sleep." And the kind, peaceful being did as I asked.

In the morning, I discovered that Dawa had diarrhea, and because I had not understood what he repeatedly tried to tell me, there were several large puddles of liquid poop in the bedroom and living room—a smell and sight I'd rather not recall. I cleaned the house and gave Dawa some pumpkin pie filling Toinette had left for him. That day, he was too tired to walk much past the end of the driveway. I sat next to him, stroking his fur. I sent him silent apologies, guilt heavy in my chest, and promised myself—and him—to be more attentive.

For the first week, Dawa alternated between diarrhea and constipation, with pumpkin as a remedy for both, until I found the right balance in his meals. But that first night, I had learned that heavy panting with his head on the bed meant, "I need to go out. Now." And we never again had an accident in the house.

As Toinette had warned me, Dawa sometimes stared at walls or his food bowl with questioning eyes. "You *just* ate, Dawa, don't you remember?" After our walks, he sometimes continued past the house as if he didn't remember where he lived. At times, he looked at me with such vacant eyes that I extended my hand to his snout, hoping the familiar scent might bring him back to the present. But other times, Dawa remembered everything, and in those moments, he was the sweetest companion—patient, gentle, and full of affection. He lay at my feet when I wrote and never disturbed me unless he absolutely had to. He had his favorite streets around the neighborhood and others he avoided, planting his paws firmly and resisting with the strength of his younger years if I tried to coax him. And on a few occasions, bursts of puppy energy at the sight of a favorite trail or neighbor dog gave me a glimpse of the playful dog he once had been.

In those moments when Dawa forgot, Minou always appeared. If Dawa faced the wall, motionless, Minou walked under his face, his tail straight up to graze Dawa's snout. The movement was slow, but always Dawa followed Minou with his eyes, then his body. Minou also chaperoned our walks, always stealthily and at a distance. If I turned to look at him, he quickly looked away or sat in the middle of the street to groom himself as though he had not been following us at all.

I never let him see me smile; I think he would have been offended. I so loved Minou in stealth mode.

With time, our life settled into the peaceful rhythm of daily routine. Dawa seemed stronger and happier than when Toinette had first left, but still physically weak and mentally confused. Minou began walking with us rather than behind us in stealth mode.

Until, one day, I remembered my assignment.

"Minou. Do you know that Dawa is very old, and that maybe he'd like to move on from this plane of existence to be free of his failing body?" I approached the subject casually, aloud, as though I were discussing with Minou a piece of news I'd heard.

His ears flattened against his skull. He lowered his body and quickly slunk away.

"Well. That didn't go well," I mumbled as he disappeared into the woods.

That night, Minou jumped on the bed for our usual snuggle and walked across my body toward my face. I cradled him in my arms and again gently suggested, "Minou. Let Dawa go to the other side."

His ears stayed upright, but he stood abruptly, slipped out of my arms, and jumped off the bed. He didn't come back for the rest of the night.

I became very curious.

It was no longer about convincing a cat to let a dog die. It was about exploring how much Minou understood me.

I let the matter rest for a few days, then tried again on one of our walks.

"Minou..." He didn't even let me finish. He slunk away immediately. And that night, although he jumped on the bed, he stayed at my feet, and neither cajoling nor apologizing could convince him to purr against my heart again.

After that, although he left as soon as I brought up the topic, Minou joined all our walks, not just some, as though he no longer trusted me alone with Dawa.

I missed snuggling him, so I let the topic drop for a couple of weeks. Eventually, Minou returned, and our peaceful routine resumed.

But time was ticking, and I began to feel I had failed Dawa, if indeed he had called me in to help his passing. So, about a week before Toinette was to return, on a crisp and sunny day when Dawa was particularly alert and vigorous, I looked at Minou walking by his side and thought—not said, but thought—"Minou. Let him go."

His ears went flat from point to point, but he didn't slink away. Instead, he turned to me and hissed. Yes—hissed.

I never brought up the topic again, but for the remainder of my time there, Minou never curled up beside me again. Toinette returned from France. Dawa transformed into an excited puppy at the sight of her. She sat beside him and rubbed behind his ears and under his belly, in secret spots only she knew—ones that made him roll over in joy.

And I sighed in relief—there was still joy in Dawa's life, and he had not died on my watch.

I left them to enjoy their reunion and moved into Leah's spare bedroom to finish writing my book.

A week later, I returned to Toinette's house to collect my payment. As I walked down the driveway, the sun bathed the deck in golden light, and there was Minou, stretched out his full length, soaking in the warmth.

"Minou!" I was excited to see him. I leaned and scratched his head, and he slowly blinked. I assumed this was a sign of reconciliation. I slipped both hands beneath his limp, sun-drenched body and lifted him into my arms. From limp to fully alive, instantly—he twisted free of my grasp, leaped off the deck, and disappeared into the tall grass. I never saw him again. His person was back. Who was I? Just a sitter with unacceptable ideas.

Dawa seemed to have forgotten who I was, but in his usual gentle manner, he let me pet him, his heavy-lidded eyes gazing up at me with quiet acceptance.

The money I earned from house- and dog-sitting bought me freedom. With *Crazy Free* finally done, I had enough to leave the growing cold and creeping darkness of the Northeast and drive to the desert, back to Sedona.

Six months later, I received an email from Toinette. Dawa had died peacefully in his sleep. She and Minou were by his side for his last breath. Perhaps Minou was right all along—some farewells were best waited for.

Chapter 16
Bark Twice—Twice

Seattle, Washington - June 2015

He was just a simple dog, the kind you'd see outside a coffee shop, tethered by a leash wrapped around a table leg. His mutt face rested peacefully on two elegantly crossed paws. His eyes were closed and his ears erect. He didn't seem to mind the cold. He simply waited for his people to return from the coffee shop.

It was warm inside the coffee shop, but still, Isabel and I cradled our cups in our hands, soaking in their heat. It had been a couple of years since we last met. I had spent my summers in other mountains and avoided driving north in the colder months. And in Seattle, the cold could come at any time of the year. Even on this early-summer afternoon, the dreary drizzle had chased us indoors for a steaming cup of hot cocoa (for me) and a double espresso (for her), as though winter still ruled the outside world.

"What do you mean, the cat hissed?" She tilted her head, eyes skeptical. "Are you sure it was because of your thoughts? There could have been another cat across the street you just didn't see."

"No, I'm telling you. This cat was upset because I was trying to convince him to let his dog die."

"Melissa." She drew out my name. "That's... a little ridiculous. Pfff!" Isabel huffed a small laugh into her espresso, took a sip, and shook her head.

In the sipping pause, I noticed that the ears of the dog outside, across the window from where we sat, stood still, whereas they had seemed to move in synchrony with my story while I was telling it. I noticed, but I didn't share my observation with Isabel.

"Alright..." she set her cup down. "Tell me again. What exactly did the animal communicator—what was her name? Sarah?—what did she say?"

"She said that to communicate with animals, the message has to emanate from the heart, not the head. Animals are natural telepaths—they feel the energy of our thoughts. But to hear their answers, we need to develop our telepathic listening."

The dog outside remained still, his eyes shut, but his right ear turned.

My explanation wasn't exactly what Sarah had taught me, but Isabel and I had experimented with telepathy before, sending heart messages across the country when we lived on opposite coasts, and with some success. So it felt like a natural entry point to approach her skepticism.

"Actually, this is what I think: I think cats understand every single word we say..." I paused for effect. "Every. Single. Word. But they just don't care about human thoughts unless it concerns them. Dogs, on the other hand, only understand a subset of our words and thoughts, but they care. A lot."

On the words "a lot," the dog's ears shifted slightly, like small radars seeking a signal.

Isabel flipped her long, dark hair over her shoulder, a faint smile curving her lips. It wasn't dismissive—at least not entirely. If I were to name it, I'd call it a smile of amused skepticism, not fully condescending, just fondly entertained.

"Alright, look." I pointed to the dog. "This dog right here, for example…" Both ears twitched. "I think he's been listening to our conversation."

This time, Isabel laughed outright. "Melissa, he's across a double-paned window." She tapped the glass lightly; the dog didn't move. "He can't even hear us."

"Hey dog," I called softly. The door to the coffee shop was closed, and the coffee shop was buzzing with loud conversations. The dog's ears twitched again, but his snout remained nestled in his paws.

"Hey dog." I lowered my voice even further. "If you can hear me, please bark twice."

The dog lifted his head, looked straight ahead—not at us—and barked. Twice.

Isabel's jaw dropped and stayed open as she slowly turned to me.

"How did you do that?"

I shrugged and lifted my palms to the mystery. In truth, I was just as surprised as she was. And we both burst into laughter.

৪০ · ৫৪

Outside of Sinclair, Wyoming - September 2018

The scene outside the diner could have been the backdrop for a spaghetti western.

The air shimmered with heat rising from the dry, hot desert dirt. Stray tumbleweeds clung to the base of barbed wire fences, their seeds scattering in the wind that had pinned them there. Young Caleen had never seen anything like it. She had never left North Conway until I kidnapped her for a cross-country adventure. Now, here we were, sitting across from each other at the almost-clean table of the only diner we'd seen for hours, sharing a plate of french fries. The fries were crispy and salted just right, but the true luxury was the air conditioning.

Outside, wavering in the heat shimmers, a slender dog rested on a concrete platform about a hundred feet from the diner window. Her front paws were crossed delicately, but her hind legs were tucked together, exposing nursing nipples to the relentless sun. Her mouth hung open as she panted steadily.

"Wow, that dog over there must be hot." Caleen pointed toward her.

"Probably is, but she's also a Wyoming dog. She might be used to it. It might not feel as hot to her as it does to you."

"Yeah, maybe."

It was Caleen's first time in a desert, and she trusted me to know these things. She finished the last of the fries and returned to the counter for soft-serve ice creams.

My gaze lingered on the dog. She seemed so peaceful over there, just resting in the sun with her snout on her crossed paws, unbothered by the world. I smiled. That dog reminded me of another dog. She reminded me of a hot cocoa and a double espresso with Isabel in a small Seattle coffee shop.

Caleen didn't know that story yet, and she loved my stories—she devoured them. I could tell her tales for hundreds of miles, and she still listened with the same delight, her eyes wide and curious. She also never complained, not even when we drove twelve or fifteen hours a day, stopped to eat only once, or slept in the back of the Catmobile at strange truck stops along the highway. To her, this was the adventure of a lifetime, and she followed my lead with absolute trust.

"One time, in Seattle…" I began as she handed me an ice cream cone, "I was with a friend in a coffee shop, telling her about a dog I knew. This dog wanted to die, but there was a cat in the house who wouldn't let him go…"

Caleen's ice cream dripped, forgotten, as she absorbed every word, her eyes fixed on me. I told her the whole story about Dawa and Minou, then continued with the next story.

"…So then I said, 'Hey, dog. If you can hear me, bark twice.' And the dog actually barked twice."

"Wow!" Caleen looked at the dog on the concrete platform outside. "Can we try it with this dog?"

I hesitated, estimating the distance. "Nah, she's too far away."

She was at least a hundred feet away, and we were inside an air-conditioned diner, with patrons as loud as those in the coffee shop had been. And this dog's ears hadn't twitched once during my storytelling—or at least, not that I could see from this distance.

"Let's try it anyway," Caleen insisted. She was so excited. Caleen believed in magic—all of it, in any form. It saddened me to think I had to disappoint her.

"Hey, dog," I called softly, not expecting anything. "Hey, dog, if you can hear me, please, bark twice."

Yes. Yes, she did. She lifted her head suddenly, looked in our direction, and barked, exactly twice.

Caleen's eyes widened in delight, and it was my turn to be stunned with disbelief.

Without a second glance, the dog rose to her feet, stretched languidly, and began walking away, her steps slow and deliberate, as though she had decided it was time to find a more private place.

ဆ · ଓଃ

I encourage you to try this for yourself, but, for the sake of full transparency, I must admit that since the day with Caleen, I have asked dogs to bark twice whenever I see them lying peacefully with their snout on crossed paws outside coffee shops, restaurants, ice cream parlors, parks, anywhere. It has never worked again.

I imagine the canine collective has made its point clear enough. It will not get any clearer by my constantly asking to repeat the magic.

Chapter 17
Momo

Yep Yep Farms, Dexter, Oregon - December 2017

Momo was a perfect circle in the center of the papasan. The wood stove was crackling. The farm was peaceful. In my fingers, my first crochet winter hat was taking form while outside, the first snowflakes of the season softly covered the world. It could have been perfect, just as it was—but my mind wondered, "Minou had clearly heard my thoughts, but he didn't want to hear what I was saying. And the dogs had barked at first, but now they don't. Why can I talk to trees but not animals? What am I missing?"

I looked up from the colorful knots between my hands at Momo on the papasan and smiled. I gathered a love-greeting in my heart and, with focused intent, sent it telepathically to Momo.

"Hey, Momo... can you hear me?"

Normally, Momo napped daily on Jason's chest. During that time, which began immediately after lunch and lasted approximately an hour, neither human nor cat responded to any calls or questions.

"Momo owns the farm," Jason often said. "We merely rent it from him in exchange for rubs behind the ears and cat food."

Although Momo owned the farm, his main duties were managerial. He sat on the dirt path linking the main house to the chicken coop and surveyed his territory, ensuring that all tasks were accomplished. If we, the farmhands, did well, we were rewarded with a visit. And in rare cases, he even let us pet him.

Momo was already an old cat when Jason and Louisa bought the farm. He had been the farm cat for the previous owners and the ones before them. No one knew how old Momo was, but with each passing year his gaze grew wiser and his stride more sinuous.

When Momo looked at me with his eyes half-closed, body vibrating slightly from the purring, I couldn't help the feeling that he was performing a deep soul scan.

In the winter of 2017, Jason, Louisa, and their baby girl, Rosa, traveled to visit family for the holidays, leaving the farm in Momo's capable paws. But because these paws didn't feed the hydroponic fish, clean the chicken coop, or pick lettuce from the greenhouse, Jason and Louisa asked me to assist him. I still slept in the Catmobile, waking each morning to a thin layer of ice in my tea mug, but the farm was right there. I stacked wood in the stove and thawed each morning, and again each evening, when I snuggled myself in blankets in front of the fire while I learned to crochet and Momo napped on the papasan.

For the first few days, Momo ignored me. I was simply the attendant to the self-serve cat buffet. I kept his bowls filled with kibble and fresh water. Remnants of animal body parts I found around the farm reassured me that his diet was well supplemented with fresh prey. Momo knew how to hunt. He didn't toy with prey the way less adept, more domesticated cats do. He killed with the savage efficiency of learned survival self-sufficiency. Momo lived in the house, but, at heart, he was still a wild cat.

During the day, while I attended to my farm duties, I rarely saw him. But although Jason was on the other side of the world, Momo upheld the daily tradition of the circular nap in the papasan. Nap time, therefore, was my best opportunity to slowly build a friendship with him, in hopes that he might someday sit on my lap and purr while I crocheted.

When I was a little girl, I was in love with the book *The Little Prince*. If a story was offered, that was the one I asked to hear, again and again. As a teenager, I memorized the entire chapter about the Little Prince's encounter with a fox, which was my favorite.

"Please—tame me!" The fox tells the Little Prince.

"What does that mean—'tame'?" the Little Prince asks.

The fox explains that to tame means to build ties. To build ties with a wild animal requires patience over many days.

Each day, the Little Prince approaches the fox a little closer until, one day, they finally call each other friends.

"One only understands the things one tames," the fox tells the Little Prince.

More than a children's tale, I stored the fox's story in my mind as a real-life manual for befriending wildlife.

As an adult, I had tried many times to tame a friend, be it a squirrel or a butterfly. But my time in the wilderness always involved movement—hiking, climbing, kayaking. I was never in one place long enough to tame a friend.

Momo came to the papasan each day at the same time. This was the first step the fox asked of the Little Prince. Meeting at the same time each day, the fox said, gets the heart ready for the rendezvous.

And so it was that I decided to tame Momo, so we could be friends, and I could hope he would lie on my lap and purr instead of keeping his naps on the opposite side of the living room.

Only then, once trust had been established, might he be open to telepathic conversation.

206

For over a week, whenever Momo entered the room, I greeted him with, "Hi Momo, it is nice to see you." Sometimes, he looked in my direction; sometimes, he didn't. Each time I filled his bowls, I opened the door and called out into the cold garden: "Momo, your food is served, if you're hungry." And every time he got up from the papasan, stretched, jumped off, and walked to the door, I repeated, "It was nice to see you, Momo. Have fun out there. Maybe I'll see you tonight."

Gradually, he softened. When I wished him well, he looked in my direction and half-closed his eyes. I imagined it meant he was smiling.

One day, he came to rest on the sofa's arm, next to me. I was able to pet him briefly before he jumped off and left. The next day, he stayed a little longer and purred. And the next day, he walked across my crochet project, which was exciting but tangled my stitches.

Then, finally, one late evening, as the farm lay peaceful and all the tasks were done, Momo walked back and forth across my crochet, then lowered himself onto my lap and purred.

I smiled, thinking. I had finally tamed wild Momo into a friend.

The very next day, still glowing with the joy of his trust, I looked up from my crochet and, with a burst of love-greeting, sent him the thought:

"Hey, Momo... can you hear me?"

He stood up, ears pinned back. No stretch, no glance— just a jump from the papasan and a straight march to the door, ears still flattened like an anvil had landed on his head.

"So... you heard me?" I asked him aloud. He sped up through the door.

"I guess he heard me." I shrugged, addressing the empty papasan.

I didn't see Momo that night. Snow covered the ground, and the wood stove blazed, but he didn't come in to warm up. I filled his bowl with kibble, but he ate a meal of his own killing.

The next day, I saw him in the distance on the farm and called,

"I'm sorry, Momo."

He ignored me.

He didn't come to the papasan for his nap either.

For three days, he avoided me. If I entered, he exited. If I spoke, he vanished. Even his path to the food bowl curved away from mine. And still, every time I saw him, I called to him, "I'm sorry, Momo."

I assumed his coldness and avoidance were direct reactions to my telepathic question. I had inadvertently deeply offended him—in his own house. There was no other explanation.

Finally, at nap time on the fourth day of his obvious avoidance, Momo entered the living room and, with regal coolness, glided to the papasan.

I kept my fingers moving as I watched him over the rim of my glasses. He jumped up on the papasan and spiraled a few times before landing as a circular cat. I was afraid to think at all. I knew he could hear me. But my mind was racing despite my best effort to keep it silent. Finally, realizing the futility of my attempt to not think, I put my crochet down, and with the most sincere and humble tone, I told him:

"Momo, I am soooo sorry. I can see that you're upset. I don't know what I did to upset you. I'm just a clumsy human, and I meant you no offense. Please, forgive me."

He turned his head and looked straight into my eyes, scanning my soul as he did. His ears were up, and by my limited understanding of cat body language, this gave me hope that my apology was accepted.

[That was rude.] The message came one word at a time, ringing clearly in my mind. The voice was neutral, neither

208

male nor female, but it had a regal tone and finality to its energy. This was not the start of a discussion or explanation but a final statement.

I had so many questions. Why was it rude? *What* was rude? Why would dogs respond but cats be offended? Was it all cats or just this cat? How would one then address a cat? Or should cats—who can never truly be tamed—never be addressed? Had I inadvertently yanked Momo back from another realm? Or had I simply disturbed the sacred nap?

I asked nothing. As the questions poured in my head like the falling snowflakes outside, I deflected them into silence, waiting with as blank a mind as I could muster for further messages from Momo.

[Don't ever do that again.] The second message was fainter but just as clear as the first one.

"I promise I won't." I wasn't sure exactly what "that" referred to, but I feared asking lest I angered him again.

He blinked and lowered his head for a nap.

That night, he climbed onto my lap and purred. It seemed that whatever wrong I had done was forgiven. I gently moved my fingers through his fur, hesitating slightly each time he shifted, careful not to disturb this newly regained peace. As he purred into my lap, eyes closed, I watched him quietly, reminded of the fox's wisdom: "One only understands the things that one tames."

But the fox had been willing to be tamed. And even then, perhaps we can build trust, create ritual, even share affection—and still only glimpse the edges of a being we tame, never the wild mysteries at their center.

Chapter 18
The Viking and the Cats

Hendersonville, North Carolina, March-May 2020

The year was 2020, and for those of you who were there, you know what that means. The world suddenly shut down. I caught an intuitive whiff of suspicion of impending lockdown while still on the flatness of the Florida seashore and fled to North Carolina, to the land of a lady I knew. If I was to be immobilized, let it at least be near mountains.

I had met the Lady of the Land, as Erik and I called her, briefly in Sedona years prior, but such is life on the road that travelers' paths cross and cross again. So when she invited me to visit her for a few days on her land at the foot of the Blue Ridge Mountains, I pointed the truck north immediately and knocked on her door that evening.

On the Land with the Lady were three other residents: Emilie, Erik, and Jewel.

The Lady introduced me to Emilie first.

"Rrrhhhellooooo?" Emilie crooked her yellow and green head to the side, using her beak to maneuver through the cage to get closer. She was an exotic talking parrot from a land far south. She had been with the Lady for at least thirty years, and the sentences she sang in the morning, when she thought she was alone, revealed the intrigues of the Lady's prior life.

210

The Lady had been extremely wealthy in a not-so-distant past, but the economic wave she had ridden to great heights had crashed suddenly. All that remained of her former life were dusty piles of materialistic mistakes stored in large plastic tubs in metal containers parked on the Land. Stacked to the ceilings were tubs of exquisite fine art paintings, pottery, authentic Native woven baskets, full-size Native American totems, delicately elegant fine China and crystal glasses for all occasions, hats, summer dresses, fur coats, and hundreds upon hundreds of high-heeled shoes, most of which had never been worn.

I had just arrived at the door of her trailer when the world's shutdown was confirmed. My few days' visit suddenly had no end date, so the Lady graciously offered me a job. If I helped free her from the burden of all these possessions and allowed her to return to the nomadic life of her youth, she would gladly and gratefully feed me. I accepted and semi-permanently parked the Catmobile in the field uphill from her trailer home, under a grandfather oak tree surrounded by wildflowers.

Every day on the Land, I sorted, photographed, and cataloged the content of the containers to sell on the web, prepared and shipped packages, and slowly, steadily, chipped away at the elephant of a task.

Erik and Jewel were an inseparable pair. Erik was a camo-clad rustic redneck, the kind who disappears into the woods with a rifle and a pack of survival gear. He was tall, tall enough to have to duck under doorways. His bright, round, curious eyes and wispy, soft hazelnut hair revealed his Norse ethnic heritage.

"Are you handsome?" I asked him once.

"I'm the right amount of handsome." He ran his hand through his hair and laughed. "I'm handsome enough that a supermodel wouldn't be ashamed to be seen with me, but not so handsome that the Girl Next Door would think me out of her league."

Erik had also just arrived on the Land. The Lady had summoned him to rescue her from a rotten tree about to fall on the roof. The roof was saved, the world shut down, and now, he was staying too.

The Lady graciously offered him meals and a place to stay, if he would please, please, clear the area around the trailer and containers of all the rusted metal, dead fridges, washing machines, and abandoned moldy chairs and sofas extracted from previously owned properties, now merely a furniture graveyard covered in rampant blackberry bushes and the omnipresent poison ivy.

And so Erik and I met, and the work on the Land began. We worked all day, then regrouped in the trailer's small living room in the evening. We sat together around a small table for candlelit dinners, like family. After dinner, one of us cleaned the dishes, then the Lady hugged us goodnight, always with much gratitude for the work done, and retired to her quarters.

Once we were alone, Erik and I, that is when the storytelling happened.

Now, I'm a storyteller, but if I'm a novel the size of the one you're holding in your hand, Erik was a full-shelf encyclopedia.

He had been a hired mercenary in what he called the Bad Land, a country in Eastern Europe he never named nor described. He had studied cellular biology, paying for his own higher education by working as a male stripper in a BDSM bar. His brilliance had caught the attention of the faculty, and he was hired as part of the scientific team that designed a microscopic laser still being tested for healing cancer cells. He was a follower of Odin, well-versed in Viking myths and mythology. He was a witch—a real witch, with the power to cast spells, the effects of which I saw. He was also a hard-working southern boy who grew up with black snakes and fireflies and who could kill a flying carpenter bee with a rifle in one shot.

Every night, until late in the night and sometimes into the early next morning, perched at the edge of my wooden stool, I lost myself in the world of Erik's stories. I saw the Bad Land in my mind's eye. I met the friends, the foes, felt the fear, and heard the gunshots. I learned about bondage techniques and marveled at his scientific discoveries. I celebrated with him the recollection of the lifelong path of slain personal demons, survived odds, satisfied women, and outgrown paradigms that had created the honorable gentleman in front of me. But, also, I laughed, a lot. I giggled in delight at his raw, honest, vivacious storytelling flare. Each story was so detailed, rich with colors, smells, sounds, and feelings that I was there. I plunged in each story as clearly as if I had passed a portal to his past and was watching his life in real-time as a present silent observer.

After weeks of daily immersion in Erik's world, I noticed that all his stories had one, and only one, thing in common. There was always at least a cat.

When bullets were whistling above his head, and his Irish brother-in-arms convinced him to desist from his mercenary contract and make a run for the border to the nearby sanctuary country, he first returned to their shack to check on the feral cats he had adopted and found them a new home. Before following women home from the BDSM bar, he always asked them to wait while he ran home to feed his cats. When he first designed the laser, a cat was purring on his lap. When he performed witch rituals to rid the Land of resident darklings, always by his side was his Jewel, his big orange cat. And when he extracted piles of rotten wood and rusty metal from underneath the containers, Jewel followed him, killing the evicted mice as they emerged.

Erik could not sleep unless Jewel was with him. Jewel curled against Erik's ribs and purred. Jewel did not fall asleep until he was certain Erik was asleep first. But, sometimes, Erik faked sleeping for the pleasure of seeing Jewel all curled and handsome by his side. It was a huge symbiotic love. And observing them move through the yard, I could have sworn they communicated telepathically all day long.

"Tell me about your love of cats."
"Mmh. Not yet."
The cats were omnipresent, yet it was the one and only topic Erik avoided, no matter how or how often I asked.

Between the daily work on the Land and the nightly storytelling, far from the world's politics, deaths, fears, and woes, two moons traveled their celestial paths in the blink of an eye. Erik cleared the Land back to a grassy, welcoming backyard. The containers were emptied and eventually towed away. Where once the ill rubbles of human mistakes had cluttered the earth, the soil breathed again. Rodents left, wild beasts returned.

[Thank you.] The plants and trees bowed a barely perceptible yet noted thank you in the breeze. I heard them.

And the Lady of the Land, at last, was freed.

Travel restrictions lifted, and the paths opened— north for me to my beloved White Mountains and west for Erik and Jewel to his home in Washington state, where his patient and dearly missed sweetheart awaited him.

On our last night, we were excited to leave but also sad that our time together was about to end, aware of the unlikeliness that we would ever again have an opportunity for such depth of exploration of each other's lives. Erik served the Lady and I quail eggs in nests of blanched spinach with a side of curried quinoa and freshly roasted garlic bread. The Lady opened a vintage wine, one of the few things she had saved from the purging of the Land. And I concluded our final meal with a cardamom-infused chocolate mousse I created from scratch with high-grade baker's chocolate and my own Costa Rican cacao beans.

The lady wished us goodnight and left. And again I asked,

"Okay. *Now* will you tell me about your love of cats?"

Erik smiled and leaned back silently, enjoying my trepidation before answering.

"Alright. I'll tell you about the cats..."

Erik was a wild ten-year-old southern boy playing in the woods with sticks, building bows, and practicing killing beasts when he found his first cat. She was a small feral cat, alone and scared. Erik sat on the forest floor next to her and gently stroked her head. His touch soothed her, so he cradled her in his arms and brought her home to his room.

It was not much of a room, just a painted concrete square with a mattress on the floor. It had no privacy and offered no safety because the greatest threat to Erik was his own drunken dad. His mom had packed her bags several years prior, unwilling to sustain the blows but unable to take her son with her. She had vanished. Dad had a job. Erik was fed, clothed, and had a roof over his head. He had stopped going to school because he was bored there, he said, and instead spent his days in the woods teaching himself survival skills. Dad was not so drunk that first night when Erik brought the cat home. He grumbled when he saw the cat then mumbled, "you better feed that cat yourself," but nothing more.

That night, the little cat climbed on Erik's chest and purred. To his surprise, Erik fell asleep immediately and deeply, the kind of sleep rarely available to kids who might get dragged out of bed by one hand while the other holds a belt, with never an explanation of why.

In the months to come, while wandering through the woods, dark streets, and back alleys of the nearby town, Erik rescued any stray cat he met, one by one, until he had twelve cats.

"I had to hide the cats in a nearby hangar, and some in the garage, so there would only be one or two in my room at any one time. Because Dad was always drunk, he didn't realize it wasn't the same cat. I could get away with it when I had six

215

or seven cats. But with twelve, I figured even drunk, it was just a matter of time before he discovered the cats, and I got a beating for being so *stupid*."

There was disgust in the word "stupid."

The story halted.

Erik stepped onto the back porch, slowly rolled a cigarette, and stared up at the stars. The warm southern breeze danced with the cigarette smoke, dissipating it in the night along with painful memories. I stayed on the stool, still in that childhood house with all the cats in my mind. I watched Erik look up at the stars. I finally understood why the story had been withheld for so long.

Erik returned to his stool, drank a little wine, and joined me back in the story, in the house with the cats.

With twelve cats, it was just a matter of time before the impending beating. The problem was that the cats didn't look alike. Two were black, some were gray, orange, calico, tabby, tuxedo, and one was all white.

"If I could just dye them all the same color," he thought one day, "then Dad wouldn't notice I have so many."

He went to town, to a small store mostly frequented by elder ladies needing supplies for quilts and such. They did have dyes for garments, but Erik had no money. And besides, he thought, the dyes were probably filled with chemicals, and he didn't want to hurt the cats. He was running through the woods toward home when, mid-jump, his pants snagged on a berry bush. He freed himself and stared at the berries— blackberries. Blackberries stained!

Erik gathered as many blackberries as he could fit in his upturned folded shirt and carried them home. There, he gathered several bags and returned for more. Diligently, he piled all the blackberries in a tub with water and moved the tub behind the house to let them soak overnight.

The next morning, the brew was done, and the water was reddish-black. The twelve cats, one by one, flat ears and tucked tails, were plunged into the blackberry dye. "And, believe it or not…" Erik chuckled. "it kinda worked." The cats didn't turn black, but they acquired a purple-greyish hue that concealed their natural color sufficiently to fool his dad's inattentive eyes.

"The problem…" Erik let out a booming laugh—a deep, head-thrown-back kind of laugh that suddenly lifted the mood back to our usual storytelling mode—"is that it rained the next day."

As the cats walked in the rain, the dye washed off. The black cats stayed black, but the gray tabbies turned slightly purple, the orange ones murky brown, and the one white cat lavender-blue, unmistakably lavender-blue.

Erik's dad came home and dropped his bag by the door. He kicked an empty bucket and turned it over, sat on it and leaned back to rest on the wall behind him. He pulled a cigarette from his chest pocket, lit it, and drew on it, when a couple of dirty, murky cats, including an unmistakably lavender-blue one walked by.

"Erik, com'out here for a sec." Erik braced himself and stepped out the front door.

"What the *fuck* is wrong with your cats?" His dad pointed at the cats with his chin.

"Yeah, I don't know, Dad. They must have gotten into something." Erik shrugged causally and walked back into the house as though nothing unusual had happened.

"And so you didn't get caught?"

"No, and as long as I fed them myself, he didn't seem to care."

"Wow! So, that's where your love of cats comes from? Because you had so many of them as companions as a kid?"

"Well… No, actually, I took that first cat home because of what happened when I was nine years old."

By then, it was about midnight. I had a seventeen-hour drive the next day, which I intended to drive in one go, and Erik and Jewel had an early flight out of Asheville. Yes, it was late, but... I stayed on the stool and stared at Erik, eyebrows raised.

"I'm not letting you leave until I know what happened when you were nine."

Erik laughed. He got up, opened the fridge, scooped the last of the chocolate mousse into two small dishes, and handed me one. We both settled back on our stools with spoons, chocolate, and a sort of silent warm friendship glow. I felt the next story was the last story, not because of the late hour, but because I sensed this was The Story, the overarching theme of an entire well-lived life. We ate our chocolate quietly, then Erik placed his bowl on the table, and we both stepped back, far back, in time.

Erik was nine years old the first time his dad took him to a zoo in the big city. They passed by the snakes, the orangutans, the elephants. All the animals were new and fascinating. His dad had also brought a new girlfriend to the zoo. The two of them had met recently and were full of spicy chemistry. They stopped in front of the cheetah's enclosure to make out.

The enclosure was wide and round, with beige packed dirt, a small pool to the right, and a cave in the back. It was surrounded by a fence, about six feet tall.

But what's a six-foot tall fence when you're a wild southern boy raised in the woods?

A cheetah left the cave and, with slow, graceful movements, crossed the packed dirt toward the gathered crowd of onlookers. She stopped in the middle of the enclosure and looked around. Erik thought she was the most beautiful thing he had ever seen. He just wished she would get closer, but she remained over there, in the center. So, logically, he climbed up the fence and back down into the enclosure.

This happened to coincide with the arrival of a big cat expert. She began her informational talk about big cats and the crowd turned to face her, including Erik's dad and the new girlfriend. Everyone faced away when Erik climbed up and over the fence.

Erik walked toward the cheetah until he was close enough to smell her breath. She was so tall that his head was almost even with hers. He looked at her big head, her whiskers, her fur, her ears, and into her eyes. She was so beautiful. He'd later learn that it's customary for mama cheetahs to smell the back of cub's necks. This is how they know whose cub this is. The mama cheetah walked closer to Erik and extended her neck over his shoulder to smell the back of his neck. Whose cub was this small human? Erik thought she was giving him a hug, so he placed both arms around her neck.

"And, believe it or not," he said, "she stayed there and let me hug her."

His eyes drifted for a moment, and his face softened.

"It was the most wonderful feeling when I was with the cheetah. It was warm and safe, and she smelled so good."

One by one, other cheetahs came out of the cave, curious about this little human. The mama cheetah stayed in Erik's embrace, and the others gathered around, encircling them.

"Oh my GOD! There is a kid in the enclosure," an adult yelled.

A man with an official zoo uniform quickly arrived through a side door.

"Kid, just slowly back away and walk backwards toward me. Just don't look the cats in the eyes."

"But... I don't want to." Erik released the cheetah's neck and shook his head at the man. The man looked scared, one foot and hand on the side door, ready for an instant exit.

"Erik! What the... get your *fucking ass* out o' there."

Erik looked back at the cat. Oh, how he wished he could stay with her. But he walked out, like the man had asked, backwards slowly until a hand grabbed the back of his shirt and yanked him out of the cheetah's enclosure.

"How dare you embarrass me like that?" A large hand met Erik's face at full force.

"We're going home right now. I can't take you anywhere without you making a fool of yourself."

Erik's dad grabbed him by the arm and was dragging him away when the lady cat expert stopped them.

"Excuse me, Sir, may I have a word with your son. It's important for my research."

"Certainly. Maybe you can teach him some goddamn common sense." He shoved Erik toward the lady cat expert, barely sparing her a glance.

The lady cat expert took Erik back to the side door.

"Well, Erik, what did you think of Soyayya? That is the name of the cheetah you were hugging."

"Oh, she's... wonderful!"

"She seemed to like you too. Say, how would you like to help me feed her and the other cats? It's about time for their meals."

And so, while Erik's dad and the new girlfriend waited on a bench, Erik and the lady cat expert visited all the big cats' enclosures. However long it took to feed them all, the lady told Erik everything she could about cats, and Erik was able to return, once more, briefly, to Soyayya's enclosure.

"This was one of the happiest days of his life." His voice trailed off, and silence lingered between us.

I realized my jaw had been open for some time, probably since Erik placed his arms around the cheetah. Tears welled up in my eyes and rolled down my cheeks. I didn't know if they were tears of joy, sadness, gratitude, or all of the above. Erik smiled, and tears welled up in his eyes. We stayed staring at each other for an instant, an infinity.

"So anyway." He shrugged. "I've loved cats since that day. And because I feel safe when they're around, I always make sure I have at least one feline friend in my life."

We both looked toward the kitchen.

Jewel stretched against the cabinet door. He had been there the whole time, listening. Lifting his head, he briefly looked at Erik, slowly blinked, then rolled onto his back with a deep purr.

ဆ · ၾ

Hendersonville, North Carolina, February 2020 (one week before departure)

A rooster sang in the distance, and a soft fog hovered over the newly exposed grassy lawn, depositing dew on each blade of grass. In his room, by the trailer's back entrance, Erik wrote a love letter on real paper to his sweetheart, as he did every morning. Across from Erik's room, Emilie walked around in her cage, throwing food through the metal bars and croaking in displeasure at the unfair incarceration. Up a step, in the kitchen, right above Emilie's cage and Erik's room, I ground cacao beans and smelled them.

I had been exploring the complexity and range of flavors in individual cacao beans and had just begun creating composite flavors. Every morning, I selected a handful of beans, smelled each one, and ground them together. I then added hot water and smelled the composite product, and learned. On some mornings, the resulting combination was so delightful that it stood on its own. Other times, I felt it could benefit from additional spices. Luckily, The Lady of the Land had several large Tupperware bins filled with exotic spices. I smelled the mixture in my mug, then opened each spice jar and let my nose find perfect pairings. Erik was my guinea pig.

"Good morning, Erik. Would you like some cacao?" I'd say. I knew the answer, but I asked anyway, in case he was not

221

at his desk writing, and so that Emilie knew I was coming and didn't get spooked.

One morning, the cacao mixture had such a complex flavor that my nose lingered over jar after jar selecting spices to add. There was cardamom, cinnamon, nutmeg, clove—well, that's chai, isn't it? There was chaga, a medicinal mushroom with a subtle smell and flavor, and great health benefits. And finally, there was maca, a root I loved not only for its nutty flavor, but also for its jet-fuel-like effect in the body. If Erik and I had only a week to clean up the rest of the Land, we needed all the fast fuel we could get. In fact, I thought, why don't I add a little coffee for an extra jolt today?

So there we had it, the most complex morning cacao yet.

"Good morning, Erik. Would you like a maca mocha chaga chai?" I said it fast, in one breath.

"Whhhhhaaaat?"

Emilie answered first. I stepped down in front of her cage holding the two steaming mugs and lifted them to show her.

"I said, 'Would you like a maca mocha chaga chai?'"

"Whhhaaaat the fuck is that?"

I couldn't believe it. I laughed and turned to Erik.

"Did you hear that?"

"I did." He leaned through the door. "And I have to agree with her."

I laughed about it all day. Later that evening, I told The Lady of the Land the story of the mocha maca chaga chai conversation.

"Oh yes," the Lady said, "one time, I asked Emilie why she was so grumpy all the time. We lived in the mountains above Ashville at the time, and it was winter, so I couldn't let her out because it was too cold. She was just being impossible, yelling all the time and refusing to eat her food. So I asked her, and she said 'Fffflorida'. I don't know how she knew about Florida, but I asked her anyway, 'You want to go to Florida?' and she looked at me sideways with her little eye and said in a perfectly clear full sentence, 'I'm a tropical bird. Why the fuck do I live in snow?'"

I wasn't there, so I cannot vouch for the veracity of the Lady's story. She claimed this was the only full sentence Emilie spoke in the thirty years they spent together. She had no validating witness but no cause to lie either, as far as I could tell.

Shortly after Erik and I left, The Lady found a new home for Emilie, and I am happy to report that she now lives in Miami, Ffffflorida.

Chapter 19
The Cats Across the Veil

North Conway, New Hampshire, for a short summer visit - July 2023

"Did you know there's a variety of magic mushrooms called the cyanescens that loves to grow in wood chips under hydrangeas?"

Hannah looked up with a giggle, a weed dangling from her gloved hand. We happened to be sitting under a hydrangea bush, pulling weeds from decorative wood chips at that very moment. We both glanced around. No cyanescens in sight—just hundreds of tiny green intruders, waiting to be yanked and sent back to the woods.

"Would you eat it if we found one?" Hannah asked.

"No way. Not without having it identified by someone who knows a lot more than I do."

"Me neither. I've only eaten magic mushrooms once. And I don't think I'd ever do *that* again."

"Why? What happened?"

She hesitated, rolling the weed between her fingers.

"Well… I don't usually like telling this story, because I'm still spooked about it. But I think you, of all people, might actually get it."

She exhaled sharply, almost a laugh.

"So… there was this cat..." She shook her head, as if deciding whether to even go there. Then, finally—

"Let's start at the beginning…"

ༀ · ༀ

Hannah's story, Portland, Maine - October 2020

It began at dusk. Hannah and two of her friends and neighbors—a couple—were curled up on couches in a warm, cozy apartment in Portland's West End. It was Halloween, the moon was full, and a dusting of snow covered the streets outside. Inside the warm apartment, the three friends shared a pecan pie and a handful of candies. It was a low-key Halloween. Hannah's only costume was a pair of cat ears in her pink hair—but Hannah's hair was always pink, or blue, or green, Halloween or not.

"I got us a special treat." The woman of the couple pulled a small purple bag from her purse and shook it playfully. "Magic mushrooms!"

She brandished the bag like the grand finale of their evening, and her partner laughed. But Hannah's hesitant smile barely curled the edges of her mouth.

"Mmh. I don't know." She reached for the bag, peering inside. "I'm soooo sensitive to substances. A teeny-tiny bit of weed makes me paranoid. I don't know if I should. I've never eaten mushrooms before."

"Then just take a microdose. You won't feel much effect at all."

The friends were already chewing their own larger portions. Hannah hesitated, then carefully extracted a sliver of stem no bigger than her sparkly pinky nail. She chewed it slowly, earthy and pungent on her tongue, then chased it down with a chug of water.

Then, they waited.

By the time the mushrooms kicked in, it was dark outside. And what better adventure than walking down an empty suburban street beneath a snowy sky about to sprinkle magic in the halo of streetlamps—on Halloween, on mushrooms?

They giggled down the stairs, wrapping coats, scarves, and hats around their still-warm bodies before stepping into the night.

A few flakes floated down, landing softly on their faces like kisses from the sky. The clouds shredded themselves thin in front of the moon, gifting the three friends flickering extra shadows, in addition to those from the streetlamps.

They strolled down the quiet street, enchanted by the way the world shimmered at the edges, until, suddenly, they hit *something*—like an invisible wall of thicker air.

"Did you feel that? What was that?"

Hannah turned around. There was nothing there, except a vague impression of Jello still wobbling from having been traversed. The air suddenly felt heavier, denser. The clouds still shredded past the moon, but the wind had died, leaving the world in a breathless stillness; no rustling leaves, no distant hum of cars, no snowflakes drifting through the air. Everything had gone silent. Yet all three felt an irresistible pull forward, as though this were the only and logical path to the exit.

Past one neighbor's house, then the next, and another. They knew the forms of this landscape—these buildings, these stairs, these balconies, these Halloween decorations. The world looked the same, yet slightly off. The angles of the porches, the placement of the windows—subtle things, wrong things. Hannah pushed her hands deeper into her coat pockets.

A shape moved ahead. It stepped out from the side street's shadows, breaking the smothering stillness. All three friends stopped.

A cat.

Shoulders relaxed with sighs of relief. It was *only* a cat.

A large black and gray, stripy tiger cat casually strolled through the upcoming intersection, shoulders rolling with each soft step. He walked like he owned the night, tail flicking, entirely at ease in his solitude. He lifted his head slightly as he walked, eyes inspecting his domain, passing over them without concern until—his steps faltered. He blinked, then snapped his gaze back, ears twitching, body suddenly still. His shoulders dropped. He stood still for a few breaths, then resumed his slow stroll—this time, toward them.

"You can't be here."

Hannah's breath caught in her throat. Had that cat just spoken with words? Or had she imagined it?

"You guys… heard that, right?"

The shiver down her spine told her the answer before they even spoke.

"Yep," one of them muttered. They both stood there for a second before shrugging in unison and continuing forward.

The cat's gaze now locked onto Hannah. "What are you doing here? You're not supposed to be here."

She looked again to her friends, but they were already several feet further toward the "exit," wherever that was. They hadn't reacted, so she was pretty sure they hadn't heard the cat's questions. But she wasn't about to be left behind. She quickened her step to catch up to them.

The cat followed.

Past a few more houses, the group of four continued their journey through the still world until they reached a two-story building slightly recessed from the others.

Hannah knew this place well. It was the fanciest on the street—a historic wonder, stately, elegant, and almost untouched by time. Dark iron gates curled around a small garden. A paved path led from the gate to a short set of steps, rising to a large, dark green door.

In the summer, the green lawn was impeccably maintained, and the blue and purple hydrangeas that skirted the foot of the building were kept perfectly trimmed. But now, in this dark, wintry world, everything looked different. The moon hung low behind the building, casting a shadow so long it stretched across the street like a stain. The green of the door appeared almost black. The iron gate, the steps, the windows—everything seemed so different. But in what way? The proportions felt... off. Just slightly. As if the house had shifted, stretching taller, leaning in. The longer they looked, the less certain they were that it had ever looked any other way.

The friends slowed, then stopped to take it all in.

There was no light inside the building. No sign of movement. No reason for anything to be watching them.

And yet—all three friends saw the movement in the second-story window. "Demons" is how Hannah would later describe them to the few of us privileged to hear the story. Swirling wispy smoke, like a dark, dense mist, undifferentiated, except for their white, glowing eyes, gathering behind the closed glass. And in the center, one set of red eyes. Fixed on them. Watching. Waiting.

A petite white and gray tabby leaped from the dried bushes at the foot of the building, tiptoed down the path, and slipped under the gate. The stripy tiger cat left the group, padding forward to meet her. Their noses touched for an instant.

"You need to get these humans out of here, *now*."

Hannah heard the words in her head, clear as a voice. But again, she seemed to be the only one. Her friends kept moving, past the cats and toward the gate as if pulled by an invisible thread.

The tiger cat let out a low, rumbling sound. "Mmmh mmmmh."

She looked up. The glowing red eyes were locked onto her friends. Hannah sucked in a sharp breath. Fear clenched around her throat. She couldn't move. Couldn't believe what she was hearing—what she was seeing.

Her friends had reached the gate. They didn't seem to notice the cats. The tiger cat slipped behind Hannah and pressed his body against her leg, forcing her forward, and out of her trance.

"Guys. We have to go *NOW*!"

The sharpness in her voice snapped them out of it. Their heads jerked back and, without question, without hesitation, they turned and hurried down the street, huddled close together.

The silence was still suffocating until a low electric buzz crackled through the air.

They turned just in time to see the streetlamps dying— one after another, two by two, in perfect, synchronized pairs down the street, toward them—"Like in a horror movie," Hannah would later say.

There was no time to think.

They ran.

They ran as fast as they could, footsteps slapping pavement, echoing through the silence, pounding against the stillness—against whatever might be chasing them. The four-way intersection loomed ahead, the last stretch of road rushing toward them.

Then—impact.

They slammed into it, that thick, Jello-like veil—harder this time, sharper at high speed. A split second of resistance, like pushing through an unseen membrane—

And then they were out.

They knew they were out.

And instantly and simultaneously, they felt the mushrooms leave them.

The trip was over.

There was wind in the trees, leaves rustling, the far rumble of a car, and all the normal city sounds. They stopped running, pressed hands on their knees, lungs heaving as they caught their breath. Hannah gulped in the cold air as though she had just broken the water surface after being trapped under. The air felt light. The night felt sweet. Even the sky seemed brighter—brighter like dawn.

And then they noticed—the sun was rising. To the east, beyond the ocean, the first pastel rays stretched into the sky. It had taken them all night to walk down their street? How?

Hannah turned in slow circles, scanning the world to confirm to her rational mind that what she had witnessed and lived was not just in her imagination, but found no evidence.

The cat was gone.

಄ · ಆ

"Whoa." I stretched both arms toward Hannah under the hydrangea, my skin alive with static, hairs from my shoulders to my wrists standing on end.

"I know. Me too. Every time. This story… I can't even."

"Then what happened?"

"We went home. But we talked about it for weeks. Just among ourselves—we didn't tell anyone else. And our stories of that night match exactly. We even independently drew what we saw in the window of that two-story building, and the drawings are identical."

"Whoaaaa." We both waved our hands in the air, shaking off the impossibility of it all. Yet, I believed her. Some stories didn't ask to be proven. They slipped right past your ears and settled deep in your cells. "That's just… wild, Hannah."

Her story settled between us and, for a few minutes, we returned to our task quietly. Only the soft rustle of pulled weeds and hands moving through soil. Dig. Toss. Ponder. Dig again.

There was a strange familiarity to Hannah's story… A story stirred in the back of my mind—one I had never told. One I had no intention of telling. Yet there it was, pressing me for a voice.

I hesitated, then laughed softly.

"Hannah…" I looked up, wiping my hands on my thighs. "You're gonna think I'm messing with you, but… I have a very similar story. It gives me the heebie-jeebies to tell it, but…" I took a breath. The words were already forming, waiting. "You want to hear it?"

She didn't answer right away—just shook her head slowly, eyes locked on mine. Then a small, nervous laugh.

"Huh… Yaaah." She shook her head, eyes wide open and both eyebrows raised. We both laughed, knowing there was no turning back now.

"Okay." I rolled my shoulders like a fighter stepping into the ring. "So there was this wooden sign…"

ဆ · ೞ

My story, Cottonwood, Arizona - May 2018

"This land is drug and alcohol free
Deep thanks for respecting
Which is Sacred"

Of course, I saw the sign. I knew the sign. I had been to Hummingbird's many times, and I agreed that drugs and Ceremony should never mix. But mushrooms weren't drugs; they were friends, medicine. Right?

I nodded to myself as I nibbled a tiny corner of a magic chocolate ball Jim had given me when we first met. I stashed the rest in the center console.

I left the Catmobile on the flat gravel upper terrace overlooking the Verde River and followed the red dirt path around Hummingbird's house. I skirted around the painted wooden sign with the clear instructions, looking away, and continued down the steps.

"It's just a micro-microdose to meet the Grandmothers with a tiny bit more of an open mind," I murmured to the tinge of guilt in my stomach.

The stairs deposited me right onto the Sacred Land, as Hummingbird called it. It was a small plot—maybe a couple of acres from the dirt road to the river—but every inch of it was curated with Hummingbird's care and love specifically for Ceremony.

I followed the scent of burning sage, sweetgrass, and dragon blood, past the Macramé hammocks in the cottonwood's shade, past the gardens and their guardian gnomes, and to the circle of women already gathered around the fire. I approached quietly to respect the sacred mood. Young and older women alike, each in turn, knelt at the altar by the Temazcal—the ceremonial lodge—and left a prayer, a precious object, or a crystal to be charged.

The Temazcal fire was already blazing, heating the buried Grandmother Stones, waking them for the ceremony. Hummingbird, kneeling between the Temazcal and the Sacred Fire, was fanning the crackling coals when she looked up and saw me standing in the circle.

"The Bobcat!" She threw both hands up with joy then jumped to her feet to engulf me in a sister's embrace. We danced in place, feet stomping rapidly in the dirt. Everybody laughed. It had been years since we had last seen each other. Although I was just passing through, I had called this special full moon Temazcal. How I had missed this land, the Grandmothers, and my sisters, especially Hummingbird.

Eleven other women had also answered the call. And here we were now, thirteen of us, barefoot and wild, with drums and rattles, dancing down the path to the sacred geometry Water Wheel by the river.

We drummed and sang, calling in the protection of the Ancestors in each cardinal direction, then Mother Earth, Father Sky, and the Heart, the Divinity within.

The rest of the ceremony, I cannot recount, so I will resume on the other side of the Temazcal.

I burst out through the heavy blanketed door, naked, covered in sweat, eyes wide in fright, and threw myself on the cool red dirt. I rolled chest to back to chest on the earth to extinguish the visions in my mind, grasping for Mama Earth—the guardian, the grounding Mother. I dug my fingertips into her hard-packed soil and gasped. In all my years of attending Temazcals in that same sacred womb, never before had I escaped the ceremony before the end of the Warrior round, the last round.

As though my dramatic exit had gone completely unnoticed, the women inside still sang and drummed their wild song to Spirit. I slowly rose from the dirt and looked to the fire. It was much smaller now, having done its job. Its embers and ashes were spread wide where the Fire Keeper had extracted the Grandmother Stones now at the center of the lodge. The flicker and crackle of the flames settled my heart slightly. I inhaled slowly, exhaled even more slowly, focusing my conscious awareness on my heartbeat to calm my nervous system. I was almost back. I needed water. The river—she would bring me back. I stood up and ran barefoot on sharp stones. The path Hummingbird had trimmed through the woods shone in the moonlight, clear enough to follow even at full speed. I reached the banks of the Verde and plunged into her cold water. The temperature shock expelled a scream from my throat. I rose back, emerged, and landed, hips deep in the river, refreshed and renewed. And suddenly, I laughed—a laugh like a howl, releasing all I had seen, feared, and escaped.

I remained in the current, enjoying the Verde's soft caress on my skin until I heard the voices of my sisters exiting the Temazcal womb. I felt much better by then, and was excited to rejoin the group.

All the sisters were now out, holding hands in a circle around the last embers. They chatted, laughed, and some still sang softly. Joy and aliveness sparkled in their eyes. As I approached, two hands released to open a space for me. Hands tightened around mine, and smiles welcomed me back. No questions were asked, and I offered no story.

As I walked back to the Catmobile, the joy and peace of the closing circle followed me home. The warmth of friendship lingered in the smile on my face. I knew I had much to discuss with my journal about the events in the Temazcal—but not yet. It believed it best to wait for daylight. Nighttime was not the time to recount scary events.

As soon as I crawled into the Catmobile, my body burrowed into the softness of my sleeping bag, and any lingering fear melted away. I fell asleep promptly and peacefully.

"Whaaack!"

The whole truck shook. With a gasp, I sat up, eyes wide, all senses on high alert. The truck still wobbled on its old shocks, but nothing else moved.

Had the driver's side door just slammed shut? I crouched to peer through the window separating me from the cab. That was odd—I didn't remember leaving it open. Had I been in the cab before the ceremony? Ha, yes—when I took that nibble of magic chocolate. Maybe I had left the cab door wide open. I did do that sometimes.

I pushed the hatch open with my foot, slid my toes over the tailgate, and dropped softly to the ground. The full moon hovered directly above the Verde River, casting a silver glow over the cottonwood canopy. Their leaves seemed luminous, almost surreal.

"Wow!" I lifted my hands, palms open, to the beauty of the night, in gratitude for whatever door had slammed to awaken me just in time to see this.

I turned back to the truck and walked to the cab. I ran my fingers along the gap where the door and frame met and shrugged. Maybe the wind had caught it and slammed it closed with a sudden gust. Regardless, it was well shut now.

The moon shone so brightly that its reflection on the truck's black paint seemed to glow. Tiny silver sparkles in the paint, which I hadn't seen since the truck's younger days, shimmered on the hood despite the thick, uniform layer of dirt covering it.

I traced a line across the moon's reflection through the dirt with my finger, then continued across the hood until my eyes caught sight of the gravel road. Like the cottonwood trees, the entire road past Hummingbird's seemed luminous, and I suddenly felt a fancy to walk down it.

Under the full moon's reign, all colors had shifted to silver tones. The moonlight revealed that the pebbles on the road were actually precious gems, and the cacti, agave, and yucca by the side of the road were radiant and wide-awake beings, engaged in conversations of their own.

I walked down the road slowly, looking left, right—everywhere. Mesmerized, but not surprised. As one who speaks with rocks and trees, I found it natural that the moonlight would highlight the true nature of these beings.

I walked some ways down the road, fascinated by it all, until I spied a small black cat peeking at me from beneath a roadside bush.

"Hi there, Kitty." I crouched down and offered my hand. She came up to meet me and nudged her head against my knuckles for a pet. "Isn't this a magical night?" I stroked her soft, shiny black fur. She looked up at me as if in agreement. Then I noticed another cat approaching—a large, sturdy gray tabby. As he came closer, I reached for him with my other hand and petted both cats simultaneously. Scrambling down the hill along the road, two more cats hurried to join the group. Even in the monochromatic silver moonlight, I could see that one was a big orange tabby and the other a petite, fluffy, pink cat.

Pink?

"Ooooh." I stood up and looked around with new eyes, "I might be in a dream. I don't think pink cats exist in physical reality. Maybe I didn't wake up when the door slammed."

The four cats now sat in a semi-circle around me, blocking the way to the rest of the road. Several more were sliding out of the shadows toward us.

"You have to go back." I knew the sturdy gray tabby had spoken the words I heard in my mind, yet he had neither moved nor meowed.

"I don't want to," I said gently. I crouched back down, reached for the orange tabby and scratched behind his ears. He began to purr.

"If this is a dream, then I want to pet *all* the cats." I pointed to the newcomer cats who had joined the half-circle. Sets of ears suddenly perked up, and several cats looked to the gray tabby. I sensed my response was unexpected.

"You have to go back," the tabby repeated, stepping forward. "We can't protect you here."

"Protect me from what?" I looked around at the serene, luminous scene. And right as I spoke the words, a faint unease crept in—a slight sense of urgency to go back.

I immediately left the cats and quickened my steps toward the truck. I thought some of the cats might accompany me, but I didn't turn to check. I looked straight ahead, and walked back with the most casual gait I could fake. A prickling sensation ran up the back of my neck. The night moved behind me with more than just paws.

I reached the back of the Catmobile before discovering what it might be. I opened the back and crawled in. The moment I settled into my sleeping bag, my body relaxed again. What a funny dream. I cocooned myself and quickly drifted back to sleep.

"Whaaack!"

The whole truck shook again. I sat up again, eyes wide open, heart beating hard. "Okay," I said aloud, "I *know* the door was shut. I checked last time." Then remembered, "last time" might have been a dream. There was a pink cat. Pink cats didn't exist in this reality. So could the door have *not* slammed the first time, except in a dream? I didn't need to ask—I knew. The door had slammed twice. And I also knew, deep in my bones, that *this* time, I was awake.

A formless presence, like a living shadow, was flying fast in circles around the truck. With each gyration, the truck rocked and oscillated. The very real, rhythmic creaking of the truck's old shocks and leaf-springs confirmed this was neither my imagination nor a dream.

I pressed a hand to my chest in a vain attempt to calm my wildly beating heart. The hair from my neck to my forearms stood to attention. I peered through the window, forcing my breath to stay quiet, scanning the moonlit scene outside. But there was nothing. Only emptiness. I lounged for the back hatch handles and forcefully locked them tightly. The pushing, the bullying, of the truck increased. With eyes still fixed on the swirling nothing outside, my hands fumbled blindly down the sleeping bag's zipper. They found the little metal tab and quickly pulled it to my chin, then wrapped the hood around my head and cinched it. I curled into myself inside the sleeping bag.

I realized I had opened a door—a crack between realms. And I had no idea how to close it. And the only act that had been different from all the other Temazcals was taking that tiny bite of mushroom chocolate. I brought my hands to prayer.

"Grandmothers of the Land, please forgive me for not abiding by the rules, if that is causing the dark entity to swirl right now. I was foolish and didn't understand the weight and power of the warning on the sign nor the consequences of my actions. Please, I ask for your protection now. Please send your cats to help me again or… whatever you feel is best."

I blinked twice and opened my eyes to sunlight shining through the side window. The sun was already far above the cottonwood trees and the temperature in the truck much too high to be cinched in a down sleeping bag.

Why was I cinched so tight anyway?

"Oh, right." I remembered the second dream—if it was a dream. I shivered and shook my hands to dispel the memory. "What a weird night. So many nightmares."

I pushed the back hatch open to let in some barely cooler air.

Still rubbing sleep out of my eyes, I extended my legs out and landed on the ground. I remembered that, in addition to magic chocolate, I had a small bag of fresh fruit and vegetables in the front cab. With that heat, they were probably withering—and fast. I walked toward the front driver's door to rescue them, but before even opening the door, my eyes caught the impossible sight, and I froze.

The hood was covered in cat paw prints. I opened the door and stood up on the frame to get a better view of the cab and shell. Cat prints of slightly different sizes and shapes crisscrossed from side to side, up and down, covering the entire upper surface of the Catmobile.

Maybe neighbor cats had jumped on the truck, making it oscillate and move, and my subconscious had spun a dreamtime story from it, leveraging on my lingering guilt.

But then, how did I explain that straight, fingertip-traced line in the dirt on the hood, under the paw prints?

ಜ · ೞ

"Spoooooooky!" Hannah rolled back onto the wood chips with a wide, open laugh, and I joined her.

"I know, right? Oooh." It was a relief to laugh after how tense we'd both been during the recounting.

"Then what did you do?"

"I called Jim. We were already broken up by then, but the mushrooms came from him, so I figured he'd know what to do." We both laughed again at the absurdity of the solution.

"And what did Jim say?"

I became solemn again, remembering how serious I had felt at the time.

"He told me to bury a piece of the same magic mushroom chocolate on the land—as an offering. He said that if I'd offended a Spirit, this should fix it, as long as I offered it with sincerity and humility. I don't know how I knew that, but..."

"But you did it?"

"Yeah. I buried a piece the same size as the one I had eaten, made a little ceremony of apology, a prayer to the land, and that night, I slept great. The weirdest part, though, was... where did all the cat prints come from? I never told Hummingbird what happened—I didn't want to disappoint her or make her think I'd disrespected her, the land, or the ceremony. But I did ask her about cats in the neighborhood. She didn't have one, and she didn't think the neighbors did either. So, I have no idea where they came from. But the paw prints were real. Hummingbird saw them too."

ಜ · ೞ

The story about the story, Puerto Viejo - December 2023

Sometimes, I wake up with these memories bursting out of me, eager to be shared, urging me to plant myself with hands on keyboard and mind open to remember and transcribe them until the story is fully told. This was the case for this story. Unfortunately, that day, I had life commitments—a yoga class I taught in the morning and an order for magic mushroom chocolates I had to create from cacao beans and dried fungi friends.

And so it was about four in the afternoon when, finally, I was able to sit at my desk overlooking the jungle and open the flow of words that had knocked at my consciousness all day long. They were ripe, and I loved writing them. I wasn't just writing; I was transported back. The jungle disappeared. I forgot to eat, drink, move. I was with Hannah under the hydrangea. And even though I hadn't been there that night, I walked down the strange Portland road again, with the cat and the group of friends.

Then, night fell, so I moved my laptop to my bed, inside my bungalow.

I lived up a hill in a place called Katuk, a small community tucked in the jungle. There were only a handful of bungalows, a single dance platform, and a shared kitchen and bathroom—but those were down a winding path through the jungle, far from my place, especially in the dark. My body was hungry, but my mind was still with Hannah under the hydrangea. I kept catching glimpses of the sign at the entrance of Hummingbird's sacred land. Taking a break for food would have disrupted my flow. I settled deeper into my bed, laptop balanced on my lap, and emailed Hannah her part of the story for review and accuracy. Then I kept writing.

The jungle, my bed, the mosquito net above it—even the mosquitoes that found their way in anyway—all disappeared. I was there, on the land with the women, dancing around the Water Wheel. The words that flowed were so precise, as if I were transcribing rather than writing. Every detail of the ceremony, every sacred move Hummingbird made, every private story she told about the Temazcal—I recounted it all. I wrote our entry into the Temazcal, the details of each round, and the steady progression from normal to... where I ended up.

I moved back in my mind to the Catmobile, as vividly as if I were there. I met the cats again, including the pink one. I returned to the truck, the night, the circling shadow, and my fear. Then—I wrote this sentence:

"I realized I had opened a door..."

Except it wasn't exactly the same sentence. It began the same, but also explained *how* I had opened the door to the darkness while in the Temazcal.

"...And I had no idea how to close it." Period. Quotation marks. Enter.

The laptop screen went blank. A small white dot flickered in the middle, then fully black.

"Whaaat?" I lifted both hands off the keyboard and instinctively looked out the window. It was absolutely dark—deep-jungle-at-night dark. And that darkness swirled. Chills ran up my spine, just like in the story. I jumped to my feet on the mattress and, in one swift move, lifted the mosquito net and leaped out of bed, away from the laptop. I shut the bungalow's door—I needed to be in a protectable space. I reached for my lighter and a bundle of sage, flicked the flame, and lit it. It was all I had. I encircled myself with the smoke, climbed back onto the bed, stood on the mattress, and waved the sage over the laptop, again and again.

The clock read 11:45 p.m. I had been writing for eight hours straight in the blink of an eye. I had saved the document repeatedly, as a reflex, every couple of paragraphs, but only on the local hard drive. My laptop had never behaved like this before, and I feared it might have died.

Before turning it back on, I took a moment to pace in my bungalow—three steps one way, three steps the other. It was a very small bungalow.

"Hi! Did I again open a door I don't know how to close? Does writing about opened doors open the doors?" I almost shouted it, hoping any ally beyond the veil would hear me.

"Yes." I heard in my mind. Unseen answers didn't seem strange, not after eight hours of straight storytelling. If a cat could guide Hannah to the Jello exit, then surely protection could be available in this realm too.

"Okay. What do I do?"

"You're safe now. But never write this story again."

I turned my laptop back on. With a sigh of relief, I confirmed it was still alive. A quick inventory—all the chapters of this book were intact, except one.

The Cats Across the Veil.

That one was blank. Nothing there. All of it—*gone.*

ഔ · ൫

Puerto Viejo, Costa Rica - March 2024 (right now)

A few paragraphs from the end of *The Cats Across the Veil,* and I'm pressing CTRL+S every few sentences, saving it to an internet drive. This time, I believe it'll stay.

The truth is, I almost didn't rewrite it. I've been afraid of it. Still am. But any story potent enough to shut down a computer and delete itself is precisely the kind of story I want to tell.

I realized that day—and you might call it superstition—that storytelling does open doors to other realms.

In the week following the original writing of *The Cats Across the Veil,* strange things began to happen. A wound appeared on the back of my calf—deep, angry, oozing. The doctor called it a spider bite, but it lacked the usual signs. We burned it with a Chinese smoke stick, never knowing, truly, what it was.

At the same time, I caught lice. Four years in the jungle with thick, long dreadlocks, and I'd never had them before. And these weren't normal lice. They resisted every remedy—bitter plants, oil, even harsh chemicals. They crawled into my dreams, feasted on my scalp, and drove me to madness.

But the worst part was the voice inside my head.

"You're gonna slip and break your tailbone." "There's black mold in the walls. You'll inhale it and die." "Nobody likes you. You see? She just walked away. She hates you."

All day, every day, gnawing on my mind. A slow, steady erosion.

And each time, I answered, patiently: "No, I will not fall." "I will die, but not from this." "She's a friend, and we love each other."

But it wore me down. And in the end, I did fall and twist my ankle, as it had predicted—even cracked a few ribs as a bonus.

Eventually, I moved out of Katuk, out of the jungle and to an apartment across the beach.

Shortly after, I met a woman who spoke in tongues and channeled an angel. "You need to pray to God. Even Jaguar cannot protect you in the realms you open when you write. Only God can." Her voice was kind but firm. She didn't know about my writing, or my connection to Jaguar.

Then, I crossed paths with a self-proclaimed shaman. He looked to the air space around me, nodded knowingly, and declared that a dark entity had attached itself to me, and he could help. I drank his strange brew—magic mushrooms, maple syrup, blue lotus, and spices—and in the fire of that medicine, I watched my body contort as the "entity" was mostly expelled.

What remained, I purged with love and gratitude. "Thank you. Thank you for making this story even more potent for me. Thank you for everything I've realized. Thank you."

Bathed in such love, it could not linger, and both the "entity" and the lice disappeared promptly without any further effort on my part.

Today, finally, *The Cats Across the Veil* felt safe enough to rewrite. I used the section I had emailed to Hannah, but left out all details of the Temazcal ceremony and any hint of how I had opened the door—as instructed.

Now it is told.

It still refuses to be copied and pasted like the other stories, but I believe, this time, it will stay here for you.

Chapter 20
The Heart of Chloe

Pacific Crest Trail, California section - 2012 (and other locations and dates.)

"I think cats and dogs are actually advanced souls, here on short-term assignments to guide us through certain phases of life—through specific lessons we need to learn. That's why they don't live as long as we do. They come, they fulfill their assignment, and they move on. Other species are so in tune with our feelings, they can provide the kind of support we sometimes don't even know we need. And each species has its own specialty, its own unique teachings. I think cats are always half on the other side—that's why they stare into space so much. And dogs ... I love dogs ... dogs are pure Love. Actually, I love them both. Equally."

I don't remember how the conversation began or how it wandered to the topic of cats and dogs. But I remember the trail—the exact shade of light brown beneath my feet, the scent of dust rising with each step. I remember the rhythm of my hiking poles—two plants for every three steps—my natural cadence on the flat. I remember the late afternoon light, casting an amber glow over the dark green pines, their wind-sculpted limbs swaying above white granite boulders that flanked the path.

The air was cooling. I had a warm hat on. But I don't remember my backpack or the weight of my entire life pressing against my shoulders because I was completely absorbed in our conversation.

Mr. Roger—that was his trail name—and I had been hiking and talking for hours. In other words, it was a typical moment on the trail. So why this one? Why did this particular thread of words, in the endless weave of our conversations, imprinted itself so deeply in my mind?

Since the PCT, Mr. Roger and I have stayed in touch, and every time his words have proved true, I've called him—astonished.

Jaya was four when my friend's world crumbled—pregnant by a man who wasn't her husband, suddenly without a car, a home, or a plan. As she wept, Jaya pressed closer, his great, knowing eyes on her, a silent promise of unconditional love. He stayed until she was whole again—until she had a kind husband, a career, and a radiant baby girl. Then, and only then, did Jaya leave.

Wally the Cat found another of my friends in a grocery store parking lot. Later, when ill-advised investments cost him his home, his car, his love, his last dollar—Wally remained.

"Honestly, I think Wally saved my life," he admitted. "I was in a very dark place, but having him by my side and needing to care for him gave me a reason to live when I no longer wanted to."

Smaug, our tuxedo cat, lived with Jack, my ex-husband, after the divorce, helping him with the transition. Meanwhile, I wandered carefree—India, the PCT, and the wild expanse of the open road. But when fortune shifted, and I suddenly found myself rudderless, Smaug vanished from Jack's new, comfortable home and reappeared—of all places—in an animal shelter in Colorado. The chip had my phone number. I was in Minneapolis, asking the Universe to, please, send me a sign when I got the call. I pointed the Catmobile south and drove to Colorado to get Smaug. That event, that decision, placed me on the new path I needed to follow.

And then… there is the case of the Viking and the cats. But you already know that story.

Yet, despite ample empirical evidence, the idea that cats and dogs were advanced souls on voluntary short-term assignments still felt like a stretch—a romantic interpretation of reality.

Mr. Roger and I often pondered this in our philosophical conversations, like this one from 2015, right after my coyotes died:

"Well, of course, there's no absolute truth," he said. "No proof. Whatever reality we choose to believe, we can and will find evidence for. We build our personal paradigms through feedback loops. The key is being conscious of those loops when we interpret facts and stories."

"Maybe. But if I had to choose, I'd rather believe that cats and dogs are more advanced than us. Before you presented the idea to me, that day on the trail, I had a sort of… disdain for dogs. I thought, 'why should I respect an animal that depends on humans for its survival?' And when I was much younger, I actually disliked cats. My mother always had one, and they moved through the house with an untouchable authority, free in ways I wasn't. They meowed and watched me with an air of judgment as if they *knew* they had more rights than I did. Honestly, I thought all cats were prima donnas until Smaug found me. But this idea that they're advanced souls is so much kinder, and more poetic. It makes me appreciate them in a way I didn't before, you know?"

"Oh, cats are definitely prima donnas." He laughed. "But still, a choice of a belief is not a proof of a concept."

80 · 03

247

North Carolina - 2021

Nancy, Mr. Roger's mom, sat in her rocking chair under the golden halo of a reading lamp. The light quilt blanket rested across her tired knees. She slid on her reading glasses and absentmindedly flipped through a book in search of her bookmark. Soon, she would disappear into another world—the written world—where handsome men swept strong, young women off their feet on sun-drenched tropical beaches—another world, far from this one.

Chloe leapt soundlessly onto Nancy's lap. Her green eyes flickered with little gold stars as they caught the lamplight. She blinked slowly, kneading the quilt with gentle insistence, then decidedly stepped onto the open book. There would be no escape just yet. Not until she was thoroughly adored.

Nancy never had a cat before Chloe. She had grown up with dogs—dogs and unsafe humans. But even her family didn't know the depths of the trauma she had endured as a child, not until after her death.

Chloe once lived across the road, in a house with other people. But when she met Nancy, she followed her home and would not leave. So, Nancy thought, "Why not? Let's try a cat."

"Mom always had so much on her emotional plate. She supported my dad, worked full-time, and took care of my sister and me. She always did everything for Dad, but in a stoic, resolved, kinda way. Because she had to. Because she needed to. My dad was just not capable of taking care of himself. And with me, our relationship was always very challenging. She tried to care for me in a way that wasn't aligned with the reality I knew was true, which of course, was different than her own sense of reality and priorities. So I moved out when I was still a teenager, which added to her heartbreak. But whenever I returned, I always appreciated how Chloe supported her. You could feel it. Chloe would climb on the book, and Mom would act annoyed, but also she seemed calmer almost instantly."

Chloe and Nancy loved each other and, for eight years, spent daily reading hours together, curled up in quiet and warm companionship. Until, on a brittle winter morning, Nancy, now retired, stepped outside to retrieve the mail.

The fall was swift. Her foot sped across the patch of ice, twisting her body as one leg shot forward while the other clung to dry ground. A sharp crack and a crunch—she landed heavily on the porch.

"Ahh." She moaned between her teeth. A sharp pain shot up her spine. She tried lifting her torso but couldn't. And she knew.

"Philip, I fell!" she called to the house. "Call 911. I think I broke my back."

By the time the ambulance arrived, Nancy had slipped into unconsciousness.

"At first, we all thought she'd come home after her back was better. But she had been in such poor health, physically and emotionally, for so long, and she had a long list of preexisting ailments that exacerbated the condition. I think also her psyche just gave up. I flew home to help take care of Dad. And I noticed that Chloe's eating had slowed down. She was much skinnier than when I had last seen her. For me, I saw a direct correlation between Mom's decline and Chloe's lack of interest in food. She was almost less present in the physical realm, less participatory in her own self care."

There was a particular place in the living room where the afternoon light streamed through the window, warming a patch of carpet about cat-sized. Chloe was lying in that square of sun, curled in perfect sphinx position, eyes closed, breath slow, when the phone rang.

Mr. Roger received the news. His mom's health had taken a turn for the worse, and the doctor advised the family to gather for goodbyes. He alerted his dad and sister, and the whole family left for the hospital.

Nancy was already unconscious when they arrived. They gathered around her bedside, and when her shallow breath faded to none, they stayed, bearing witness to the moment she slipped away.

"After Mom's death, the shift happened more rapidly. Chloe's eating came to an almost complete stop. I was able to give her a few nibbles, but she wasn't interested. It was obvious to me that it was related to Mom's death... She had come, she had done her job of emotional support, and now it was time to move on. Of course, my dad doesn't have that view of reality at all. And even the vet had a hard time believing it. But she inspected Chloe, and everything seemed normal, physically. She said she'd never experienced this before—a cat willingly starving herself."

In the wake of Nancy's passing, there was much to arrange. As executor, Mr. Roger spent his days meeting with morticians, lawyers, realtors—handling logistics while accommodating visiting relatives. Yet, through the whirlwind of responsibilities, he kept a close eye on Chloe.

One night, just as he was drifting to sleep, she padded through the open door and nestled against him. This was unexpected. Ever since Chloe had joined the family, Mr. Roger had invited her into his room countless times, even tried coaxing her gently—but she had always refused. She slept with Nancy or on the sofa.

But that night, she stayed. All night.

And the next night, she slept with his dad.

"So, she was displaying different behaviors than before, and it made me wonder. I wanted to know if there was a separate medical problem with Chloe in addition to the grief we all felt. I got the number of this animal communicator from a friend. I told her that my mom had passed and that the cat refused to eat. That's my personal technique. I figured I'd say as little as possible so there's no bias. Basically, the animal communicator had a blank slate, and I was able to assess if she was really talking with Chloe or not. The whole conversation was recorded. I'll send you the recording if you'd like."

℘ · ℃

The recording transcribed [intact — only filler words were removed]

"I'm sorry to hear about your mom."

"Thank you. It's definitely been an emotional whirlwind. A first-time experience for me, losing somebody that close and having a new reality to sink in."

"Yes. Have gentleness with yourself. I'm so glad you reached out. Do you have any questions about the process right now?"

"No, I've witnessed your process before with my friend, so I'll just follow your lead here."

"Okay. So Chloe was mostly your mom's cat is what I gathered."

"Yes, I mean, she liked my dad too, and over the years, felt increasingly like the family cat, but dominantly yes, it was my mom she was close to"

"And... you're wondering how she's doing?"

"Yes, she's been losing a lot of weight. She's not eating or drinking much at all. I just want to know where she is in her head space. Can she, in her psyche, turn it around to where she's more motivated to be here, on the physical plane, which includes the eating and the drinking."

[silent pause]

"Okay. The first thing she's showing me is that all of you are sharing this grief. I feel in her a heavy numbness that starts in her head and flows down. She's processing the energies of everyone, so she's right there with you. And she's showing me, it's not just one thing going on with her, it

251

changes. Sometimes, she's in the spiritual realm, where she's connected with your mom. She actually knew when your mom transitioned, because she's been connected with her the whole time. Part of this is because, she says, her and your mom used to sit together a lot and there was a sort of energetic exchange going on which helped to ground your mom."

"Yes, I can see that."

"Yes, they had a very nice flow and relationship. Part of Chloe's sadness is because after your mom left the house, Chloe could still feel your mom, but your mom couldn't feel Chloe, so she is sad that she wasn't able to help your mom in that way. There's a lot of feelings she's processing around that. But your mom can connect with her in spirit now, they no longer need the physical presence. Chloe is saying they are going through a healing process together right now. And I've heard this from other animals, and from other mediums who deal with people—I'm not a medium for people—there is some kind of process after transitioning and it varies from animal to animal and person to person. The way the animals describe it is a sort of... healing process, whatever that is.

So, there is a time period... I've connected with animals right after they passed and sometimes their energy feels like they're connecting almost through water, or that they are very far away, and they show me they are in their process. So what Chloe is showing me right now is that she is not only here in the physical plane, with you and your dad, and others who are grieving your mom, but she's also with your mom as she's going through this spiritual process. So, literally, she has one foot on Earth and one foot in the other realm. That is why she's not connecting with food. It's beyond just that she's depressed or feeling grief."

[silent pause]

"She's saying that you might notice that she's almost in a trance sometimes. She's just staring off into space. And you might notice she's not even aware of you. She says when she's in that state, she's working in the other realm with your mom."

"Okay. Yes, that fits with my observations of her in the past few weeks. My next question is… I wonder about her sustainability in this physical form. Is it in her mindset that she'll willingly continue to be here physically?"

[silent pause]

"So, what Chloe is saying is that she's aware that she is physically declining because she's not taking care of herself fully in the physical realm. Animals are very present. She is saying, right now, I am doing what I need to do with your mom and I am doing what I need to do here. What it feels like to me is that she will, at some point, have to make a decision as to whether she wants to join your mom in the spirit realm or return fully here. But for now, she has to do this process with your mom. She's acknowledging the importance of her physical presence for both you and your Dad. She's doing her best to stay in the physical, but until the process with your mom moves forward or gets to a point where she can shift that percentage of how much she is in the physical versus the spiritual realm, she will remain in the current state she's in. So, I can express to her your concern if you'd like… How long has it been, you said, that she's not been eating?"

"She might be eating or drinking a little bit when I'm not looking, because I'm not observing her every moment of the day. When I carried her down here a little while ago, under her chin was a little wet, so it's possible she drank a little water, but there was definitely a shift when Mom passed. I want to honor Chloe's process but also would like to ask if she's willing to maintain the bare minimum to be able to stay in the physical."

"Yes, I'll convey to her your concerns about that now. And I'd also like to do a physical body scan on her to see if there is another physical issue going on, if that's okay."

"Sure."

[silent pause]

"I don't… she's not highlighting anything with digestive issues. It feels like her system is working harder just because she's not taking care of herself as well, but she's not highlighting any physical reason that causes her to not eat. So, let me ask her again."

"Thank you… I'd like Chloe to know that my only objective is to help her, to care for her in finding the balance that works for her with all of that she's juggling."

"Oh. I can feel that her heart is so huge. I can feel her heart opening wide and she really appreciates you reaching out to her in this way."

"You mean this conversation, the exchange happening right now?"

"Yes. The messages I am receiving are directly from her. She wanted to explain that she's helping your mom, but is also very grateful to you. The energy that she's showing me is like you created a big circle with your arms and allowed your parents to be in this safe space, her included. And she says that you all poured so much love into that circle to make it work, and that it hasn't been an easy decision for you to come here and do that. I'm feeling a lot of gratitude from her for your awareness of her needs, and the respect for her situation in the midst of what you are going through. And she is showing me… does she have like a… There's like a nice sunny spot, and there is a plant there."

"There's a place on the living room floor where the sun through the window hits, and she likes to be directly in the sun on the carpet. That is one of her favorite things, to lay in the sun, there, on the carpet, where the sun comes through. Another question I had… my parents have been feeding her… the same… probably, you know… boring name-brand dry cat food for the whole time that they've had her, and I'm wondering… is there something we could be doing differently in the food department that she would appreciate?"

"It feels like you're already tuned in with her because she is showing me that what she needs right now is food with more moisture. So, if you see her, laying in the sun, or relaxing, offer her just a spoonful of food. Small offerings of wet food here and there. And be patient with her timing, because what I'm hearing from her is even though your mom's spirit has transitioned, she is still in the beginning of her process. She's saying really just a spoonful because everything is overwhelming right now. Everything in small increments. Very small steps, very small increments, and that gentleness of asking her 'would you like to try this?' She appreciates that… it's that continuous tie to the physical that will help her start to come back in fully when your mom's process goes through, but… it's… I mean, there is no time over there, in the other realm, no linear time."

"So, basically, it's just trusting Chloe with the process?"

"Yes"

"And with a little bit of assistance here and there, she will find a way to get what she needs to sustain herself physically even while she's one foot in one world and one foot in the other?"

"Yes. I feel from her that she'll eventually have to decide which way. So, if you start to see a big physical decline, know that she's made the decision to go fully in the spirit world with your mom. But I don't feel that from her right now. She's still choosing to be in both, even though it's a challenge."

"Well, could you convey to her my gratitude just for the fact that I am now aware of where she's at. Just knowing where she is takes the edge off my concerns, so in that way, I feel her support, just by the fact that this communication is happening. If you could convey the sense of gratitude that comes with that to her."

"Yes, that was beautiful. It gave me full-body goosebumps when you said that. She's receiving that fully and… yeah, there is so much gratitude, really so much gratitude just for everything, on her part as well. She is showing me what a loving flow between the three of you, her, your dad and you, and… Yes, just a lot of gratitude."

"Last night, she slept on my bed. And she's never done that before. Could she say what that was about? What was her motivation behind being present in my space in a way I'd never seen before?"

[silent pause]

"So hmm… this is interesting. What I feel from her, is that it's related to the process your mom is going through during that time. It's almost like your mom was reliving every single moment of your life together."

"Of my life with her?"

"Yes. *[chokes with tears and emotion]* I'm sorry… It's just so beautiful. Chloe is showing me, your mom is reliving every moment from the time she was pregnant with you, the whole way through. And Chloe is making the connection stronger by being in your physical presence. So it feels like your mom was going through a huge review. No, not review, but like… a process of reliving and feeling each and all of the moments with you."

"Which was a whole emotional spectrum, from challenging to positive."

"But, in that process, it's just love. You know, just love. Just like a big… Love. And so having that physical connection through Chloe helped your mom's healing process too. And Chloe says that is something she can also offer you. She says it's harder for humans, especially in grief, to feel the connection, so she's saying she's connected with your mom, strongly, and if there's any time you want to say something directly to your Mom or feel something with your mom or feel your mom's presence strongly, she says, she's here to help you."

[tears and emotions pause]

"Mmmh. Thank you for that."

"It's really beautiful. You know, each communication is different. I've never heard it put that way before, that process. That's really beautiful."

"My mom had a lot of challenges in her life and it was really encouraging and positive to observe their relationship over the years—Chloe and my mom. She was totally tuned into my mom, providing endless emotional support. It was like this constant gift that Chloe was giving her."

"Yes. Chloe is saying that you mom needed a lot of heart healing. Dogs, cats and animals in general help us do that, but, she says a lot of the healing needed was… I don't know if you know this or not, or can confirm this, but it had to do with your mom's parents and her grandparents, like the way she was brought up, there were jagged edges there."

"Yes, I have become aware of what that is just recently."

"And what Chloe is saying is that this is a big part of your mom's process, and it's all being resolved. The way she's showing me is that all those jagged edges, all that sharpness, all that darkness, all the pain—all that is falling away and your mom is starting to… now she's only feeling the love. It's only the love. So when Chloe said that your mom was reviewing her life with you from the moment she was pregnant all the way through, and you said, 'Oh! Even the challenges?' Chloe is saying that the process is that all that shifts to just love. All the challenges, jagged edges, all those sharp things that hurt, literally fall away. The soul is cleansed. She is saying that all that stuff that your mom went through, long before you, ugly things from her childhood, she says, all that is being resolved. It's all being resolved for her.

[Tears and emotions pause]

"Thank you. That helps more than I know how to express at the moment. "

"And Chloe is saying she is glad that you've opened up the door to this type of communication with her, and that type of communication with your mom too, on a spiritual level. She's saying that it will flow better for you now, even with the grief."

"Okay. I have a lot of respect for other species. We're all each other's teachers and students at the same time. I always feel that when another species lives with a human, they are, on some level, a willing collaborator. And it's been clear observing how Chloe's presence has contributed to this family. And I'd like her to know that I have recognized this all along."

"She's saying that she's always felt very respected, very acknowledged, by all of you."

"She has all these little quirks and characteristics that I don't necessarily understand, like when I pick her up and she sounds like she's protesting, but then at the same time, I'm not sure she's actually protesting. Historically, she's been very vocal. And I've always been curious, 'what are you saying?' Could you ask her, maybe, what kinds of things she's communicating when she's vocal, if she could nutshell that."

"*[laughs]* She's saying, 'well… you guys talk.' *[laughs]* Animals connect and communicate telepathically, humans talk. *[laugh]* She's like, 'you guys talk all the time, so that's what I do too.' She's like, sometimes she just wants to converse, sometimes she's expressing a displeasure… like, sometimes, she doesn't want to be picked up. 'I was fine here, why did you move me, just because I'm small, just because you can?' And sometimes she recognizes the need for you to hold her. She's saying it's different each time. Sometimes, she does want something and she's trying to tell you. And if you get too involved with… sometimes animals say that we stare at boxes. If you're staring at a phone or a computer screen, they feel us. And if it's causing us anxiety or emotional stress, they might say, 'Hey, you're getting stressed, I think you're staring at that box too much.' Sometimes it's like just, 'Hey, have you looked out the window? Have you?'"

"Okay, and… is she okay with the fact that we don't know how to interpret her vocalness?"

"She's saying that instead of going into your head to try to figure out what she's saying, you can check in with yourself, then check in with her. If you find yourself stressed, calm yourself down, and see what happens. That might be what she was trying to tell you. If you find you feel good, you're in a flow, maybe she just wants to connect with you when you're feeling that way and is saying, 'hey, how is it going? Oh, this feels good!'. She's saying to check in a little deeper with yourself rather than keep asking her what she means. If you check in with yourself, then check in with her—place your attention on her—and you find, 'Okay, I was feeling this way and suddenly I'm feeling something different.' then, that's her. The new feeling is hers. Does that make sense?"

"Yes. Which is closer to your process of how you do what you do, I guess."

"Yes, it's exactly what I do. Everyone has this ability."

"So this leads me to a question… it might be a bit of a tricky question, a sensitive question. The very premise that we're embracing here, with the work that you do, this idea that we can communicate directly with other species, seems to be an inherent capacity all humans have, it's just a matter of whether it's in dormancy or we develop it. This is not something that a large percentage of the population embraces. That we're having this conversation and this session, in this format, is not something I feel comfortable telling everyone I know. And this is coming from my own fear of other people's perceptions, of course, but for example, my dad—he's very conventional and I don't think this is something he could or would embrace. I told him I would talk to someone to get some thoughts about Chloe, but I didn't say specifically that it was direct animal communication. And so, my question is how do I represent this conversation, this session, to him, or to those who wouldn't embrace the underlying premise? So, on one hand, how do I even tell my dad about this, when… I don't want to… and on the other hand, I believe we're in an era now when we no longer should hide in the shadows. It's time to speak our truth. Now is the time, more than ever, to say it like you see it… and yet it's still very scary for me. So, seeing these vastly contrasting narratives of how the universe operates, I feel sometimes caught in between them, and it's very uncomfortable."

"I get it. I went through this when I first started doing this. I had to 'come out', in a way. I learned that I don't have to prove anything to anyone, and to each his own, you know.

259

If someone's not open, then I don't talk about it. You can, if you already know that your dad's not open, you can say, 'well, she's sad and affected by her loss.'"

"Yes, and he's been able to see and acknowledge that."

"So, keep it in the physical realm, like, 'Well, Dad, Chloe is just like us. She needs some gentleness right now and we're gonna keep feeding her a little bit at a time and we're gonna keep offering her spoonfuls as we work through all of this stuff.' But, you don't have to share, if you don't want to, or if it makes you uncomfortable. You can listen to this recording again, and sort it, like 'Okay, they might be open to that.' Or you could just let them listen to the recording for themselves."

"Oh, yes, oh boy, that's a 'Oh boy!'"

"You don't have to put yourself in the middle."

"That would be putting myself in the middle. But I understand, and thank you. Thank you. This conversation helps tremendously. And one last thing, is Chloe okay with me coming down on the floor and just wanting to pet her and be present with her sometimes?"

"Oh, my God, yes. She says yes. Absolutely."

"Okay. Alright. Thank you. Thank you so much."

⁎ · ⁎

Chloe maintained a bare minimum of physical presence for a few weeks after the first session. Mr. Roger fed her spoonfuls of wet food and gravy-covered treats. He lay on the carpet next to her, and gently rubbed her calico coat. When he did, she purred faintly.

She held out as long as she could, holding space for both the humans who stayed and the human who had left. Then, suddenly, her condition deteriorated further and she completely refused to eat. Mr. Roger once again contacted the animal communicator.

It was a short conversation with only one clear message.

"I'm ready to go home," Chloe said.

She died peacefully shortly after the second animal communication session—her assignment kindly and successfully completed.

Part 5

ALLIES, GUIDES, AND TEACHERS

Chapter 21
Allies

Envision Festival, Uvita, Costa Rica, March 2023

"Alex, how much free will do you think we have as sovereign individuals? I mean, do you think our decisions are actually ours, or are they influenced by energetic waves in some sort of collective field or matrix? Are our lives just steps in Pachamama's evolution agenda, or God's plan? And even if we have free will… who's this "we"? Our cells? The viruses and bacteria we carry? The food we ingest? Don't microbes alone outnumber human cells? Do they all get an equal vote in our decisions? What if it's actually the plants and fungi we ingest running our lives—like those ants that get hijacked by mycelium. You know? … or maybe I think too much. Maybe there's no greater meaning or deeper connection to anything, just random coincidences and instinct responses."

I exhale, staring up at the night sky.

Alex slowly lifts his head from his pillow and squints through the openings of our tents, which face each other. He blinks a few times.

"Oh—I'm sorry. Were you sleeping?"

It is four in the morning on the last day of the Envision Festival. I've been dancing all night, and the festival's supercharged energy, combined with the endorphins coursing through my body, has unleashed an inner supra-dimensional questioning monster.

Alex laughs. "Are you on mushrooms?"

"I'm not."

It's not the first time I hear this question. But in truth, I am 100% sober, unless prolonged ecstatic dancing counts as a psychedelic.

He studies me for a beat, then shakes his head. "Mmh. I can never tell with you. You always ask the kinds of questions people on mushrooms ask."

ഓ · ഇ

Puerto Viejo de Talamanca, Costa Rica, October 2022

Here in Costa Rica, I live across from Cocles Beach in a lovely little apartment with walls painted bright aquamarine and shaped like ocean waves. It's always a bit dark and cool, which is not my preferred setting, but perfect for my current business. My friends call it the *Maya Wonka Cueva*—the cave of Maya Wonka, the magic mushroom chocolate maker.

So, what were the chances, if life were ruled by coincidences, that Flor would land in the apartment right next to mine?

I was sitting on the tile floor, a headlamp strapped to my forehead, halfway through loading a batch of cacao beans into the melanger, when a petite, vivacious woman appeared in my doorway.

"Hola! Soy Flor, tu nueva vecina!"

I looked up, temporarily blinding my new neighbor with my headlamp.

"Ayyy!" She squinted, throwing up a hand, and laughed— a delightful little silvery sound. Oh, I already knew I was going to like her. I gestured for her to come in.

266

"OooOoooh!" She leaned forward, marveling at the fragrant, swirling mass of cacao. Then her gaze wandered— past the shelves, the plants, the small jars, the bags of cacao beans, the business notebook—until it landed on the bed, where a fresh batch of mushroom chocolates lay neatly wrapped in foil. The picture of psilocybin mushrooms on the labels said it all.

Her eyes darted back to me, and a bright smile appeared on her face. Without a word, she lifted her sleeve, revealing a mushroom tattoo. Then she grinned and gestured for me to follow her next door.

Flor's apartment was a mirror of mine—same wave-shaped walls, same cool, cave-like feel. But where I had a painting of a jaguar, she had hung a garland of paper-cut amanitas, boletes, and some imaginary mushrooms. And where my plants stretched toward the light on hanging shelves, she had a collection of her own mushroom paintings and sketches.

Flor, I would soon learn as our friendship grew and my Spanish improved, is an artist. Not just an artist—a mushroom artist.

She sketches mushrooms, paints mushrooms, prints mushrooms on journals, notebooks, and bookmarks. She creates coloring books filled only with mushrooms, murals for businesses where each letter blooms with vines and fungi. She sells her stickers and illustrated notebooks at the Saturday farmer's market, her table a vibrant shrine to the fungal kingdom.

And right next to her table are Calvin and his lovely wife, Cristina. Their table is stacked with natural soaps, tobaccos, teas, and medicine pouches. What isn't on their table is magic mushrooms. So you'd never guess that Calvin is the best mycologist in town, and my supplier.

Flor, the mushroom artist, living next door. Calvin, the mycologist, selling beside her.

How did we all become neighbors? Was it for some Greater Purpose? Did the mushrooms themselves orchestrate this?

Or do we still choose to believe in coincidences?

ဢ · જ

Puerto Viejo de Talamanca, Costa Rica, October 2022

Right in front of Flor's and my patio, a four-inch wide trail winds through rocks, dirt, moss, and grass. I smelled them before I saw them—a musty, earthy sweetness, unlike any fruit or dessert, yet one I know well. It's a scent I first encountered as a taste when I was a child in New Caledonia.

In my tropical childhood home, any bread left unattended on the kitchen table would soon be overtaken by ants. The rule was simple: "If you eat my food, I will eat you." I mostly ate ant-bread because it made me giggle. Yes, there is a sweetness to them, because of the formic acid, but the aftertaste is unmistakably, disgustingly insect-like. I haven't eaten ant-bread in years, but the ants' sweet scent remains a deeply imprinted childhood memory.

That's how I knew. Even though the path was empty in daylight, the scent told me exactly who had cleared it.

One night, I returned home late from dancing at Katuk, a wooden platform deep in the jungle where I teach yoga and where the community gathers for ecstatic dances and cacao ceremonies. Flor's light was already off. The night was still. But the air was alive—thick with the sweet, pungent scent of ants, stronger than ever. I knelt by the cleared path and switched on my headlamp.

There they were—hundreds, if not thousands of ants moving like a determined yet chaotic army. Each ant heading to the right carried a small piece of leaf, while those returning to the left, unburdened, weaved through the carriers, pausing to touch antennae with each ant they passed before continuing on their way.

In the days that followed, ants were on my radar, and I started to notice them everywhere. Similar ant trails crisscrossed the jungle—worn, bare paths just like the one at my doorstep. As a thru-hiker, I had seen trails evolve from mere trampled grass to bare dirt paths as thousands of footsteps gradually killed and prevented vegetation from regrowing. But these were created under the heavy footfalls of humans, horses, and dogs. These ant trails were just as bare. How many ants, even factoring in the weight of the leaf, would it take to carve such a bare dirt path through the thick jungle?

One day, I followed a trail of ants from the gathering tree, across the jungle, and to a mound of dirt debris. There, the ants disappeared. I knelt beside the mound and peered down the small, dark opening at its center.

"What do you guys do with all the leaves?" I asked aloud. "Do you eat them? Do you feed them to your queen?"

It didn't occur to me yet to look for answers on the Internet. I had communicated successfully with ants before— once during a fast in Death Valley and again on the Pacific Crest Trail. I assumed I could get my answers straight from the source.

But these jungle ants were on a mission. They stopped for no one and had no time for conversation.

On another occasion, on the jungle path up to Katuk, I spotted a snake. He moved perpendicular to an ant trail, his body flowing like liquid over the dirt—until he reached the moving colony. He paused, and seemed to be waiting. I rode my bicycle closer and stopped just a few feet away. The ants marched on in an unbroken line. Completely still and quiet, I waited to see what the snake would do.

Finally, a gap appeared between the ants, and the snake slithered through, not disturbing a single one. The ants didn't slow down at all; the snake had to adjust his pace. I lifted my bicycle and carefully stepped over the moving river of ants. Both the snake and I continued on up the hill.

The next day, the unstoppable colony had vanished. A straight line of abandoned leaves lay scattered across the path as if dropped mid-march.

Why?

Why had they left these pieces behind? Was there a strict cutoff for the ants to return to the hill, forcing them to abandon their loads? Was the leaf storeroom full?

Why, why?

ଫ · ଔ

Puerto Viejo de Talamanca, Costa Rica, November 2022

A couple of weeks passed, and the ants continued marching through the jungle with their leaves and unsolved mysteries, as they did in my mind.

One night, after an ecstatic dance at Katuk, five of us lingered on the platform, unwilling to break the spell of movement, sweat, and shared rhythm. Someone suggested a bonfire on the beach. Someone else mentioned mushrooms. A plan was made.

Vitali and Blue built the fire. Nikita and David stirred miso soup in a pot over the flames. Aniel and Claire arranged blankets and pillows on the warm sand. And I? I brought the mushrooms.

We sat in a circle, wrapped in the quiet glow of fire and friendship, the night thick with salt air and possibilities. I spread the mushrooms on the blanket, dividing portions under everyone's curious, trusting eyes.

The shares were uneven, but no one questioned it, trusting in my intuition.

Claire received the smallest dose—it was her first journey. Vitali, who had once cultivated mushrooms in Russia as a black market business and consumed them in copious quantities, received the largest. Blue, who facilitated mushroom ceremonies to heal the planet through group meditations, got the second largest dose. The rest of us received equal portions: Aniel, a seasoned mushroom harvester with a keen eye for spotting gold growing from cow dung; Nikita and David, both experienced myconauts; and me, the mushroom lady for the night.

We cradled our soups and mushrooms, raising them to the circle.

"Thank you, mushrooms, for the sacredness of this moment and this deliberate gathering of special people on this exquisite night!" Nikita spoke the prayer.

We raised our bowls even higher and drank.

As I sipped the wonder broth, my gaze drifted from face to face. The firelight flickered in their eyes, and I couldn't help but feel that each of us had been specifically called by the mushrooms, not just to this circle but in life in general, for profound reasons beyond our conscious reckoning.

We finished the soup, ate the mushrooms, and lay back on the blankets in peaceful contentment, waiting for the journeys to begin.

With the warm soup as a carrier, we didn't wait long. One after the other, the contagious psilocybin giggles found us, until the circle rippled with laughter, light and open, like children set loose on a playground.

Then Claire began to sing. And we all hushed to listen.

Her wordless, ethereal song held us, transported us to a magical realm where synchronicity was the norm—ocean waves crashed in exact cadence to her tune, and even the stars seemed to twinkle brighter and in sync. One rhythm, unified, from our heartbeats to the cosmos.

I lay there, dissolved into the moment, feeling the pulse of everything, when, suddenly, Blue rolled over onto his belly, bringing his face only inches from mine.

"Maya," he said, eyes intense and tone filled with revelation, "did you know that leaf-cutter ants don't actually eat the leaves?"

I blinked, caught off-guard. I hadn't mentioned any of my ant-related mysteries. How did he know that particular question had been dancing in my mind just then?

I nodded—of course. We had ingested the same mushroom. Invisible threads wove our minds together, dissolving the illusion of separation. My mind was our mind.

I just smiled. Then in unison, we turned our gaze to the ocean.

For a while, we just watched the waves, then Blue rolled over again and continued.

"Yeah, they actually gather the leaves to make a mulch, and with it, they grow mushrooms."

I smiled wider. *"Mushrooms!"* he repeated emphatically. The word hung for a second in the salty air, then, as if on cue, everyone burst into laughter.

Ants growing mushrooms. Of course, they did. What sentient being *wouldn't* want to grow mushrooms?

A few days later, Lexi and I lounged in the shade at Chino Beach, a serene corner of the Caribbean protected by a coral barrier. A kilo of sweet mamon chinos sat between us to sweeten our already perfect day.

"Lexi, Blue claims leaf-cutter ants feed the leaves to a fungus they grow. That seems incredible. Do you know anything about this?" I asked while peeling one of the vibrant red fruits.

Lexi was a horseback riding guide and an experienced plant and animal communicator. If anyone would know, she would.

Her face lit up. "Yes! Funny you ask. I've been fascinated with them lately and did some research. Get this—the fungus they grow dates back twenty-three million years. Whenever an ant leaves the colony to start a new one, it carries a piece of that fungus with it. So, all leaf-cutter ants, everywhere, cultivate the exact same strain. Isn't that incredible?"

I popped a mamon chino into my mouth, savoring its juicy sweetness as Lexi went on, her eyes bright with excitement.

"My favorite part is the minims. If you look closely at an ant trail, you'll see tiny, tiny ants riding on the leaves. They're called minims. They clean the leaves before feeding them to the fungus. If the fungus gets infected, the whole colony can collapse overnight."

I pictured them—miniscule sentinels, diligently grooming each leaf as it made its way through the jungle. The level of coordination, the sheer precision of it all—their entire life dedicated to keeping a fungus alive.

Blue's revelation had seemed almost mystical, but Lexi's details felt straight out of science fiction. Yet, a quick internet search confirmed it. Not only had leaf-cutter ants been tending a twenty-three million-year-old fungus, but some sources even suggested the fungus actually controlled the ants, overriding their instincts. Some articles labeled the ants as the fungus's "slaves" or "zombies."

I prefer the term allies.

I don't know how scientists determined that the fungus manipulates the ants' minds, but I *need* to believe "allies" is the correct term.

ಬ · ಛ

Casa de Luna, California, May 2016

I was in my mid-forties the first time I ate psilocybin mushrooms. Up until then, I had such an unpleasant panic-paranoia reaction to Cannabis the couple of times I tried it, even in minuscule doses, that I never wanted to try any other mind-altering substance. My reasoning was that weed was so common, and people who smoked it seemed to enjoy it so much, if I couldn't even do *that*, I'd better not try anything "harder."

But on one sunny Californian afternoon, as my friend Kyle and I had just returned from an adventure to Cuba, during which we had run out of money, slept on sidewalks, bribed our way onto a sailboat back to Florida, and hitchhiked across the entire US continent, I felt invincible. I felt like I could handle anything, even mushrooms.

Kyle had carried magic mushrooms to Cuba to enjoy them on an inviting, white sand beach, but I had refused to partake, and he had refused to take them alone. Mushrooms, he insisted, were about connection, like the mycelium from which they came. They had to be shared. He had waited until either I changed my mind, or he found other friends to join him. Both happened the same day, as Kyle and I rested from our journey at Casa de Luna, a thru-hikers' gathering outpost on the Pacific Crest Trail, and Papa Joe's house.

Kyle brewed a light tea with the mushrooms and handed me the smallest of the three cups. I took a few cautious sips while the men finished their cups in a few gulps. All three of us then sat outside in the sun, and the men lit cigarettes. I loved both these men and had warm memories of Casa de Luna from my days hiking the PCT. There couldn't have been a better setting for my first time.

Kyle had warned me that I might feel a slight nausea at the onset. But I felt nothing; I just slowed down, and everything slowed with me. The low sun kissed the grass. The men drew on their cigarettes in silence, even the smoke rose in a slow contemplative motion.

Papa Joe slowly handed Kyle his lighter back.

The lighter was green with three stripes—a red, a light green, and a yellow stripe.

The background green of the lighter was exactly the color of the grass we were sitting on. The yellow was exactly the color of Kyle's windbreaker. The red was exactly the color of Papa Joe's sweater. And the light green was exactly the color of my Patagonia jacket—Exactly! I intercepted the lighter in front of Kyle's hand and without a word held it to each of our garment pointing out to the men the impossible coincidence of color matches.

"Wooooooooaaaaahhhhh!" Papa Joe slapped his forehead then exploded his hand in the air, both mimicking and explaining what had just happened to our minds.

That was the precise moment when I became an ally. The mushrooms' little giggles tickled my heart. What a delightful magic trick they had performed with the lighter. And yet, I understood there was no magic. This extraordinary coincidence, like all so-called coincidences, was normal. Lack of coincidences was simply a symptom of lack of attention.

I looked from the men and the magic lighter to the rest of the garden. I could see the real world. I didn't discover it; I remembered it. Oh, what joy! Reunited at last! To whom? To what? I didn't know. It didn't matter. The only importance in this matter was that I could see the real world, and I wished *everyone* could have the opportunity to see it too.

"Maybe," I thought, "maybe I've been chosen to help others see the beauty of the real world." It was a bright thought, brighter than normal thoughts, one that sat deeper.

"Yes." It was so clear and obvious. "I should take a mycology class and learn how to grow mushrooms. Not just magic mushrooms—all mushrooms. I could sell them in tea form in colorful little packages, and whoever drank them would discover the real world and, in turn, feel compelled to share. And like mycelium, gladness would spread, connecting us all and changing the world exponentially from each source person.

I said nothing then, but I was sure this was my path.

In fact, I remained silent for hours. When Papa Joe retired to his room to nap, Kyle and I moved to the soft grass in the sun. Kyle lay in the grass. I sat cross-legged, motionless, and I looked—looked and looked—at everything, intently, while the sun slowly traveled to the treetops on the other side of the yard.

The grass under our bodies was greener than any green grass I had ever seen, not even in the wet Pacific Northwest known for its vibrant greens. Each blade of grass was arranged at an angle that matched the angle of one of the trees in the forest behind us. One-to-one. Exact correspondence. The tangy aroma of green green grass and the subtle scent of soil in the shade of trees harmonized in the breeze like two compatible notes on a piano. The clouds in the sky were exactly in proportion to the size of sky available and surrounded by the bluest blue I had ever seen. The leaves swayed in the wind like a quiet melody. Each leaf a unique instrument in the symphony of that tree. Each tree an essential part in the grand opus of Creation. *This* was the Earth I lived on. And how had I never noticed before that it was a Designer Earth, where everything matched perfectly?

Well, except for the fence.

There was a metal fence between us and the woods. A man-made fence, clashing with the rest, a false note in the perfect Symphony of Things. I followed the fence with my eyes to a metal gate. The curves of the metal gate might have appeared elegant if I had been in a different state, but the discrepancy with the rest of the Natural Symphony was jarring. A nauseated disgust rambled in my stomach. I observed the disgust. Was I discovering a Universal Truth or simply seeing a reflection of my own prejudice against human-made anything that interrupted the natural world? After all, humans were natural too. So why did our creations clash with the Designer Earth? Did we not also belong in the Greater Order of Things? Or were we, humans, purposeful flaws? Were we the mole on the face of Supermodel Mother Nature, the mole that enhanced Her beauty by breaking her perfection? And what if the imperfections were on purpose so that some of us humans would find purpose in restoring the perfection? A gift from Mother Nature to us, lovers of hers.

In that moment, I decided to not only grow and sell mushrooms, magic and otherwise, but also to dedicate the rest of my life to the protection of the natural world, in whatever form I could. It felt important. More than important, it felt essential, primal, a matter of life or death for all species. Tears filled the corners of my eyes from overwhelming gratitude that this Grand Purpose could be mine, if I chose it.

Through all these insights and epiphanies, I still hadn't spoken a word. Finally, I felt I needed to share and ask Kyle what *he* thought of our Designer Earth. I rolled over in the green grass toward him. Kyle's eyes were fixed on the perfectly proportionate sky. A peaceful smile rested on his lips. I opened my mouth to ask him if he thought human-made creations clashed with the greater Symphony of Things, but the words were left silent when my eyes caught the golden sunset light reflected in his red beard.

Did you know that red beards are not actually red? One hair might be blond, tangled next to it, one might be almost pink, another dark brown, another ochre, another pale yellow, white, etc. And only as a whole does a beard look red.

"What?" Kyle backed away from my intense glare and gaping mouth.

"Your beard… it's… spectacular."

"Ah. So, you're feeling them." He laughed and lay back in the grass. I laughed too. And we continued laughing for several minutes, as I joined him in sky contemplation.

Shortly after our stay at Casa de Luna, Kyle and I parted ways. I returned to guiding in Sedona, and he went back to Missouri. My mushroom journey faded, along with the lofty promises I'd made on Papa Joe's lawn. But Kyle, a seasoned ally, wasn't ready to let go so easily.

"Com'on, Bobcat. Move in with me," he insisted over the phone. "I've got a dark, cool basement—perfect for mushroom cultivation. We can grow all kinds—magical, medicinal, edible. I have the space, but I need your science brain to make it happen."

"Kyle! I'm a geophysicist, not a mycologist. I studied electromagnetic waves, volcanoes, and glaciers, not fungi!"

I didn't move to Missouri.

Growing mushrooms, making a living from psychedelics—that was not my path. No. Instead, I drove to New Hampshire, parked the Catmobile, and set out to hike the Appalachian Trail southbound from Maine. My journey was cut short in Vermont, where a mysterious illness landed me in the hospital for a week.

The day after I was discharged from the hospital, I met Jim.

ଐ · ଓ

Puerto Viejo de Talamanca, Costa Rica, May 2022

The trees here, in Costa Rica, are unlike any others I've known. Except for the stand-alone banana and coconut trees, which are not even trees—the former being an herb and the latter a grass—the trees here are complex, vertical, green metropolises.

At the heart of each metropolis stands a giant main tree or several with interwoven roots. Around this centerpiece, leafy vines with symmetrical leaves cling and meander upward, overlapping with thicker sinuous root-like vines. Ferns rest in and burst from crevices where branches fork from the main trunk. High above the salty ocean air, the canopy fan opens, casting cool shade on the smaller plants below. Mushrooms grow from the trunk, ants carve winding paths into the bark, and lizards, monkeys, birds, and insects inhabit this vibrant, living tower in joyous cacophony.

Each tree is a complete ecosystem. And I've been staring at a particularly complex tree-ecosystem for at least ten minutes from the balcony when Joe joins me, morning coffee and a cigarette in hand.

"What'chu you looking at?"

"This tree here. It's… breathtaking. I can't even…" A tear of awe rolls down my cheek.

"Are you crying?" Joe leans over the balcony to look at my eyes. He looks at the tree, then back at me. "Are you on mushrooms?"

"No. I'm not."

He lights up the cigarette. "I can never tell with you. You always look at the world like it's the most fascinating thing you've just discovered."

He's right. I do do that. It's just… Once you've seen the Designer Earth, you can never truly unsee it.

૪Ͻ · CZ

North Conway, New Hampshire, September 2016

"I wish I had $600," Jim said casually while rolling a joint in the passenger seat of the Catmobile.

We had met four days prior. This was our first date—our four-day first date.

"Yeah? What would you do, if you had $600?"

"Buy mushrooms! A friend just texted—he's got a pound of cubenses for 600 bucks. We could sell them a gram at a time and pay for traveling out West together."

He licked the edge of the paper and sealed the joint with slow precision. My mind swirled. $600? Buy mushrooms? Travel out West—*together?*

Crazy!

Well… But then… I had flown to Cuba four days after meeting Kyle, and that had led to memorable adventures. My mind landed on the number.

$600. That was exactly the amount of money I had left from my aborted AT hike. *Exactly.* I didn't believe in coincidences any more then than I do now, so, without a word, I reached behind Jim's seat, pulled out the envelope with all the money I owned, and dropped it onto his lap.

He paused, lifted it, opened it, and looked inside. "That's $600." I pointed to the envelope. His eyebrows shot up, and a wicked grin spread across his face as he turned to me.

"You... Little Witch!"

And so, they found me again. A pound of cubenses joined us in the Catmobile, dried crisp in their plain brown paper bag.

To celebrate their arrival, Jim gifted seven of my friends and colleagues from The Local Grocer about a gram each. We gathered on Micah's lawn, held our mushrooms high, and, looking into each other's eyes with a nod of readiness, crunched our mummified friends.

This was only my second time eating magic mushrooms—just four months after my first experience with Kyle in California. Five of the seven were first-timers. Two began giggling, then burst into uncontrollable laughter almost immediately. Another, who had taken a double dose, curled up with a lawn chair as if it were the love of his life. The last two inflated a raft and spent the rest of the afternoon reclining in it, pointing at passing clouds in the perfect sky.

"I think I broke your friends." Jim laughed. He seemed pleased with the scene.

Although this was my first macrodose, I felt nothing— except responsible for my younger friends. They weren't *broken*, but they were altered, and by some ancestral maternal instinct, I remained fully alert and watchful until, one by one, they drifted back into themselves and made their way home.

With everyone safe, I returned to the Catmobile. I lifted the maple branches long enough for Jim and me to climb onto my bed, then let them spring back into place above my pillow.

Then, and only then, did my stomach lurch from the psilocybin.

I rested a hand on Jim's chest while my eyes drifted from the maple tree just outside the Catmobile to the leaves hanging over our heads. A tree feeling emerged. It felt like curiosity, like tendrils of an exploring presence aware of me.

This was the first time I spoke with a tree—a point of first contact, a simple hello, and a recognition that much more was possible.

That day, on the lawn with Kyle, I had promised to help others see the beauty of the world, to grow and sell magic mushrooms, to protect the Living Earth. Such noble, yet youthful dreams. As though I, with my limited human perspective, could accomplish such a task single-handedly.

"I should microdose mushrooms every day. Trees communicate with each other through the mycelium; probably I can too," I thought as I lay back. "Maybe if I could communicate with them, they could guide me on how best to protect them. If mankind understood the sentience of trees—not just intellectually, but through direct experience—the whole planet's consciousness would shift, and the natural world would never again need protection."

Jim stirred and opened his eyes. I turned to wrap my arm around him.

"Hey, can we save a few grams for me? I want to microdose until we leave to learn to speak with trees."

I believed then that these thoughts were mine. Were they? Did my need for a greater life purpose ignite the fire, or was it them, the mushrooms, seeding instructions in my mind, nudging me on a path, initiating me as an ally?

❧ · ☙

Denmark, Maine, November 2016

Jim never wore shoes. The mane of his white dreadlocks swayed past his tailbone rhythmically as he walked through the woods in front of me. His bare feet crushed the rusted red and brown leaves on the ground. Fall had come and gone, and soon, so would we.

Crunch. Crunch. Pause.

He bent down, plucked a mushroom from the moss, and popped it into his mouth. Another few steps, another mushroom, another bite.

I quickened my pace to catch up. "What are they? The mushrooms you're eating, what are they?"

He twirled the slender stem of the one he was still holding, inspecting it with exaggerated curiosity. "I dunno."

I frowned, shaking my head, but I smiled too. Such a Jim answer...

"How do you know they're edible then? Can't some mushrooms kill you in, like, two minutes?"

He turned to face me, the faintest smirk curling his lips. "I just ask them."

"And they answer you?"

"Of course, they answer. You just have to listen." He laughed and threw the mushroom in his open mouth theatrically.

Jim is an advanced ally.

ᛒ · ᚳ

Puerto Viejo, Costa Rica, March 2023

The moist heat, thick as honey, sits heavily on the Caribbean, slowing everything to a lazy crawl. Luckily, inside the Maya Cueva, a couple of fans keep the chocolate—and human—from melting. Outside, on our shared patio, Flor leans over the table, her forehead creased in concentration, seemingly immune to the heat. A set of colored pencils is scattered across the table like a spilled rainbow.

I watch her work for a moment, the tip of her tongue caught between her lips, the page before her an intricate tangle of blues and greens.

"A new design for your stickers?" I ask, dropping into the chair across from hers at the art table.

"No. It's a commissioned piece for a new restaurant in town. They want a mermaid for the bathroom."

Flor lifts the paper toward me, but her eyes stay on the drawing, her pencil hovering midair as if still shaping the lines. A swirl of blue waves flows across the page, and in the center, an elegant fishtail, each scale a different color, tapers into—*a mushroom?*

She grins. "Es una hongirena."

A full-hearted laugh rolls me back into the chair. "Ha! A mere-shroom! That's brilliant."

"Síiiii!" She lets out a small, triumphant giggle. :I tried to draw a mermaid, but it was so boring. So—" she flicks her wrist, outlining the hongirena's gills with a deliberate, steady hand, "—I fixed it."

She leans back, tapping the pencil against her chin, eyeing her work with a satisfied nod. "They know my style. They know I draw only mushrooms. And if they don't like it? I do. I'll refund them and keep it for the magic mushroom coloring book."

"A magic mushroom coloring book? With cubensis and amanitas, like that?"

Flor shakes her head, already flipping to another page. "No, no—magic mushrooms." She turns the sketchbook toward me. A mushroom with a unicorn horn on the cap. A family of happy Amanitas nestled in a jungle. A mushroom with butterfly wings, hovering mid-flight.

"Real magic mushrooms."

I press my hand to my chest, feeling a warm glow of friendship rise. "Forita, I love them."

She flips back to the hongirena and fingers through the pencils—mushroom cap yellow, here you are!

"You know, I'm writing a chapter about mushrooms right now, and you're in it."

Her pencil pauses midair and her eyes grow round. "Me?"

I laugh. "Of course. How could I have a chapter about mushrooms without the mushroom artist?"

I tilt my head, curiosity stirring. "How did it start for you? What was your first time like? How did you end up drawing only mushrooms?"

Flor's fingers drift to her lips. She looks past me, past the patio, past the heat, past now—searching. Then, with the smallest lift of her brows—

"Ah, sí. I remember… It was only a year ago, and it really wasn't that special." She shrugs. "I was with a friend, we ate the mushrooms, and then—" She pauses, frowning slightly, as if the memory is still puzzling. "Even though it was a really hot day, I got cold. I put socks on. That was weird. I never wear socks."

I wait for more. A revelation. A cosmic unfolding. A vision that changed her life.

Nothing. Just socks.

"And after that, you started drawing mushrooms?"

She lets out a sharp little laugh, shaking her head. "Oh no. I've been drawing mushrooms for years." She leans back, tapping her pencil against the table. "When I first arrived from Argentina, four years ago, I lived in a jungle cabina with no Internet. It was far from the beach, no distractions, nothing to do." She lifts her hands in a helpless gesture. "So, I walked. I stared at plants. And then, one day, I saw the cutest little mushroom peeking from behind some leaves. I lay down on the ground and drew it. And that was it. I never drew anything else again."

She glances at her sketchbook, almost amused. "And now? Now it's my business. It's a good business."

I study her for a moment. "So… you don't eat magic mushrooms?"

She tilts her head, as if the thought hadn't even occurred to her. "No. They're not very interesting to me. And—" Her lips rise into the faintest smirk "—I don't like having my feet cold."

That was *not* the answer I was expecting.

I glance at her sketches again—the hongirena, the mushroom-butterfly, the joyful Amanitas. A whole world of fungi, born from her hands and unaltered mind.

How peculiar. A non-journeying ally.

∞ · ∞

Puerto Viejo, Costa Rica, April 2023

Flor is at a mushroom conference in San José. Her art was noticed, and she was invited as a guest vendor. She was practically vibrating when she left, eyes wide, hands fluttering as she talked about the opportunity.

The patio has been quiet since. I miss her laugh, the rhythm of our conversations, the way she holds her pencils mid-thought, as though the drawing were speaking to her and guiding the next line. But work has kept me busy.

This morning, Calvin dropped off two ounces of mushrooms—one of Cambodians, the heart-opening mushroom, and one of Golden Teachers, the shamanic mushroom. I spent the day grinding, weighing, and folding them into chocolate, the kitchen thick with the aroma of cacao and the satisfaction of productive days.

Now the work is done. The evening is settling in, soft and orange. I step out of the *Cueva*, stretching my arms, inhaling the salt air.

When a strange, little shape at the base of the wall catches my eye.

I step closer and lean in to find—a mushroom!

Growing straight out of the concrete.

A little *Amanita pantherina*—hallucinogenic but highly toxic—is growing straight out of the concrete, its cap round and golden, its stem curved ninety degrees so that its cap seems to hover parallel to the ground. It is so perfect, like one of Flor's sketches come to life.

But how? How did it get here? Does this mean the entire wall is saturated with unseen mycelium, threading through invisible fractures, waiting for an opening to bloom?

And what are the chances that of all the places, this little fungi friend would bloom right here, exactly between the two allies?

ꙮ · ꙮ

If you're wondering. No, I am not on mushrooms.

Despite their place of honor in this book, I sell magic mushrooms but rarely eat them myself. So if this story seems psychedelic, it is not by my doing. This is just how it wanted to be told. This is how mushrooms tell stories, by threading events into a single mycelium mat.

Chapter 22
One Gram per Ocotillo

Anza Borrego, California - March 2019

The gentle boil of the water in the titanium pot on the one-burner stove on the Catmobile's tailgate was the only sound I could hear in the vast Anza Borrego desert. I sat on the tailgate next to the stove and breathed slowly as though I were calm and confident. But my wildly dangling feet and tapping fingertips betrayed the truth of my inner state. I was nervous. I thought I was calm. But, of course, I was nervous. I mean, it's not every day one voluntarily chooses to disappear into the desert to die.

I had a preference for the ideal setting for my purposeful ego death. I wished for a mound wide enough to park the truck, one that offered an unhindered 360-degree view of the surrounding desert.

Since first being exposed to the concept of a purposeful ego death, I had studied the matter and learned that psilocybin-induced ego deaths were the result of inner rather than outer journeys. The journeyer was to block out the outer world by closing the eyes under an eye mask and by filling the ears with music carefully curated to induce and enhance psychotropic openings. All sources recommended the help of a professional or at least a seasoned sitter, someone present to hold the voyager's hand. The sitter was the anchor of compassion in the physical world that allowed the journeyer a deep dive. The warmth of a human hand was the reassurance of safety not available to the other senses.

I neither had nor wanted a sitter. I believed any human would be a distraction, and I was certain I could go deeper by myself. I lived alone. I had walked thousands of miles alone. I trusted myself in aloneness. Yet, because I had chosen to be as far away from humans as the backcountry roads of Anza Borrego allowed, my ancestral instincts urged me to seek a high vantage point with unobstructed views. If someone else was in this desert, I wanted to see them first, even though I planned on being inside the truck with closed eyes and blocked ears.

I also wished for the death of my old self to coincide with the sunset. I liked the poetry of the parallel—the sun, my visible known reality, setting, and the moon, the potential hidden in my subconscious, rising. I calculated that, optimally, I would take the mushrooms about thirty minutes before sunset so that the last of my old self could be sent off with gratitude. Thank you for all the experiences, lessons, joys, sorrows, adventures, loves, and heartbreaks. Goodbye, and here is an explosion of colors in the sky to celebrate you. I sought the backdrop to my sunset scene as I imagined it, complete with a few silhouetted ocotillos and maybe the howls of a coyote just as the moon rose.

That would have been ideal.

But I left the little town of Jacumba too late in the day and searched for my high vantage point in the desert for too long. I tried a few locations close to the park's entrance, but, energetically, none felt right, so I drove on. The dirt road became rockier and narrower. It followed the edge of a crumbly, precipitous canyon. I focused on the rocks ahead, choosing my line of travel carefully to keep from falling into the canyon below.

I didn't find any mound. Instead, I drove along the canyon's edge for miles, until the sun glowed dangerously close to the horizon. Having failed in my quest for perfection, I pulled off the road on a random, good-enough, flat spot across from the canyon. I rushed to the back of the truck to boil the water, make the tea, and drink the mushrooms before sunset.

The bottom of the sun touched the horizon. I opened the Ziploc bag. These were the last of the Jim mushrooms. The bag held about ten grams.

"How fitting," I thought, "that the man who ushered in the heartbreak that finally revealed to me my codependency pattern also provided the medicine to dismantle it."

I waved my hand and wiggled my fingers toward the orange sunset, sending gratitude to Jim, wherever he was. The pain of missing him was still sharp, but now I understood, or imagined, that I had likely attracted him exactly to expose the pattern, to give myself the opportunity to sit with these mushrooms, on this Pink Moon of March, to change my life forever.

I held the bag to my heart to speak an intent, but the sun was already only half a disk, and my mind was blank. Instead of an elaborate request regarding codependent relationships and freedom from patterns, I simply asked the mushrooms:

"Please help. I know that you know what I need. Probably better than I do." Then, as is my custom, I asked "And in exchange, what would you like?"

[Trust] was the simple energy I felt in return.

[Trust all night.]

[Trust even with dosage.]

I closed the lid of the micro-scale and opened the mushroom bag. One dried mushroom after the other went into the hot water, and still I felt [more,] [more,] [more.] Then, suddenly [Stop!] I zipped the rest of the mushrooms in the bag and let the chosen ones steep. The sun disappeared, and the quiet began. I slowly drank the brew, holding my mug with two hands like a precious ceremonial vessel. I chewed the rehydrated mushrooms slowly, exploring their spongy texture on my tongue and their earthy, musty, slightly bitter taste—almost like damp soil—on my palate. Then I wiped the stove, pot, and mug clean and put these last vestiges of my soon-to-be former life away, back in the drawer under the mattress.

I relaxed into the silence and afterglow of the setting sun. I was committed now. No turning back. My feet slowed their swinging, and my shoulders relaxed. I was probably safe; I was with the Catmobile. I caressed the truck's metal with my fingertips.

How wonderful to be reunited with my truck after months of separation—my Catmobile, my love, my home and companion.

Since early February, Hippie Long Stockings and I had been sleeping on camping pads in the open desert. We had begun with our hands touching the thick metal fence separating Mexico from the United States and, for about a month, had walked northward.

Before that, in January, we had lain on our bellies in Hippie's partner's living room in Jacumba, on a carpet of topographic maps, looking for trail and dirt road crossings where we could stash gallons of water for our upcoming adventure. We had then driven Hippie's truck to all these locations, from the border to the northernmost point in Death Valley and back to Jacumba, where we began our walk.

On August 8th of the year prior—08/08 also known as the Lion's Gate—I woke up in the Catmobile in North Conway. My first thought was "Ooh, it's the Lion's Gate. Whatever is offered to me today, I will say 'Yes.'" It's a game I play every year on 08/08.

Half an hour later, I received the call.

"Hey, Bobcat. I just learned about a long trail called the Desert Trail. It looks badass! It's not even a trail. It's like a set of friggin GPS points from Mexico to Canada parallel to the PCT, but in the middle of nowhere. I looked into it. It's only been walked twice, and both times by men. What do you say? Wanna be the first women to walk the Desert Trail?"

"Yes. Yes. Yes. Absolutely Yes!" was the obvious answer.

I would likely not have quit the Desert Trail without extraordinary circumstances. My ego was tightly wrapped around the potential future pride of being the co-first woman to walk the Desert Trail. And I trusted that Hippie Long Stockings was the perfect partner for this adventure. We had crossed deserts on foot together several times. We had similar pace, grit, and almost supernatural immunity to heat—*almost*. We had already agreed—no matter what, we would step across the Canadian border together so there would never be a Sir Hilary Tenzing Norgay debate about our feat.

We began our adventure in joy and excitement but also in pain. Hippie's L5 vertebrae was slipped out of line and pinching the nerve that ran down her left leg. She had a scheduled surgery in late April but was unwilling to delay the start of our hike. Another couple was planning for the Desert Trail. We knew them, and one of them was a woman. Oh, Ego, how far will you push us? The day before the border, Hippie received a cortisone injection directly into her spine. With the pain temporarily numbed, she shouldered her heavy pack, and we began walking.

My pain was in my heart. Just a classic story of heartbreak—you know the one. A man and a woman fall in love but are incompatible. One of them sees this and reasonably decides to leave, triggering deep wounds in the other, wounds that long predate the relationship.

So while Hippie trudged in the intense heat with muffled groans and mumbled "You Fucker…" every time an uneven rock shifted her pack onto her lower back, I distracted my unhinged hamster wheel of a mind with audiobooks while we hiked.

How to Change Your Mind, by Michael Pollan, dropped my
jaw in amazement as often as the beauty of the landscape we
crossed. It was in this treasure of a book that I first learned
that with four grams of psilocybin, the brain resets itself to
the neuroplasticity of that of a four-year-old, a stage in human
development when neural pathways are still highly fluid and
malleable. Studies had shown, Pollan explained, that when the
brain was returned to full plasticity, previously ingrained
neural pathways could be rewritten, rerouted, and rewired.
Automatic trauma-responses could be erased and life-long
addictions cured overnight.

Four grams of psilocybin—just four—and my mind
could be reborn anew.

"Bobcat, I don't feel so well." Hippie sank at the foot of
a spindly ocotillo and slowly collapsed into a fetal position on
the bed of rocks under the shade of her umbrella.

"Is it your back?" She had already walked over a hundred
miles with the faulty L5 and had not once complained aside
from groans and mumbles.

"I'm kinda cold." I knelt beside her. Her face was too
red, glistening with sweat, yet her body shivered. We both
knew these symptoms and how serious it could get out there.
But neither of us said anything. Naming it would have made it
real, given it power. And we were too far from help for that.

She took a sip of water, swallowed carefully, then pulled
herself up. She winced as she shouldered her pack, and we
kept walking. There was no other option.

I checked the map. Mecca, our next resupply point, on
the shore of the Salton Sea, was still half a day away. But there
was a canyon a few miles ahead. If we could reach shade, she
could rest and cool down. I glanced at her again—her jaw was
set, her focus turned inward. I didn't press her. I just walked
behind her, keeping pace, listening for any hitch in her breath
that might signal she was getting worse.

We just needed to reach that canyon.

Hippie slept in the canyon's shade all afternoon, shivering inside her down sleeping bag wrapped inside mine, even as heat waves shimmered a few inches off the canyon floor in the sunny section. I sat nearby, watching the light shift, waiting.

Once the sun had set, we hiked out by headlamps, moving slowly through the desert toward the highway along the Salton Sea. By the time we reached the road, it was two in the morning. We dropped our packs and slipped into our sleeping bags under short shrubs by the highway but stayed fully dressed and with packs ready in case we needed to move quickly. The area didn't feel safe, and neither of us slept. Hippie was still nauseated, but at least she had stopped shivering.

In the morning, with a supernatural push on Hippie's part, we hitched a ride, and another, and another. Five in total, each depositing us a little closer to Jacumba. By late afternoon, we were standing in front of her partner's house.

"It's gonna be a few days, Bobcat. You're welcome to chill here while you wait, if you want."

"No. I think I want to go to the desert and try to die an ego death."

Hippie glanced to her partner with a puzzled look. I didn't explain.

The moon rose as the sun set, so the desert never turned fully dark. It just shifted—from color to orange to greyscale. I lay on my mattress in the truck, closed my eyes, began the music playlist I had prepared, and waited.

I didn't wait very long.

As soon as the mushrooms gave their first lurch in my stomach, something erupted in my lower belly. My heartbeat quickened, and every hair on my arms and the back of my neck bristled. I ripped the earbuds out and bolted upright. And I listened.

The desert silence I normally adored now rang hollow, like a marble tomb. I knew the feel of adrenaline that

293

accompanied the intuition of imminent danger. This was different. This was… Pure Fear. It was not *fear of something*, but the essence of fear, debilitating fear. From my gut, it surged up my spine, cinched tight around my sternum, and shot icy shrapnels down my legs, my arms, to my fingers and toes. And then even beyond. The fear was an independent entity emanating from my body like a shock wave. It bounced against the night, returning to me stronger with each harmonic amplification.

A scream of terror rose in my throat, but I stifled it, inhaled, and swallowed it. My mind began its storytelling.

It said I couldn't scream—a scream might drown out the sound of approaching steps. I needed to know about approaching steps. It said I was a woman, alone, in an altered state, in a desert I didn't know—a desert I didn't trust—and so close to the border. Worse, if I screamed, it said, I could alert harmful humans of my presence. I rubbed sweaty palms against my legs and pushed the back hatch open. My eyes scanned the darkness, searching for a reason, a justification. Searching for what I feared finding: a shape hidden behind a creosote bush, a drunken, horny man with no respect for life because he had nothing worth living for.

"Worth living for…" That last thought snapped me back to reason. Even with fear clawing at my gut, I had my love, my truck, to protect—my one responsibility in this world.

"Okay." I calmed my voice—low enough to hear myself but quiet enough to stay private. "Mushrooms, if this fear comes from you, I will trust you, as you asked, but I need to keep the truck safe."

[Step outside.] I felt an energy call me from the desert. I climbed over the closed tailgate and stepped into the night. An ocotillo stood to the right of the truck.

"Did you call me outside?" I stood, minuscule, at the foot of the ocotillo, and spoke to its flowers twenty feet above my head.

[I did.] I felt its answer, but more than the perceived words, it was its warm, kind presence that instantly soothed me.

[We will keep your keys.] I felt a pull to the front of the truck, where another equally tall ocotillo stood in the moonlight. I walked to it, knelt, and buried my truck keys at its foot. No matter what fear whispered in my mind, no matter how wild the terror grew, driving away along the canyon's edge in my current state was the greater danger.

Of course, I knew where the keys were—I had placed them there myself. But if panic took hold, if the urge to flee overpowered me, I would have to walk past two friendly ocotillos and under one full moon. That, I believed, would be enough to bring me back to my senses.

"Am I actually in danger here?" I asked the first ocotillo.

[You will not be tested while in-between worlds.] The ocotillo's felt answer was crystal clear, as they usually are when mushrooms aid with translation. But still, I hesitated. What if I was completely delusional and actually in physical danger, not from my self-inflicted state, but from, well… actual dangerous humans.

[You will not be tested while new programs are installed.]

I didn't fully understand what the ocotillo meant, but its tone was so kind, so reassuring, that, in spite of myself, I felt safer.

I bowed in gratitude to my spindly friend. After all, I had eaten these mushrooms to heal a deep wound. Did I expect it to be easy? This was the journey. And the only way out was through.

I climbed back into the truck, but I didn't lie back down, nor did I block my ears. Instead, I sat cross-legged, facing the back hatch, and stared at the fear inside my body.

I decided I would not move a muscle. I would sit and stare with my inner gaze until the fear passed. But after staring for a while, a new sensation stirred beneath it.

In my mind's eye, I saw a "pocket" burst open at the base of my womb, the same location where the fear had first erupted. And I realized … there would be no approaching steps, nor dangerous humans, nothing. Because the truth was that I was completely alone.

Absolutely completely alone. I was alone in the world. Maybe I had always been alone. Maybe I had clung to people, grasped at love, just to avoid feeling what had been obvious all along.—that I was alone. Maybe *everyone* was alone. All humans, walking their separate paths, wounded and untethered, distracting themselves with work, relationships, routines—anything to escape the inescapable truth: *We. Are. alone.*

This time it wasn't my sternum that tightened, but my heart. Oh, the ache. The ever-tightening vice grip. There it was—the ultimate curse of separation inherent in the human condition.

And so, I stared at that, too.

In my mind's eye, I saw the shape of Ultimate Loneliness in my body. It was a poisonous black smoke snake, rising, swirling, whistling, choking life and sounds. The smoke rose up my throat and filled my brain.

"Well," I thought, "I might as well die if this is what life is about. What's the point?"

And I meant it in that moment, not in a morbid or suicidal tone, just as a simple realization of the truth about the meaninglessness of life. Without the Other, self-love had no scale. How much did I love myself? Who cared? There was no one to reflect it. Without the Other, whether we lived or died didn't matter at all.

[Step outside,] an ocotillo called.

I shook off enough despair to push the back hatch open and stepped into the fresh air.

It was a different ocotillo that had called—not the first one to the right, nor the one that kept my truck keys. This one was to the left of the truck.

[Moon.] The felt sense from that word was silent. The ocotillo was simply pointing at the moon with its many skinny, flowery fingers. My eyes followed them up. I exhaled.

Seriously—how impossibly beautiful was that moon?

The ocotillo smiled. The moon reflected off the metal of the truck, draping silver reflections on all its rounded edges. The truck smiled too. And suddenly I wasn't alone anymore. I was surrounded by friends. Quiet tears of gratitude ran down my cheeks.

I was understanding a profound truth, maybe not about the world, life, or humanity, but about my own inner workings. I had never been alone because I believed in the sentience of all beings, animate or inanimate. And because I believed it, I perceived it.

I looked up, smiling. "Oh, Moon. Ppphhew. This is intense." I laughed. "Whose idea was this again? Oh, right. It was mine." I laughed again, and the moon smiled like a loving mother.

[Eat something. It'll take the edge off.] The ocotillo directed my gaze back to the truck. I nodded. Yes, eating was an excellent idea. I only had a pack of Girl Scout cookies with me because the store in Jacumba had been closed on my way out of town. I sat back on my mattress, cross-legged and facing the closed hatch, and ate the entire pack.

Slowly, the moon traveled across the sky. Like waves, the Debilitating Fear and Ultimate Loneliness, as I named them then, washed through me, again and again. At times, if it became too intense, I stepped outside, spoke with the ocotillos, and looked at the moon.

Then with renewed courage, I returned to the inner dark and stared until the emotions began to feel more like a fascinating art project than anything that could actually affect me —just an experience to observe, dissect, name. I watched how my body reacted. I memorized it so that I could recognize it later, in real-life situations.

This was the mushrooms' gift. The fear and loneliness had likely lived in me for decades. The mushrooms hadn't created the emotions, they only opened the doors of perception and revealed them. So the pocket that had burst must have held these emotions hidden from my conscious mind, and from there, had guided my choices in life, including my choices in mates. I understood.

If you could imagine feeling debilitating fear, heart-wrenching loneliness, and deep love and gratitude all at once, you might come close to what I felt that night. Then, add the crystal-clear metallic green of the mint taste of the Girl Scout cookies, and you're even closer.

The mint taste was crystal-clear metallic green. The taste was cold, like the texture on the sharp edge of a metal coffee table. The fear was a dark brick red, dense, and gritty like a cinder block. The loneliness was black, smokey black.

"Mmmh." My eyes snapped open. "Synesthesia!" So my mind had reached the stage where the input from external and internal senses was received and processed by all sensory modalities in my brain at once. This was the state of neuroplasticity Michael Pollan had described in *How to Change Your Mind*—the exact state I had intended to reach.

A grin spread across my face.

"This means," I whispered, "I can now rewire my brain."

My grin unlocked a cascade of colorful fractals. This is what a decision to heal looked like—colorful, curly, repeating patterns, starting from the seed dis-ease and unfurling, with each iteration, into its diametrical opposite.

Fear held and birthed: *I am always safe*.

Loneliness held and birthed: *I am deeply loved*.

I held the new programs in my open palms and, for a time-irrelevant moment, became fascinated by the words.

298

What were words? Symbols and sounds out of one's mouth, creating images in one or the other's mind. Wasn't that synesthesia? Were all languages synesthetic?

I gave gratitude for the sounds and symbols of my new programs, then began knocking the knuckle of my index finger between my brows repeatedly, right in the location of the third eye.

Why was I tapping my knuckle on my forehead? I had no idea. I just knew that, without physical reinforcement, the new programs wouldn't take.

I knocked and knocked and knocked, until, finally, I stopped, unsuccessful.

I stepped out of the truck and visited the ocotillos. My body was tired, and my mind was shrinking back to its limited, normal perspective.

This was puzzling. Why wasn't my body uptaking the new beliefs that it was safe and loved?

"I don't know." I raised my shoulders, palms open to the moon. "I just don't know."

She was almost all the way across the sky. I guessed that only a few hours remained before dawn. Sunrise. The beginning again. Sunsets in the desert always seemed so orange, while sunrises seemed softer, more pink.

"Haaaaa." I saw it.

The end had a different color than the beginning. That's right... I hadn't begun my life in English. My parents spoke French. That pocket—wherever it had come from—was from the beginning of my life. That's why it sat at the base of my spine. And so, to dismantle it, I needed the language of that era.

"*Je suis en toute sécurité.*" "*Je suis profondément aimée.*" My knuckle knocked. I disliked speaking French, even though it was my mother tongue, but I was committed to reprogramming myself, no matter what it took.

But even in French, these new programs resisted getting installed. Still, I knocked, and knocked, until, eventually, I felt a subtle shift in my being.

The base of the horizon glowed pink as the sun neared the edge of this reality, but the moon lingered in the sky to witness dawn. I pushed the hatch open and dropped the tailgate. I sat in the comfort of the morning silence, dangling my feet as I watched the light march across the land toward me.

It was done—whatever it was.

80 · 03

Once the sun fully bathed the truck, I jumped off the tailgate and walked to the front ocotillo to retrieve my buried keys.

That is when I noticed the impossible symmetry.

The front right ocotillo was exactly in line with the corner of the front right bumper. The back right ocotillo was exactly in line with the corner of the back right bumper. The same was true of the other two corners and other two ocotillos. Four ocotillos, standing at the same distance and the same angle from the truck, like four corner posts of purposeful protection. I had pulled in randomly, yet, here they were.

I walked around the truck several times, jaw open, rubbing disbelief from my eyes.

The coincidence—if I even believed in coincidences— was so far beyond the range of possibilities that, for a moment, I felt dizzy.

"There," I said aloud to hear my own symbols, "if you don't believe that you are always safe and deeply loved after this… I honestly don't know what would do it."

80 · 03

My first act when I arrived in Jacumba was to quit. I no longer cared about being the co-first woman to hike the Desert Trail. I don't believe Hippie understood my decision—neither did I at the time—but she respected and supported it. Instead, I drove north and crossed Death Valley on foot, by myself. Death Valley—the place where I was conceived, according to my dad. My place of beginning.

Both Hippie and I ended up hiking across Death Valley solo that year.

Our friend Steady, as far as I know, became the first woman to hike the Desert Trail. She hiked it for the pleasure of hiking, and I don't believe she even knows she was a first.

Also, I did eventually weigh the remaining mushrooms in the Ziploc. Six grams were left, so I must have eaten four that night. Four grams. One gram per ocotillo.

I believed then, as I drove away from Jacumba, hiked across Death Valley, and later on the Pacific Northwest Trail, that these four grams had sealed a cycle, rewired a wound. I believed my experience was a final period to a long-standing pattern. As I am writing this book years later, I now understand it was, in fact, the beginning of everything that followed.

Chapter 23
Enter the Jaguar

Envision Festival, Uvita, Costa Rica, February 2020

You wouldn't expect to meet a leprechaun in the heart of the Costa Rican jungle. Yet, this is exactly how this story began.

The man wore Kelly green pants rolled at the ankles, possibly to accommodate his short stature, and a rainbow tie-dye shirt, perhaps to increase his visibility among the festival-goers. Above his head, glued to a wooden stick, was a glittery rainbow over a well-executed drawing of a mushroom—the famous white-dotted, red-capped *Amanita muscaria*, the universal symbol for magic mushrooms, even though most people's experience is with the psilocybin variety, not Amanita.

We locked eyes as he walked by. His mischievous smile pulled on the edge of his goatee—a smile of recognition. He stopped in front of me, nodded, and pointed a finger toward the sign.

"Do you need Magic?"

I had watched him approach. He had passed through the crowd like a wolf on the hunt, looking left and right, but letting his sign speak for itself. He had not engaged with

302

anyone, until he saw me. I felt profiled. Did I look like someone who needed Magic?

"No, thank you," I answered automatically, though his eyes held mine. I hadn't planned on taking mushrooms, not tonight.

"Ha," he chuckled softly, not moving. "You might not think you do, but…" He leaned closer, voice dropping to a conspiratorial whisper. "These are *Taj Mahals*."

His voice pressed on the name with the weight reserved for sacred, rare, or even famous strains. I had never heard of Taj Mahals.

"Do yourself a favor. Try them. They're truly spectacular beings."

It might have been a sales tactic, but he seemed relaxed and genuine, not pushy in any way. And he had profiled me accurately. If an ally had recognized me, it was worth paying attention. Guidance was guidance, whether mine or his.

I bought one chocolate ball.

"They're very strong." He closed the satchel of magic chocolates and readjusted the strap on his shoulder. "1.5 grams each, and I highly recommend you eat no more than half to begin with."

Eat only half?! Ha! That leprechaun clearly didn't know me. He didn't know that just a year prior, I had sat with four grams and four ocotillos by myself in the desert, that mushrooms had taught me how to speak with trees, that I had crossed an entire continent with a man who sold magic mushrooms to pay our way, that I…

Thank Goodness, Jenna found me before I ate the whole thing.

"Sunset?" Jenna had found me through the crowd. I tucked the chocolate ball into my pocket and fell in step with her toward the beach.

"I saw you talking to the magic man. You actually bought one?" She grinned, tilting her head toward my pocket.

"I mean... he found me. And he said I should eat only half. Would you share it with me?"

She laughed. "Absolutely!"

Jenna and I had met at the festival's Spa booth, where we traded a few hours of work each day for our entrance tickets. We'd clicked instantly and arranged to sync our day off to explore the festival together. The leprechaun had crossed my path on the eve of our one day off.

Jenna and I stopped just before the sandy path to the beach. I split the chocolate ball and handed her half.

We each cupped our half-ball in closed hands and brought the mushrooms to our hearts to set our intents. Why were we eating these sentient beings? And what did they wish from us in exchange for their medicine?

Before I could even think of an intent, I felt the mushrooms' giddy energy pulse through my hands.

"Wow!" Jenna laughed, and we both snapped our eyes open.

"I know! Wow!"

We closed our eyes again, and I silently spoke to the mushrooms. "Hi. My name is Maya. Maybe you know me. I've journeyed with your kind before, with respect, in ceremony to explore my own shadows. But you... you feel so vivacious. This time, may I please experience what party people use mushrooms for? Show me the colors, the fractals, the kaleidoscope. I want to dance! Show me your magic—let's have fun!"

[Giggles. Joy.] Oh, they had heard me.

"And what would you like in return?"

[Your body. Full control.]

The sun set over the jungle and the impossibly wide beach as the tide pulled the water and all the fire-spinning, hula-hooping, wild people hundreds of feet away from the jungle's edge.

Jenna and I left the beach and the howling crowd right as the last speck of light dove into the ocean. We crossed the festival grounds back to the quieter yoga and spa section and arrived just in time.

"Maya, I feel them. It's started for me. I… I need to meditate. I know we agreed we'd dance, but I need to meditate right now."

"Yes, of course." I followed Jenna to a set of cushions under a tree. She closed her eyes and became completely still. I waited for a while, but she gave no sign of resurfacing, so eventually, I got up and left.

When we regrouped the next day, Jenna shared that she had stayed on that pillow under the tree in deep meditation for fifteen hours. She had never before meditated for more than an hour but felt no soreness from being in the same position all night.

What follows is what happened to me during these same fifteen hours.

I left Jenna on her meditation cushion and drifted toward the nearest music stage. The festival had several, each pulsing with its own rhythm and vibe. I started at El Cielo, in the yoga section, because they played music I knew—earthy, grounded sounds from real instruments.

El Cielo stage stood inside a large, elegantly carved wooden shala. The place was already packed when I arrived. I stepped onto the platform and found a small opening in the back of the crowd to ease into the rhythm.

So many youthful, attractive people had gathered in the shala. They moved like water, effortless and free. Suddenly, I felt clunky, my limbs too old, too uncoordinated, too aware of themselves. How odd—I had always loved dancing, yet my body hesitated as if waiting for permission. I closed my eyes and swayed my hips just enough to feel part of it anyway while I waited for the familiar psilocybin nausea.

305

Within the first song, a tingle sparked in my back teeth, and my stomach gave a little lurch. This was the signal I had expected—the cosmic memo to my conscious mind that I was knocking at the doors of extrasensorial perception, and that they were about to be flung open.

"Here we go." I breathed out, pulse quickening.

Some mushrooms take you on a journey kindly. They guide you up the ramp slowly and let you acclimate to the new reality.

There was no ramp with the Taj Mahals.

As soon as my stomach gave that first lurch, the physical form of humans around me grew fuzzier in concentric circles from my vantage point. I could see each person with my own opinion-informed eyes, but also through the mushrooms' vision.

They were enamored with this slender woman I had met and disliked. A fire keeper I had thought manly, they revealed as macho and insecure. Ah, but Antonia—my dear, sweet friend Antonia—they confirmed was also a shining soul.

I stared at one, then another, but my interest in humans quickly faded. I longed for the company of trees instead.

I looked up. Above the dancers' heads, the carved wood of the shala stirred to life, breathing in tempo with the music. I matched its rhythm and danced with the wood, ignoring the humans around me, while the fuzziness continued to grow outward.

When the fuzziness reached the stage with the DJ and the loudspeakers, the music turned liquid. It poured from the speakers onto the wooden floor, a molten river of iridescent rainbows, spreading across the floor like the stretched fingers of a flood.

I stood still, watching with some trepidation as the liquid fingers raced across the floor toward me. I both feared and hoped the music would consume me.

The colorful liquid music reached my bare feet, seeped through my soles, and flowed up my legs like warm sap being drawn toward branches and canopy. When it reached my heart, I fell in love. I loved that liquid music like the dearest, most coveted lover. I placed my hand over my heart, thumping with bright green love and gratitude.

The liquid continued into my arms, shoulders, and neck and began moving them. My body was an instrument played by liquid sounds, its movements graceful and free. I was danced, surrendered to the music's will.

My fingers carved through the air, leaving trails of sparkles and colors that lingered like faint traces. I crossed back through them, creating ripples, harmonies, and eddies.

Through the wonder, I became aware of an odd grin stretching across my face, and for a split-moment, I almost felt self-conscious. But just then, the music stopped, and so did my body.

I again stood still, barely breathing in the interminable silence between songs.

Tribal drums pulled in the next song. The drumbeats pulsed up from the wooden floor, rising in cylindrical tunnels of colors. My feet stomped and splashed through them like puddles, and suddenly, I was lifted, twirled, and woven through the crowd.

When I closed my eyes, the music was alive with rainbow fractals. When I opened them, humanity's oddities made me giggle.

Time unraveled. I was flying through colors, levitating, pulsating—

Then, suddenly, I awoke. I remembered the world, and where I was in it. I remembered the Taj Mahals.

The mushrooms were giddy in my mind. "Let's go explore!"

Yes, there was so much more to see. Without a second thought, I jumped off El Cielo's platform and skipped lightly through the crowd, giggling as I disappeared into the night.

At the next stage, the Lapa stage, the music pulsed with a much faster tempo, world beats remixed with heavy drums and bass. No sooner had I arrived than my body morphed into a large African Mama. She had such a different body rhythm than mine. Her feet hit the dirt with perfect cadence, and her wide hips rolled farther than mine ever had or could.

The music changed. I was an Egyptian belly dancer, fluid like a silk veil. Light, sinuous, sensual. Then a delicate geisha. A weightless ballerina. A fiery, fierce flamenca, stomping and clapping in syncopated synchronicity.

With each new song, I was a different woman—all of them dancers. Until, suddenly, I was a cacao bean. I was still dancing, but I tasted bitter, dark brown, heavy, earthy. Not like chocolate—no, a far more potent taste. At the time, I had never tasted or even seen a cacao bean. But as one, I felt wise, old—not just old, but Great-Grandmother-old—and very, very powerful.

I swayed in place, feeling this new rooting presence within me. My body's wild dance tapered, shifting from performance to communion. My arms and legs moved in the subtlest ways, now tracing only the undercurrents of the music. I felt the mushrooms' playful nod.

It was time for the big stage.

The Sol stage.

I had watched it from the edges all weekend, intimidated by its massive spectacle of laser lights, pulsing heat, and relentless synthesized sounds. It was the culmination—the stage with the headlining bands. I had wanted to step into that scene but hadn't yet.

But now, I was Cacao—rooted, fearless. I weaved through the thick crowd until I was right below the stage. All around me, fire erupted from columns scattered across the ground. People jumped around the columns, their movements mechanical, repetitive, in cadence with the techno beat. Speakers thumped shock waves that pressed into my chest.

308

Up on stage, fire dancers spun their flames until they blurred into sigils I intuitively understood. The dancers and their fires moved like a series of flickered slides, not smoothly like habitual reality. Reality was deconstructing. And I knew, from the sigils, a new one would emerge. What did that even mean?

I was no longer dancing. I stood in the crowd, absorbed in the sigils. The steady kick drum thumped on, relentless. But the metal edge of the music clashed too sharply with the organic thrum of mushrooms and the spirit of Cacao in my body. The rhythm turned ugly. A wave of nausea swelled. I turned and quickened my steps away from the stage, hands and elbows forward like a shield. I had to get out of there. I needed to find something older, something that breathed.

I spotted a tree in the distance, in a peaceful shadow, away from the metallic clash of sounds and flames. I felt it notice me too. It seemed to be waiting for me.

It was a giant tree with roots draped around its trunk and spiraling outward. I sat on one of the roots and exhaled slowly.

"Ffffffffffh. Wow. Taj Mahals," I told the tree.

[Jungle,] the tree replied.

I sensed there was more. I slid off the root and nestled myself on the ground, wedged between two roots, like a small child in the arms of a Grandmother about to tell a story from her childhood.

But this story had no words. It moved in currents, weaving through me like a dream with images of macaws, monkeys, and hummingbirds, green vines, ferns, and swampy soils.

I knew this place. I knew the jungle the tree showed me even though I had never stepped into it, only glimpsed it at the festival's edge, behind the safety fences.

My conscious mind stirred, slowly returning. I was more aware of my body in this world, yet the sense of roots

309

elsewhere lingered. Perhaps the jungle was a place I had once known—or one to which I belonged?

I pressed my palms to the top of the roots and extracted myself from the tree's embrace. I now felt the fatigue in my dancing legs. The sounds of the festival were growing quieter, and the horizon glowed brighter with the promise of dawn. Taj Mahals no longer held supremacy over my body, but we still shared one mind, like two friends walking side by side, exchanging ideas.

We decided to return to the tent to rest at last, with a stop at the art gallery.

I had visited the gallery the day before, and I remembered thinking the art looked psychedelic and that it was likely meant to be experienced with an altered mind.

Well, I had an altered mind, and the gallery was on the way.

The day prior, the art had seemed busy, chaotic, tangled, and nonsensical to my human eyes. But now, with psilocybin vision, I saw the hidden patterns, the meaning beneath and beyond the paint. Surely, these artists had help from their own allies in the creation of such multidimensional messages. I drifted from painting to painting, enthralled by the hidden worlds I could now see, until, suddenly, I stopped, spellbound.

A jaguar, as tall as a door.

My breath caught. The air around me buzzed. Slowly, I lifted my gaze.

His face was right up front, poised, patient. One paw hovered, the other pressed down, mid-step, ready to cross the threshold. A quiet sigh escaped my lips as my eyes widened. This was no ordinary cat. Beyond the paint, electric greens, deep blues, and molten oranges pulsated in patterns that shifted the more I stared. The spots on his fur were portals, some fractal, others geometric. His mouth was slightly open, revealing elongated fangs that seemed too sharp for a paintbrush. But his striking golden eyes were the most alive, fixed on whoever dared meet his gaze.

Jaguar—part paint, part animal, and, to one with an ally from beyond the veil, a full totem. He was a shamanic sentinel. He didn't just look; he saw.

Our eyes locked. His unwavering golden eyes were now only looking at me. And I couldn't move. I stared. People walked by. Some stopped, glanced at the jaguar, and moved on. I kept staring. I stared for so long that, eventually, his eyes moved. I didn't see them move; I *felt* them move. Jaguar scanned me up and down, investigating, sizing me up.

Then, slowly and deliberately, he stepped out of the painting and moved forward until his eyes were mere inches from mine.

My head moved back ever so slightly—a reflex really— and both voices spoke in my mind at once. One laughed. "Wow, the visuals with these Taj Mahals are out of this world!" But the other, even-toned and reverent, said: "This is Jaguar. DO. NOT. MOVE!"

The part of my mind that commanded "Do not move" kept my body frozen—on high alert, humbled, and deferent, as one would be before a Great Teacher.

Because that part of my mind remembered Jaguar like it remembered the Jungle.

Then Jaguar spoke. Not in my mind or ears, but right through my third eye, in the center of my forehead.

"You—you will be back here exactly one year from now, and you will study Cacao, and you will become a chocolate maker."

Even in his commanding tone, I sensed I had a choice. I could refuse, but of course, I wouldn't. To be chosen by Jaguar to study Cacao was such an honor—even if I knew nothing about cacao, even if I had no idea where I would be or how I would return here a year from now. I had to accept.

I bowed deeply to Jaguar. And I stayed bowed until he slipped back into the painting.

A small part of me remained aware of the physical realm—of people walking past, stepping around me, glancing back with amused smiles at the strange woman bowed before a painting.

But the rest of my mind, which remembered Jungle and Jaguar, knew—a shift had just taken place, monumental, life-changing, and irreversible.

I didn't know what it meant. Only that my soul had already agreed.

Chapter 24
Cacaocito

Envision Festival, Uvita, Costa Rica - February 2020

"You—you will be back here exactly a year from now, and you will study Cacao, and you will become a chocolate maker."

I bowed deeply to Jaguar, breath suspended, and stayed bowed until he completely dissolved into the painting. When the last of his whiskers had faded back to mere paint, the trance broke.

I looked around the art gallery. A few stragglers lingered past the end of the last music sets. The paintings hung, lifeless, one-dimensional. In the distance, a gong echoed, calling early risers and all-nighters to meditation. The world was ordinary again—well, almost. A pulse of joy still echoed in my chest, the quiet certainty of a new adventure. And I refused to believe it had only been a psychedelic mirage.

I brought my pressed hands to my heart, bowed again, this time only with my head, and whispered, "Thank you, Taj Mahals. Thank you, Leprechaun. Thank you."

By the time I sank into my sleeping pad, a wide grin still on my face, sunlight had already breached the jungle canopy. A few ants bit me, as was customary, but I faded before their sting subsided. I vanished into a deep sleep, a portal to another world—one of dancing, fractals, and colors.

The howler monkeys woke me a couple of hours later. I stretched in the thick jungle heat as the night's memories flickered back. I felt refreshed, energized, and excited for life.

I quickly dressed, slipped out of my tent, and crossed the festival grounds to the nearest row of porta-potties.

In the mid-morning hour, the festival was quiet, and sleeping dancers still in their party attire could be found everywhere—in hammocks, in the shade of trees, on benches, or even curled up in the dirt.

"Maya!" Jenna's voice rang out, bright and sparkly, as she spotted me.

I turned and caught her in a joyful hug.

"I meditated all night!" she said, beaming.

I laughed. "And I met a Jaguar!"

We danced a little jig, then linked arms and walked toward breakfast. After rice and beans and a juicy slice of watermelon, we strolled through the waking festival, still sharing our stories, hands gesturing, eyes wide, words punctuated by gasps and bursts of laughter.

"This here wee flower is the flower of the cacao tree. Put it in yer belly button… like so… and leave it thir for two days."

I felt Jaguar's energy press against me, as palpable as if a flesh-and-blood animal walked by my side. He stood to my left. I didn't tell Jenna about my companion, yet she switched sides, unconsciously making room for him. His quiet pull guided us toward the tent.

"Let's go in!"

It felt like my decision, but I understood the mechanism. I was being led.

We ducked under the low tent and settled in the back.

Cross-legged on a low wooden stage sat a woman about my age—or so I guessed from her short pixie white hair, though her sharp blue eyes, twinkling with mischief, felt much younger. Her hand was up her shirt.

"Jus' be sure to not forget it in thir," she continued, her slight Scottish accent trilling the words. "Mibbe ye'll find it all moldy some weeks later. Ooh, no."

The audience burst into laughter.

"This will alleviate two kinds of stress in the body—only two kinds. Stress from overwork and stress from having too many responsibilities."

She reached into the cloth bag by her side and presented us with a set of oblong, pointy leaves. The smaller ones were pinkish; the longer ones dark green and leathery.

"Cacao is a great medicine. We know it for its seed, the cacao bean, but the whole tree is full of gifts." She rolled one of the younger pink leaves like a fruit roll-up and popped it into her mouth. "The young leaves are mucilaginous. This means they help keep the body hydrated. In this humid climate here, we don't know that with all the sweating, we're dehydrated, but we are. Eating the young leaves will remedy that."

She passed a handful of pink leaves to the audience. Jenna and I split one. As I chewed, it turned slicker than I had expected—almost slimy.

"When the leaves are older, we dry them and make Cobacco. Like tobacco but with cacao leaves. Smoking Cobacco can even cure asthma."

She reached into her bag and pulled out a yellow pod about the size of her hand.

"This here, is the cacao pod." She turned it over in her palm, then, with a swift cut of her machete, split it open. Lifting one half of the shell, she held up the exposed white fruit. I leaned in, fingers pressing into my knees, afraid to miss a single word.

"The fruit is called Baba. There are about twenty seeds in each pod. The kids here pack cacao pods as their lunch. They

315

eat the fruit and throw away the seeds. So if yer looking for young cacao trees, look around schoolyards…"

She continued the lesson as the open pod traveled through the audience. I plucked a slimy fruit from the shell—my first cacao fruit. It tasted like the lychees of my childhood. Jenna had already eaten hers and bitten into the seed to reveal the deep purple of raw cacao.

"I will pass some chocolate around now. Again, my name's Ancel—c'mon up if you have any questions. I promise I won't bite. Except you, the handsome lad in the kilt over there. Ye, I'll bite."

Everyone laughed, except for the young man in the kilt.

I tasted Ancel's chocolate and closed my eyes. The moment it melted on my tongue—dark, like ancient, earthy magic—I found myself rising, weaving through the audience before my mind caught up. This woman *was* cacao—wise, soft, kind, spirited—and I just had to ask…

"Hi. Do you take interns?"

"YES!" She almost shouted her answer. A tingle of excitement ran up my spine. The teacher! I had found the teacher, and so soon after bowing to Jaguar.

Ancel scribbled her email address on a wee piece of paper and handed it to me. As I tucked the paper into the hidden fold of my yoga pants, a light breeze stirred. Jaguar, I imagined, had just brushed by.

୫ · ଓଃ

Corcovado, Osa Peninsula, Costa Rica - February 2020

"I own a hotel in the jungle. If you want to come for a few days and set up a tent in the yard, you're welcome. I have room in my car, and I'm leaving right now."

Lena, looking like an angel in her flowy white dress, had just loaded her massage table in the trunk and was holding the door open. Jenna, Antonia, and I exchanged glances. We had already packed and cleaned everything in the Spa and had been sitting on our own packed bags, enjoying what we thought was the last of our time together. Antonia had surf lessons to teach in Santa Teresa, but her schedule was flexible. Jenna had a guiding job waiting in San José, but not for another week. And my flight back to the U.S. wasn't for another four days. So why not?

With a flurry of giggles, we tossed our bags into Lena's car and squeezed into the backseat.

The paved road led us south to the Osa Peninsula, then shrank into a rugged dirt track winding through thickening jungle. We crossed rivers without bridges and climbed ever deeper into the green. With each switchback, the air grew thicker, the trees denser, the jungle more lush. Vines hung from the tall canopy like curtains protecting another world.

By the time we reached a small gravel parking lot surrounded by vivid hibiscus, fragrant magnolias, and lush, feathery ferns, I felt we had arrived at the very heart of Pachamama. We stepped out of the vehicle, wide-eyed— Lena's Ecolodge wasn't a "hotel." It was an altar to the jungle herself.

For a moment, we simply stood, absorbing it all, held in awe. But Lena was already at the entrance, calling us in. We dropped our bags and stepped into the spacious dining room, drawn forward by the view. On one side, laughter rose from an open kitchen, where local women prepared food with knowing hands. On the other side, a half-moon wooden platform extended above the canopy, offering a sweeping view of the jungle. Macaws and toucans soared at eye level over the treetops. Morpho butterflies flitted among the trees and over Lena's flower garden. Trees of all sizes and shades, like a sea of green, swayed as one living canopy.

We walked to the very edge of the platform and listened. A howl in the distance, a rhythmic knock, a raspy croak, a trill, a series of chirps—all blending into a ceaseless hum. I knew these sounds. I had seen these birds before. Yet I hadn't.

317

Lena joined us with a tray of steaming cacao. She placed a small, round pottery mug into my hands.

"This cacao…" She lifted her mug, cradling it in both hands before continuing. "It is grown here, on our land, by the local women. They tend the trees, harvest the pods, ferment the beans in the sun, and shell each one by hand. Traditionally, only women worked with cacao. We grow ours in the spirit of their ancestors."

I ran my fingers over the rim of the mug. The weight of it in my palm, the warmth, the scent. This was medicine, not just a drink.

"They say the spirit of cacao is a grandmother," Lena continued. "She opens the heart to ever greater love."

We raised our mugs to the cardinal directions, Father Sky, Mother Earth, our hearts, and each other, then, as one, we brought the cacao to our lips.

I took a slow sip. Earth. Bitter. Rich. Along with the warmth, a sensation of joy and peace entered my being and settled into my heart. This cacao. That view. The sisters. The jungle. And Jaguar, lounging on the edge of the platform, his tail dangling, at ease in his own home—Aah.

I closed my eyes and let a tear of gratitude fall into my mug.

We drank slowly, savoring each sip, murmuring our "mmmhhs" and "aaaahhs" until Lena's laugh brought us back to the moment.

"Oh… also, there is no yard for your tents. So instead, I arranged for a room to be prepared for you."

She had tricked us in the most generous way.

That evening, we climbed a winding stone path lined with bright red heliconias, past guest cabinas, until we reached the yoga studio, perched at the top of the world. The studio extended into the largest jungle-viewing platform at the lodge. Far above the canopy and flowers, it overlooked the entire valley, all the way to the Pacific Ocean.

Lena had to return to the restaurant to greet each guest, but we lingered at the platform's edge, three jungle sisters woven together by laughter, feet dangling, drinking in the jungle's sunset like the nectar of life itself. As the sun slid toward the horizon, mist spilled from the mountains, veiling the jungle below. Then, at the last moment, the clouds parted, and the sun slipped into the sea.

As soon as the light faded, a symphony of insects rose from the understory's shadows, billions of songs, all layered into one vast chorus, with cicadas at the head of the orchestra.

The magic continued the next morning as Lena led us down a sun-dappled jungle path of roots and damp moss. Jenna danced ahead, barefoot and gracefully light. Antonia followed, her laughter ringing through the trees. I trailed behind, listening.

Jaguar was near. I could feel him.

I let myself fall further back from the group's joyous chatter until I was alone with the jungle. I walked softly and scanned the undergrowth, expecting at any moment to catch a glimpse of fur or a low, rumbling growl. But he didn't show himself—at least, not in the flesh. Still, I knew he was there, watching, his amber eyes half-closed in quiet approval.

The murmur of rushing water grew louder, and I quickened my steps, suddenly eager to rejoin the sisters. I rounded a bend, and the jungle opened to a stairway of waterfalls, each spilling into the next over smooth river rocks.

They were already in the pools, naked, swimming, sunbathing, or meditating cross-legged on the smooth stones.

We played all day. We splashed, swam, napped, and slid down rocks to explore the lower pools.

As the afternoon softened toward dusk, Lena again surprised us with cacao.

She set a small, woven rug on a flat rock in the middle of the river and arranged our mugs in a circle around a mini altar

319

of fresh flowers and sacred objects. A carved, painted, wooden jaguar no bigger than my thumb sat in its center.

Ha. There he was.

I bowed to the little jaguar and smiled. Good. I was still on the Path.

This time, Lena had prepared the cacao the way the Aztecs drank it: warm and spiced with chili, cinnamon, and vanilla. She poured it from a thermos, and as the sun slid behind the jungle and the cool dampness of the night settled, we wrapped our hands and hearts around the warm magic in our mugs.

We drank slowly, then returned to the path, singing to Pachamama and the spirit of Cacao all the way back to the lodge.

"Would you sell me some of your cacao beans?"

Jenna's eyes sparkled as she turned to Lena at the breakfast table. In addition to being a backcountry guide, Jenna was an herbalist and a chef. Finding the highest energetics in ingredients was her life calling and mission. And these beans were pure love.

Lena hesitated. "Well…" She glanced at the sacks behind the lodge. "I don't usually sell our beans. They belong to this land, and I feel we honor them when we drink them here."

Jenna placed a hand on her heart. "I *promise* I will honor them. I will prepare them with the utmost love and respect and only share them with the highest intentions."

A slow nod. Lena agreed to sell Jenna five kilos of her sacred cacao, at $20 a kilo.

I checked my bank account and emptied my wallet on the bed in our room. The festival had cost me a lot more than I had expected. I had precisely $32.88 left, total, everywhere. So I had a choice: One kilo of cacao, or a meal. One kilo of cacao, or a bus fare from the airport to my truck in Pensacola.

I bought one kilo of Lena's shelled, sun-toasted cacao beans. And, after two idyllic days with the jungle sisters at the

Luna Lodge, in the heart of Pachamama, I bought a bus ticket for $12 back to the San Jose airport.

⟨ᴏ · ᴄ⟩

Pensacola, Florida, February - March 2020

"…and so that's how I ended up with only 88 cents to my name. But I have cacao beans! Look…" I opened the Ziploc bag and dropped a few beans in my hand to show Jeannie.

I had been so lucky—Jeannie, who had my Catmobile, happened to return from her own travels the same day I did, and just in time to pick me up from the Pensacola airport.

"Aren't they amazing? Yeah, so I don't have any money right now… I don't know… When I hold these in my hand, I can't even worry."

Jeannie chuckled, shaking her head. "Now, that's a wonderful story. And don't you worry—I'm a Southern woman, and nobody goes hungry in mah house."

That night, we feasted on a steaming pot of gumbo, rich with crawfish, crab, and shrimp, and shared stories and laughter well into the night.

My first night back in the Catmobile, parked in Jeannie's driveway, I placed the cacao beans in a red cherry wood box with a Tree of Life carving on the lid and fell asleep with it beside my pillow.

The cicadas pulsed, their song rising and falling in waves. Were they here, in the Florida night, or was I dreaming already? A warm jungle breeze brushed gently over my arm. Ah—I was dreaming. How else could I feel a breeze beneath the covers?

Jaguar emerged from the shadows, his muscles rippling with strength and grace. With a presence that commanded respect, he crossed my dream, slowly, deliberately. He didn't meet my eyes, didn't speak, yet I understood his unspoken instructions.

Each morning, I was to eat one cacao bean—only one— and let Cacao teach me.

When I awoke, even before my eyes adjusted to the light, I rolled over and opened the red cherry wood box. A deep cacao aroma unfurled into the truck, rich and grounding. Instantly, I felt joyful. I ran my fingertips over the beans, and the scent intensified as if the very act of touching them stirred them to life.

They were all so lovely. It felt impossible to choose just one. My fingers hovered, then settled on a deep purple bean—the color of the raw seed I had tasted fresh from the fruit during Ancel's talk. Its surface was veined with micro-cracks, some forming near-perfect hexagons. I lifted it to my nose, inhaling slowly, letting its scent fill me.

I nibbled a corner first, testing the bitter against my tongue, then chewed the whole bean. It was softer than I had expected, yielding easily to my teeth, with almost no crunch. But as it was my first whole bean, I had no frame of reference, no way to judge whether this was normal. I couldn't analyze yet; I could only observe.

Jeannie had a little kitchen remodeling work for me, paid generously, on top of the daily Southern feasts and an open invitation to raid her pantry whenever I pleased. I gladly accepted and stayed in her driveway for another two weeks.

Each morning, before picking up a paintbrush or screwdriver, I met, studied, and ate exactly one cacao bean. No two were the same. Some were brick red or purple, others dark brown or almost black. At first, I only tasted bitter— some rich and dark like fertile soil, others sharp enough to pucker my whole face. But as the days passed, my palate began to decipher subtleties. A bean could open with a flash of sharpness, then bloom into a soft floral field, and linger with a smoky hint of cedar. Another might begin like damp earth, then melt into fruit, a tart little ember that faded into honey at the very last moment.

I ordered a book on cacao, eager to learn more. *Forastero, Criollo, Trinitario*—I rolled the words in my mouth, as if they might taste as rich as the beans they named. According to the book, my beans were Criollo—heirloom treasures celebrated as the finest in the world. I read about the history, the cultivation, the alchemy of chocolate-making.

But the next morning, when I opened the wood box and inhaled that sacred aroma, I realized that no definition, no expert's words could teach me what the beans themselves already were. I set the book aside and never picked it up again.

Each morning and each night, I told my cacao beans, "I love you." And oh my, did I mean it! And because they answered with pulses of aroma, I knew—without a doubt—they loved me back.

Jeannie's cabinets changed color beneath my brush, drawers gained new handles by my screwdriver, but my mind was elsewhere, wrapped in the velvet world of cacao. Their scent lingered on my fingers and their taste on my tongue. I was giddy and ridiculous, a teenager consumed by the infatuation of first love.

Jaguar had shown me the path, and now it gleamed ahead, straight as a river of gold from Jeannie's backyard to Ancel's farm. All I had to do was work at The Local Grocer Café over the summer, save enough for the flight to Costa Rica and the apprenticeship, and become a chocolate maker. No obstacle in sight.

And every time I thought about it—how perfectly, impossibly, beautifully it was all aligning—I cried in gratitude. Every single time.

After two weeks at Jeannie's, I found the precious wee piece of paper with Ancel's email address and sent her a message titled: "The dream of learning all I can from you."

"Hello Ancel. My name is Maya. I spoke with you at the end of your cacao talk at Envision. I asked, 'Do you take interns,' and you said, 'Yes!' So, here I am. I would love love love to volunteer at your farm. I feel I'm at a turning point in my life, and Cacao is calling me. Could I come this fall? October maybe? And stay a month or several? If it's best for you or the farm, I can come earlier. I have skills and can be useful..."

I sent the email on March 1st, heart pounding, already tasting the jungle air, already hearing the rustle of cacao leaves in the wind. The path was set; the email was merely a formality.

Except... I never received an answer.

∞ · ∞

Hendersonville, North Carolina - April-June 2020

My blissful time of painting kitchen cabinets and eating cacao beans in Jeannie's driveway was cut short by the increasingly alarming world news. COVID had entered the world stage and was rapidly shutting it down. I fled north to the Blue Ridge Mountains of North Carolina, where I met the Lady of the Land and Erik who loved cats. And there, I stayed.

At the farm, the land took its time waking, and so did I. I usually opened my eyes to the sun already tickling the flowers in the field, stretched, rolled closer to the Catmobile's side window, and watched the world unfold from my pillow.

Squirrels—I think the same two every day—chased each other through the oak's highest branches, leaping from tree to tree, their chatter breaking the stillness. Cardinals landed on the lowest branches, bursting into song before vanishing in red streaks. Bees danced over the wildflowers. Cats crouched low in the grass. Somewhere, a human whistled.

[Peace. Exhale. Rest.] The oak hummed.

Once I had my fill, I rolled to my other side and reached for the red cherry wood box.

I ran my fingertips over the smooth shells, greeting each one before choosing one bean. I held it in my palm, pressing it between my fingers, feeling its presence. Every cacao bean carried the same fundamental essence—ancient, feminine, and wise—but within that, each had its own individual personality. Some felt lighthearted, others deep and brooding. Some called to me; others sat in patient silence. I wasn't just meeting seeds but new friends, one by one.

One day, as I watched the two squirrels chase each other through the canopy and the bees gather on wildflowers, a thought surfaced like a revelation.

"Oh! Cacao beans grow in pods—they're social beings. So they're meant to be experienced together."

Was the thought mine? Perhaps. But I still believed I was following Jaguar's path. I bowed and smiled.

"Thank you. I see the next step now."

From that morning on, I chose my beans in handfuls. I greeted them, felt into their energies, then hovered my nose over the group to marry their scents. Most days, one or two beans returned to the box for future matching.

When I felt satisfied with the pairing, I dressed, slipped on my headphones, and moseyed over to the trailer's kitchen. Ever since Costa Rica, I played nothing but what I called Cacao music—grounded earth songs with wooden flutes, drums, didgeridoos, and softly picked guitars to a background of jungle sounds. I could have sworn the beans tasted sweeter when I played them Cacao music.

I ground the selected beans in my cacao-only grinder— no coffee, no spices, nothing to taint the sacred aroma was allowed near it. I brought the water to a boil and let it cool exactly five minutes.

325

Through trial and error, I had learned that if the water was too cold, the cacao fat stayed firm, leaving gritty nibs to sink to the bottom of the mug. Too hot, and the volatile aroma burned off, leaving bitterness behind and taking the magic with it. But a barely quivering boil left to settle for five minutes unlocked the richest flavor without compromise.

Once the temperature was just right, I turned to the spices. For this step, my nose again led the way. I hovered over the steaming cacao, letting its scent settle deep into my senses, then, carrying its essence with me, I drifted past the Lady of the Land's endless spice jars, searching for the ones that would answer it in perfect harmony.

"Good morning, Erik. Would you like some cacao?"

Every day, I prepared three mugs of cacao—one for me, one for the Viking, and one for the Lady of the Land. Hers often sat untouched until later in the day, but Erik and I drank ours at optimal temperature.

One sip, and his verdict followed. "Mmh. Too much cinnamon in this one." Or, "I liked yesterday's better. What did you change?" And sometimes, "This is it! This is the best yet."

Erik drank his cacao like a connoisseur, even though he had never laid eyes on a cacao bean before I arrived. I drank mine like a scientist, gradually inching away from mindful ceremony and deeper into methodical obsession. The process took over. Bean counts, grinder settings, water temperature, the songs playing, the weather, my mood, and, most importantly, Erik's feedback—each scribbled in my notebook like an alchemist refining a formula. What had once been guided by instinct and presence became a puzzle to solve, a mystery of ratios and heat.

Somewhere in the pages of my notebook, Jaguar faded. So slowly, so quietly, I didn't notice right away.

As the weeks passed, the trees thickened with fresh leaves, black snakes and fireflies returned, and the warm breeze of southern nights caressed the Land once more. The world stirred from its slumber—COVID restrictions lifted, the lockdown unlocked, and a $1200 stimulus check landed in our bank accounts. The work on the Land was finished just in time, and we were free to fly.

Erik caught the western wind and flew to the arms of his beloved to build a life and be cherished, as he deserved and wished. I caught the northern wind and drove the Catmobile, the cacao, and myself to the White Mountains of New Hampshire.

On our last night, I made a cardamom-infused chocolate mousse, a final ode to months of cacao exploration. A breath of spice lifted the fruity notes, egg whites rose into peaks, light as air, and a single crushed Costa Rican bean crowned the top. I followed no recipe, only the felt guidance of Cacao itself.

Erik slowly rotated his glass, inspecting it like a fine vintage. He plunged his spoon in, took a bite, and closed his eyes. A slow grin spread across his face.

"Bobcat, you did it. *This* is the best yet."

᛫ ᛫ ᛫

North Conway, New Hampshire - July 2020

"Micah, can I make the chocolates for the Café?"

"No, Paul makes the chocolates."

I paused for a moment.

"Yeah, I know… but Paul doesn't actually like making the chocolates."

Micah smiled. Oh, he had seen me coming. All I had talked about since my return was cacao.

"I think Paul does a good job. Besides, we need to keep him employed full-time, and there's just not enough work for him in the kitchen without the chocolates."

"Mmm… Well. We'll see…"

A few weeks prior

After months confined to the farm in Hendersonville, I took to the White Mountains like a wildling set loose. I climbed, hiked, camped. I disappeared into the woods for days at a time. The scent of pine replaced the stillness of lockdown, my feet moving freely over dirt and granite. Every so often, I emerged—filthy and grinning—to Leah's house, where I washed my gear, scrubbed myself clean, and restocked from the stimulus check before vanishing again.

With each passing week, my body rewired itself to the rhythm of the hills. My legs reclaimed their strength. The last of the summit snow surrendered to rushing streams. The black flies awoke. And suddenly, summer was in full session. It was time to return to civilization and find opportunities to fill my bank account—three months of wages and tips ought to be enough for a flight to Costa Rica and an internship on a cacao farm.

So, I packed my backpack, hiked—danced, really—down the mountain and straight to Leah's house.

Summer brought flowers and vegetables to gardens. At the time, The Local Grocer Café sourced most of its fresh organic produce from its own farm. Everything in the kitchen was, at most, a couple of days out of the soil or off the branch. I started working there for a small salary and a bag of fresh vegetables for each day of work.

Summer also brought tourists in droves. We called it Revenge Tourism. City dwellers from New York to Boston, starved for open space after months of lockdown, flooded the little mountain town like water from a broken dam. So I began working as a barista at the Café in addition to the farm. I made hundreds of lattes, cappuccinos, macchiatos, mochaccinos, and americanos.

And on Fridays, I had one additional task—the careful display of chocolates.

I pulled Paul's chocolates from the walk-in cooler and arranged them in the top right corner of the bakery display case. Back then, there were only a few varieties—just the classics: the plain dark Bliss, the ever-popular Peanut Butter Cups, and Almond Joy with shredded coconut.

That's when the thought first appeared.

I bought one of the Bliss chocolates for my lunch break and sat with it, the way I once had sat with my beloved cacao beans. I closed my eyes and ran the chocolate under my nose. It smelled sweet, but the deep, earthy warmth of cacao wasn't there. I let it melt in my hand, then took a bite. The texture was smooth, the taste leaned toward bitterness. Not bad, just lacking in subtle layers. I waited for the heart-opening surge. But the chocolate was silent. No joy, no warmth, no wisdom. It felt… bland. Maybe even a little sad.

As the last of the chocolate faded on my tongue, the thought slipped in: "Maybe Paul didn't love making chocolate. Maybe, to him, it was just another task. Maybe chocolate needed someone who adored it, who listened to it. Maybe it needed *me*."

But immediately, that idea was backed into a corner. "Wait a minute. I've never actually made chocolate. I just know to grind cacao beans and melt them in hot water. Paul is a trained chef with decades of experience."

A low, barely audible growl appeared in my mind, along with the fleeting vision of ivory-white fangs opening and closing. A slight hiss to finish, and the vision was gone.

A plan was already forming...

"Micah, can I make the chocolates for the Café?"
"No, Paul makes the chocolates."

I paused for a moment. Yes, I understood that Paul needed to remain employed. This was not personal. I liked Paul. It was just that… I closed my eyes, tuning in to my surroundings.

A slight brush of fur, a tail flicking lazily from a high branch. Yes, Jaguar was here, waiting, watching what I might do next.

"Mmm… Well. We'll see…"

The next day was Wednesday, my day off from both the farm and Café. A quick call to my friend Andra, Micah's neighbor, secured a kitchen for the day. I had a secret weapon I'd used once before: cardamom-infused dark chocolate mousse.

I bought the highest-grade baker's chocolate, the darkest local maple syrup, and fresh cardamom pods. I chose the best cacao beans from my red cherry wood box and played my favorite cacao music, letting the jungle seep into the store-bought chocolate.

The beaten whites stood like perfect, firm peaks. The cardamom slowly swirled at the end of my spoon into the molten chocolate. A few drops of rose water joined the dance—rose, to open the heart and soften resistance, just in case.

The mousse was flawless—even better than the one I had made for the Viking and the Lady of the Land. This mousse wasn't just an offering; it was an argument, a spell of persuasion.

This was how the spell would be delivered, as I envisioned it: when Micah came home, I would greet him in the driveway with an elegant, long-stemmed glass filled with cardamom-rose-infused dark chocolate mousse. He would roll down his window. I would hand him a spoon. He would plunge the spoon into the mousse and, with one taste, the kitchen would be mine.

When five o'clock struck, I turned off the cacao music, decorated the glass rim with a small, wild rose, and posted myself in the driveway.

Micah drove up. He stopped right where I had hoped he

would, with his window in front of the mousse. The electric window rolled down interminably. Finally, it reached the bottom, and without a word, I handed Micah the spoon. But he didn't take it. Instead, he stared at me, eyebrows furled.

"Alright, Bobcat. How did you do it?"

"How did I do what?"

"Paul quit today. He got a kitchen manager position at a new upscale restaurant in town."

I blinked, spoon still in my hand.

"So congratulations, you're the Café's new chocolate maker. And… you start tomorrow."

Chapter 25
Stay on the Branch

North Conway, New Hampshire - June-December 2020

The moist jungle soil cradled my crossed legs. Curly vines grew from the ground on either side of my body and slowly slid over my legs toward my hands. With a delicate spiraling motion, they wrapped around my wrists, growing thicker, holding me in place. They reached my elbows and stopped. I flexed my fingers instinctively, a flicker of movement before remembering to be still. The leaves on the vine tickled my skin.

Those tickling leaves—how could they feel so real?

Somewhere in my mind, I knew I was sitting on a cushion in Leah's living room. Although my eyes were closed, I knew a candle burned in front of me, a glowing companion to my now-empty mug of ceremonial cacao. I remembered the second empty mug and the set of freshly drawn oracle cards on the coffee table. I could picture Leah's slight frame comfortably lodged into the sofa.

And yet, just as real were this moist ground and these binding vines.

Why was I bound? I had to wait, I was told. For what? By whom? I was not told. I only understood that I needed to become calm and still before the next step of the journey could be revealed.

The jungle pressed in around me, thick with damp earth and the scent of green. I exhaled slowly, willing my body to settle. The vines loosened their grip slightly.

As I dropped in, deeper and deeper, a presence emerged in front of me, as though the air itself had acquired greater density.

My spine snapped upright as a wave of joy surged through me. *Jaguar!* It had been so long! I almost called out, almost jumped forward in my mind to hug him—

I caught myself.

Thank goodness for these vines holding me, saving me from my own foolishness. Jaguar was neither pet nor friend. He was my guide, and he belonged to realms I couldn't have navigated alone. I returned to a proper deferent stillness, then nodded a respectful greeting.

His amber eyes were steady, patient, as if he had been waiting for me. His tail flicked once, lazily, barely stirring the leaves. Without a sound, he rose, stretched slowly and deliberately, then turned back to the jungle. The rolling motion of his shoulders parted the leaves, creating a path. He didn't demand that I follow him or beckon me in any way— he simply knew I would.

The vines fell off.

Although my physical body remained on the cushion, I quietly uncrossed my legs and stood up in my mind. With hands behind my back, long strides, and head respectfully bowed, I followed Jaguar into the jungle.

We had only walked for a few minutes when a joyous giggle brought me back to the living room. Jaguar vanished.

I opened my eyes. The kitchen clock claimed forty-five minutes had passed. The candle still flickered. The air smelled of cacao. I glanced toward Leah. Her hands traced cursive glyphs around her body, as worlds still unfurled behind her closed eyes. A few s*hhhht*, s*hhhht* and *ffhhh* sounds, and her hands lowered and rested on her lap, fingers forming a heart.

Suddenly, she giggled again, head falling back in delight. She opened her eyes, beaming.

"How wonderful!" She rubbed her palms together. "There were vines and flowers. Flowers of all colors, all around my body. And there was a jaguar." She caressed her cheek, still smiling. "He licked my face with so much love."

I stared at her and blinked. He licked her face? "Ouch," said my ego. *I* had brought Jaguar back from Costa Rica. He was *my* guide. A lick of humility for me. In truth, I hadn't felt Jaguar's presence since North Carolina. Had he followed me all along, waiting for my mind to be still enough to perceive him? Had we both returned at a preordained time? Or had he been here this whole time?

I glanced around Leah's home—Leah's *temple-home*, brimming with feathers, drums, crystals, totems, talismans, and spirals painted and carved into wood.

If Jaguar had waited anywhere, I imagined it would have been here.

For weeks, I had roamed the White Mountains—hiking, camping, climbing—fully feral, fully wild, ecstatically joyous. I hadn't carried cacao with me or given much thought to Jaguar's path. But now I was back in civilization, with two jobs lined up, one at the farm, one at the Café. My life resumed.

Leah had probably known. Not about Jaguar's path specifically, but that my energy was flying too high, that my body had returned but my spirit was still in the woods. Which is probably why she had suggested we meditate with cacao, to help me ground again.

Leah wasn't just a meditation teacher and university professor—she was a powerful shamanic healer. I had seen her dispel darkness with words from another realm, release buried traumas with drums and chants, and bridge worlds for those seeking lost loved ones. I had meditated with cacao for months, but only with Leah did I journey so deep, so vividly. She moved between realms like... well, like Jaguar.

Of course, he had licked her face. They were probably old friends.

ॐ · ℃

The next day was my first day back at The Local Grocer Café.

Within weeks, Paul quit, as I recounted in the previous story, and I became the Café's official chocolatier.

Was it the cardamom chocolate mousse spell, a lucky coincidence, or Jaguar? I'll never truly know. But I didn't believe in coincidences, and as Micah didn't like cardamom and refused to taste the mousse, I drew my own conclusion and, with hands together, sent my most heartfelt thank you to my guide.

That evening, in Micah's driveway, neighbors, friends, and their spoons gathered around the elegant glass and the last of the chocolate mousse to celebrate my new position.

"The thing is," I admitted, "I've never actually made chocolate before. I just know how to grind cacao beans and melt them in hot water."

"Don't worry about it." Lilly waved a hand dismissively. "I used to make the chocolate for the Café. I'll come by tomorrow morning and show you how."

I handed her the last bite of mousse. "Lilly. That would be so helpful! You're my savior!"

I climbed into the back of the Catmobile, parked in my usual spot next to the Maple tree, connected to Micah's Internet, and launched YouTube on my laptop.

How to make chocolate? Enter.

The art of transforming cacao beans into chocolate wasn't just a craft—it was pure alchemy. I had assumed chocolate melted in hot water, but no—it was a colloid, a delicate suspension of fine cacao particles. To create a smooth chocolate, the cacao had to be ground to the nanometer range in a specialized machine called a melanger—a process known as conching. During conching, the cacao's pH, oxidation levels, and, therefore, flavor profile morphed.

And that was just the beginning.

Then came tempering, the dark magic of chocolate-making. YouTube dropped me into a world of white-coated chefs debating molecular structures and crystalline formations, of heating, cooling, reheating of six different ways the polymorph cacao molecules could align, with only one—the elusive, self-organizing Beta V—responsible for the snap, sheen, and smoothness of proper chocolate.

Oh my!

The deeper I went, the more it became clear: chocolate-making was manipulating entropy, bending matter to will. There were four-year French culinary programs with entire semesters dedicated to tempering alone. I had one night, YouTube, and Lilly.

Eight o'clock arrived sooner than I wished. Armed with about six hours of YouTube knowledge and three hours of sleep, I donned my official brown apron and entered The Local Grocer Café's bakery section. Lilly had already prepped the essentials of my training and was waiting for me.

There were no cacao beans, no melanger. At The Local Grocer Café, chocolate was made from cacao butter and cacao powder: Melt the cacao butter and coconut oil, add and mix in the cacao powder, maple syrup, a little of this spice, a little of that extract, following the proprietary recipe, and *Voila!* Chocolate.

"What about tempering?" I asked Lilly.

"Oh, we don't do that. We only sell raw chocolates, so they stay in the fridge and don't need to be tempered. They do melt in the hand, but they have this yummy fudgy texture and all the benefits of raw chocolate. Customers love them!"

"But… then they don't have Beta V crystals."

"Ha!" Lilly laughed as she shouldered her pack. "Sounds like you already know more about chocolate than you need to work here." She placed a reassuring hand on my shoulder and leaned in as though to reveal the most important secret.

"Just have fun!" She grinned and walked away.

And just like that, I was left alone in the bakery.

I took a deep breath and looked around. No, I hadn't studied in a prestigious French culinary program, but Jaguar had said I'd become a chocolate maker, so I assumed some spiritual guidance would be offered. I pressed play on my favorite cacao music playlist, taped the recipe at eye level, and began making chocolate.

That first day, everything went smoothly. The cacao butter melted perfectly, the powder dissolved effortlessly, and the cacao mass turned silky, as homogeneous as if it had been conched in a melanger.

For practice, I decided to temper it. It would still be raw, I had read, as long as it stayed below 107 degrees. Sitting in the walk-in cooler, the bowl warm in my lap, I swirled the chocolate in slow figure-eights, pouring all my love for Cacao into the motion. At 82.4 degrees, I returned to the bakery, where, by pure luck, the ambient temperature held steady at a perfect 88.

The tempering worked on my first try, and I naively assumed this whole process wasn't as finicky as they made it sound.

"How's your first day?" Micah stepped behind me, peering over my shoulder into the bowl of chocolate.

"I think great. You want to try?"

He scooped a spoonful and tasted it. His eyes widened. "Oh my God, Bobcat. This is sooooo delicious. How did you make it taste so delicious? Did you use the same recipe?"

"Yes, but I played cacao music while I made it. It reminds the chocolate of its origin as a jungle bean."

Micah chuckled and nodded. "Of course you did."

That first day, I created ten flavors, all of them smooth, well-tempered, and delicious. Within days, the case was empty. I was ecstatic.

The following Thursday, I swaggered into the bakery like Ms. Wonka herself. I had spent all week dreaming up flavors—rum, coffee, chai, orange—recalling every chocolate I had ever loved. With the Café attached to the Local Grocer, I had access to almost endless shelves of spices and extracts. I was ready to create serious magic.

Jaguar might have thought I needed another dose of humility.

A couple drops of water landed into the cacao mass, and almost instantly, it seized, clumping into a thick paste-like mess. Scrambling to make a new batch, I raised the stove's flame to speed up the process. I blinked, and the cacao butter's temperature soared to 145 degrees. Too late for raw chocolate. I sprinkled in the cacao powder anyway, whisking furiously, but the mass remained stubbornly grainy. I swirled stressed figure eights in the walk-in cooler, but the bakery's temperature hovered at a stifling 92 degrees, melting my Beta Vs faster than I could create them. At last, with the clock speeding toward my due date, I admitted defeat and poured the best I had into molds.

By the end of that second day, there was chocolate on the floor, the walls, and my face; dishes piled high in the sink; and only four types of chocolates were presentable enough for the case.

That week, we sold "raw" chocolates stored in the fridge. The lie weighed on my conscience, but Thursday was over. The kitchen would not be mine again until the following week.

"It's alright." Micah leaned against the counter, unfazed. "You're just learning. You're gonna break a few eggs before you make an omelet."

He shrugged. "I'm not worried."

৪১ · ৫৪

There were three jaguars in Leah's living room.

The first was large, a male, I assumed. He circled my meditating body, each step as light as a shadow. The second, smaller, female, sat ten or so feet in front of me, paws together and back straight—regal and sovereign. Her eyes rested beyond Leah's sofa, gazing into another world, yet her focus remained on me. The third was a cub, acting like a cub. He bounded up the stairs and tumbled down again, spine as fluid as water. He ignored me entirely, yet his presence grounded me. He felt like the most powerful of the three.

As Jaguar continued to circle, sit, and tumble, layers of myself began falling away like extraneous skins—I was Woman, Storyteller, Scientist, Explorer, Adventurer, Friend... Off, one by one, discarded garments crumbled on the floor in a ring around me, on the path of Jaguar. Beyond all the layers, I floated, weightless in a timeless void, until a small flame flickered. I remembered the candle on the table. I was that flame—a flame surrounded by shed skins. The jaguars had left. I guessed they were responsible for the shedding, but why?

No answer was given.

Instead, I felt my Woman self wrap itself around the flame. Woman self—make chocolate gently, with a loving and soft feminine energy. The Explorer followed—make chocolate boldly. The mind mostly repeats patterns and recreates known flavors. Let the ingredients guide your imagination. The Storyteller—make chocolate that tells a tale. Lead the palate on a journey—salty to spicy, bitter to sweet, crunchy to smooth. Always finish with either the fire of lingering spice or the warmth of loving sweetness. The Scientist—

The scientist? I had studied geophysics. How could my Scientist self help with chocolate? Ah, yes, I saw... I had studied volcanology, including the chemistry of polymorph molecules. And I had studied glaciology and ice rheology.

339

Chocolate, like ice, was a viscous mass with temperature-dependent structures.

It all connected.

Seriously, how long had I been primed to become a chocolate maker? How far back in time could Jaguar reach? I had not studied in a four-year French program. No. Instead, I had collected random skills my whole life that all culminated now—in Chocolate.

The jaguar cub tumbled down the stairs again and landed in front of me, golden eyes gleaming.

He looked up at me, head tilted, and without a sound, I felt his laughter.

"Hey… don't take yourself so seriously."

Then he was gone.

వ్ · ૪

July 2020, my first month as a chocolatier at The Local Grocer Café, remains a highlight of my life. I woke up every day thrilled to be alive. In the mornings, I walked through my woods, welcomed as one of their own, trading stories with pine scent and swaying leaves. Then, all day and all night, I dreamed in chocolate. Everything I saw, everyone I met, every dish I tasted became inspiration for a new creation. On Thursdays, I sat in the walk-in cooler, bowl on my lap, swirling chocolate in slow figure-eights, singing cacao songs, fully in love.

Slowly, from the small corner of the bakery case to which chocolate had once been relegated, we took over. One shelf, then another, until the entire case was filled with strange and delightful flavors—coffee and star anise, chipotle and goji berries, fresh basil and mountain rose, turmeric golden milk, and my favorite: the four-Cs with cayenne, chipotle, cinnamon, and cardamom. The four-Cs told such a layered, complex story.

Every week, new chocolate flavors flew off the shelves faster than I could invent them.

"You are glowing!" Leah often said when we met for our cacao meditations.

I believed it. I lived in a state of passion, and it suited me well.

But on August 4th, a swift windstorm tore through town, knocking down several trees. Leah and I stood by her kitchen window, watching the trees sway. She lifted her hands toward the storm, incanting spells of protection I trusted. The Catmobile was safe in her driveway, and I was safe in her house. In town, not far from where the Catmobile and I usually spent the night, a tree fell on a house. Micah's mother was in that house, exactly in the path of the fall. She died instantly.

Our little community was deeply shaken. In the aftermath, friends and coworkers stepped forward to cover Micah's shifts and responsibilities at the Café and support him emotionally while he grieved. None of us took a day off for the entire month of August.

On Thursdays in August, I woke at dawn, worked a few hours at the farm, then rushed to the bakery to make chocolate as quickly as possible before covering the Café's closing shift.

Every night, I returned to the Catmobile, exhausted, with no aspiration but to rest. Gone were the days of whimsically strolling through the aisles of The Local Grocer, listening for the call of special ingredients. Gone were creativity, stamina, and joy.

At the peak of tourist season, only the essential best-sellers filled the case.

Yet, none of us complained. We worked, we supported each other, we carried what we could.

On September 4th, three days before my fiftieth birthday, I sat cross-legged on my meditation cushion in Leah's living room. This was our first meditation since the windstorm. My mind felt thick with fatigue, and my heart was restless—like a loaded paintbrush, itching to smear itself across any open space.

"I don't get it." I exhaled sharply. "I sent Ancel an email, a Facebook message, an Instagram message—nothing. I even tried calling. Nobody answers. Maybe Jaguar didn't lead me to Ancel. Maybe I was just high on mushrooms and saw what I wanted to see. Maybe I misunderstood. He said I'd be back 'here,' but he didn't say Costa Rica. How big is 'here'? Maybe he meant anywhere in Central or South America... Or maybe I imagined the whole thing. Leah, what if there isn't a jaguar?"

Leah smiled and continued shuffling the deck of oracle cards.

"Why don't you ask?" She held the deck out to me.

I hesitated, then pulled a card at random.

Leah pulled a card for herself. "And don't you make chocolate already?"

"It's not the same. I'm not working with cacao beans. At the Grocer, I'm a chocolatier, not a chocolate maker. There's a difference."

I flipped my card over. *Pachamama*. At its center, a dark-skinned woman with jaguar spots smiled. Above her head, Jaguar rested—watching me.

೮ · ೞ

She was back, but alone.

The female Jaguar sat, again, ten or so feet in front of me, paws together, back straight, eyes fixed beyond Leah. I waited for her to move, to signal, to beckon. She remained still. Her chest moved with each slow breath, steadily, effortlessly.

Was she waiting for me? Maybe I wasn't still enough. I exhaled slowly, settling deeper, mirroring her posture as I had done when the male Jaguar had first returned. She remained motionless, poised as a statue.

Wasn't she going to lead me somewhere? What was I not seeing? My fingers flexed slightly, then curled into my palms. I was right there, fully present, ready for the next imminent step.

Tic. Tic. Tic. Leah's clock on the wall dragged each minute forward. A hint of a cramp tightened my thigh. I shifted ever so slightly to free my leg from the cushion.

A low growl rumbled through my mind. I stiffened and snapped my leg back into lotus position. Alright, she wanted me to wait.

Tic. Tic. Tic. My legs fell asleep. Armies of marching ants tortured my ankles and knees. I ignored them. The pulse of my heartbeat oscillated my upper torso. This was the only movement she allowed. If I moved at all, if my mind wandered at all, she either growled or turned her stare toward me until I was still again.

The longer I sat, the more restlessness stirred beneath my skin—an itch to go, to move forward, to be done with this. This was my meditation, after all. I could move if I wanted, couldn't I?

My jaw clenched, fighting the creeping impulses of impatience, but curiosity still was greater. Alright, I would wait. I recalibrated my focus, shifting all my attention to her steady presence, searching for a sign, an unspoken cue. I felt into her energy, the way I had learned when speaking with trees. But all I perceived was the effortless rhythm of her presence, the way she filled space without pressing against it. She wasn't waiting; she was being. And in her stillness, she revealed how unstill I was. Stillness wasn't forced waiting; it was wholehearted surrender. I understood.

She blinked slowly. Her energy softened.

She stretched, turned, and unhurriedly walked back into the jungle. But just before she vanished, she glanced back. Her gaze met mine, and her wordless download filled my mind.

"Stay on the branch, just as I taught you. Wait for the right prey. Conserve your energy. Don't jump off to chase

343

meaningless squirrels. Wait for the right prey. You will know when it's time for action. Stay on the branch until then."

In my mind's eye, a vision appeared—Jaguar, draped across a thick branch, eyes half-closed, tail swaying. Watching. Being.

Leah giggled, and the vision dissolved.

I was back. The *Pachamama* oracle card and my empty cacao mug rested before me, as though they, too, understood the stillness beyond waiting.

Leah stretched, pressing her palms into the sofa to lift herself.

"Well, did you get some answers?" she asked.

I shrugged. "I think so… I'm just not sure what it all meant."

‽ · ‘ϓ

September flew by and straight into fall. The days shortened. The leaves changed wardrobe. Micah returned to The Local Grocer, and I settled into a lighter part-time schedule—one day at the farm, one as a chocolatier, weekends as a barista, and the rest roaming the Whites with my backpack.

I also began training Dave, our resident baker, in chocolate-making, so that when the cold chased me south— which loomed closer every day—The Local Grocer wouldn't be left chocolateless.

On farm days, I arrived early to meet Farmer Russ and receive my instructions for the day—weed in the tomato greenhouse, harvest beans, pick raspberries, whatever was most needed. Then, Farmer Russ left to tend to other work, and I was delightfully left alone with the plants for the remainder of the day.

Of all the farm tasks, harvesting basil in the greenhouse was my favorite.

I moved the upturned bucket to the next plant and carefully pinched off the stem right above the nascent leaves. Instantly, the basil's flowery fragrance filled the greenhouse. My fingers pinched another branch, and another, letting the little leaves grow for another round.

My fingers worked, but my mind explored. That day, it was a podcast, *The Mushroom Hour*, with guest Oliver of the Fungi Academy.

I had chosen this podcast because Oliver had a kind voice filled with a spark for life. I moved the bucket over. Next plant. Oliver's early life, born in Estonia, starting with nothing, then bravely leaving everything behind to discover the world. Next plant. His healing journey with magic mushrooms. Next plant. Lake Atitlan, Guatemala, the creation of the Fungi Academy, the sharing of the magic, the birth of a community—with classes and long-term residency. Next plant. Whoa! Oliver was also a chocolate maker. Chocolate-making was part of the Fungi Academy curriculum... Magic mushrooms and chocolate in one place?

My heart picked up speed. A rumbling of excitement... Guatemala?

I stopped mid-pinch, basil leaves trembling between my fingers. But... what about Ancel's Farm? I tried to picture myself in Costa Rica, deep in the moist heat of the jungle womb. The image didn't quite land. But Lake Atitlan? It spoke of eagles, lake shores, volcanoes... and they even had mushrooms. Jaguar had said I'd be back "here." Did he mean "here" as in this rush of excitement? The thrill of the path revealed? He'd said I'd study cacao and become a chocolate maker. Ancel had not answered, and here was a real school with a chocolate-making curriculum.

There were no bigger prey I could see from my branch.

That same day, I sent the Fungi Academy a message and filled out the application for residency. We exchanged a few emails. It was immediately apparent to both that I was a perfect fit for the Academy, and they for me, but Guatemala's borders were still closed due to COVID restrictions. We agreed to chat again as soon as the borders reopened to iron out the details of my internship.

I was off the branch and running straight to Guatemala in my mind.

ঙ · 03

I poured hot water over the cacao in our mugs while the Catmobile waited in the driveway, packed and ready.

"I've saved all my tips this summer, and with selling New Year's fireworks for Aaron in Florida in a couple of weeks, I'll have a nice cushion to land in Guatemala. I should be able to live well for the first few months. And by then, I'll know how to make chocolate—maybe even turn it into a living! Wow. It's happening, Leah! I'm going to be a chocolate maker!"

I left our mugs on the counter and spun into a little jig of joy around the kitchen island. Leah laughed.

"That's wonderful, Maya! Wonderful!"

We carried our mugs to the living room and arranged ourselves with pillows, cards, and a candle as we always did. Leah nestled into the sofa, settling in for what would likely be another wild, multidimensional journey with cacao.

This was our last meditation together—for how long? Who knew? Six months, two years, forever? I took it all in: Leah's slight frame, her curly, purple-silver hair, the spark of mischief in her blue eyes, the flickering candle, the well-worn deck of cards in her hands. How lucky was I to have such kind and powerful friends? A tear slipped down my cheek. I smiled silently. Words would have been inadequate. We drank our cacao and closed our eyes.

Leah's mind soared as always—that day, she might have met dolphins, grown flowers, or touched a star. I sat quietly on my pillow. No Jaguar, no vines, no message, no lesson. Just the rhythmic *tic, tic, tic* of the clock upstairs and the sweet nectar of a shared moment. I already knew I was going to Guatemala. No further revelations were needed. I rested on my metaphorical branch, gratefully aware of how far I had come so quickly and excited for the next step of the journey.

Leah stirred, signaling the end of our meditation. She giggled as always, traced glyphs through the air with her fingers—*Shhhht, shhhht, ffbhh*—then rested her hands in a heart shape in her lap.

Through the window behind her, the first snowflakes floated down softly.

It was time for me to fly south.

Chapter 26
The Frog That Erased It All

Daytona Beach, Florida, January 2021

Infinity swiftly moved his right crutch to his left hand, pushed the heavy wooden door open, slipped both crutches back into the appropriate hands, and led us across the red entryway.

We were a sight, the three of us. Infinity, our leader in this adventure, was—and still is—a one-legged living art piece. Approximately eighty percent of his body is tattooed, including his shaved head and face, with tribal markings on his cheeks and nose and a repeating fractal pattern on his first eye—as he calls it—in the middle of his forehead. I followed close behind, elongating my gait and flipping my long dreadlocks to appear more confident than I felt for the sake of the worried little sister behind me. Flora, the last to go through the entryway, was a petite Indian woman with a shy smile and large brown eyes framed by impossibly long eyelashes. She was merely twenty-one at the time—fifteen years younger than Infinity and thirty years younger than me. She had met Infinity a week before and me only the day before. Yet, we had connected instantly. She had trusted me with stories of her turbulent childhood, and I had embraced her as soul family.

We crossed the living room toward a back door, as instructed. We passed a large round bed with red pillows and silk fabrics pretending to look appealing. Across from it, a tall tapestry of an Indian deity mounting another in sexual rapture covered the entire wall. I didn't have time to notice much else before we reached the next door. My chest constricted. I already disliked the energy of the place. Was it too late to back out?

We passed the next door and crossed a small room with beds, a computer, and some blood-drawing equipment. Before I had time to turn around, we were out in the backyard, where the ceremonies took place.

As I became more experienced with sacred medicines, I learned that it should never be a decision to partake nor a curiosity to satisfy but always an undeniable call from the medicine itself. Had Kambo actually called me? All these years later, I'm still not sure.

At the time, my wallet was comfortably padded from selling fireworks in Tampa—enough for a flight to Guatemala and tuition at the Fungi Academy. I was physically exhausted and needed a quiet place to park the Catmobile and rest for a few days. My friend Infinity had just arrived from Sedona and was staying at a friend's house by a peaceful lake in the Ocala forest.

"Come and rest here. There's everything we need—a free house, a pantry filled with food, woods to play in, a lake to swim in. It's heaven here. You'll fucking love it!" He concluded his offer with his signature little giggle, and there was nothing else to discuss.

When I arrived at the lake house, Infinity had already met the Frog once. A row of four burnt dots lined his upper arm, right down the axis of a tattooed pyramid.

"It's incredible! You have to try it. You both have to try it. It's safe. I just did it. And I'm going back on Monday for round two, and maybe three."

The sparks of enthusiasm in Infinity's eyes were contagious. Flora and I glanced at each other, smiled, then nodded.

"Okay, why not. We're in."

The Maestro of the ceremony was lying in a hammock next to a small jacuzzi when we exited the house into the courtyard. He lifted himself upright and gave Infinity a brotherly bear hug. As he hugged Infinity, our eyes locked. A look of surprise flashed across his face.

Infinity turned to the outdoor kitchen to greet the man's partner. The man and I were left face to face. We stared at each other for a moment, smiling.

"Do I know you?" We spoke in sync, then laughed as we realized our matching words. I was almost certain I had never met these intense gray eyes or these graying, bouncy brown curls before. Yet, as a whole, the Maestro felt deeply familiar.

"Must be in a past life, I guess." I shrugged and turned toward the kitchen to hide my immediate attraction to the man.

I approached the kitchen and casually climbed onto a stool, peering over the counter at the contents of the pot on the stove. The aroma was Italian, rich, and grounding.

"Hi. You must be Elizabeth. Infinity has told me wonders about your cooking."

"Thanks." Her shoulder-length hair was pulled back in a ponytail. It seemed to pull on her eyes and lips, narrowing them as she stared at me.

"I'm John's partner." She pointed toward the man with her chin—Ha! So, that was the look.

"Yes, Infinity told me, and you're part of the ceremony too, right?"

"I'm a trained blood chemist. I take blood before and after the ceremony so we have physical proof of the efficacy of the medicine. It's an additional $100 if you want your blood analyzed."

"Hah. Interesting. I'm confident my blood's clean, but that's wonderful you can do that."

"I also help with the ceremony. I specialize in physiognomy. I can read people's personalities and traumas by looking at their facial features." She enunciated "phy-sio-gno-my" carefully. "This helps us support our guests with the healing needed."

Her eyes widened slightly, and she lifted her shoulders from her cooking stance, standing squarely to face me—ladle still in hand, gaze locked onto my face.

"Are you reading me right now?"

"Yes. I mean, I can... You are… needy. And a masochist."

Needy? Masochist? What? If I'd had fur at that moment, it would have bristled. But all I had were words and a casual tone.

"Mmh, I guess physiognomy must not be an exact science then. I am the opposite of needy. I am self-sufficient to a fault."

"Yes. That's a common counter-reaction to neediness. The person fears their neediness to be seen and judged, so they take on airs of not caring. It's very common."

Infinity, who had been greeting the cats and dogs on the property, returned just in time to halt the runaway conversation.

Half an hour later, the image of Flora's blood cells floated peacefully on the computer screen in the little room. Elizabeth outlined certain cells with the back of her pencil. Here were toxins, and there were clumped cells where they should have been evenly distributed. She then tilted her head to the side, looked at the screen, and turned back to Flora.

"Did you have a violent childhood?" Flora froze, and the question hung. I began to cry. Was I crying for me, for Flora? I didn't know why but wished I wasn't—not in front of Elizabeth anyway.

351

"Mmmh." Elizabeth looked at my tears and nodded in agreement with an unspoken thought. Flora remained frozen, so, eventually, Elizabeth placed her hand on Flora's knee. Both women's faces softened.

"It's okay, Flora. You only answer if you feel comfortable. Whatever it is, with intention, Kambo can help you clear it."

Hop hop hopping in on one leg, Infinity came through the door.

"We're ready to go. Everything's ready. Come on! Let's meet the Frog!" He gave a pirouette and gestured for us to follow him. I laughed at his antics, wiped my tears, and followed the hopping friend back to the courtyard.

In the courtyard, two rows of pillows and white buckets awaited the guests. On a small table, a paua shell held a smoking sage bundle, next to a fan of feathers, vials with cork lids, and two narrow bamboo pipes, one with a forty-degree elbow, the other straight. Infinity, Flora, and I, each in turn, stood in the purifying sage smoke fanned by the feathers, then joined the two other guests—a man and a woman—who had arrived while we had been in the blood-drawing room.

"Welcome, everyone!" John took one of the vials in his hand, wrapped his fingers around it, brought it to his heart, and closed his eyes. We all fell silent. When he inhaled, we followed his inhale. When he exhaled, we followed, each with a long sigh—Aaahhhh.

"I honor this medicine and the lineage by which it came to me, with gratitude for the healing I have witnessed. May my hand be guided by the ancestors in the tradition. I now invite you to join me in ceremony with an open mind and an open heart. Leave your expectations behind. Trust that Kambo knows what you need."

John then recounted the story of Kambo, as it had been told to him when he trained with his Maestro in the Amazon jungle.

A long time ago, deep in the jungle, a respected shaman was led into the forest by the Grandmother vine, Ayahuasca. His people were sick, and it was his responsibility to find a cure. The plant led the shaman to a river, to a frog in the river. The plant instructed the shaman how to collect the frog's poisonous secretions without hurting the frog. The plant then granted the shaman a vision of how to apply the poison on a small burn—called a "gate"—on the human skin so that it might enter the body to detoxify, purify, and restore it to optimum health. The shaman thus cured the village.

This is still how the medicine is served.

"May I serve you Rapé (pronounced Hapé)?" John knelt in front of me with an open vial and one of the narrow bamboo pipes.

"Sure. What is it?"

"It's a powdered ceremonial tobacco—Mapacho—one of the master plants. It purifies the body and spirit of negative energies. I will blow the Rapé into one nostril, then the other. Inhale, exhale, inhale again, then hold your breath for the count of three as I blow."

I breathed in slowly to calm my nervous heart and looked John in the eyes. He smiled and nodded. He poured a small mound of tobacco into the palm of his hand, scooped half of it with the end of the pipe, then approached my face.

Pppffff. A raspy, acrid taste burst into my right nostril, up to my eyeball, to the back of my skull, and down my throat. I held my breath for the count of two, but my body coughed the taste before I reached three. I spat brown saliva in the white bucket next to me and heaved a few times. I spat again and looked at John with my non-tobaccoed eye. "Did we really have to do both sides?" I asked without a word. But John had already reloaded and was approaching my face again. *Ppppff.* The taste was just as harsh on the left side, but already, a sensation of cool, white peace permeated my right side. The sensation spread until it filled my whole head, extended above my head, and descended into my heart. The group, John, Elizabeth, the dogs and cats faded. All I felt was the energetic equivalent of fresh, soothing, clear mint inside and around me. I sat in lotus position, eyes closed, soaking in the delight of the sensation until it dissipated. Even as it left, I still felt cool, calm, collected, and ready for whatever came next.

Next was Sananga.

John explained that Sananga came from an Amazonian vine. Its potent extract was traditionally used as eye drops to sharpen vision—enhancing contrast, deepening colors, and heightening the perception of movement. Many Amazonian hunters still relied on it before setting out into the jungle. It also cleared dark energies, making it an essential part of the ceremony.

I lay my head on the pillow, tilting back to receive the medicine, then turned to the side to watch the process, starting with Infinity. Two drops. He opened his eyes, and his body began writhing with pain. "Aaaah," he moaned through his teeth, pounding fists on the mat and kicking his one leg up in the air. Flora was next. Two drops, and she, too, moaned and writhed. She pressed her hands against her eyes and rolled back and forth onto her back. Elizabeth knelt in front of my face.

"Is it necessary?" I asked.

"It only lasts thirty seconds." It was Infinity who answered, breathlessly. He was already on the other side. "It's worth it, Bobcat. Try it."

"You are not obligated to anything." Elizabeth waited, eye dropper in hand, ready to either retract or advance.

"It's okay. I'll try." I closed my eyes. One cold drop landed in the inside corner. Another cold drop in the other inside corner.

"You can open now," Elizabeth said. And I did. Then immediately closed them again.

Pain—there was nothing else. Pain of such a magnitude that I couldn't move, breathe, think, or understand. The torture was so intense that I remained absolutely still and silent, lost in the agony of the moment.

And then the moment was done. I gasped and opened my cleared eyes. Infinity had sat up to watch my reaction. I blinked a few times and turned to look at him. His blue shirt did seem bluer, and his outline crisper. He giggled and rolled back down.

Finally, it was time to meet the Frog.

The next day, John admitted that he had incorrectly assumed I was a person of high tolerance to medicines, as I had, by outward appearances, little reaction to the Rapé and Sananga. In fact, I was so sensitive that I had been unable to move—not in the rapture of Rapé's fresh coolness nor in the excruciating pain of Sananga. Two gates would probably have sufficed. I received four.

The small stick burned my skin, and the little scoop applied the frog's poison to the wounds. Then we waited, and drank water—a *lot* of water.

"Everybody, drink as much water as you can so the toxins released by the medicine can get flushed out." A voice drifted in. Who had spoken? My head was swimming. A woman sat next to me. I thought it might be Elizabeth, but she looked different. Oh, I was fading fast. I was vaguely aware of a worried look on my face. Someone gently took my hand.

"Are you drinking water?" I understood the question but had no control over my arms or hands to find the bottle. My body was so heavy. It leaned as if it were about to fall. Another gentle hand pressed against my back. The touch was comforting but not sufficient to keep me upright. I was collapsing, dizzy, nauseated. Who was that again, next to me? Retching and vomiting sounds surrounded me. Ha, yes, the ceremony—a murky memory—there were other people here, all vomiting in buckets. My back slumped onto the mat. The hand was gone. The blurry world narrowed, and I, too, was gone.

When I opened my eyes again, I was curled in the fetal position. A warm blanket had been placed over me. I felt peaceful, clear-headed, with no trace of the medicine left in me. Behind me, people were still vomiting in buckets.

I sat up to take in the scene and briefly scanned myself. Whatever experience my body had with Kambo, I had missed it. Down the line of buckets, four human frogs still emptied their watery entrails with body convulsions. It was not a hallucination. They looked like frogs. Their lips were huge, the skin under their eyes swollen, their cheeks puffy. They sat above their buckets, arms on each side, holding themselves up. I checked my cheeks with my hand, pinched my lips, and patted under my eyes. My skin seemed flat. I didn't look like a frog. I had skipped even that.

"Frog Sleep," Elizabeth explained. "It's rare, but it does happen. Basically, Kambo does such an upgrade that the human needs to be moved out of the way … You fainted, in other words."

Elizabeth poured soup into our bowls as the group sat around a large wooden table that evening. With rehydration, the human frogs had regained their normal appearances. Everyone was hungry. Everyone had stories.

"I used to be a hard-core alcoholic and drug user." The man to my right turned toward me. He was a professional bodybuilder with a gentle demeanor. "Kambo cleared all that. Now I come back just for maintenance, but I've been five years sober. And I have no cravings at all."

"Same for me." The woman across from me said in a thick Russian accent. "Kambo saved my life. I was going very bad path with cocaine before I come here."

Infinity tore off pieces of flatbread, dipping them into his soup. "Wow. Good for you both!" He turned to John, "Say, John, I was thinking—could I try just one gate tomorrow so I can feel the medicine without the purging?"

"Of course." John nodded. I looked at him. He looked so… ordinary, whereas he had seemed so handsome before

356

the ceremony. And Elizabeth—she was pretty, casual pretty. I no longer felt upset that she had called me needy and a masochist.

"I won't do another ceremony," Flora stated bluntly. "I'm going home." Her blood results didn't show much improvement from the initial sample. The only thing that changed was her sudden desire to return to winter in the Great North, whence she came. Just that morning, she had told us there was no way she'd return there; she was spending the winter in Florida, and that was that. She left early the next morning. Neither Infinity nor I ever heard from Flora again.

"I'm done too." My tone was flat. My heart simply said no. No Rapé. No Sananga. No Kambo. No, thank you.

℘ · ℭ

Ocala Forest, Florida, January 2021

Once Infinity had met the Frog on a one-gate journey, we returned to the house by the lake in the Ocala forest. For the following four days, I slept an average of eighteen hours a day. I didn't question it, nor argue with my body about it. It needed rest, so I only ate and slept. Then, for the next three days after that, I slept twelve hours a night, walked around the lake, and sat quietly on logs.

After a week, my physical body felt renewed, my mind crystalline clear, but my spirit was vacant—my "I"dentity erased. I knew my name—my many names—but who was that? Who was Melissa? Who did she wish to be? Did The Bobcat still enjoy living in her truck? Did Maya actually care about studying Cacao? Did any part of me want to travel to Guatemala? Or travel at all? And if I didn't want to travel, what did I want? Nothing. Nada. Blank.

I sat cross-legged, perched on a log above the lake, and whispered,

357

"Who am I? Who am I? Am I this body sitting here?" I cringed—what if I was just this mundane body sitting here? "Am I spirit choosing to have a human experience?" I shook my head—and do what with it? There was no fog in my mind. I perceived with complete clarity that I knew nothing.

I sat cross-legged in the Catmobile and wrote in my journal,

"Who am I? Last known place of contact with Aliveness —> Cacao. Jaguar."

I boiled water on my camping stove on the tailgate, poured it over ground cacao beans, and held the small mug in my hands as I had so many times.

"Mama Cacao, Jaguar, please, guide me again." The brew physically warmed my heart but offered no existential answer. There was no hint that there ever had been or ever would be a Jaguar.

"Infinity, I think the Frog erased me."

"Fuck yeah! That's awesome" Infinity had returned from Kambo filled with inspiration, dreams, and travel plans. My jaw clenched. No, it wasn't awesome. That damn Frog had erased my Jaguar. And Infinity couldn't understand. He lived by the seat of his pants. He lived in his truck most of the time, with no address, no destination, no purpose… like me. That was it, wasn't it? Without Jaguar, without Cacao, without a greater purpose to my life, I was just a rudderless, homeless, fifty-year-old woman with nothing in life but a truck.

"Leah, the Frog erased my Jaguar." I erupted in sobs. Tears streamed down my cheeks as I snorted loudly. Snot and tears covered my phone. Leah waited until a break in the woeful cataclysm.

"I don't think that's the case, Maya." I couldn't see her, but I imagined her sitting in her big chair in the temple-house, moving her hands in the Ether, gathering information.

"How do you know?" I sniffled.

"Because I can see your Jaguar. He's on a branch. He's waiting for you to come back. And…" She was silent for a moment, and in that pause, a memory stirred—a meditation in her living room, just a few months prior. *Stay on the branch.* Jaguar had used those exact words. I had never shared that with Leah, yet here she was, speaking them now. It couldn't be just a coincidence. My heart settled, just a little.

"…what I sense is that Frog and Jaguar are working together. They're in cahoots. You're still being guided, and this was a necessary next step on your journey."

"Okay." I sighed as I wiped the tears off my cheeks with the back of my hands. "Okay."

For the next few days, Leah's words kept me afloat, a life raft in the sea of no-self. Until, finally, on the morning of January 12th, a small crack opened in the void.

"Bobcat! Do you want to walk across the Big Cypress Preserve with Elijah and me?"

My eyes drifted from Aaron's message to the placid lake. In the early morning, a wispy white fog still covered its surface.

"How about that? An adventure just landed in my lap," I said calmly to the lake. Now, historically, such an offer would have ignited my heart and made me jump for joy with a resounding "yes". I tilted my head to see the lake sideways. A different perspective. How odd, I wasn't sure what to say, yet I watched my finger press the small phone icon next to his message.

"Hi Aaron… so, Big Cypress… hmm… Maybe I do? What is it? What's the plan?"

"Oh, you know, just a breezy forty miles of swamp walking with alligators and snakes. Just the wildest and most remote section of the Florida Trail. But it'll be fine. Absolutely fine, Bobcat. Everything'll be just fine."

"That's a lot of 'it'll be fine,' Aaron. Are you trying to convince yourself?" I laughed.

"Look—Elijah and I are going. And you need to come…
Come on! You'll have fun. You've done crazier things, right?
And I'm sure the swamp water isn't that cold, practically
almost lukewarm. Tell you what, I'll let you pick first camp on
the islands and personally serenade mice to our tent, away
from yours. What do you say? Come on!"

"Okay, okay, Mister. Hold your horses. Give me a
second."

I shut my eyes and listened to my heart. Although Frog
had erased even my wildness, a faint feeling urged me to say
yes, and, slowly, a smile appeared on my face. The truth was,
walking in swamps with Aaron and alligators seemed almost
saner than sulking by a lake about the loss of a jaguar to a
frog.

"Alright, Aaron. Let's do it! I'll meet you in the
Everglades. I can be there by tonight. But if you've lied and
the water is cold, I'm turning around, and you'll be the only
alligator chum."

∟ · ∞

Big Cypress Preserve, Florida Trail, January 2021

"I'm not a masochist!" My voice echoed through the
towering cypresses as I thrust my thighs through the almost
lukewarm, murky water.

"Sure, Bobcat… And I bet you're not needy either."
Aaron's yell floated back from twenty feet ahead. In the
leader position, he walked through clear water, easily avoiding
fallen trunks, roots, rocks, and sunken holes. But with each
step, his waterlogged shoes churned up the bottom mud,
creating a six-foot wide corridor of swirling opaque swamp
for Elijah and me.

"I think I should lead, Pikachu. Clearly, you're distracted
up there, judgment clouded by too much sarcasm. You might
miss a snake—again."

Elijah giggled. His tall, lanky teenage body parted the swamp water, kicking up yet more mud into my path.

"I'm focused, Bobcat. No danger noodles here."

"Danger noodles" was Aaron's term for venomous snakes, a name he had coined on day two, when we all almost stepped on a cottonmouth. Elijah chuckled—he laughed at all his dad's bad jokes.

"Oh, right... like you said there weren't any alligators right before one *hissed* at me? Or like you said there weren't any mice on the island right before one chewed a hole through my tent? Lies, Pikachu, all your words are lies."

This time, Elijah laughed out loud and turned toward me. I smiled and winked at him.

Swamp walking required physical strength and stamina of the spirit. We pushed on in knee-high currents, past exhaustion, soreness, and sometimes sunset, to the next island, the next camp for the night.

This I had expected. The surprise was the sheer delight in the experience.

With each step, water flowed through the mesh of my trail-running shoes, rhythmically massaging and enlivening my toes, soles, and heels. I imagined the Swamp herself gifted us this cooling current that pulsed like deliberate caresses. Maybe she was saying, "Thank you!" "Thank you for your unwavering commitment to meet me, far from boardwalks and visitor centers, in my most wild and pristine state."

Within a couple of days, we became adept swamp dancers. We mastered the slip-sliding mud shuffle, trusting our hiking poles to keep us upright and dry. We followed the current, contouring the cypresses' colossal feet and the mangroves' elevated roots. Occasionally, we ascended to dry ground, traversed grassy prairies, snacked, and napped in the shade of oaks and palm trees. And all throughout, our laughter rippled upward and over the swamp's surface, causing alligators to dive under, storks to scatter, and even the short-tailed hawk to forsake its hunting perch.

We walked and laughed, and not once did I wonder who I was. What I wanted was simple: safe passage during the days and dry ground for the nights. I forgot about Frog, Cacao, even Jaguar. Until one day, as if following an unseen current in the swamp, I veered off the main mud path behind Aaron and Elijah and stumbled upon a hidden glade among the cypresses.

I stood in its tranquil water and looked up to the ring of air plants right above my eye level. There, resting on a throne of green moss, her delicate roots wrapped around a trunk in intimate embrace, sat the most exquisite of them all—a white ghost orchid.

I approached her pale petals slowly, jaw agape and eyes wide. How could anything so fragile and small be so resilient and adaptable? How could one blossom shake one's soul more than miles of pristine wilderness? If Nature was my church, this flower was one of its patron saints. In a split-second sacred moment, I found myself mirrored, the portrait of my personality unveiled anew.

I recognized that each decision I had made with curious excitement—from choosing to learn to talk to trees, to walking long trails, flying to Costa Rica for Envision, and crossing the red room that led to the courtyard where I had met the Frog—was part of a continuum. That continuum was the path. How did I know? Because it had led me, exactly, to this white orchid.

I realized I had abdicated my decision-making process to Jaguar. Following a guru, even one as wise and powerful as Jaguar, had never been my style. I was not an orchid in potted soil on a windowsill. And so Frog asked, "If it wasn't for Jaguar, would you study Cacao? Without step-by-step guidance, would you fly to Guatemala? What would *you* decide? Let's find out…"

"Okay. So… you saw the white orchid, and that's how you knew that the frog erased the jaguar so that you could choose to decide to study cacao again. Did I get that right?"

Aaron rolled to his side to face me, propped his body on one elbow, and raised an eyebrow. Only two miles separated us from the terminus parking lot, but none of us wished for the trail to end, so we lingered in the grass, eating any remaining snacks in our food bags and recounting our favorite swamp moments.

"Yeah. I mean, when you say it like that it does sound strange…"

"No, Bobcat, not strange at all." Aaron turned to Elijah and silently mouthed "very strange" while twirling a finger by his temple.

I threw my apple at Aaron, and our laughter once more rose, disturbing the hunting hawk for the last time for this journey.

‽ · ℭ

Pensacola, Florida, January 2021

"Welcome, dear friend." Jeannie waltzed across the living room to greet me, her long gown floating behind her. I pushed the mosquito screen and stepped in just in time to fall into her embrace.

"I was expecting you two days ago. My, I was starting to worry."

"I know. I'm sorry, I didn't have cell reception. I just fell in love with the Everglades. Jeannie, it was incredible! I was already driving here, but I didn't want to leave, so I turned around and went back and camped two nights in the Long Pine Key Campground, where I didn't have cell reception. But, well, now here I am!"

"Aah am glad. And how long do I have you this time?" She pushed the screen door closed before the mosquitoes could follow me in.

"Well, I need to send a message to the Fungi Academy to confirm they have room for me, but I'm thinking max a week. And thanks, Jeannie, so much, for keeping the Catmobile again while I'm gone."

"Mah home is your home. Tell you what, why don't you freshen up? I've got a clean towel ready in the shower for you, and I'll fix us supper. Sushi bowl? Raw salmon and spicy boiled shrimps?" The twinkle in her eyes was almost suggestive, but I knew to read pride in it—she had once again surprised me with all my favorite fixins.

While Jeannie left for the kitchen, I dropped my tired body on the sofa beside sweet Sadie Sue, the fourteen-year-old beagle.

"Sadie! Do you know I'm going to Guatemala?" Her droopy eyes lifted, and I petted her head. "Yes, it's true... look!" With Sadie Sue's mild interest spurring me on, I opened my email on my phone and sent the Fungi Academy this message:

"Hola! Do you remember me? We spoke last September and agreed to speak again when the borders reopen. I included our emails below, it's easier that way. The borders are open. Coming to you is still my plan and dream. Are you hosting residents again? My backpack is ready. Let's talk!

With gratitude for and trust in whatever might come,

I hope to hear from you soon.

Mush(room) love - Maya."

In that moment, the path was once again so clear that the smell of Lake Atitlan's shore was as real as that of the spicy boiled shrimps drifting from Jeannie's kitchen. And, as I had still a few minutes before supper was ready, with a heart beating fast with excitement and eyes filled with the gratitude of dreams about to come true, I opened the Fungi Academy's website.

Closed.

The impossible word glared at me. The Fungi Academy was closed.

The following announcement appeared on the front page:

"Oliver, Brother, Lover, Healer, Leader, Visionary, and Founder of the Fungi Academy tragically fell to his death in the early morning of the 25th of December. He hit his head on a rock, whereafter he died in the Lake he held so close to his heart and soul …"

The message continued, but I couldn't read on. My heart constricted. I had just lost a best friend I hadn't even been granted a chance to meet. And an entire community who could have become family was in pain, grieving. At least the void of the Frog had been neutral. This was a next-level dream destruction: one life-changing human eclipsed in an instant, and hundreds of paths, mine included, suddenly left dangling in shock.

I grieved the death of Oliver as I would a close friend. I honored his loss by letting the severed path dangle for a few days. I made no attempt to reroute.

Jeannie had work to keep my hands, if not my mind, occupied for a few days. With a heavy heart and frequent tears, I dismantled her old patio furniture, hauled the rusty pieces to the curb, pressure-washed the outdoor rugs, and set up new shade.

As I worked, I imagined Frog's beady slit eyes on me, his green leathery skin almost luminescent in the dark jungle. "So what now? There is no Guatemala. Will you still choose to study Cacao?" And I knew the answer was "Yes!"

I would study Cacao no matter what. And as I was no longer traveling to Guatemala, and no other teacher had stepped forward, I would do it myself with YouTube, just as I had when I became a chocolatier at The Local Grocer Café. I bought a melanger on eBay and had it shipped from India to Jeannie's door. I found a cacao bean supplier in Eugene,

Oregon, and ordered half a pound from each of six countries to test and taste before deciding which to purchase in bulk.

"Look, I cleared up this whole shelf for your chocolate machine. I'll tell all my friends. Oh, maybe we can sell chocolates at the Saturday market. We'll be right on time for Valentine's Day!' Jeannie giggled and whirled around the kitchen table, holding the hem of her dress in one hand. "Oooohh. Aah am so excited I'll be living with a chocolate maker!"

The mailman strained under the weight of the heavy box. I waited for him at the top of the few steps to the front door.

"Are you Melissa?" He gently deposited the box covered in custom forms, random numbers and "Fragile" packing tape at my feet.

"I am. This is my chocolate machine." My feet danced as I signed on the screen with the stylus.

"Are you a chocolate maker?" He placed the stylus back in his chest pocket.

"Now I am!" I pointed to the box.

"Well, then I hope for some free samples. That was a heavy box, you know!" He laughed as he returned to his mail truck.

My first act as a chocolate maker was to dismantle the melanger. Despite the "Fragile" tape, the journey from Delhi to Pensacola had broken my machine. I spent my first night with the machine on the phone with patient Indian technicians. One screw, one piece at a time, guided by back-and-forth chats and videos, I plunged into the depths of its machinery. And all along, I thought, "What a gift! Day one, and I've already learned how to fix this machine myself!"

My second act, of course, was to finally load it with beans. The inaugural batch was from Uganda. It had the most pungent aroma of all the test batches I had ordered—a strong and deep chocolate fudge and date aroma, almost masculine in its essence.

As the conching began, the aroma expanded into every corner of Jeannie's house, out the front and back doors, and even to the open Catmobile.

I lay in the back of the Catmobile and smiled. In twenty-four hours, I would taste my first organic, handmade, bean-to-bar chocolate. And in the meantime… I reached for my phone and opened Instagram. I didn't spend much time on social media, but this momentous event had to be shared.

Except, I didn't share because right as I opened the app, a post appeared at the top of the feed from Ancel—Ancel, the chocolate maker from Costa Rica I had met right after Jaguar came out of the painting. And what did Ancel's post say?

"Looking for one intern."

When I arrived in Puerto Viejo, two weeks later, Ancel and I laughed as we recounted my interview. It wasn't much of an interview…

"So, do you have any questions for us?" Ancel and two other women leaned forward toward the screen.

"Well, I can make up questions, but I already know I'm coming to study with you. I mean, I don't want to sound cocky; of course, you'll choose the best candidate, but I already know it's me, so… huh… I'll stop talking now."

I hadn't expected the interview to be via Facechat. I'm of the age where long-distance interviews are obviously phone calls. But, there I was, tee-shirt covered in cacao shells, in the back of my twenty-square foot home, babbling to a woman I so wished to impress.

"Is that a ukulele?" As I had been talking, the team at the other end had also been studying my living quarters behind me. "Can you play?"

"Not yet, but I'd be happy to bring it and learn while I'm there." Ancel laughed and relaxed back in her chair. The interview continued with many superfluous questions I no longer recall until it came to a natural close.

"So, how long will you need to decide? I mean to choose who will come be your intern?"

"Oh, I think we already know." She smiled to each of the two young women by her side, then looked back to me.

"Oh, I hope it's me. Is it me? It's me, isn't it?" All three women laughed.

"Yes. Yes, it's you!"

೫ · ೮

Puerto Viejo de Talamanca, Costa Rica, February 2021

I parted the light mosquito mesh and stepped onto the platform that was to be my room for the next few months. "The Bird House" Ancel called it, because it had only one bamboo wall, the others made only of mosquito mesh, and because it sat right by the pond, where twelve ducks, seven roosters, twenty-two hens, and two geese—not counting the fresh chicks and ducklings—came daily and loudly to refresh themselves.

I dropped my backpack and sat on my bed. I couldn't believe it—I was here!

I pulled my journal from the front pocket of my backpack to capture the exact moment of my arrival and wrote on a blank page:

"2/22/2021 - Ancel's farm."

I stopped and stared at the date. 2/22. What a special number! Then suddenly—wait a minute!—I flipped through the pages of my journal, traveling faster and faster back in time, to… 2/22/2020.

That was the day when Jaguar came out of the painting and said, with a precision too great to dismiss as coincidence, "You—you will be back here exactly a year from now, and you will study Cacao, and you will become a chocolate maker."

Chapter 27
They're All in Cahoots

So, I made it to Costa Rica, just like Jaguar had said I would, and dropped my bags at Ancel's farm right on schedule. What had Leah called it? Ha, yes—"in cahoots." It had taken a mushroom, a jaguar, a pandemic, a kilo of cacao beans, a trusty kitchen manager, a frog, and even a ghost orchid to get me here. I could imagine them all, high-fiving each other.

I mean, it worked. I learned to make chocolate with Ancel—my dream teacher—and launched my own chocolate company, "Namù Cacao Love." Namù, because it means jaguar in the Bribri language—the Bribri, the indigenous people of Talamanca, who just so happen to grow the most exquisite Criollo cacao beans, perhaps in the world.

I returned to the States with a suitcase crammed with cacao blocks and Bribri beans. Soon, the melanger was humming non-stop. My chocolate was fantastic, orders poured in, and within a few months, I was living the dream, happily ever after.

End of the story, right?

Well, not quite. It turned out there was a bigger plan all along. The ones in cahoots knew I wouldn't have answered that call, so instead, they had lured me in with chocolate.

So, let's rewind to where it should've ended but didn't—back in Ancel's kitchen.

1. Samantha

Ancel's farm, Puerto Viejo, Costa Rica - February 2021

"What about you, Maya?" Samantha asked while carefully stirring the beans over the flame, "Would you ever try Ayahuasca?"

"Me? Nah, that's not for me." I laughed and leaned in to scoop up the intoxicating toasted cacao aroma to my nose. "I've had enough spiritual experiences from fasting, hiking, mushrooms, and cacao. I don't need something as potent as Ayahuasca."

Samantha raised an eyebrow, pausing her stirring for a moment. "Really? I would have thought, with all your adventures, you'd be at least curious."

"Ayahuasca is for people who need deep healing, you know? People who haven't faced their traumas yet. I've done all that work. My life's pretty sweet, honestly. I've got it handled… And the cacao's ready, by the way. You smell that? That's the brownie signature smell signal we've been waiting for."

We poured the toasted beans onto the tile table to let them cool.

Samantha had just learned the art of chocolate-making in one of Ancel's classes. I had spotted her right away—the way her chocolate-brown eyes lit up when Ancel introduced the mother cacao tree, her giggles when the truth was revealed about mosquitoes being its pollinators, and her furious note-taking in a Jaguar notebook. She was a Cacao Sister, and before we even spoke a word, I'd already decided we'd be friends.

And I needed a friend. As much as I adored making chocolate in Ancel's kitchen, some days, those twelve ducks, seven roosters, twenty-two hens, and two geese—plus the fresh chicks and ducklings—drove me near to madness.

For a whole month, Samantha joined me in the kitchen to make chocolate, and every Saturday, we explored Puerto Viejo together. She loved parties on the beach and reggaeton; I took her hiking and kayaking. And we talked. About everything.

But, too soon, the day I had dreaded arrived. With ticket in hand, bags overflowing, and a tropical tan, she was set to return to Austria.

Playa Negra, Puerto Viejo, Costa Rica - New Moon, March 13th, 2021

Samantha spread the circular mandala tapestry on the black sand beneath the dark sky speckled with countless stars. She planted a few candles in the sand and smudged our two-person New Moon circle with sage.

"Om gam ganapataye namaha…" she chanted while arranging cacao beans on the center altar, along with a journal and two pens. I joined in the chant, eyes on her graceful movements.

"…shanti shanti shantiiii." Our song ended. We reached for each other's hands across the altar and giggled.

"Thank you." I smiled. She knew what I meant: thanks for all the laughs, for listening to me rant about Ancel's chickens, for the adventures, for everything.

"Thank you," she echoed softly. And I also knew what she meant.

We tore two pages from the notebook and each leaned closer to a candle to write our New Moon intentions.

Samantha read hers aloud first.

"May doors to new business opportunities swing wide open and be revealed. May my particular skill set serve the Greater Good. May Ganesha, remover of obstacles, clear my path to success. And may my sister Maya and I reunite this year, wherever fate leads us. And so it is. Namaste."

With palms pressed together, she bowed to the flickering flames and the spirit of Ganesha, then folded her paper and, with an open hand, invited me to share mine.

"Thank you for my life," I began. "It is perfect as it is, and I am grateful for it all, but, if it aligns, I would welcome a true partner. Not any partner—I call in the embodiment of the Beloved, my Divine Partner, my Transcendental Soulmate." I turned the piece of paper to read the addendum along the edge, "And also, this year, or whenever Divine Timing allows, may Samantha and I cross paths again. Aho!"

We chuckled. "Sounds like we'll meet again for sure. We both wished it." Samantha smiled, raised her arms to the stars, and, in a loud voice, claimed it.

"And so, it is done!"

From the altar, we each chose a cacao bean and planted the bitter, aromatic seeds of our intentions into the depth of our being.

Samantha flew back to Austria the next day. Then, a week later, she called.

"Maya! You won't believe it! I got a full-time job in Milan. Everything I wanted—art therapy, meditation, women's circles. It's going to be a dream! And you must come visit—maybe in November?"

"And so, it is done!" I replied, echoing our black beach ceremony, and we both laughed.

A week after Samantha's wish came true, I slept with Joe. "See? You got your wish too!" Samantha teased.

"Oh, no! No, no… Joe is definitely not the Beloved I called in. But I guess if you make a wish and get something else, you're probably being shown what stands in the way of what you actually wished for."

I was so wise that day. What a shame I forgot all about it so soon after.

2. The Roosters

Ancel's farm, Puerto Viejo, Costa Rica - March 2021

As I said, I adored making chocolate in Ancel's open-air kitchen. The six melangers humming non-stop, the hundred-kilo bags of beans and cane sugar, the cacao trees just outside, and the lush jungle all around. I still miss the place to this day.

But the chickens—*Ugh!* The chickens. I just couldn't.

Clucking, crowing, shrieking, scratching, pecking—constant noise converging on the pond by the Bird House. It pierced through my exhausted sleep, night after night. I tossed and turned, clenched my fists, and buried my ear-plugged head ever deeper under the pillow to escape the nightmare.

Some nights, I'd lose my mind and run outside, screeching like a banshee, broom in hand. On other nights, I'd meditate on the hate. "This is a new emotion," I'd coach myself in a soft voice. "Understand Hate. Embrace it."

But like water torture, each cluck was a drop eroding my sanity.

During the day, while I made chocolate, I tried to block them out with music, but they were inevitable. They jumped on tables, pooped around the melangers, knocked over compost buckets, nested in piles of laundry. And no one else seemed to care.

"Why do you have so many chickens?" I once asked Ancel.

"They're pretty." She shrugged and pointed to the obviously pretty chickens.

And even Nina, the young Russian woman who also lived on the farm—she loved the birds so much that she had trained a couple of hens to nest on her bed. She wanted to live like Baba Yaga in a hut standing on chicken legs. From the kitchen, I could see her, sitting in the dirt with the chickens, stroking their feathers gently and cooing sweet words. And the chicken loved her back and followed her around the farm.

The truth was, I'd always disliked chickens, and especially roosters. It wasn't just their incessant clucking; it was their little beady eyes, their jerky movements, the way they pecked at the ground, and most of all, the way they paraded their cocky strut around the farm, like they owned the place. In the past, I'd laughed it off as just a quirky part of my personality. But here, at the farm, surrounded by the enemy and observing Ancel and Nina's love for them, I had to admit my repulsion was a tad irrational.

"Why do I hate you guys so much?" I once asked Leroy, the one chicken who actually left the kitchen when asked. "Cluuuuck," he answered and strutted away.

I lasted a month and a half until, one morning, after another sleepless stretch of clucks drilling into my brain, I knew. "I have to leave, or I will lose my mind. I'm done."

My return flight wasn't scheduled for another month, but I figured I'd learned enough to become a chocolate maker in the States. I could buy beans from the Bribri tribe; I had a melanger in the Catmobile; I even had a name already picked for my chocolate business: "Namù Cacao Love."

There was nothing else keeping me here.

Nothing, except my flight, which, I had forgotten, was non-changeable and non-refundable. High season was in full effect, and any one-way flight back to Florida cost twice as much as my original flight, an amount I no longer had. I had paid for the internship and, ever since, had lived off the fruit and veggies grown on the farm. I couldn't even afford to move out.

I was stuck. Completely trapped. And just as I stood there, sinking into the absurdity of my situation, Joe appeared.

3. Joe

Joe was an enigma. He worked at the farm occasionally, helping with odd jobs. He was punctual and efficient, his permanently creased forehead a testament to how seriously he took his job, and life in general. He only paused to roll cigarettes, which he smoked from the corner of his mouth, head tilted as he contemplated his tasks. He never smiled, rarely looked up, and if he spoke, it was in short, clipped sentences.

I was so taken with chocolate making that, at first, I didn't pay much attention to him. I just noted that he was … different. There was something about him, maybe how he carried himself with regal countenance despite his slight frame, or perhaps it was his quiet ways that intrigued me.

Eventually, I gave him my phone number—not for any romantic reason, but because he had a bicycle for sale, and I needed one. Instead, he used my number to ask me out. I declined at first, but he insisted, and so we went out twice: once for karaoke—he sang, I didn't—and once to El Bucanero, where I sipped a smoothie while he emptied several beers.

Although Nina teased me about my "dates," I thought nothing of it. Joe was thirty-four; I was fifty. I assumed he was just being friendly, taking me out because Samantha had left, and he thought I might need company and relief from the farm.

That was the state of our connection on the day I realized I was stuck in paradise.

Puerto Viejo, Costa Rica - March 2021, and beyond

I licked my pistachio ice cream as the crystal clear waves kissed my toes, half-buried in warm sand.

Costa Rica. Paradise, they called it. And yes, from the sea to the jungle, it was picture-perfect. But I was stuck in it.

"Alright," I muttered to my ice cream, surrendering. "I don't believe in accidents, so there's gotta be a reason why I need to still be here." My stomach felt heavy, but the gelato was handmade and delicious, and that helped.

I felt him before I saw him. As the words left my mouth, I slowly turned. There was Joe, casually strolling down the beach, with a swagger and a wide grin, which was odd because Joe never smiled.

"Maya!" he called, his voice unusually chipper. "Whatcha doing here?"

"Contemplating the inevitability of reality," I replied in a flat tone. I didn't expect he'd understand, but he chuckled and nodded. "Yeah …" Then he grinned again, flashing a straight row of tobacco-stained teeth.

"Well, you seem happy today."

"I am happy!" He leaned in, blue eyes darting, and whispered, "I'm on acid. And I've got more… wanna join me?"

"Mmh." Intriguing offer. Normally, I'd have said no. LSD was synthetic, and I preferred medicines from the Earth. But I needed *something* to shift, and if this substance could make Joe smile, maybe I ought to give it a try.

"Alright," I nodded, "but not today. I need to make chocolate for the Saturday market. How about Saturday evening?"

"Saturday it is. I'll save you a square." He winked. Then, without warning, he hugged me. I lifted my ice cream cone awkwardly out of his embrace, but smiled anyway.

"Okay… Let's see why I'm here."

Joe and I sat cross-legged on his bed, his eyes steady, as he handed me a minuscule sliver of acid on his fingertip. I took a deep breath. My heart pounded, and my nerves twitched.

"You've got me, right? If things get weird, you'll take care of me?"

He nodded, firm and sure. "I promise I won't leave your side."

"You have a lot of experience with this?"

He let out a low chuckle, "Yeah, you could say that. Acid's what got me off cocaine. I traded one habit for another, but this one's healthier. It's just… they're both so easy to find here, you know? It takes a lot of self-control to stay away."

I still couldn't fully read him, but there was a certainty in his gestures, a quiet steadiness in his almond-shaped eyes. Whatever else Joe was, in that moment, I trusted him.

As soon as the acid hit, we left his room and ventured through the chaos of Semana Santa (Easter Week party)— drums thumping, bass pounding, drunken people spilling into the streets. Joe's hand was always there, guiding me like a compass in the storm. Even when we came across the ambulance, the flashing lights, and the body under the white sheet, Joe was there, steering me as I giggled at the absurdity of it all. My dilemmas, this town, the roosters, life, death, this… increasingly handsome young man—what a ridiculous game reality was.

Much later, in the wee hour of the morning, we sat again cross-legged on his bed.

"You kept me safe," I said with a giggle.

"Of course." He lit a cigarette and calmly pulled on it. Smoke escaped his lips. She rose like a sensual dancer toward the ceiling. I tasted her on my lips and licked them. A fire was igniting deep within me and spreading to that locus between my legs. It might even have flushed my face because Joe asked, "What are you thinking right now?" He tilted his head as though he were trying to read me.

"I'm thinking I probably should get home." I stood up suddenly and grabbed my bag. In one smooth move, he was right behind me, motorcycle keys in hand.

"I'll take you; it's safer."

The pink of dawn was already spilling into the ocean when we reached Playa Negra. Joe's back was warm against my chest. I looked up to the last stars and spread my arms to catch the wind. Mmmmh. Maybe Paradise wasn't so horrible after all.

The farm was eerily quiet when Joe dropped me off. Where were all the chickens? Asleep? That would have been a first. And the kitchen was locked by a large metal door secured with a padlock. I didn't even know the kitchen could be locked.

I looked up to the door and giggled. "Seems I switched universe. What else is different?"

Back in the Bird House, I flopped onto my bed, greeted Annie and Nancy, my spider roommates, and checked my phone. A message from my friend Susan in Maine, to whom I had cried my woes the day prior, blinked in waiting. She'd worked airline magic and got my flight moved up to Tuesday for just a hundred dollars. She even covered it, saying she trusted I'd repay her "when your chocolate empire is up and running."

I blinked. Read it again, then screamed and flailed happily like a flipped beetle. "Cluuuk?" A chicken responded from under the bed, but for once, I didn't care.

"I really wanted to kiss you last night." Joe stretched a corner of the crumpled bedsheets, wiping off sand to make room for me.

"Then why didn't you?"

"It was your first time on acid. That would've been rude."

I was back on the same corner of the bed I had left just that morning. My excuse? I had forgotten my earrings. I hadn't meant to leave them, not consciously anyway. But, here we were, back staring into each other's' eyes, except this time, he was shirtless and reclined, comfortable in his domain.

"Would you stay the night?"

"Huh... you know I'm fifty-years-old, right?"

"So?" He pulled me closer. "Maya, this isn't a relationship."

Everything I needed to know was in that sentence. This isn't a relationship. You're flying out in two days. You'll never hear from me again. So, live a little. Have some fun. All this and a lot more too. A lot more I wouldn't understand until this non-relationship had fulfilled its ultimate purpose.

But, in that moment, I simply shrugged. "Alright. Why not?"

I called Samantha from the San Jose airport. When she was still in Puerto Viejo, Joe had tried to seduce her, but she liked "brown boys," as she called them. His fair complexion, blond hair, and blue eyes had him at the bottom of her long list of suitors.

"O.M.G.! You slept with Joe? How was it?"

"It was a bit like... like wrestling a jaguar on fire."

She laughed. "Sounds like that would be your style."

"It's exactly my style." I laughed too.

"See? You got your wish!"

"Oh, no! No, no… Joe is definitely not the Beloved I called in. But I guess if you make a wish and get something else, you're probably being shown what stands in the way of what you actually wished for."

"Truth!" Samantha agreed.

"Realistically, though, it was just a one-night stand. I bet I never hear from him again."

I was so wrong about that.

By the time I landed in Pensacola, I had several messages from Joe. And before my chocolate company even got off the ground, my phone was filled with flirtatious messages and nude photos.

At first, it was all sexual—backstories, kinks, fantasies—but soon, we started talking. He was a hand-on-the-heart, salute-the-flag, southern boy. He believed I should get vaccinated—it was criminal not to. I should also vote and pay taxes. Given the chasm, we should have withered and died quickly. But we agreed to disagree and kept talking.

Then, right as the Catmobile and I were crossing South Carolina on our way to New Hampshire, Joe landed a bartender gig there, in his hometown.

His dad, a preacher man, never knew the level of sinning that took place in the back of that little Toyota truck parked on his lawn.

In the morning, Joe and I again said goodbye forever, and I drove on.

While Joe made a name for himself behind the bar, I climbed fifty mountains to welcome in my fifties (all New Hampshire's 4000ers and two more for good measure). The higher I climbed, the more I watched myself slip. Each time I reached a summit, I checked my phone for a message from Joe. And when his name popped up, my heart raced. I hadn't felt such butterflies in years. If Joe's name didn't pop up, I'd worry I had already been replaced by a younger lover.

Then, in September, Joe landed in New Hampshire on a one-way ticket.

I always suspected he was asked to leave his parents' pious house because of his nightlife habits, but he always denied it, claiming instead he had left specifically to come climb mountains with me.

That first night, we snuggled in the Catmobile, staring at the stars. When he started singing—songs about dragons and princesses, about how Love tames the Wild—I thought my heart might burst. Who was this man? Not the same Serious Joe I'd met at the farm.

For the next month and a half, we spent every moment together. We climbed mountains, made love, cooked s'mores on the campfire, and watched the leaves start to fall. Joe smiled and laughed every day. No drugs, no alcohol, just him. He was attentive to what I liked and disliked; he asked many questions, more than he shared; and he woke me up daily with tickles and silly songs.

"Can I still stay? Are you going to kick me out now?" he'd often ask, jokingly but with a hint of worry in his voice.

I'd engulf him in my arms. "Kick you out? No way. Who'd steal the blanket and leave a mess in the Catmobile?"

Frost filled the truck's windows, and crunchy brown leaves covered the ground. November was approaching quickly, and no matter how snuggled Joe and I slept, winter's icy fingers sneaked in through the cracks.

I was already packed for Italy—Milan to visit Samantha—and Joe had landed a bartender job in Arkansas. I could have flown to Rome from Boston and left the Catmobile in Leah's care, but I wasn't ready to let Joe go. So I called Samantha, postponed buying my flight to Italy, and drove Joe to Arkansas instead. That got me another week with him.

At the end of that week, we stood outside a diner, layered up like two birds about to migrate, our summer warmth clinging to us like memories that'd fade away too soon. Joe pressed his hands deeper into his pockets. There was no future promise in his smile.

"Well, this is it, then." I twirled the Catmobile's keys around a finger. I sensed he was already gone, yet I couldn't help but press a little more.

"So, what are the odds? What percentage likelihood do you think that we'll ever see each other again?"

He pulled me in for a hug, still smiling, still quiet. No answer. Perhaps he couldn't give one. Perhaps he was relieved.

I drove off and didn't look back. I was sure, this time, it was done. I had been gifted a strange, wild summer fling and nothing more. But for what purpose? What had been shown? What had I learned? I'd always been able to see the bigger picture, but in this case, I couldn't. Could a fling just be a fling? I shrugged, lifting my hands off the steering wheel, palms open to the mystery of it all.

4. The Vaccine

2021—oh, what a divisive time that was. Half of my friends, including Joe, rushed to the nearest pharmacy to get the COVID vaccine, as, clearly, it would've been irresponsible not to, while the other half of my friends fell on a spectrum ranging from distrust of Big Pharma and government to full-blown conspiracies about mind control and hidden agendas.

Where did I stand? I stood in love, with my nose in the melanger, watching the swirling mass of my own handmade chocolate, or on my phone swooning to Joe's advances. The world's drama played in the background, with no more relevance to my life than a badly dubbed soap opera I had no interest in watching.

I wasn't specifically anti-vacc, I just believed that, with proper nutrition, I could keep my immune system in a state of optimum defense better than any vaccine. And as I had been in close proximity to confirmed positive COVID sufferers with no consequences, I trusted my body's resilience over society's prescriptions for health.

Until Cacao stepped in.

Tamworth, New Hampshire, September-October 2021

The cacao in my small ceramic mug was so dark that, at first sip, I thought it tasted like coffee. Yet I had shaved this cacao from the same ceremonial block I used daily. And I had made that block myself at Ancel's farm before I left Puerto Viejo. I took a second sip—definitely much darker than normal.

There was no logical reason for this, but I had learned to pay attention when reality switched suddenly.

I closed my eyes and concentrated on my breath. Inhale—the scent of the forest. Exhale—land deeper into the cacao. Without just a few breaths, a black hummingbird with jewel-like feather tips appeared on my mind's inner screen, then as swift as the wind, it vanished. In the swoosh of its departure, a voice said,

"You'll need to get vaccinated, Child."

What? Vaccinated? I squinted, keeping my eyes shut. The voice had been crystal clear, but… "Child?" Neither Jaguar nor Cacao had ever called me "Child."

"Okay, whoever's talking, I hear you, but I'm not going to do that." I wanted to see if this was the kind of voice that could be disobeyed.

"You will need to get vaccinated," the voice repeated, kindly but firmly. "On the day of vaccination, you will drink five times your normal amount of cacao to help flush the physical components. Then you'll need Ayahuasca to clear the energetics."

"I'm not really comfortable with this vaccine idea. I don't know what's in there, and…"

"There is nothing man-made that plant medicine cannot clear or cure."

Beyond the words, the idea landed in my heart as an absolute truth. There *was* nothing plant medicine couldn't cure. Would I subject myself to it, though?

"Does it have to be Ayahuasca?"

"It does."

I let out a heavy sigh, "but… Ayahuasca is expensive, and I'd have to fly somewhere, and sit with a Shaman, and all this… ceremony, drumming, singing, and vomiting in buckets. It sounds so unpleasant, and I just don't think I need it."

Suddenly, I was back on the tailgate, in the forest. There was no answer to my last plea. Where had this come from? Who had spoken in my head? Who was calling me "Child?"

Joe arrived three days later, and for a month and a half, we had pillow talks on all topics, except those that might have tensed the very small space we shared—like the vaccine. Until, about a week before we drove south together, Joe asked to be taken to the pharmacy for his third booster.

On the drive there, unprovoked, I started an argument.

"I don't care what you do, I'm not getting vaccinated. And it's not because I believe it contains a mind-controlling chip. I just have full sovereignty over this body, and nobody will force me to inject anything into it…" I continued my rant all the way to the pharmacy. Joe didn't say a word. He just observed as I delivered a full-volume medley of popular arguments I didn't even believe.

But right as we parked in front of the pharmacy, my own thoughts interrupted the monologue: "Wow. Look at me go. That's a lot of resistance. What am I resisting so hard? And what would happen if I went the other way?"

I pulled the hand brake, paused, then looked at Joe. "Okay. I'm going to get vaccinated, but I'm getting the

Johnson & Johnson, because it's only one shot, and I'm doing this only once…"

Strangely, that morning, although I had absolutely no intention of getting vaccinated, I had found my meditation cacao to taste unusually light. I had shaved more, then more, for a triple dose of cacao. Later that day, while waiting for Joe in the Home Depot parking lot, I had found two bars of my own chocolate mysteriously stashed in the Catmobile's center console, and I'd eaten both.

As the strange words slipped from my mouth, "…Johnson & Johnson, because it's only one shot, and I'm doing this only once…" I realized I had eaten exactly five times the cacao I normally did that day, as per the instructions, so I added, "… But, I'm *not* going to Ayahuasca."

Joe raised an eyebrow and shook his head. "Oookay. The way your mind works sometimes is like… I dunno, like a Rubik's cube on acid." He chuckled. "And… Ayahuasca? I don't think they have that here, but you do you, Maya."

The next day, while Joe dealt with only a mild headache, I collapsed. I shivered, shook, vomited, and still managed to drag myself to the woods for diarrhea. My fever spiked, my mind swam in delirium, and my temples shrank in the vice grips of a migraine so intense that I believed I might actually die.

That day remains a blur. I only vaguely remember Joe's worried, furrowed brow and that, at a loss, he eventually drove me to Leah's.

The next morning, symptoms had subsided. I assumed my immune system and cacao had flushed out the offensive substance. All that remained was a dull pain like a metallic sensation in the lower bones of my eye sockets.

Was this level of discomfort really necessary for my journey? It seemed so, because with that one epic puncture in my flesh, everything else quickly fell into place.

5. Convergence

I dropped Joe off in Arkansas, drove to Florida, made chocolate in Jeannie's kitchen, and practiced Italian every day, but I didn't buy my ticket to Italy.

I tried, but every time I found a cheap flight, by the time I landed on the purchase page, the flight was full or canceled, or my computer battery died, or Jeannie called me for dinner.

Then, Samantha called.

"Hey," she sighed. "I can't take the job in Milan." Her voice was heavy with disappointment.

"Why? What happened?"

"They're requiring everyone to get vaccinated now, and I just… I can't do it, Maya. It just doesn't feel right."

I leaned back against the Catmobile, letting the news sink in, finally understanding why I couldn't book a flight.

"What are you going to do?"

There was a long pause on the line. "I'm going back to Costa Rica. It's the easiest. I can pay $100 in expat insurance and get in without proof of vaccination. I've already booked an Airbnb in Puerto Viejo. I think I'll just hang out there and figure out my next move. You should come. The studio has two beds, and it would be cheaper if we shared."

Back to Costa Rica? That had not been on my radar. But, out of curiosity, I checked available flights. $333 for a round trip leaving on 11/11. With numbers like those, I couldn't deny the Universe's nudge. I had enough for the flight and half the Airbnb, but I didn't have an extra $100 for expat insurance. And then I remembered: I had a vaccine card! I checked the Ministerio de Salud's rules. The card needed to be at least fifteen days old by the time of travel. I counted

backwards to the date of my vaccination from 11/11...
fifteen days. Exactly.

Cocles Beach, November 12th, 2021

Samantha turned the key in the lock and opened the door
of our home for the next month. I stepped in first, and froze.
A huge grin spread across my face.

As tall as the wall, as majestic as ever, a fabric painting of
a jaguar hung directly across from the entrance.

"Jaguar!" With eyes wide with delight, I turned to
Samantha. "Jaguar's here. That means I'm on the right path."

Samantha laughed and dropped her bags. "Well, perfect!
You sleep with your jaguar, and I'll take the queen bed."

There was a short knock at the door, and a voice as sweet
as honey drifted into the room.

"Hola, soy Yolanda." A woman about my age in a
colorful tunic stood in the doorway. Her face was soft and
radiant. I assumed she was our host, and as Samantha didn't
speak much Spanish, I stepped forward to greet her.

"Everything perfect?" Her smile was as sweet as her
voice. "Did you find what you need?"

I laughed, pointing to the painting. "I found Jaguar.
That's all I need."

Her eyes lit up. "Jaguar is the protector. Do you already
know him?"

A hundred stories flashed through my mind, but I kept it
simple. "Yes, I'm a chocolate maker. My company is Namù
Cacao Love. And Namù means..."

"...Jaguar," she finished for me, "in the Bribri language.
My husband and I, we own Namù Ecotienda in town."

I blinked, speechless. What were the chances?

"We're already family then." Yolanda's eyes sparkled.
And there was something more—a quiet, unspoken energy,
drawing me in. She readjusted the bag slung over her
shoulder, keys rattling in her hand, and for a brief instant, I

felt I knew her. I had known her, always. We *were* family, beyond the Namù name.

"Bueno, I'm off to an Ayahuasca ceremony, but I'll be back tomorrow. Anything you need, you just let me know."

Cacao had once again led me to Jaguar. And… to Ayahuasca?

"Ayahuasca for just one night?"

She nodded. "Yes. We meet in Bribri with our friend Jordi."

"Is Jordi the Shaman?"

She paused, and her eyes deepened as though she were looking for the answer in another realm. "Jordi gathers the vine and prepares the medicine, but we each hold our own ceremony. No Shaman, no drumming, no ícaros. Just us, the jungle, and La Abuela."

She placed her hand on her heart. Before I knew it, we were holding hands, and a promise was being made:

"I'll come with you one time. Not today, but soon."

The words felt right.

Yolanda simply smiled, knowingly.

As the door closed behind her, I shook my head, returning to my senses.

"I think I just told Yolanda I'd go to Ayahuasca with her."

"But you said Ayahuasca wasn't for you; it was for people with deep traumas," Samantha remembered.

"I did." I scratched my head, puzzled. "I don't know why I told her I'd go. I guess I just got caught in her bright energy… But no, obviously, I'm not going to Ayahuasca."

Oh, how much work it must have taken those in cahoots to line everything so perfectly, only to hear, "No, obviously, I'm not going to Ayahuasca." I imagine they must have shaken their heads—whoever they were—then nodded to each other.

For resistance of this magnitude, they would have to resort to drastic measures.

On my first full day back in Puerto, I received a text from Joe. I had only heard from Joe sporadically since I drove away from the diner in Arkansas.

"Hey, Maya. Guess what? I got a job at El Bucanero in Puerto. I'm on the bus right now. Can you believe it? Back to Puerto. Maybe you should come and visit." The tone was set by a smiling purple devil Emoji.

"Hey, Joe. Guess what? I'm already here."

And just like that, everything shifted again.

Samantha and I had looked forward to our reunion, but living together wore out our friendship fast. She lived for reggaeton bars, and I didn't drink, and I couldn't twerk. Plus, Joe was in town. We led separate lives in the same studio until she left town. She met a man, followed him to Guatemala, and quietly left my story.

So, it was Joe and me again. Well… Joe, me, and the ladies from his hostel—a new batch every week. He took them to nightclubs and beaches, for their protection, of course.

"They just don't realize how dangerous it is here. This isn't Europe," he'd say.

Sometimes I met them at a club, but he always walked *them* home.

"I've seen you climb mountains, Maya. I know you can take care of yourself. But if you want me to walk you, I will."

"Nah, I'm fine. Take the ladies back," I'd say proudly. He was right; I wasn't a damsel in distress.

I slept in his bed when invited and asked no questions. I would not be the one to tame a wild man. Even when tiny plastic bags of white powder, unfamiliar hair ties, flower scents, and his fading libido surfaced in his messy sheets, I

389

shrugged it off. His hair was getting longer, mosquito spray had a slight flowery scent, and he was working now. Of course he was tired.

If jealousy thumped in my heart, I sat cross-legged on the beach and meditated it away. I refused to let anything spoil my precious romance with Joe.

In this way, I lasted another month after Samantha left. But, as Joe wanted to keep his privacy, I had to rent a room elsewhere and watched my funds evaporate in the tropical sun.

When my return date came, Joe carried my bag and walked me to the bus. He stood in the sun, a waving retreating figure, until the bus turned along Playa Negra. As I sank into the bus seat, part of me teared up, but another part sighed with relief.

I landed back in the States with ten kilos of Bribri cacao beans, right on the Winter Solstice.

6- Resurgence

This time it was really goodbye. Costa Rica, Puerto Viejo, Joe? Wonderful memories. I wasn't going back. I had a business to run, clients to keep happy—all in the US. Soon, the melanger was humming in Jeannie's kitchen, orders flooded my phone, and chocolate ruled my life once more.

But a few days after I landed, Florida experienced record-cold temperatures. Even with a space heater in the Catmobile, my now tropically acclimatized body shivered, and my teeth chattered.

A friend in New Mexico asked if I wanted to house-sit for her.

That same night, on the Florida news, the anchorman reported that frozen iguanas were falling out of palm trees.

Beside his concern for the iguanas themselves, he pointed to the weather map: cold was here to stay.

The next day, I drove to Silver City, New Mexico, not realizing it sat at six thousand feet in elevation, with a mean mountain wind chill factor. Even in the house, the melanger struggled. I sacrificed my space heater to its cause and slept in a fully zipped zero-degree sleeping bag.

Next, I drove to Sedona. Surely, Arizona had to be warmer.

I was greeted by snow in the desert. I retreated to a friend's house and built a cardboard fort around the melanger to contain the heat where it mattered most: the chocolate.

And that's right about when Joe asked me to come back to Puerto Viejo, to the warm tropics, to be his next-door neighbor.

It was folly, and I'll tell you why.

I didn't expect Joe to return to the flirtations of a year prior, but I hadn't anticipated he'd disappear completely either. In Florida, I tried to play it cool—maybe he'd met someone. If I truly loved him, I'd want the best for him, right? But as the cold froze my body, the dread of not knowing froze my heart.

So, I asked.

Yes, he had joined Tinder for "casual fun," but I was still his closest friend.

"Would it help if I told you when I meet someone, so you don't wonder?" Joe offered.

This worked for a while—until I arrived in Silver City and Joe disappeared again. My gut told me something serious had come along.

I asked again.

Yes, a young woman with a frizzy afro had moved in next door. How convenient. They made love every day, watched movies, sang songs, visited secluded beaches.

"She's not my girlfriend any more than you are. Look Maya, I'll be straight. You're the person I trust the most in the world, but I'll never be with you. We're very different people, and I'm looking for someone with more similar interests."

It made sense. I was looking for the same. I thanked him for his honesty.

The frizzy romance fizzled and, with the low season, Tinder dried up. It wasn't long before Joe reached out again. By the time I landed in Sedona, his messages came daily, pulling me back into the memories of sleeping in his arms in the tropical heat.

"Maya, I think you should come back," he wrote one afternoon. "The apartment next to mine is now open, and I want to make sure I have a neighbor I actually like. We could hang out all the time."

Oh, I knew it was a terrible idea. I could see the heartbreak from two thousand miles away. And yet, I was drawn to it, pulled in by a tractor beam stronger than any reasonable counter-argument my mind could concoct.

"Okay. I'll come, but you must promise you won't have sex with another woman where I can hear you."

"I promise. We'll be our own sanctuary."

The thought appeared in my mind: "Fastest way out is through."

I landed in Puerto Viejo on a one-way ticket with melanger and all my chocolate-making utensils in tow.

That first night, Joe was gone. He had met a lawyer from San Jose right about when my shuttle dropped me off and, as per our agreement, had gone home with her so I wouldn't hear her moan.

It was a flawed agreement from day one. Almost every day, Joe had a new "friend." He'd come home around two in the morning, scratch at my door, slip in my bed, and whisper, "I love you, Maya." I still believe he meant it, in his own way.

Day by day, the pain grew. It hit me in waves, sickening and surreal. Yet, a part of me felt this was necessary. Why? I couldn't say.

"I made a new friend today." Joe lay down behind me, wrapping his arm around my torso. "Her name's Sky, she's woowoo, like you. I think you'd like her. Do you want her phone number? She's new in town, maybe you two can hang out."

I lifted myself on one elbow and turned to face him. "No, Joe. I don't want to hang out with your lady conquests, thank you very much."

"It's not a conquest, we just went on one date at the beach. That's all."

That was all but, by then, it was more than I could take.

How did I know the woman in the green flowy dress, pedaling through town with a smile as wide as the sun itself, was Sky?

"Sky!" I called before thinking.

She glanced in my direction and crunched her brakes to a screeching halt. Then, with eyes fixed on mine, she dismounted her bicycle and locked it to the nearest pole.

I ran across the road and stood face-to-face with her. I thought I might dislike her because of her connection with Joe, yet here she was, all smiles.

"Who are you?" She tilted her head, studying me like a curious animal.

"Hi Sky. I'm Maya." I realized I didn't want to speak about Joe. I wanted to meet this woman, not because he had told me to, but because I recognized her magik simply by the way she pedaled through town. "Would you like to get a smoothie with me?"

"I would be delighted!"

As we sat together, a tension I didn't even know I carried simply melted away. Sky was from New Hampshire. She

393

knew the White Mountains, North Conway, and my trees. She was a little piece of home. We spoke about our trees while sipping mango smoothies.

Then, eventually, her brow furrowed, and she asked, "How did you know my name is Sky?"

"You went on a date with a friend of mine, Joe." His name tasted bitter in my mouth, and I saw she'd caught my discomfort. "He said I'd enjoy meeting you. I guess, for once, he was right. When I saw you, I don't know how; I just knew you were Sky."

"Well, it was hardly a date. We sat on the beach, then I jumped into the ocean, and…" she rolled her eyes, "he kept telling me I had to get out because the sea was too rough."

"Was it rough?"

"It was rough for him because he was fighting it. But…" she looked at me intently, leaned in, and whispered, "I can speak with the ocean."

I smiled. "I understand. I can speak with trees. I have for years."

Her already large blue eyes opened even wider. "You understand! You know!"

I nodded slowly as warmth filled my heart. I already loved this kindred-spirit woman.

"I'd always heard the ocean's call, but for so long I didn't know her language. Then three days ago, I sat with Ayahuasca with my new friends, Jordi and Yolanda, and oh, Maya… everything shifted. Back in New Hampshire, I was trapped— like a bird in a cage—always chasing another dollar. Aya lifted the veil. She unraveled me and wove me back together, lighter, freer."

She raised her hand, delicate as a breeze, fingers floating upward. "Now, I'm weightless. I can speak to the ocean. I want to hold on to this—anchor this feeling—before I go back. That's why I'm sitting with Aya again next week." Her words trailed off into a thoughtful pause, and her bright eyes settled on mine. "I'm feeling called to offer… Would you maybe want to come with me?"

I held her gaze and let her words settle while the ones in cahoots held their breath.

This was the third time Ayahuasca had appeared in my field. Yolanda and Jordi… I had said I didn't want a Shaman, drums or ícaros. Well, such a place had appeared. I had said I had no big traumas to heal. Then how did I explain Joe in my life? "Plant medicine can cure anything." Cacao had said. Could it cure even this?

"Okay… Yes." I nodded slowly, "I think Ayahuasca's been calling me for a while." I laughed. "I'm totally scared, by the way, but yes, I would love to go to with you."

Sky and I spent the evening together, and by the next morning, we were together again on the beach, eating magic mushrooms and uncovering each other's worlds and secrets. One day blended into the next, and before we knew it, we had spent a whole week wrapped in the joy of each other's company.

By the time Yolanda pulled up to our rendezvous point, I felt closer to Sky than to friends I'd known for years.

"Hola!" I waved to Yolanda through the window, but she stepped out, arms open wide, and embraced me. The twinkle in her eyes told me she had always known I would keep my promise to meet La Abuela.

As we drove deeper into the jungle toward Bribri, I couldn't help but smile. From Mushrooms to Cacao to Jaguar and now to Ayahuasca—what a journey! I glanced at Sky, then Yolanda, and sighed in relief. Wherever my journey meandered from here, whatever else the ones in cahoots had in store for me, at least I now had these sisters by my side.

Part 6

ABUELITA CURANDERA

Chapter 28
Little Monkey

Bribri, Costa Rica - March 2022

In the heart of the jungle, on the wooden platform, atop the purple altar rug, surrounded by feathers, copal, and candles, she awaited our gathering. Thick, rich, and reddish-dark in her hexagonal glass bottle, she awaited the ones she had called.

Jordi uncorked the bottle. With calm, well-practiced movements, he rolled a piece of tissue and wiped the edge of the wooden chalice. Sitting at the edge of my mat, eyes wide with excitement, I watched his every move. My heart pounded so hard that my torso oscillated, back and forth over my folded legs.

"Shadow dancer twirling me. From the bitter swallow of the dark night's tea. Flesh and bone now I have no form, but the notes of the flute song playing…"

From the silence, Sky's angelic voice rose and mingled with the smoke of the copal. Together, they danced in the flickering candlelight, up to the ceiling, then beyond, to the jungle and stars. I glanced at Yolanda, then Sky. They both smiled. Sky reached for my hand, sending her medicine song in my direction. Because she had surrendered to the medicine before, had emerged, and been transformed, she trusted.

I trusted, too—in the way one trusts a roller-coaster when the last click stops and the ride is suspended at the edge of that first drop. Ayahuasca had called me, and I had come. There was no backing out now. Although the journey had not yet officially begun, everything—Sky's song, these ceremonial objects on the altar, Jordi's measured moves—everything already seemed otherworldly.

"Maya." Jordi invited me with an open hand to the altar. I crawled forward from my mat to the edge of the altar rug and knelt, back straight and hands on my thighs. He smiled reassuringly. His eyes, fixed on mine, seemed to see through me, beyond me. He held the bottle up for a moment, and I imagined he was telepathically asking Ayahuasca, "This one? How much should I give this one?" Whatever answer he heard would be correct. He poured the thick liquid a little past halfway to the top of the chalice. He pressed it to his heart, eyes closed as in silent prayer, then offered it to me with a smile.

I cradled the chalice and pressed it against my own hard-beating heart.

"Abuelita Ayahuasca. I've come to meet you, but I'm a little scared, to be honest. Okay… Deep breath… I can do this… I'm a little scared, but also I trust you. Whatever healing you think I need, whatever happens, I welcome you. It's an honor to receive your medicine. Thank you for calling me."

I brought the chalice to my lips and took a small sip. Suddenly, breaking the solemnity, I turned to Sky. "Whoa! It's delicious!" Everyone laughed. I had heard tales about the bitter brew that opens the mind, the acrid medicine that transforms lives. "Just drink it fast, and don't think about it." I'd been told. But in that moment, Aya delighted my taste buds with the sweetest, earthiest jungle cacao nectar.

I drank the rest to the bottom of the chalice and handed it back to Jordi, then quickly bowed, hands pressed in gratitude, and returned to my mat.

Sky was still giggling from my reaction. She leaned toward me and whispered, "I had a dream a week ago, when we first met, that you and I were here together, and that you said exactly that." She squeezed my hand. "That means we're exactly where we need to be."

Then, she stepped forward to receive her dose of Ayahuasca.

Jordi only spoke Spanish, and fast, but I understood his instructions. We were to lie for the first couple of hours, still and quiet, and wait for Her. La Abuela worked in her own time.

With sweet cacao nectar lingering on my tongue, I lay on my back—hands by my side, eyes closed, completely still—and waited.

In a perfect world, I would have been relaxed and ready, mind open, fully present to receive this medicine. But in reality, my mind wasn't relaxed at all. It swirled ceaselessly with thoughts unrelated to Ayahuasca, this moment, or this platform.

Forty-eight hours prior to Ayahuasca

Sky and I stood on a log and sang to the trees that had witnessed unspeakable horror. She sang for hours, and I held the trees in love and compassion, hoping to ease the dark, oppressive energy upon them. She sang until dark, until the trees felt lighter. Then, respectfully, we placed our hands on their trunks, waved goodbye to the island, and walked back to our bicycles.

Although psilocybin still partially shared our minds, our journey was winding down. Our stomachs grumbled, reminding us we had fasted before taking the mushrooms that morning.

"Let's go eat. And let's ride fast! I love the feel of the wind on my face when I'm on mushrooms." Shaking off the heaviness we'd witnessed, Sky swung her leg over her bicycle, and off she was like the wind toward town. I jumped on mine and pedaled as fast as I could to catch her.

"Where do you want to eat?" she yelled back.

"Let's go to El Bucanero."

The Caribbean cuisine and ocean view at El Bucanero were wonderful, no doubt, but I chose it because Joe worked there. I flipped my dreads and smiled. The Golden Teachers made me feel graceful and feminine, like Sky, and I wanted Joe to see me in my glowing state.

El Bucanero was packed. Joe raced between tables with drinks and food. With only a quick hello, he took our order and raced on. Amidst the clunking of forks, clattering of bottles, rapid footsteps on the wooden deck, and ever louder drunken conversations, Sky reached across the table and gripped my hands. The smiles in our eyes matched. We were an island, two daughters of Pachamama in a sea of drunkenness. Throughout the meal, we leaned to stay close.

We finished at the same time, stood up, and turned toward the exit. I had already taken a few steps, opening a passage through the sweaty crowd and leading Sky by the hand, when I remembered Joe.

I turned around to see if I could find him and interrupt his race just long enough to wave goodbye.

Joe was right there, right behind me, with his mouth on Sky's.

She pushed him away, her eyes searching mine. Without a word, I turned away and left the restaurant. What could I have said? Sky followed and linked her arm with mine, silently reaffirming her loyalty. I held her close as we walked through the bustling night world of Puerto Viejo. I saw nothing, felt nothing, thought nothing—just hollow stupor.

Several hours later, a rap-a-tap on my door woke me up. I rolled over and checked the time. Classic—the 2 a.m. booty call.

"Maya? Maya?" Joe called through the mosquito net window. I didn't answer. I didn't feel anything, except for that fat tear rolling down my cheek, around my face, and into my ear.

Twenty-four hours prior to Ayahuasca

The sun was already high above the jungle when I heard Joe's door creak. Cigarette smoke wafted from our shared gravel patio. I shook my head. There was no point in addressing it; I knew what he would say. "We're not in a relationship. You don't get to tell me who I can and can't kiss."

I'd heard it all before. It was an endless loop, a scratched record of dead-end arguments, and there was nothing I could do about it: we were not in a relationship.

I swung my door open to let some light in. Joe was already showered and on his bicycle.

"Hi Maya!" he called as he turned out of the driveway. "Let's hang out later. I missed you last night—you didn't wake up when I came home." He flashed a smile of yellow teeth—a ray of sunshine after the rain, that smile. My mind saw this man was not my type at all, yet my heart fluttered at the mere sight of him. What sorcery was this?

"I guess I just love him." I shrugged, sighing. "I suppose you don't choose whom you love."

That day, I made chocolate, dragging my heavy heart from stove to fridge, then back to bed. I sat cross-legged and meditated on the pain—the piercing dagger through my breastbone. "Why are you here, pain? Why can't I just accept the friendship with casual sex that's being offered?"

"Betrayal!" my heart answered, and it sank even further with the weight of heartbreaks of every woman, everywhere, who had ever caught their husband in bed with another lover.

"But… Joe isn't my husband." I opened my eyes to the realization. "Ah! I see. This is much bigger than me. I'm tapping into some sort of collective trauma. Well, if I'm feeling it this deeply, maybe it's because I've been entrusted with it, like a sacred task to heal a collective wound. Not just for me, but for all the women who've felt this pain."

This was a new thought. It helped—I felt lighter already. I took a deep breath and returned to my chocolate.

Rap-a-tap on my door in the dead of the night.

"Maya! Come hang out."

I sat up, eyes rolling, but I got up anyway and stepped next door. I brushed off the cigarette butts, discarded beer bottles, and empty cocaine pouches, pulled the dirty sheets back over the corners of the bed, and lay next to him. He smelled of patchouli—another "friend," no doubt. Joe definitely seemed drawn to the hippies, like Sky, like me. He curled up against me and pulled me deeper into his arms. I felt his back relax. Sanctuary, he'd called it. Here we were again.

What was different that night? Why didn't I just hold him and enjoy the moment while it lasted? Was La Abuela already at work? Did she reach back in time and compel me to suddenly sit up?

"Joe, I can't anymore."

He blinked in surprise. "What can't you?"

"This. I can't." Suddenly, I was yelling. "You being with all these women, kissing Sky—my friend—in front of me. You're free to do what you want, but I'm done. I can't be your friend anymore."

I stood up and started for the door.

He rose behind me, his voice rising with him. "I've been honest with you from day one." He stepped in front of me. "So do *NOT* threaten to take your friendship away!"

The rest of the argument spiraled into our well-rehearsed endless loop until, as he often did, he collapsed in the entryway, his back rounded, his head bowed.

And as I always did, I sat beside him and placed my arm around his shoulders.

"Hey. Alright. I'm not taking my friendship away. We're connected, you and I. But my heart hurts. I need to heal it. You understand? My heart hurts, even if it's not your fault."

On the platform, waiting for Ayahuasca

The woman next to Sky burped and vomited into her bucket. "Are you okay?" her boyfriend whispered. Sky's breathing had shifted to the quick inhales and forceful exhales of effort. Yolanda and Jordi were quiet. I felt nothing. Just thoughts swirling through my mind like dark clouds: Joe kissing Sky, Joe curled by the door, "You're my best friend. Don't take your friendship away."

I waved my hand above my closed eyes to dispel the thoughts. Here I was, in the Costa Rican jungle, having ingested one of the most powerful Shamanic medicines on Earth, and what did my mind obsess about? A boy.

A mixture of shame and anger knotted my stomach. I imagined Ayahuasca scanning my body to assess what healing was needed, and what would she find? A petty little girl with romance problems, not an empowered woman who has faced and cleared her shadows.

What if Aya decided I wasn't worthy or ready for a shamanic journey?

Hours later, the soft chirps of Spanish brought me back to the room. Jordi had lit a candle and was offering each a second cup. Both Sky and Yolanda sat up and drank another.

"Jordi," I whispered when he reached my mat, "I feel nothing at all. Nothing. Is this normal?"

"It's not very normal, but it does happen." The slight rise in his eyebrow told me it wasn't normal, but he didn't want to say so. I took the chalice in my hands and again pressed it to my heart. "Ayahuasca, I really wish to meet you. I'm sorry I can't quiet my mind. I'll try my best."

The second cup was only slightly sweet. The dark brew's bitter pungency lifted my throat and filled my mouth with saliva. What had happened to the jungle cacao nectar? I swallowed, lay back down, and watched Jordi replace the cork. The second cup, with such a different taste, had come from the same bottle.

I closed my eyes and committed to diligently silencing the drama. Whenever thoughts of Joe surfaced, I forced myself to listen to the night jungle sounds. The chirps of crickets, the random wooden knocks and high-pitch trills, the "groooot" of the frogs—they felt so deeply familiar, like this jungle had always been my home. My body and mind relaxed.

I invited her again, "Please, Abuelita, I would like to meet you." I repeated it like a mantra, matching the rhythm of crickets, until, eventually, a thought of another kind crossed my mind:

"What if *this* is my journey? To accept that nothing is happening or will happen, to just handle disappointment gracefully. That would be a journey indeed." I placed a hand on my heart. "If this is the experience I'll have, then it must be the experience I need, so thank you, Abuelita, I will have it." And I relaxed fully, finally surrendering.

No sooner had I surrendered than an intense buzzing—too loud to be an insect, too quick to be anything else—appeared and hovered right above my third eye. I had expected a shift in perception or consciousness, not an actual physical manifestation of Ayahuasca.

"Maybe it's just a bug that, by coincidence, stopped right there." As though in answer, the buzzing flew around the room, circling the other participants once, then returned to hover exactly above my third eye.

So, it wasn't a coincidence; it had begun.

I opened my eyes to see if the world looked different. The ceiling beams still appeared straight and real, but the fire's glow had changed. The once orange, random flickers now moved in organized waves, forming sacred geometric patterns in dark greens and bright reds. These colors weren't on the ceiling but in my mind, yet I saw them projected onto the physical world as vividly as if they were truly there.

The whole universe was contained within the platform and surrounding jungle, illuminated by the flickering flames, yet it was vaster than any reality I had ever experienced. It buzzed and merged with worlds beyond the veil into one unified cosmology where everything, from the smallest atom in my beating heart to the distant stars, was alive, conscious, and thriving with purpose. I was swimming; my body felt wobbly, but my mind soared, drunk with vitality, clarity, and fractaled colors.

I closed my eyes to see the colors better. Beyond my heartbeat, pressure squeezed my heart while my ribs spread apart as if unseen hands were at work inside me. The process was painless, and I sensed—or imagined—Ayahuasca was scanning me.

"Aaahh Ah! I'm going to restructure your being to your original blueprint." A voice that wasn't mine spoke in my mind. The image of a curved metallic scaffolding appeared at my core. Curved bars on each side of my spine, like the twin helices of DNA, connected by shorter bars extending from ribs to ribs, moved about each other as Ayahuasca organized them.

"Excuse me, young lady, I found some psilocybin in your room." Her voice turned stern.

I winced. It was true—I had eaten magic mushrooms just two days prior, with Sky, on the beach. I braced for repercussions, but then, to my surprise, her tone softened.

"It's alright, Child, but next time, please come to me clean."

I nodded, silently promising. Her fingers returned to the scaffolding. She moved each piece, just slightly, into a more balanced, harmonious arrangement.

"Are you… fixing me?"

"Fixing? Well, I'm gonna try, but have you seen this mess?"

I hadn't expected Ayahuasca to have her own voice, much less humor and Caribbean sass. I giggled, and my body relaxed. Somehow, I knew I was safe with this Caribbean Mama, no matter what happened.

"Before I *fix you,* though…"

Invisible fingers appeared below my cheekbones. They pressed down, then outward toward my temples. Ever since I had received the COVID vaccine, six months prior, I had felt cold metal embedded in the lower portion of my eye sockets. As Aya pressed, the metal moved out of my flesh. I opened my eyes and mouth, rolling them around, looking for the familiar unpleasant sensation. It was gone.

"Thank you! Cacao said you would," I told Aya in my mind, and suddenly I realized… that was who had called me "Child" that one day on the tailgate in the woods of New Hampshire. It was Aya all along. I grinned—one mystery solved!

Immediately, the fingers reappeared, this time at the corners of my smile. One side of my mouth lifted toward my eye, then the other, and back and forth, one up, one down, none of it my doing.

"Mmmh, mh. I'm gonna fix your smile." Both sides of my mouth lifted, pressed into a forced smile by the invisible fingers.

"What's wrong with my smile?"

"It's uneven. You've got a crooked smile, Child. It happens when love from your parents isn't equal. You know this—you always smile more on the right than on the left?"

I knew this, from photos since I was a child. I'd always had a crooked smile but never thought much of it. This made sense. I was definitely a Daddy's Girl, whereas Mom, well…

"Now, they both loved you in their own way. All that criticism and discipline, that's how Fear loves. The idea is to give you the tools to be safe in a scary world. It's a love that tries to protect."

"But… my world isn't scary."

"That's right, so you couldn't receive her love. That's why your smile is crooked."

I realized my sister had always been closer to our mother—and her smile was crooked on the other side. Did we all just walk around with our personal histories written plainly on our faces, silently advertising our wounds and needs to the world?

My jaw dropped in awe at the profundity of this realization, and immediately, a dark-skinned hand closed it shut.

"Close your mouth, Little Monkey!"

As she spoke the words, my eyes grew huge and round, my ears elongated, hair tickled my face, my chin shrank, and my cheekbones protruded. My face… I was a little monkey! I giggled and smiled—a monkey smile, with gums showing and pointy teeth, yet perfectly even on both sides.

The scaffolding vanished, revealing a void nestled between my ribs, then a room. I blinked but couldn't yet see. Mama's voice filled the space with a wordless melody. A sweet African lullaby caressed my ears with its soothing cadence. Everything became serene. Time itself paused to bask in Mama's song. Warm arms wrapped around my body, gently cradling and rocking me, back and forth, with a rhythm as ancient as Earth itself. I rested in this safe cocoon of love—a love deeper and sweeter than I had ever known.

The room shifted. Colorful wooden blocks lay scattered across the ground. I gathered and stacked them between my small brown legs. Mama's song floated from the kitchen. I looked up from my blocks. Mama swayed her hips to the rhythm while stirring a steaming pot. The scent of Caribbean spices filled the room, warm, sweet, and familiar. She was Ayahuasca. I saw her as a person, but the energy that emanated from her was wiser and more ancient than any human. Yet in that moment, to me, she was Mama.

My adult consciousness dissolved. Through the wide eyes of my two-year-old self, I saw Mama, tall and graceful in her green and red apron over her flowery dress. A cascade of tight brown curls, pulled back with a ribbon, framed her glowing, ageless face. As she turned toward me, laugh lines crinkled the edges of her eyes. She smiled, and her love, like a tangible substance, crossed the room and enveloped me. Her love was so vast, boundless, and safe that I began to cry.

Mama left the kitchen and gently squatted in front of me. "What's wrong, Little Monkey?"

"It's just... I've never felt a love so big before." I laughed and cried simultaneously.

She cradled me in her arms and kissed my tear-streaked face, then looked me in the eyes with a stern gaze. "You should never cry from love. Love should be normal, you hear me?"

Mama and I were in a lush garden of green grass and vibrant red flowers. I was shrieking with joy, running away. She could have caught me, but she let the chase play out, fingers outstretched. Love. Those fingers, that game. Everything was love. And my physical body on the mat on the platform felt wrapped in it. I began crying again, then remembered I shouldn't cry because love was normal. I sniffled and wiped my tears, then sniffled again.

"Blow your nose, Little Monkey!"

I had no tissue. I opened my eyes and glanced around the wobbly platform, searching for some. Jordi, looking like a translucent ghost, was walking toward the woman in the back, who had been sobbing. Her boyfriend was vomiting. Yolanda seemed peaceful, but Sky was groaning.

I sat up, craning to see Sky's face. She had chosen the tallest mattress and now lay on her back under a white blanket, so luminous and radiant. She was an Elf Queen from the water realm. That was her true nature. I had suspected as much from the depth of her ocean-blue eyes and her slightly pointed ears, but now I truly saw her. I smiled an even smile—what a gift to have met Sky! I sniffled again.

"Blow your nose, Little Monkey."

A roll of toilet paper sat on the center altar, but it was so far away, and I felt so drunk from the medicine. My body collapsed back onto the mat.

"I don't wanna get up. I wanna stay here with you," I sniffled.

"What kind of rebellious child do I have on my hands here?" Mama's tone was firm, and I saw her slender figure with both fists on her hips and her foot tapping. But I knew she was joking, pretending to be upset with me.

"Well, I'm almost a teenager now. I'm supposed to rebel."

Her hands dropped from her hips, and her arms wrapped me tightly in her love again. She flicked her tongue. "Tsk. Child. That's a mistake humans make. A well and evenly loved child doesn't become a rebellious teenager. There is individualization and more independence, sure, but all in a healthy way."

I felt my teenage heart and knew she spoke the truth. As a teenager, I defined myself in contrast to the rules and restrictions. But now, I was once again becoming my own person, and this time on a solid foundation of love. I didn't feel like rebelling; I felt like exploring, discovering, and telling Mama all about it.

"Good. You understand. So, go. Blow. Your. Nose!" A hand like a vine unfurled and pointed to the roll of toilet paper.

"No." Imitating her, I pressed my fists to my hips and tapped my foot under the blanket. If she was a jokester, and I was her child, then I, too, had that spark.

Suddenly, my whole body turned. My hand lifted on its own, reached for my long-sleeve shirt, brought it to my nose, and blew my nose loudly into it. This was my favorite long-sleeve shirt. I, of my own accord, would never have blown my nose in it.

"Oh my God! She can move my whole body." My jaw dropped. And immediately, Mama closed it, triggering a cascade of giggles. She morphed my face into a young monkey, then a jaguar cub, with tickling fur and whiskers— the more I laughed, the more she played—oooh, I was an owl, a toucan with my nose as a beak, a boar with tusks growing from my lower teeth, and back to little monkey, with gums showing an even smile. It was the equivalent of spiritual tickling. She did it to make me laugh.

And laugh I did—out loud, a full-belly laugh—as my face transformed from monkey to jaguar, owl, boar, and back.

The woman in the back was still sobbing. I imagined my laughter would make it worse for her. I placed a hand on my mouth in compassion for others' pain. I didn't want to be a selfish teenager. I caught my breath and willed myself back into a respectful silence. But the immense joy couldn't be stifled, and in spite of my best effort, I began laughing again.

I propped myself up on one elbow and glanced at the sobbing woman, checking if she was looking at me disapprovingly.

She wasn't—and shared the next morning that my laughter had helped break through her hard dream and lighten her cleansing journey.

She wasn't looking at me; Sky was, with a radiant smile.

The next day, Sky recounted her experience of that moment. Ayahuasca had been tuning her bones like one tunes a musical instrument, stretching and compressing each until its frequency matched that of the Earth. This attunement was vital for the work she would one day be called to do—holding sister circles and tuning in to the Earth for guidance. But at that moment, the process was excruciating, akin to growing bone pain radiating through her entire body. She accepted the agony because she understood the gift offered. Until my laughter pierced through her pain, instantly dissipating it. She opened her eyes, turned toward me, and smiled.

Sky—my Elf Queen sister. I slid off my mat and scooted toward her. I felt Mama's hand help me cross the distance. She was encouraging me to connect with Sky. Without a word, we found each other's hands, pressed our foreheads together, and closed our eyes. At first, her body still trembled from the bone-tuning portal she had just crossed. Soft hues of tan, pale yellows and pastel blues emanated from her and flowed into my being. Her colors mingled with the vibrant green and bright red of my own sacred geometry patterns, then together, they ebbed back to her, like waves passing between us. I grounded and settled her; she softened my sharp edges, until our breathing matched, restful and soft.

I felt Mama retreat. She wanted me to experience sister's love apart from mother's love. How long did Sky and I rest like this? Hours? By my reckoning, we always had, and always would. Sky and I were sisters in all times, dimensions, and universes. Not even the most intimate moment with a most beloved lover in the physical realm had merged me so completely with another being.

In an instant, my entire concept of sisterhood shifted. I had, historically, befriended very few women. Women were always more beautiful than I was, and men always preferred them. I saw these stories I had believed to be truths evaporate, smoke in the wind, nothing tangible. Sky's hand in mine, her supportive smile, her healing songs—these were tangible. These were the true essence of sisterhood.

After an eternity, Sky sighed, and we slowly parted, rolling back to back, still connected yet returning to our own journeys.

Mama wasn't back, and Sky had left. For the first time since I was a Little Monkey, I was energetically alone, yet this was a very different alone than I had known. I thought I knew "alone." I had hiked hundreds of miles alone, lived in the desert purposefully alone. Being alone had made me feel safe: no one to judge, criticize, or even attack me. But even as Mama was quiet and energetically absent, her love was a solid anchor in my heart, and I knew this shift was permanent.

"Mama Aya, I'm curious. You give me your love, a mother's love, and I feel Sky's love, a sister's love. You've given me a second family, but why a family of only women?"

"Because you don't have a father wound."

"Are you sure? By everything I've read, my pattern with men, and I mean mostly this last one, suggests I do have a father wound. And I don't understand why. I love my dad."

As I spoke the words, my heart filled with my own love for my dad and… Aya's love for my dad. My jaw dropped, but I quickly closed it myself. Aya knew my dad! Of course, she did. She had access to all my memories. Or maybe she knew him because the sea told her. My dad and the sea—that was a serious love affair. I saw him in my mind's eye, curls in the wind, whistling a happy tune, free as a bird on his boat. He looked at me and winked.

Aya's love wrapped around me like a warm embrace. It was snuggly soft, unconditional, undeniable, and it now lived deep in my DNA.

My dad's love was different. It was supportive and playful, like a wide, dreamy playfield of infinite possibilities.

"You're right." Mama took me in her arms. "Your dad's energy *is* a dreamy playfield of infinite possibilities. You grew up with two masculine energies, one gentle and playful, the other strict and disciplined. One in a male body, the other in a female body. But you didn't have a Mother's Love, until now. And this reaches far beyond your physical life as you currently understand it."

Tears of gratitude welled up as I felt Aya's love flow through me and up my ancestral line. My mother needed this love too, and maybe her mother before her, and all those before them. Aya pursed my lips into a kiss and blew some of her Great Love into the ether, through my heart and to my mom, wherever she was. Then to my dad, with a bow of gratitude for being my best friend, always and still.

Both images faded.

"Little Monkey, come here. We need to talk about this boy of yours." Mama opened her arms, inviting me onto her lap. I felt I was too old to still be called Little Monkey, or to sit on her lap, but I had been wondering if she would explain about Joe.

"Listen. You won't understand everything now, but your heart will remember." She leaned back, rocking me gently, her loving brown eyes fixed on mine.

"The love you share with that boy is real, but not as you understand it. Reality has layers. Years from now, when you recall this conversation, you'll perceive it differently. As you evolve, you'll grasp more depth beyond the words and images. And at each stage, what you can comprehend will be revealed to you. So, listen well, Child."

In my mind's eye, Joe appeared as a little boy. The tall legs of his dad walked by. Joe looked up, but couldn't catch his dad's eye. Joe couldn't catch anyone's eye. Little Joe was different from anyone in his family, and they couldn't see him. So he just stacked the colorful blocks. As he did, his face aged. His chin became thinner, his jaw squarer. The outer edges of his eyes angled up into that classic, sexy almond shape I found irresistible. He grew lean, sculpted muscles. It was all by design.

Attention—his very survival depended on it. How to catch attention.

I saw Joe's lean body walking through the crowd, his bright smile—yellowed teeth and all—seducing women. He was a master with a well-hidden wound to those who could not see. Our history flashed before my eyes. I was a prime candidate. What was it? Was it my crooked smile that advertised my love template was incomplete? "You are needy and a masochist." I remembered Elizabeth's words. She had known simply by looking at my face. Or was it Kambo, the Frog, who had spoken through her?

Mama showed me, without a word. Unconsciously, Joe had taken a whole year to learn me. What pleased me, what triggered me. From the way we first made love to our mingled songs rising to the stars from the back of the Catmobile. These were my dreams, not his. So he had embodied my dreams, and, of course, I had adored him for it.

But attention, like cocaine, was ever required in greater amount to satisfy the same craving once the current dose had become the norm.

"Drama is the highest form of attention a human can get," Mama said. "But only one with a love deficit will bite. You, my Little Monkey, have settled for love crumbs because you didn't trust you could get the whole baguette."

Our entire history flashed before my eyes, then slowed down, zooming in on the last twenty-four hours. I had mentally cast myself in the role of the crazy jealous woman. What was wrong with me? He had been honest; he had told me we weren't in a relationship right from the start. It was his right to see or kiss whomever he chose. Now I saw the twist. I didn't yell at him because he kissed Sky. He kissed Sky so that I would yell at him.

We stood again in his filthy room, me yelling, and him shrinking by the door. The world disappeared in my rage, and at that moment he had all my attention, 100% of it. The craving was fed, for now.

I pursed my lips as Aya had done and blew some of her love to these two people locked in their drama cycle. They didn't know. They just didn't know.

And I saw he wasn't the first one. I had worshiped friends and lovers alike in my eagerness for love crumbs my whole life.

Mama wrapped me tightly in her warm love, then extended her arms to look at me with pride. I was grown now, and the imprint of her love made me strong.

"You can send Joe some love, but remember, you're your own priority. It's not your job to fix him or anyone else. You think because you're so adaptable, you can take it on, always putting others' needs first. You think it's helpful? It's not. Listen, Child, no one will make you a priority if you don't prioritize yourself."

"I don't always put others' needs first," I mumbled defensively.

"Mmmh, mmh?" Suddenly, my sassy Caribbean Mama was back, pointing out that I was lying directly on the wood of the platform to be close to Sky, while Sky rested comfortably on the Queen's Mat.

"That's different," I argued, then scooted back to my mat. As I did, my blanket fell off, exposing my skin to several mosquitoes. I gently brushed them off with the back of my hand.

"Mmmh, mmh?" Aya took my hand and, with one slap, killed the mosquitoes on my arm.

"You even put mosquitoes first. Enough. You're too powerful to play wallflower."

My jaw dropped again. Had Aya just killed mosquitoes? But... weren't all creatures to be protected?

417

"Close your mouth, Little Monkey." She hadn't said it in a few hours, and it did, still, make me giggle. "You gotta set some boundaries. Even with mosquitoes."

"Mama Aya? I know it's going to be morning soon and you'll fade from my system, but before you go, why did you say earlier that I was too powerful to play wallflower?"

"Again, Child, you won't understand everything. But here's a glimpse of one representation of who you are in the spiritual world. Knowing this will be enough for now."

In my mind's eye, I saw myself, an Earth being, running through the jungle, agile and light on my feet. Large leaves parted as I navigated intuitive paths to the clearing where the clan gathered. The jungle opened where light reached the trampled grass. There, I slowed down and caught my breath. Jaguar entered the clearing from the other side and approached me. We placed our heads together, jaguar's large and powerful head against my small skull. With the greeting over, I threw my arms around his neck and scratched behind his ears. He growled slightly, then let himself drop onto the grass, offering his underbelly. Kneeling by his side, I nestled myself against his warm fur for a quick rest.

I saw the dream was real.

This is how we rest and sleep—we, the People of the Jaguar. We own nothing but the dark orange and ochre pieces of cloth that cover our dark skin. Our jewelry is made of vines and wood offered by the jungle. We are the Guardians. In spite of our slight stature, we are fierce and strong. The jungle is our home—this jungle, here, in Bribri specifically. Just behind the veil, we harmonize with trees and animals, using telepathic abilities yet to be discovered in the default world. Some harmonize with the sea, the air, the mountains, the desert; we are the People of the Jaguar.

The sun on my eyelids made me sleepy. I rolled to the side, seeking the soft comfort of my friend's underbelly. I was there and on the platform simultaneously. I opened my eyes and looked at myself on the mat on the platform, next to Sky. And I, on the platform, looked back. This one of me there, in the jungle, she had jaguar spots on her temples. I caressed my own temples as the image faded. What remained was a deep sense that this jungle, here, in Costa Rica, and in Bribri, especially, was home. And that there was a deeper purpose, yet to be discovered, to my being here.

"Goodnight, Little Monkey." Mama's embrace wrapped me once more in her immense love, and this time, I didn't cry. "I'll see you soon, Child. This time, you came to heal. Next time, you come to play."

80 · 03

Puerto Viejo, Costa Rica - twenty-four hours after Ayahuasca and beyond

"You feel different." Joe and I stood on the beach under the moonless sky, feet deep in wet sand, eyes up to the stars.

"I am different." I felt very tall.

"Sorry I didn't see you all day. I was out with a friend." I smiled, remembering one of Mama Aya's pieces of advice.

"What do I do if Joe tries to hook my attention?" I'd asked.

"You show him your fangs, Little Monkey."

I smiled in Joe's direction, all teeth exposed, lips even on each side. I felt Aya's love in my heart and compassion for this man. But I also saw the game he played—so I played back a little.

"Ha. I didn't notice. I was in my hammock at the beach all day. Wasn't today just the best day?"

"Mmh mmh."

We were silent for a moment. I was aware of his every move. He shifted from one foot to the next, then placed a hand on my lower back. I moved forward, legs deeper into the sea, away from his flirting hand.

419

A group of people ran by us, laughing on their way to the dark waves.

"Oh. I know this laugh. That's my friend Marli." He pointed toward a woman, one of the laughing figures silhouetted against the waves.

Marli was nothing to me. I looked up to the stars.

Long silent minutes came and went with the ocean's flux, and suddenly, Joe collapsed.

He hunched his back and wrapped his arms around his knees. He looked like the little boy I had seen with the blocks.

"What's going on?" I sat next to him but didn't touch him.

"I don't know. I feel weird. You're different, and I don't know what to do."

I showed him my teeth and gently reassured him. "It's okay. There's nothing to do."

For the next month, despite my small size and Caucasian skin, I walked through town feeling like a tall, sultry, magnetic, mixed-race beauty—the lovechild of my Caribbean mama and sea-loving dad. I bought a few pieces of clothing in the proper People of the Jaguar colors, and watched my whole world transform by no effort of mine.

A week after Ayahuasca, Sky and I hugged goodbye as it was time for her to return to New Hampshire. That same day, an unexpected high-paying job offer came to Joe. He flew to the US within a week. Two days after his departure, I met a man who had a dream cabina for rent on Cocles Beach, my favorite beach. I moved in that day.

Calvin the mycologist trusted me with a fresh batch of his magic mushrooms on credit. With the cleaner space and my own kitchen, I made love-filled chocolate and mixed in the potent fungi friends. As much as I had struggled to sell chocolate, magic chocolate flew off the shelves of my new fridge. And soon, I lived a very different life from the girl who had been Joe's next door neighbor.

I lived the life of a woman who knew her worth and loved herself.

For now, anyway…

Chapter 29
Once, When I Was Tree

Bribri, Costa Rica - May 2022

I caressed the papery belly of the elliptical leaf hanging over the platform, and with one foot, pushed my thin mat underneath the branches.

Sleeping under leaves was a familiar setup, and this shrub radiated such a joyful, playful energy. I imagined it would be a delightful journeying companion. It hadn't been there two months prior, when I was a Little Monkey. Maybe it had been too short to be visible from the platform. Or maybe my attention had been so focused on the brew inside the glass bottle and the stories that unfolded that I had noticed nothing else.

Jordi appeared around the walled side of the platform. He held a smoky shell and blew on the copal incense, directing the smoke to clear any unwanted energies before our ceremony. He blew the smoke toward the plant and my mat underneath it, then smiled and caressed a leaf.

"Chacruna." That was her name. He pointed to the bottle on the altar and, in rapid Spanish, introduced me to Chacruna.

Ayahuasca, he explained, is a decoction of two plants: the vine Ayahuasca and the shrub Chacruna. Like sisters, they dance in unison in the brew. Chacruna offers the DMT—the vivid colors, the sacred geometric patterns, and the epiphanies. Ayahuasca, the Vine of the Soul, neutralizes enzymes in the stomach, allowing Chacruna's essence to reach the human psyche. The Vine is also responsible for the most profound DNA upgrades.

So, my bedside companion was the medicine herself. I looked to her with new eyes of respect. I had chosen my place on the platform well.

Jordi continued with the copal smoke toward the sacred fire, around the fire, toward the jungle, and back up the steps to the platform. He circled our mats as we organized ourselves for the night. Once La Abuela joined the dance, tasks in physical reality would be challenging. Buckets, tissues, water, blankets, extra layers, and headlamps all had to be within easy reach.

We were just three participants this time: Nikita, David, and me—the same Nikita and David who had cooked miso soup on the night with the magic mushrooms on the beach. Nikita spread a blanket on her mat and began writing in her journal. David, right beside her, created a backrest against the wall with pillows and blankets. I lay on my mat and let the energy of Chakruna gladden my heart. It wasn't just Chakruna; it was this entire setup—friends on the platform, leaves over my pillow, the jungle all around... it reminded me of happy days with leaves and friends in North Conway.

I followed the vein of Chakruna's leaf to her thin trunk with my finger and sent the image of Whittaker Woods to Chakruna. Plants always seemed to appreciate stories of their distant relatives.

My thoughts drifted to my beloved Catmobile. I smiled at the sweet memory of the Catmobile backed against the maple

423

tree, but gradually, my smile pressed to a bittersweet line as the image changed to the Catmobile now, alone under a tarp in Sedona, awaiting my return.

For ten years, the Catmobile and I had been inseparable. But now there was magic chocolate, jungle, tropical beaches, dancing, an income, and friends. Of course, Puerto Viejo was too small to keep me forever, yet I couldn't imagine I'd return to a solo, penniless life in the truck.

Those ten years of roaming had been needed. They had blanked the slate of who I had been before, and any notion of who I ought to be. Cacao and the others in cahoots had led me here. But despite the immense gratitude I felt for their guidance to this point, I couldn't help but sense—or maybe hope—I was meant for yet greater things.

I had come to Ayahuasca with no pressing question, no preformulated intent, but here was a question to the scope of a Great Teacher—what was my purpose? How could I best share the gifts of the road and the lessons of the jungle in service to the world?

ᘓ · ᘔ

"Maya." Jordi wiped the chalice as I crawled forward to the altar. He poured the dark brew halfway up the chalice, held it to his heart, and handed it to me. I reached for the chalice with both hands and brought it reverently to my heart.

I had been warned by many. "Oh yes, she loves you the first time, then she kicks your ass." "She said next time you'd play, did she? Oh, good luck! She plays hard sometimes."

With eyes closed, I felt her warm energetic embrace. I didn't believe this *Curandera*—this Healer—would ever do me harm.

"Abuelita Ayahuasca. Mama Aya. Thank you for calling me again. It's an honor to receive your healing, and whatever you think I need, I trust you."

I brought the chalice from my heart to my third eye, lifted it to the jungle, and drank the thick brew in one gulp.

I lay back under Chacruna's leaves, peaceful and patient.

As with my first journey, I felt nothing for hours. I stared at the stars, the jungle, the silhouette of banana leaves against the dark night sky. Nikita vomited twice, David's breathing tempo changed several times, and Jordi played the flute, then the harmonica.

Still, I waited.

Jordi relit the candle and offered each one a second cup. I drank another half chalice of medicine and lay back down.

℘ · ℘

She entered through the soles of my feet as though I were planted in moist jungle soil. She slowly twisted up my legs, to my pelvis, my heart, around my lungs until my chest was filled, then up my throat and to my third eye. From there, her presence expanded outward.

Her tendrils curled, swirled, and explored until every corner of my being was filled.

A face appeared briefly. She was green, ageless, with soft, symmetrical features, and with pupils like stars. She smiled, and I felt her benevolent curiosity in my heart, then she faded, replaced by fractals.

Instead of geometric patterns, the fractals were spirals in various shades of green with occasional pinpoint flashes of bright jewel-like emerald light, like fireflies in a forest.

I waited and observed as my whole wobbly, buzzing universe filled with the elegance of dancing, unfurling ferns, curly vines, and leaves. I waited for Aya to guide me to insights and epiphanies, to reveal what healing we'd accomplish, but she continued mesmerizing me with designs of increasingly delicate beauty.

So after a while, I spoke first.

"Hola Ayahuasca, hola Mama Aya. Please… What is my purpose here on Earth? What can I do to benefit the whole? Is Cacao the best career for me? Any guidance you…"

425

"Child, I don't give career advice."

Suddenly, my Caribbean Mama was back, complete with sass and hands on hips.

"Besides," she continued, "you can't even breathe right. Learn to breathe, then maybe we'll talk."

"I don't... breathe right?"

"No, look at you, your breath barely skims the surface of your lungs, and half the time, you don't breathe at all. You only take deep breaths when you're gathering courage. Shallow breath isn't natural breath, you know."

Well, it was true that I sometimes woke myself up gulping for air. And I had noticed in meditation that my breath was shallow. But it was my breath, so it was normal to me. And I had asthma as a kid, but I had grown out of that decades ago.

"Learn to breathe." My lungs, of their own accord, took a deep, long inhale. "Then it won't matter what you choose to create with your life. Whatever you choose, you'll be able to breathe life into it, literally, and it will be successful."

Aya pursed my lips, ready for a pointed exhale, but in that micropause between the inhale and exhale, Jordi began playing the harmonica. The exhale stalled. With each long harmonica note, my lungs filled more and more. My belly rose to match my chest, and both became so full that the outward pressure physically hurt.

Aya then blew a sharp, sustained stream of air toward Jordi. *Ffffffffh.* That breath I knew meant "Thank you!"

"Harmonica!" my mind marveled—it was the only instrument I'd ever learned to play. How fascinating that I had chosen a wind instrument. Perhaps, unconsciously, I had always known I needed to learn to breathe.

"Whatever or whomever you wish to support, this is how you breathe life into it."

"And what about things I don't wish to support?"

I felt her smile. She lifted the corners of my mouth, and I expected her to say, "Show them your teeth, Little Monkey." But I wasn't a Little Monkey. This was a different journey.

Shhhhhhheee. A wild cat hiss escaped my lips instead.

426

"Like that," she said. "That's how you set your boundaries."

I wondered if anyone on the platform had heard me. It had been a loud hiss. But when I checked, no one moved. All were immersed in their own journeys.

I lay back down under my leaves, facing the jungle.

The green fractal vines continued dancing in my mind, in my relaxed body, in my loved heart. Sky appeared in my mind. She had been busy since she returned to New Hampshire, and we had only spoken a few times. My Elf Queen—she would have loved this green, spirally journey. I filled my lungs, pursed my lips, and blew a long Breath of Love to Sky. Then another to my dad, one to Leah, one to my plant-loving friend Kaja, and... I hesitated... what about Joe?

Joe was back in town. He had either been fired or quit the job in the US after a month, and returned to Puerto Viejo with cash in hand. He had rented a new apartment with a big-screen TV and a revolving door—not an actual revolving door, just a regular sliding glass door that opened for a different woman every night.

His game was the same, but I played differently. I listened to his stories of conquests, observed the sudden turning of his phone with incoming secret messages, and received the reassurance that I was his best friend, and that he loved me, but I didn't react. I starved the attention-craving beast inside of him with detached smiles and casual nods. Inside, I churned and burned and ached, yet I persisted in sitting on his sofa and sleeping in his bed, locked in no longer by his charm but by the morbid curiosity of watching the addiction die—mine or his, I wasn't sure.

So, what about Joe? Should I send a Breath of Life loaded with compassion, since I understood what plagued him, or hiss to set clear boundaries and keep him and his kind away?

A melody from the harmonica cut through my thoughts. I realized I wasn't breathing. How long had I been holding my breath? Maybe the whole time I'd been thinking about Joe. Letting go of those thoughts, I filled my lungs until they ached, then exhaled a Breath of Life toward... Jim.

Ffffh... Thank you, Jim, for speaking with trees and spreading mushrooms in the world." I felt Aya join me. She smiled—ah, she approved of that friendship. Once more, my lungs filled, and on the Breath of Life, she added a special flavor of joy, that of unexpected gifts.

"What did we just send Jim?"

She didn't answer, instead, using my hand, she selected one of my longer dreadlocks, and tickled my third eye with it. Jim was also the reason I had dreadlocks. I had fallen in love with his first, then let my own curls begin to lock. Aya tapped on my third eye with the end of it. I giggled and pushed her away with my other hand, then laughed. How strange was this scene—my hands pushing each other in a playful battle?

"I like these." Aya twirled the end of the dreadlock in mid-air over my face, then caressed my head. "This hair of yours, it has power. It acts like antennas to the natural world, and it looks like vines. I like it."

My hand was left to hold the antenna-vine in mid-air, as Aya regrouped in my heart. Instinctively, I wrapped my lock around Chacruna's thin trunk. How I wished I could just connect this way, like in the movie *Avatar*, and know all of Chacruna's thoughts and feelings from the inside.

I had tried speaking with trees and plants in the jungle, but they never seemed to hear me, except for the ones near the beach or where humans lived. In the deep jungle, they communed with each other with a constant buzz of energy but paid me no mind. What would it take to get the jungle plants' attention? Did I need to select one and insist—

Harmonica notes rose over the night jungle sounds.

How odd. Last time, Jordi had only played the harmonica once, but this time—

"It's for you." Ayahuasca interrupted my thought. "The harmonica plays whenever you forget to breathe."

I checked my breath. It was so shallow as to be practically nonexistent, again.

"Ugh. This is so much work, having to remember to breathe all the time."

"Is it too much work to be alive?"

I paused and pondered for a second. "Well, actually... yes. Sometimes, it is too much work to be alive. I have nothing pulling me forward, so what's the point of life?"

"Learn to breathe. Breath happens in the present moment. Life happens in the present moment. When you breathe mindfully in your Point of Life, anything you wish to create will then pull you forward."

"Aya, that's a circular argument."

As if to answer my thought, a cascade of green spiraling vines suddenly filled my mind. Correction: not circular; upward spiraling.

As the harmonica's last note tapered to silence, I filled my lungs, pursed my lips, and blew a Breath of Life to the plant world with gratitude—to all my friends in Whittaker Woods, the majestic oak at the corner of Mechanic Street, a few special junipers in Sedona, the West Coast redwoods and ponderosas, even the condescending Joshua trees of Death Valley. Aya filled my heart and mind with her green, spiraling love. How fortunate were we to live on such a verdant, abundant Earth surrounded by peaceful tree people? Chacruna's gift, DMT in my brain, was allowing me to perceive this immense Green Love.

"Right... DMT." Suddenly, a slight nausea of disappointment washed over me as I realized all of this was just DMT in my brain. All these colors and revelations, just me entertaining myself, just my imagination on drugs. Last time I had imagined myself a new mom, and now I was imagining a conversation with a plant teaching me how to breathe. But I had always wished for a new mom, just as I had always wished to speak with plants. So there was nothing tangible here, just internal processes.

The harmonica began again. Exactly—like the harmonica! Jordi played the harmonica for the group, it had nothing to do with me. I probably always forgot to breathe, but whenever I heard the harmonica, I placed my attention on my breath. Then I drew inaccurate causal correlations and imagined he played specifically for me, because "Ayahuasca was teaching me how to breathe."

To the tune of a long high note, I opened my eyes to locate Jordi. Sometimes, with Ayahuasca, sounds appear to emanate from locations away from their source.

I imagined I'd find him on his mat, which would validate my skepticism, but the harmonica was directly above my face, only two to three inches away. He was so close that I could feel the wind from the notes on my forehead. I tilted my head back. Jordi's knees bracketed my head as he leaned forward to play directly over me.

"Okay," I said out loud. I snapped my fingers and pointed to the harmonica. "So, not just in my head. Got it!"

With eyes closed, Jordi drew a long breath and blew a melody over me. In return, I inhaled deeply and softly blew a Breath of Gratitude to the man and his harmonica. He smiled, stood up, and returned to his mat.

So Aya was real. My muscles softened and sank into the mat in deep relaxation. Matching my renewed surrender, Aya engulfed me with bliss and love of such a magnitude that I could have sworn it was greater than the greatest love I had ever felt—which happened in her very arms, just two months prior.

She had once gifted me motherly love of an almost human kind, but *this*—this felt like the love of Pachamama herself, the embrace of an entire sentient planet, a love that carried the energy of belonging. I felt and knew, beyond a doubt, that I was part of a far greater whole… what had I called it before? Yes, the Great Symphony of Things. I was part of that.

The Great Symphony—Macaws and morpho butterflies, trees and shrubs, flowers, jaguars, ants, coyotes, cats and dogs, sharing breaths, mingling, balancing each other in perfect harmony. And me, us, the appreciators. Flowers didn't perceive fragrances; morphos might not realize the beauty of their iridescent blue wings; trees didn't hug themselves.

So if I shared breaths and purpose with all these kindred beings, why had I said, and meant, that sometimes it was too much work to be alive?

The mood and colors darkened quickly. The flip side to the Great Symphony came into focus. The physical world in its current state was off balance. Humans running in hamster wheels to earn a few dollars to buy food, while mechanical machinery plowed endless monochromatic fields. Humans locking doors with keys and chains, barricading themselves, sinking in plastic sofas, and staring at blinking screens, while the Milky Way sparkled for no one. Plastic water bottles floating down rivers where sick fish jumped to escape the ever-growing dark foam from sewers and the goopy drips from trash bags. I felt increasingly nauseated and reached for my bucket, just in case.

"What's your address?" a voice suddenly asked. "I live in my truck," I replied. "We don't have a check box for that. You're not in the system. You don't exist."

"What's your address?" the voice repeated. "I live in the jungle." Denied again.

Saliva filled my mouth. I sat up and moved my legs around the bucket.

"Aya, could you heal this in me? Just like you gifted me a new childhood and installed so much self-love and confidence, could you gift me a new life perspective? Could you anchor the Symphony of Life as my permanent paradigm? I enjoy the colors and fractals, I really do, thank you, but while I'm here, I don't want to squander my time with you. Can we work on something important?"

"Work!" Lifting one of my locks, she twirled it a few times above my face like a whip, then slapped it across my nose. The gesture was so playful that the nausea instantly dissipated, the colors regained their vibrancy, and I lay back down.

"Work, work, work." She slapped my nose in rhythm with her words. "Child, that is all you do. Internal work, every day. It isn't necessary. I told you, you're here to *play*. So, let's play. Any experience you wish. What would you like?"

"Anything? I can experience anything?"

"Anything that is not work." She tickled my nose with the curl at the end of my lock.

I looked to the jungle and pondered. Maybe Aya didn't understand my request because she had never been human. She had never needed money. No one had ever asked her for her address. Maybe when you were a plant, human drama seemed odd and irrelevant.

A smile appeared on my face…

"Aya, I'd like to know what it's like to be you. I'd like to know how plants experience life and the world. Could I be a tree?"

"You can't be a tree, because of the rubber suit, but you can experience Tree, the essence of being a tree."

Before I could ask, Aya pinched the skin on my belly with my hand. "This rubber suit." She kept pinching all the way to the side, where she grabbed a handful and shook it. "Human skin is so strange." I laughed, and with the lighter mood returned, Aya gently engulfed me in her love again.

"Be Tree then."

An explosion of spiraling curls filled my being. The display was breathtaking, and for once, Aya let me hold my breath. Green as an oak canopy in the heart of July, leaves pulsated, spiral-danced, and wove into one another. A flash of gold, and soon the scene changed, unfurling fiery hues of reds and yellows. Then leaves began their descent, drifting to the ground in slow figure-eight spins. Deep browns and a sense of grounding, the rich scent of earth mingled with tiny electric pinpricks—these were the tickles of mycelium in the soil. Oh, what a spectacle in my mind. Yet I was still only a spectator, and appreciator.

"Aya. I see it, but I don't feel Tree."
"You do, Child, but it feels normal to you."
I stood, tall and slender, in a boreal forest of evergreens. My ears tapered to delicate points, and as though tiny corks had been popped out of them, I heard the natural world's slightest, subtlest songs—the sounds of Whittaker Woods in my mind and those of the jungle around the platform simultaneously. A golden headdress dipped to a point, cradling a bright emerald jewel on my third eye. I lifted the hem of my gown and stepped a bare foot forward. The emerald fabric flowed like mist, ethereal and lighter than silk. My bare feet sank into the moist forest soil, each step a deeper communion with the standing ones, my kin. I had no destination; I was content just walking. I had no question; I was powerful, grounded, wise, and anything I wished to know was already known through the soles of my feet.

Except, I did have a question—I, on the mat on the platform.
"So... Am I Tree? Is this what I'm seeing and feeling right now?"
Tendril answers twirled up my legs and entered my heart. "You are Plant in many of your parallel lives—what humans call past lives. You are Plant more than anything else. That's why this state feels natural to you. That's why you so ardently

433

wanted to speak to trees, and why it came to you naturally, more so than with animals, or even humans. You have cellular knowing of how we, plants, communicate. This essence (I understood Aya meant the sensed vision of the woman in the emerald gown) is your Plant self. This is how we see you."

I inhaled deeply as tears gathered in the corners of my eyes. Never in my wildest dreams could I have imagined I was such a beautiful plant.

My hand twirled over my face, each finger opening a flower until the last one wiped the tear that had escaped down my cheek.

Coming into the scene with a confident yet bouncy stride, a man I knew well—he was my mate in that world—joined my vision. His ageless skin glowed. He tightened his oak-green garment, which was coarser and more fibrous than mine, then extended a hand. I knew if I took his hand, my being would become lighter. This hand would guide me on wild adventures and catch me if I fell. That man—or male Plant being—was the mischievous leaf inexplicably waving from within the canopy, and, simultaneously, he was the rooted oak, sentinel guardian of all that is green and natural amidst the expanding world of humans.

"This—this is available to you. So why do you chase after lizards?"

Before I could ask Aya what she meant by "lizards," the man had stepped in front of me. With his face so close to mine, I softened, and, from my Plant self, a peach and crimson hibiscus flower bloomed. I was the flower—soft like my petals, receptive, connected, open, patient, colorful. Yet I was still wise, grounded, and powerful, like the plant that produced me. I had never felt so completely feminine before. As I leaned forward to meet his loving gaze, the pollen I

434

carried at the end of my filaments became tangled in his hair, and we both laughed.

"Why do you chase after lizards?" Aya repeated. "*This* is how you attract a true mate."

"By being like a flower? Just sitting there looking pretty?"

Several green spiraling tendrils whipped around me, and Aya expanded in my mind at the exclusion of all else. The man was gone. I sensed I had offended her and cringed at my lack of grace. But she forgave me quickly; I was still just a human in a rubber suit, after all.

"No, no, no." Using my hand, she picked again one of my locks and slapped me across the face with it. I giggled, and, instantly, the awkwardness dissipated.

"'Sitting there looking pretty' is not what flowers do. Flowers master the Art of Being and Broadcasting. They broadcast their essence's signature with such specificity that only those truly attracted to them are invited to the banquet of who they are."

Aya paused while the dreadlock pressed on my third eye so that I would remember these important words. Then, with an inquisitive tone, she continued, "What fragrance do you wear now?"

"Sandalwood."

"Why?"

"Because... it's my favorite fragrance, and even though I trust you, I was a little nervous coming here, so I dabbed on some sandalwood to make me feel more grounded and maybe safer."

"So you're wearing a fragrance that you're attracted to—a male essence that makes you feel safe. That is what you seek, not what you are. Sandalwood doesn't attract sandalwood. Do you understand?"

"I do. But how do I know what I should smell like?"

"I can't tell you that. You have to discover your own fragrance."

"Okay… so let's say I find my signature fragrance. Then I just wear it and wait?"

Again came the dreadlock across the face.

"No, no, no. Flowers don't wait; they radiate. They bathe in the sunshine wearing their most vibrant colors, sway to the caress of the breeze, entice with fragrance, sweetness, and beauty. But never do they wait. It is their very nature to be attractive. Waiting would imply their grace depends on whether or not they receive the visit of a bee. You have been the bee, Melissa the Bee, Maya the Bee, Wyld like the best honey. Be the Bee, wild and free, just know you will have more success in finding a true mate if you are also the Flower."

A bee flew over a field of dandelions, and I followed it in flight. The sea of green at the foot of the plants receded in the background, a mere showcase for the irresistible flowers. The bee descended, zeroing in on a particular bloom. It landed on the soft petals and immediately began gathering pollen. Its legs quickly became dusted with golden grains as it moved efficiently around the flower's center. And off it flew.

"Aya… the bee flew away."

"Yes. That is what bees do. And you'll notice, the flower isn't longing for its return, or wondering if the bee will call, or checking its cell phone every five minutes."

"Ha ha ha!" I mocked Aya's sudden sass, but she continued, "And you'll notice, she's not worried about the bee's whereabouts. She doesn't feel less attractive when the bee lands on another flower."

"Okay, okay, I get it. Bees pollinate and leave. But I'm not a flower, Aya, I'm a woman, and I'd prefer to attract a mate that wants to stay, not some sampler-pollinator."

"Hey!" Although she was green and fractal-spiraling, I felt my Mama Aya come through. "If you're asking a plant for relationship advice, I'm telling you what we do. If it doesn't fit for you, then find your own way."

436

I laughed out loud. I laughed so loud that it might have sounded like sobs because Jordi kindly knelt next to me.

"Maya, is everything okay?" he whispered.

"Yes, thank you." I chuckled. "Everything is wonderful!"

Aya retreated from my consciousness. I imagined she was giving me space to truly land with this new perspective.

I reviewed the files in my memory of previous behavior with men, and mentally replayed each scene casting myself as the Flower, watching how the outcome changed.

How long did I play this game? Irrelevant—time didn't exist anymore. I played until the rain.

A few drops fell on the tin roof, surprisingly syncopated to the sounds of crickets. Then a few drops turned to the typical jungle downpour. Curtains of water flowed over the plants around the platform.

"Rain! Rain is so wonderful. Go outside, don't miss it!" Aya spurred me on with giddy excitement. I slowly lifted my body swimming with medicine, swung my legs off the platform, and stepped into the rain. Wobbling with each step, I planted myself in front of the jungle, and let the water drench me.

It was not wonderful. It felt cold and wet. My cotton clothes clung to my skin. Although the rain and warm air were decidedly tropical, I began to shiver.

"Aya… this isn't very pleasant."

She caressed my head gently. "That's right, I'm sorry. I forgot about your rubber suit. You can't feel the rain physically, like we do. But close your eyes, and feel it with your heart."

I closed my eyes and listened to the rain. It had a voice like a choir, with resonant and grounding bass, rhythmic patterns, and soothing hums. I was no longer cold. Each drop was an influx of energy, of pure potential vitality seeping into my being, recharging, cleansing, recalibrating.

437

I opened my eyes. The luminous grass at my feet was alive. Tiny pinpoints of white light, like electric impulses, rose in vertical waves from each blade.

"Wow. How beautiful you are!" My words floated down to the grass as violet pinpoints of light, and the grass responded by thickening its upward waves. I looked to the jungle. Similar currents of sparkles emanated from each tree and floated in directed currents between them.

"Are you communicating with each other? Is that what I'm seeing?"

Several of the nearby trees "turned" toward me. The feeling was similar to what I had experienced on mushrooms in the Whites, except this time, I could see the form of their attention, and I was eager and ready for it. As the trees turned toward me, their currents shifted, and part of their light waves seemed to be "blown," like a breath, in my direction. I inhaled their gift, filled my lungs, and instantly felt energized.

On that breath was also knowledge. They explained that tree breath is directional. Trees and plants consciously direct their breath, granting more life-force to those humans they deem worthy of support. Breath is the fire of creation, and by fanning their allies' flames, they influence and change the world.

I had received the support of plants my whole life. That was partially why I had found the Secret Room, to have the experience of directional breath from plants at an early age, before too much programming could cloud it. I had always wondered how I could walk for months in the woods and emerge revitalized rather than exhausted. Now I understood.

Yet, the far-reaching effects of tree support worked on a timeline beyond the reckoning of human perception.

One inhale lasts all day. One exhale lasts all night. One breath cycle, twenty-four human hours, is one tree unit of time. Yet, from the perspective of trees, only this present moment exists.

In each moment, trees perceive all inputs—sounds, smells, feelings, thoughts—as waves of undifferentiated information packets within a plant-specific energy spectrum. We, humans, have gating mechanisms that sort inputs so as to not overwhelm ourselves. Trees perceive with their entire being, from roots, to bark, to leaves. They are wide open and attuned, and their deciphering mechanism is so sophisticated that each moment contains all information, including the past and future as we understand it.

We also have this ability, but we've forgotten. We also receive inputs through hair, skin, and felt sense, in addition to the five specialized sensory receptors. And with DMT on the brain, the gates drop. For me, sounds, smells, and feelings appear as colors, and time dissipates.

The concept of the passing of time does exist for trees and plants, but it isn't related to the counting of time units, rather it is proportional to the quality of breath.

We, humans, breathe so much that we are only able to sustain short lives. And for those of us with shallow breaths, we create so little in those short lives. We also breathe so fast— about 15 breaths each minute. That's a 28,000:1 breathing—or life-speed—ratio, compared to a tree.

From a tree's perspective, human lives appear like the movement of a hummingbird's wings to us—a blurry impression too quick to differentiate. They read us from the energetic imprints that linger in the wake of our passing, and direct their breath accordingly.

Only when a human truly takes the time to sit in the shade, lean his or her back against the bark, and slow their breath, only then, can a semblance of an equal connection be made, and the benefits of the tree's directional breath fully perceived.

"Does it mean if we breathe slower, we live longer?"
"That is absolutely what it means."

I felt Aya support my physical body as I suddenly grew weak. I wasn't weak from lack of life force, but from an overflow of information my system wasn't designed to handle, even with the DMT. I knew I had received it though, and remembered Aya had told me that I wouldn't understand everything, but that it would be stored in my heart and revealed in stages as I evolved.

I climbed back on the platform and dropped onto my mat. My clothes were soaked, and again, I began to shiver. I changed my shirt and wrapped my body tightly in the blanket. I felt swaddled and loved. Images and epiphanies had settled. Only a deep, blissful peace remained, and a sense of being connected to everything.

Much later, Jordi knelt next to me and whispered a word. Was it my name? I sat up to face him. He continued with words, maybe sentences, just a series of sounds in tones of blues and greens, which I guessed must have been in Spanish.

"Oh no," I thought, "I don't understand human language anymore."

He waited a moment, and as I was not responding, he repeated the sounds.

"Okay," I thought, "I definitely don't understand this language, but if I'm still Tree, I should be able to read him energetically."

As Jordi waited for my answer, I placed my hand on his heart and listened. He placed his hand over mine. And just like that, I knew—it was almost morning; he was inquiring if I needed anything else; and if not, he wished to retire to his house for a little rest.

"Haaa!" I nodded and blew him a Breath of Gratitude. With over twenty years of holding Ayahuasca ceremonies, Jordi was fully attuned to the vine herself, and I felt he knew exactly what my answer meant. He laughed, then went home to rest.

I lay back down under my leaves for the final few hours before dawn.

♾ · ♾

Around 8 a.m., the same day

In the morning light, David and Nikita stirred and sat up slowly. I pushed my blanket aside and sat next to my leaves. We looked at each other and, for no apparent reason, started laughing. Each time one of us stopped, another started again, so it took a while before we could speak in words.

"Wow," David began, shaking his head. We chuckled again.

"Good morning, Nikita. How was your journey?" I asked.

"Not at all what I expected. I asked Aya, 'What is my life purpose?' and she—"

"What? I asked her the same thing!"

"You're kidding, right?" David chimed in. "I did too!" And again, we rolled with laughter.

"Well, I hope you two did better than I did," Nikita said. "She told me, 'What do I look like to you? A tarot card reader?'"

"Ha ha! Yeah, she told me, 'I don't give career advice, and besides, you can't even breathe correctly. Learn to breathe, then we'll talk.'"

"Oooh, ha ha ha. You two are lucky. She told me, 'I won't even address this question, and from now on, you must only speak Spanish to me.'"

We laughed until our backs were rolling, hands slapping, and tears streaming. Finally, we caught our breath.

Nikita was the first to speak again. "Oooh! She showed me how I hid under the covers because I feared the mosquitoes. Then she asked, 'How will you become an entrepreneur if you can't face life's small annoyances, perfectly impersonated by these mosquitoes?' I saw I was afraid of life. But she worked the fear out of me. That's what's in the bucket, I think. And she said once I find my courage, anything I choose to create will be successful."

"She didn't even address the question with me." David leaned back against the wall. "She just stood there with her hands on her hips and insisted I had to speak Spanish."

"Like this?" I mimicked Mama Aya's gestures as I had seen them.

"Yes, exactly like that. And I saw her too... first time I've seen her, and I've sat with Aya before. She looked like a Caribbean woman in a green and red dress with big flowers. And she was so loving. The first thing she did was remove the COVID vaccine from my body. I guess it was stuck in my calves. I felt her fingers press it out through my feet. And now it's gone."

I pointed to David and snapped my fingers. "Okay, Aya, so you're not just in my head. I got it. You planted clues so I'd believe."

An immense joy filled my heart. Aya was real!

And I hadn't even left the platform yet.

A couple of hours later, on the same day

My hammock, strung between two coconut trees, swayed gently in the sea breeze. I turned my phone on for the first time in twenty-four hours—one tree breath—and wrote a message to Jim. Jim and I hadn't spoken in years, not since we broke up, except for a brief exchange when I had taken mushrooms on Hummingbird's sacred land.

"Jim! Hi! So, I was with Ayahuasca last night. I think she sent you a gift, but I don't know what. Do you?"

I immediately received a voice note from him:

"So it was *you*! Last night. Yeah, I got it. Out of the blue, one of my step-siblings had a stroke of compassion and decided to give me part of his inheritance from my mom, even though she'd kicked me off the will when she was alive. And I needed it too. So, thanks, Bobcat. Thanks!"

A few hours later, still on the same day

A stack of chocolate bars waited to find their home in gold wrappers, as my fingers, slower than usual, attended to business matters. My mind, though, still smiled from the memory of spiraling vines and leaves.

"Excuse me?" A man's voice cut through my reverie. "I don't usually do this—approach strangers—but, I'm holding a meditation circle at 4 this afternoon and… I just felt I needed to invite you."

I looked up. The man was striking, with a bright white smile contrasted against glowing mocha-colored skin and short dreadlocks like a helmet of antennas.

I normally wouldn't have attended a meditation circle. Aya knew this, so she had sent a handsome man to invite me. I felt slightly manipulated, but I giggled and nodded. "Okay. I'll come."

He took my number and sent me his address.

Except, by 3:30, the sky was falling in torrential deluge. Sure, rain was wonderful, but even more so from the warmth of my bed, where I had just woken up from a nap. I rolled over to face the gray sky. No way was I riding my bicycle in this, no matter how handsome the man was.

"You're going. Non-negotiable." It was Aya's voice.

By the time I arrived at the man's house, drenched, a young woman was already sitting on a cushion on the patio, waiting for the meditation circle to begin. She had soft, light brown hair and a rose-colored shirt. Her back was straight yet relaxed. She exuded strength, confidence, and soft kindness all at once, and I knew, she was a powerful Flower.

"Hi. I'm Sydney."

"Nice to meet you. I'm Maya. Do you live here?"

"Yes, I've been here for over a year now."

"I'm surprised we haven't met before, it's a small town. What do you do here?"

"I'm a breathwork facilitator. I make people breathe."

I burst out laughing. "Of course you are!" I extended my hand, "Hi. Ayahuasca sent me. She said I need to learn to breathe."

Sydney laughed too and took my hand. "You're not the first one she sends me, but you are a very important one. I need just one more one-on-one session to complete my two-year training. What are you doing this Thursday?"

"Breathing with you, I guess."

Thursday of the same week

I left Sydney's house feeling high on life, healed, loved, renewed, and with conscious, connected breath still vibrating in my cells. I flew down the steep gravel road and came to a screeching halt before the main road, gravel flying and brakes moaning.

A young woman was already waiting at the intersection. She turned to see who or what had caused such commotion, then laughed when she saw it was just a wild woman on a bicycle.

"Hi!" Her high voice was as soft as the fabric of her flowy dress.

"Hi. You look familiar." ("Because you're yet another Flower archetype," I thought)

"Yes, we met at the dance last week. I'm Kaina. You're Maya, right? You sell the magic mushroom chocolates."

"I am. I do. That's me."

"I wanted to speak with you. Do you ever do trades?"

"Maybe. What would you like to trade?"

"Would you trade for a session? I'm a Psychic Aromatherapist. I create custom fragrances for people. So, I read your aura, and we explore who you'd like to become, then together we create a mix of essential oils that energetically represents the best version of your future self. What do you think?"

Again, I had to laugh. "Seriously? That's just... yeah...
So, how many magic chocolate bars would you like?"

A month later

Kaja and I shared a vegan lunch on the balcony of Como
en Mi Casa, one of our favorite restaurants. From one topic
to the next, our conversation flowed and eventually landed on
psychedelics and their effects on perception.

"...That's a good question. I mean, for me, synesthesia
always defaults to visuals, to colors, but yeah... would a
musician default to sounds, and see the colors as notes
instead? And that's just because we're limited to the five
senses. Once, when I was Tree—"

Wherever that sentence was going, it was suddenly
interrupted by Kaja's chuckle.

"That's such a wonderful phrase, 'Once, when I was
Tree,'" she repeated with flair. "It sounds like a book title.
Maybe you should write it. I'd read it."

We both laughed. We do say strange sentences in public
in Puerto Viejo—sentences about Jaguar and Cacao and
lessons from plants wiser than ourselves.

I laughed, but I also made a mental note. Kaja had
formally studied Storytelling; I trusted her instinct for a catchy
title. "Once, When I Was Tree." Yes. It did sound like a book
I'd love to write.

The very next day, I cozied myself among cushions on a
shaded wooden platform by the beach, laptop ready. I closed
my eyes and pictured a book. It began as an old leather-bound
grimoire with thick, yellowed pages. When I tried to focus on
the cover, it transformed, sprouting blue iridescent dragonfly
wings that grew and grew, until they extended well beyond
the platform.

So this was the book's energetic form. How wonderful! I
couldn't wait to meet it.

I filled my lungs completely and blew a Breath of Life onto my screen. Then I opened my eyes and placed my fingers on the keyboard. Words flowed immediately as if they had been locked behind a dam, waiting to be released.

"In French, the time of day right after the sun has set, but while its afterglow still illuminates the land, is called *entre chien et loup*..."

And so the writing of this book began. I wrote the whole *Coyote* chapter in one sitting, almost as it appears now. I sobbed when the coyotes died and giggled when I invited the Trickster into my life. I wondered, "Oh my. What kind of book starts with Coyote?"

From that moment, chocolate became secondary, everything became secondary. This book and I, we had found each other. I was as obsessed as when I wrote my first book and remembered that I adored writing.

So, Ayahuasca doesn't give career advice. Or does she?

Ffffffffffffh. Here is a Breath of Love for you.

Chapter 30
Of Lizards and Care Bears

Puerto Viejo, Costa Rica - August 2022

"Mmh… we're close… but I feel it's still missing just a hint of…"

Kaina lifted one of the bottles she had arranged in a row on her sarong and waved it under her nose. Her eyes narrowed, and her mouth twitched—that wasn't it. She picked up another bottle, smiled, and looked at the label.

"Ha, Cacao! Of course. Cacao is one of your allies, no?"

I nodded excitedly—this magical woman spoke my language.

"And… I'm feeling Geranium to finish. Geranium's spirit helps us forgive so we can free ourselves of old patterns."

She added a few drops of each, brought the mixture to her nose, and giggled.

"That's it! Alchemy complete. I present the future you."

She offered me the slender bottle with two hands, and I received it in the spirit in which it was given. My future self was woodsy, earthy yet floral, playful and uplifting, with a tinge of intoxicating. I inhaled deeply, and my body melted.

"Oh, Kaina, this is incredible. I want to roll myself in it. I want to wear it every day. I—" I suddenly clenched the bottle to my heart. "But you're leaving, what happens when I run out?"

She laughed and brought her forehead to touch mine, the way sisters do. "Maya, someone like you? I have no doubt by the time you run out, you'll have outgrown it."

A buzz in my pocket interrupted the moment, effectively ending it. Kaina gathered the bottles while I checked my phone.

It was a message from Joe.

"Hey Maya, I'm at the bar here with a friend I'd love you to meet. Come and join us."

"Let the Games continue," I thought. "I guess secrecy no longer gets him enough attention, now I'm invited to meet the conquests."

I shook my head, then opened my hand still clenched around the bottle, revealing the amber potion. With one quick dab, I covered the palm of my hand with my future essence and rubbed it on my hair, face, and arms. I shared about the message with Kaina as we stood up for a goodbye embrace.

"So you're going to meet the new girl?" Her eyebrow lifted, protective.

"No, I'm going to meet the new me."

And with a six-foot-tall walk bathed in power essence, I left Kaina for the bar.

Valeria was an orthodontist from Argentina. She was intelligent, educated, kind, and traveling alone for the first time.

"You know about cognates? Ha! Yes, I've always loved Linguistics."

Valeria and I connected immediately, leaving Joe to sip his beer alone, out of our conversation.

"Well, that went better than I thought." Joe leaned toward me as soon as Valeria excused herself to the bathroom. He sounded cheery, but I caught the subtle slump in his shoulder as he watched her go.

"Oh yeah? Why wouldn't it go well? I'm happy for you. She's wonderful!"

For the next seven days, Joe romanced Valeria, and on every occasion except the most intimate ones, I was invited to come along. Sitting on the same sofa in front of the large screen TV, he kissed and tickled, and she giggled.

"I'm so glad you came, Maya. My best girl and my best friend. This is a special time."

I faked a smile and wondered, "Why again, do I do this?"

Ayahuasca might have asked the same question.

I later learned that if insights from a journey were not fully integrated, old habits and patterns resurfaced and worsened. Ayahuasca healed the core self, so old behaviors and thought patterns stood out in stark contrast—highlighted for urgent attention.

I didn't know this yet, though. All I knew was that the moment Valeria's shuttle left for the airport, Joe invited me back into his bed. Once, twice, then, suddenly, no more calls, texts, or invitations. I saw him from the road sitting in his usual corner of the bar; he hadn't left town. So if it wasn't me, who walked through the revolving door now? His curly-haired boss? His long-legged coworker? That girl over there on the beach with the thong bikini? My muscles tensed in the presence of any young woman. Anybody could be her.

But only a section of my mind spun with irrational jealousy; the rest shrugged and shook its head. "Mind, what are you doing? Who cares who he sleeps with? Good riddance. For real, stop it!"

All night, I tossed. All day, I paced in my room, checking my phone as though staring at it could induce a message. Then I sat on my bed and knocked on my skull.

"Enough. Stop it."

It didn't stop, so, as a last resort, I called Joe.

"Hey Joe, look, I'm going through something. I think it's related to my last Ayahuasca journey. I'm going a little insane with endless thoughts of you and other women, so I want to…"

449

"You don't get a say in who I see..." His tone was flat and dry.

"Yes, yes, I know. I'm not asking you to change; I'm just informing you that I'm going crazy and that I need to stop all contact for two weeks to see if I can get my wits back."

His tone rose rapidly. "You're doing it again! Don't threaten to take your friendship away. That's not fair."

I shook my head. "Have you heard nothing of what I just said? This isn't about you; it's—"

"I'm a Leo. Everything is about me!"

We had arrived—the nuclear core of Leo logic to end all discussions.

"Ugh. I'll talk to you in two weeks." I hung up.

I opened my eyes the next morning feeling refreshed and relaxed. I scanned my mind. No thoughts of Joe. And in the newly vacant space, a hundred good ideas bloomed.

"I'll make rose and mint chocolate today. A new flavor." "Ooh, and I can redo the labels—full color this time." "Tonight, the Bees chapter. I feel the words are ready." I tossed the sheet to the side and jumped out of bed. "But first..." I slipped on my bathing suit, crossed the road, and dove into the sea.

Two weeks flew by in a joyous blur devoid of Joe. I only remembered him on the last day, from a hammock on the beach.

"Oh wow. It's been two weeks already."

I reached for my bag under the hammock and typed a quick message:

"Hi, Joe. I said I'd contact you in two weeks. It's two weeks today. But I'm going to continue with the no contact— I feel better this way. Thank you for understanding. I wish you well. Take care."

I stared at the message, finger hovering above the "Send" icon. Even though it was true, I could have stayed silent and achieved the same distance—without the stab.

I could have. But I didn't. I hit "Send," rolled back in the hammock, and crossed my hands behind my head. The sun streamed through the coconut palms. The calm, clear water caressed the sand. Such an idyllic day.

Unfortunately, we only truly know if we're healed when tested. Swaying in the hammock, sun on my skin, I couldn't have imagined the trials just around the corner.

The first was a machete's blade against my cheek while a masked man pulled me by my hair. A few feet away, another machete, held by another masked man, sliced the shoulder straps of Sydney's bag. We stood tall. We kept each other safe.

Only long after the men had vanished through the trees with our belongings, did a raw emptiness settle in my heart. The wild jungle, once my home and refuge, now felt menacing. I found myself anxiously locking my apartment's door and yearning for a protector—a male presence that could stand between me and the world's madness. I despised that feeling, the longing for something—or someone—I had sworn I didn't need.

Then a few days later, my computer—my lifeline to the rest of the world—went dark.

In the U.S., it would have been a quick fix, a matter of a day, but in Costa Rica, things unfold in their own time. Between delayed shipments, incorrect parts, flooded bridges, and national holidays, a full month passed... until August 4th. Joe's birthday.

That day, I felt deep in my bones that *this* was the day I would return home with a computer. "Your computer is ready. Just go get it," the voice in my head assured me. But the man at the repair shop gave me the same apologetic shrug as before. "Tal vez mañana. Maybe tomorrow."

I pedaled away, my mind spinning in confusion. "If it wasn't for my computer, why send me out here?"

And as if in answer, there was Joe, standing outside the bar, beer in hand.

I muttered under my breath, "Alright, Universe. I'm listening."

I parked my bicycle and walked toward him with purpose. He saw me and stiffened—hesitation, maybe even fear. He took a step back as if bracing for impact. But I wasn't here to confront him. I opened my arms and smiled.

"Hey." My tone carried the peace I meant to offer.

He hesitated, then stepped into the hug. His body was tense at first, but slowly, I felt him melt into my arms.

"Hey." His voice was quiet, almost disbelieving. "You're here. I didn't think you'd come back."

"It's your birthday." I shrugged to hide my racing heart. "I'm not a jerk."

He pulled back slightly, still holding my arms, eyes searching mine as if trying to figure out why I'd come. "I've missed you, Maya. You staying? I'll buy you a beer." His voice was cheerful—too cheerful, almost like a dare; he knew I didn't drink.

"Sure, I can stay a while. My computer's broken, so it's not like I can work or write anyway." I meant it as a joke, but the words weighed like stones in my mouth.

"Oooh. That's rough." He winced. "You want to borrow mine? I don't use it much. You can keep it for a few days. Just swing by my place tonight, I'll have it ready."

The offer hung in the air. My mind paused, teetering.

I really needed a computer.

Checkmate.

Sitting in the hallway of Joe's apartment, I watched him roll a joint, a bottle of beer by his side. I knew the scent of his tobacco, the rhythm of his rolling fingers, the flicker of blue in his eyes under the corridor's neon light, the slight tilt of his head. I knew them all by heart.

"That really hurt, Maya—you just leaving like that." He brought the joint to his lips and licked the paper shut. His eyes flicked up to catch mine.

I crossed and uncrossed my legs. He shouldn't have been this attractive, realistically. So, I wasn't fully cured. I looked away, toward the ominous clouds unfolding in the darkness.

"Absolutely not!" a part of my mind rang in alarm. "Relax," another part replied. "I wasn't even thinking of staying the night."

I took a breath and looked back at Joe.

"We're okay," I simply said. Thunder cracked in the distance. I stood and picked up my bag. "But I should go. Looks like I'm going to get drenched on the way home, so best I don't take your computer now. But can I borrow your headlamp? I've been scared of the dark since the attack."

"Do you want me to ride home with you?" I knew he would, if I asked, but I needed time to regroup.

"No, I'm fine, thank you... just the headlamp."

As I rode home, rain stinging my face, I felt my mind lose its grip down the slippery slope.

"It's really not that bad with Joe. I mean, I could probably hang out again. Occasionally. Maybe dinner. Maybe a movie..."

ॐ · ॐ

The next morning, I woke up to a message from a stranger:

"Hi, my name is Lillian. The hotel owner here gave me your phone number. I'm looking for a large dose of magic mushrooms, enough for deep shadow work, maybe even an ego death. What do you have available?"

Shadow work? Ego death? In this vacation town, I rarely received such requests. Sure, mushrooms could take her there—I had walked that path myself. But it wasn't for the faint of heart. I felt it best to meet her in person, to make sure she got what she truly needed.

"Where are you now? I'll come over. Let's meet and chat."

We met on the beach and sat in the shade of a coconut tree. Lillian was tall and fit. Her posture was strong and assured, so I was surprised when her eyes filled with tears. I looked up at her and smiled encouragingly—tears were welcome here.

"I think I need help." She wiped the corner of one eye. "I'm a successful businesswoman; my husband loves me; I'm respected in my community; but... I hate myself lately, like I don't fit in my own life anymore. I've become this angry, edgy wife and mother, and that's just not who I want to be."

As she spoke, an image flashed in my mind: a thick vine, powerful and wise, spiraling up the trunk of a jungle tree.

I knew that vine—Aya!

I assumed this was a sign, a call from La Abuela. And I assumed it was for Lillian.

I waited for her to pause. "If I may... I'd love to sell you a large quantity of mushrooms, but I think what you actually need is Ayahuasca."

She sighed. "Yes, I thought of that. But Ayahuasca ceremonies are so expensive, and you have to book months in advance. I don't have the budget, and we go home in three days."

A smile spread across my face. She had not been sent to me by chance. "Well, things work differently here in Puerto Viejo. Let me just send a message."

Jordi replied almost instantly, as I thought he would. He didn't usually hold private ceremonies, but I imagined if Aya had appeared to me, he would likely also have received the message.

"You're all set," I told Lillian. "My friend Jordi can hold a private ceremony for you tonight. That's where I go. It's such a wonderful place. The platform is surrounded by jungle, and the vine grows right there. You can see her."

Her eyes widened slightly.

"The first time I went, I had a lot of insecurities and self-hatred too—I didn't even know. But Mama Aya loved me so deeply, it changed my life. I believe she can change you too. And please, call me tomorrow. I'd love to hear about your journey."

Lillian's shoulders relaxed, and a small sigh escaped her lips, yet a slight uncertainty lingered in her eyes. "The thing is..." Her lip quivered with a flicker of unease. "I once had a scary experience in the Amazon with a fake shaman. I'd feel better with another woman there. Would you come with me? I'll pay for your session."

As she spoke, my phone buzzed with a message from Jordi.

"If you'd like to come with your friend, you don't need to pay anything. Just come, Hermanita."

℘ · ℭ

Bribri, Costa Rica - August 2022

"Maya," Jordi called. I crawled forward to the altar and smiled at Lillian to reassure her.

"Would you like a hero's dose today?" Jordi had already poured the thick, dark brew three-quarters to the top of the chalice and waited, bottle suspended.

"Sure, why not." I didn't know what a hero's dose was but imagined it meant an even greater, deeper experience of Aya. And that sounded wonderful.

Jordi poured the medicine to the brim and carefully handed me the chalice.

"Aya, Abuelita Querida. I've come today not for me, but for my sister Lillian. Thank you for all the love you've given me. My intent today is to energetically support my sister who's doing such brave work. Please help her heal, as I trust you have called her here. Thank you for all the healing and love you spread in the world."

455

Then, in two long gulps, I emptied the chalice. My face contorted with the intensity of the bitter brew. My tongue stuck out, and my eyes shut tight. I breathed deeply and swallowed. A hero's dose was a lot of medicine. When I reopened my eyes, Jordi was smiling. I gave a small bow of thanks and crawled back to my mat.

As I sat back on my mat and Lillian stepped forward to receive her medicine, a tiny movement caught my eye. A baby lizard, no larger than half my pinkie, had climbed onto my pillow, and with his head stretched high above his short legs, he stared me down with bulging eyes. I turned to him with a raised eyebrow—"That's my pillow, little fellow."

But Lillian had received her chalice and was holding it to her heart, silently praying. I waited until she had returned to her mat, then faced the tiny cutie.

Oh, he was doing push-ups to intimidate me. I giggled. "You're very small, you know. Go. Go. That's my pillow."

I waved my fingers in front of him, but he didn't move, so I carried the pillow off the platform and shook off the little guy back into the wild.

I returned to my mat with a smile and made myself comfortable for what I imagined might be another long wait. I listened to the jungle's song—the hum of insects, the creaks and rustles of the night. My breath slowed.

Within a few minutes, my toes, of their own accord, began moving up and down. Pressure on my tibiae followed. She was already inspecting me. She lingered in my empty stomach, skipped my heart altogether, and stopped in my teeth.

I felt her pull my canines, press on my molars, then back to the canines, which she wiggled in their sockets, and to the molars, which began to buzz. And all the while, inexplicably, I thought about lizards.

Maybe it was because she had lizard-like movements within my jaw. Both the previous times, Aya had flowed while exploring me. This time, she moved in short bursts, then stopped and pressed or pulled or buzzed. Or maybe it was simply because a baby lizard had just been on my pillow, and he was still on my mind.

"Do lizards have teeth?" I wondered.

I actually didn't know if lizards had teeth, and I thought I knew a lot about them. I shrugged—well, I'd look it up later. Aya was here, and my heart swelled with love just knowing she was with me again.

"Hi Mama Aya. Hi Ayahuasca, Abuelita Curandera…"

Silence.

There were no words, no movement, no communication of any sort in the physical or mental world. I was simply silenced. I pressed my mouth shut, eyes wide as I looked around the ceiling of both my mind and the platform, wondering what had just happened.

I observed silently as Aya moved on to pressing my teeth one by one, starting with the bottom row. She pressed my jaw tightly shut, and kept it shut while fingering the square angle of my jaw bones. She squeezed then pulled the point of my chin. Suddenly, she blinked my eyes a few times, then pressed them tightly tightly shut.

She was in my eyes! My smile returned. "Maybe she'll heal my eyes and improve my vision!" I had no doubt she could.

Silence.

The mood quickly shifted. As my body began swimming, angular shapes danced in my mind. Interlocking triangles in pale yellow and teal expanded and contracted, birthing more of themselves. The vision was bright—the kind of bright in hospital corridors: pale bright, flooding, and cold.

The body scanning continued. My abs contracted, then my hip sockets moved about, pressed and pulled.

I remembered reading a post by Alejandra, an Ayahuasca facilitator in town who had trained with Shipibo Maestros in

Peru. She had written that Ayahuasca scanned first the physical body, then the mental and emotional body, and finally the spiritual body. If the physical needed clearing or healing, she attended to it first. Only once it was cleared did she address the subtler layers.

"Maybe that's why the physical scan always takes so long with me," I thought. "I'm pretty clean in the physical, but she has to fully explore it before she gets to where we're actually doing work."

Arrogance.

Arrogance whipped in my being. With it came the wordless energy of "Arrogance to think your intellect is adequate to comprehend the medicine."

And at the same time, a neutral voice spoke: "This is what it feels like inside a Lizard. Understand this, and you'll understand this boy you chase."

So this was about Joe? She had called him a Lizard once before. And I had spent the prior evening with him. Was this an intervention?

I felt into the energy swirling in my body. It felt like a chin held high, tightly pressed lips, and downward disdainful eyes. There was neither warmth nor care here. There was only decorum. Shoulders back—a stilted and angular elegance. I found the heart—no love there either, just a sort of cold appreciation for whoever serves a purpose at that moment.

But this was not Joe. Joe had his faults, but he smiled, snuggled, tickled, and loved. He was neither haughty nor cold.

I felt even deeper and found the template.

Power. Attention. Recognition. These were the endgame. Smiles, snuggles, and tickles were merely pawns on the unconscious chessboard.

"Power, attention, and recognition without love? But... I don't care about these things."

"That's because you're a Care Bear," a voice answered, and in its tone, the words rang like an insult—A Care Bear: A fuzzy, fat, spineless, fluffy simpleton. "Oh hi, let me love you, please."

I felt nauseated. This energy inside of me was not compatible with me at all. Joe and I were not compatible at all.

I rolled over like a limp mass and stared at the bottle on the altar.

"Aya. I got it. You explained it twice before, but this time, I finally got it. I will never find the love I seek with that man. Thank you for showing me that I…"

Arrogance.

Arrogance—of thinking my puny intellect could even fathom its motives.

With that one word, the cast order was established, along with the expectations that came with each. I looked again to Aya. Why wasn't she releasing me? I had learned. I understood.

Suddenly, my stomach clenched as I realized… Because we were just the two of us, Jordi hadn't purified the space with the copal smoke. What if this wasn't Aya? It definitely didn't feel like the Aya I knew. What if an opportunistic evil entity had slipped in? I swallowed hard, fear rising.

Arrogant and cowardly. Spit.

Cowardly?

That, I was not. Entity or not, this Lizard was inside me. And despicable Care Bear or not, I still believed love could cure all. I inhaled deeply and blew a Breath of Love to the Lizard.

"Hi!" I whispered aloud. "Whoever is inside of me, if you're Lizard or Reptilian, I'd like you to know I've always loved your kind, since I was a child. I even have a lizard tattooed on my back. You see it?"

Insolence.

Insolence—I felt a sharp pull on my ear, like when I was a child and my mother dragged me by the ear to some catastrophe she believed I'd caused or a mess left—intentionally no doubt—to mock her. I felt a pinch on my neck, and the image flashed in my mind of my mother holding a kitten by the skin of its neck, rubbing its nose in its feces on the living floor so that it would understand the errs of its ways. These were simply teaching methods necessary for the taming of wild things.

And simultaneously, I saw the feces in which my nose was rubbed. First the image of the baby lizard I had just unceremoniously tossed in the jungle. Then, the scene, a couple of days prior, of a young gecko perched on the edge of an open jar of psilocybin-infused honey on my kitchen counter.

"Don't eat that," I had told the lizard. "You'll get high, and I don't think that's healthy for you." The lizard had looked at me, flicked its tongue in my direction, then plunged back into the honey. I had taken a photo because he was so funny and cute.

It was the "funny and cute" that snagged. I should have served, revered, venerated him, just by the very fact that he was Reptilian and I was not. Albeit small, he was still a representative of a superior race.

All this was explained without words.

Then, suddenly, having made its point, the entity vanished.

Angular sickly teal and yellow fractals still swam in my mind, but the entity—or energy—was gone. I waited, then scanned my body. I found no trace of it.

This was worse. I didn't believe it would have just left, so where was it lurking? What was it up to?

I was a child curled in a closet. I hid and listened for the steps of the adult who might enter the room. What would it be today? A smile or a beating? I so hoped not to be found.

Then I remembered, the child would grow and be set free, but I was already an adult; there was no escape from this for me.

I was stuck. I tried rolling to one side to find a measure of comfort within the discomfort but discovered I couldn't. I was energetically pinned, chained flat on my back—"That's right," the entity snarled, "useless slaves are not freed; they're locked away. Your worth is less than the mental power it would require me to figure out another use for you."

So this incarceration was final and likely fatal. Would I welcome death as a release? There had to be a way out. These were still my body, my mind, weren't they?

I felt nausea rising but was too paralyzed to sit and find the bucket. I had no power over my own body. But my mind... my mind was still observing.

"No es compatible," I whispered. I could only speak Spanish; English was blocked. In all the scanning, silencing, and subjugating, the entity had overlooked that I spoke other languages.

"No es compatible," I repeated louder. Whatever this was, it was not compatible with my home-system, my core self, and just knowing I wasn't like it gladdened my heart with a glimmer of hope. Just knowing that, thanks to this experience, I would never be with another Joe brought a smile to my lips.

"No es compatible, así que lárgate." I inhaled deeply for courage and pushed my weight up until I was seated. I moved my hair out of the way and brought the bucket between my legs. My head was swimming with shapes and medicine. "Lárgate. No es compatible." I hissed, and my mouth contorted as my throat lifted. "I welcome you to get out now," I finally cried out in English.

My mouth opened and closed, hissing, fighting me.

Fff ffff ffffh. Jordi sat up and blew a series of short breaths in my direction. I nodded—yes, thank you, the trees had taught me this system. These I knew were Breaths of Help— Thank you. I began to blow Breaths of Help to myself between hisses. The taste of vomit filled the back of my throat. I'd never eaten a lizard, yet I knew, if I had ground ten lizards into a paste and eaten it, that would've made this vomit taste.

"You're disgusting," a cold voice echoed in my mind. "And you shall not command me."

I remained polite, my voice even, calm but firm. "I welcome you to get out now."

Finally, my whole body lurched forward, again, and again, and again, and again. And all the while, my toes moved up and down.

A thick, dark bile covered the bottom of the white bucket. Darker than anything I had eaten or drunk, not even the medicine herself.

Jordi knelt next to me and placed a hand on my shoulder.

I looked at him and laughed. Not a laugh of joy, but of deep appreciation for the process at hand—this purging, clearing of Lizards, whatever they were. And for the intense inner theatrics the medicine employed. Jordi laughed with me. He knew. He'd seen it many times.

Heavy, empty, and limp, I collapsed onto my mat and exhaled deeply for the first time in hours. Jordi stood slowly and returned to his mat.

I rested for a moment, alone with my thoughts for the first time since it began, and remembered Lillian in her own journey across the platform.

"Oh no, I told her about this huge love from Mama Aya, and brought her here to this… Lizarddom. I hope she's okay."

I rolled over to see her. Her eyes were closed and her body rested, facing me. In my mind, I sent her love and courage. But the more I looked at the shape of her body on the mat, the more I realized she looked a bit like a lizard. She had the same build as Joe—the same long, firm, slender torso, shorter legs, a square jaw ending in a pointy chin, and those large almond-shaped eyes.

"Ugh!" Lillian was Lizard! It was suddenly so obvious. I could spot Reptilians from their physical shapes. My face contorted in disgust. When this was all over, I'd have to avoid her. Well, she was my ride, but after we returned to town, I'd avoid her then.

I turned away from her and looked to the jungle. The trees offered no support—no sparkly Breath of Life for me. I tried to drop into my heart to inspire—or coax—them into helping me. They didn't respond.

What was I doing? Trying to manipulate trees? Was the whole field of the platform so steeped in Lizardry that even I was succumbing to it?

"On the other hand," I thought, "If Lillian is Lizard, she's probably at home in this field. She won't fight it like I do, and maybe even have a pleasant, fruitful journey—assuming Lizards take care of their own."

I rolled onto my back and stared at the ceiling. Despite the enduring nausea, discomfort, and pulsating pale, angular geometry, I noticed I'd just had a series of uninterrupted thoughts about Lillian—no silencing, no exclamation of my arrogance or insolence. I intuitively knew this journey's flavor was set for the night, but with most of the Lizard now in black bile form in the bucket, I believed the worst was over.

"This isn't hopeless after all," I comforted myself. "It's just going to suck for a few hours, but tomorrow, I'll be fine again. And since this is the experience Aya is granting me today, you know what? Let's have it. Let's see what I can learn from Lizards."

This last thought did not go over well. Nausea tsunamied to my throat, and both my arms snapped to the side of my body.

"You couldn't learn from us even if we wanted to teach you. Remain in your place, or there will be repercussions." There was a spit on "rePERcussions."

It didn't have me completely though. I wiggled my fingers, lifted my arms slightly, and fired back, "What repercussions can be worse than what I've already gone through?"

"Maya?" Jordi's soft voice interrupted the inner argument. "Would you like a second cup?"

I absolutely did not want a second cup, yet my body sat up, and by my own mouth, these words were spoken: "Sí, porfa, media copa." (Yes, please, another half chalice).

Repercussions—My hand took hold of the chalice and forced the thick liquid down my throat. The moment the medicine hit my stomach, I began gagging and dry heaving in convulsions.

Fffff ffffb fffhhhh. Jordi blew to help. I opened my eyes and nodded to let him know I was okay. He stood up and walked to Lillian to offer her a second cup. I swung my legs to the other side of the mat and pulled the bucket between my knees.

"I welcome you to get out now. You are not welcome in my body." I tightened my stomach to force my diaphragm to contract and expel the dark brew, but my hand reached for my water bottle and washed the medicine deeper into my stomach.

Oh, it had me now.

I collapsed back onto the mat and hid my face in the pillow. It didn't even bother turning me this time; it pinned me, right where I was. Chills ran across my arms from the cold night's breeze. Mosquitoes bit my face with reckless abandon. I had no agency to pull the blanket up or defend myself. Repercussions—I was nothing. Nothing worth caring for, defending, or protecting.

"Wow," a barely perceptible thought floated through the back of my mind, "this is intense. It must be for my benefit though, or it wouldn't be." I saw the tiny, still inextinguishable flame of hope in my heart, but immediately hid it, convinced that if it were discovered, the entity could blow it out, or distort it. Then I would never recover from this. My psyche would remain distorted for the rest of my life. So I pushed it to the bottom of my being and pretended it didn't exist. I just lay there, powerless rather than surrendered—surrender still implied a choice; I had no such privilege.

I lay there, and waited.

Maybe Mama Aya would reappear in her green and red dress, hands on hips, and she'd say, "Well, Child. Have you learned your lesson? Will I see you with that boy again? Lizards don't love, they only seek attention. Do you get it now?"

And I'd say, "Yes Mama, yes. I got it, I got it." And she'd wrap me in her love again.

But hope is a privilege too; I knew she wasn't coming.

I waited and endured, trapped within the structure of the nauseating angular shapes in my mind. Minutes felt like hours.

"I need to reground," I thought. "I wish there was a drum beat. Drumming always helps me ground."

I heard the soft swish of Jordi's blanket as he rose. He walked to the back wall, retrieved a shamanic drum I hadn't noticed before and tapped a gentle beat while circling the platform.

How did he know?

Tum, tum, tum. Each beat brought back fragments of

myself. *Tum, tum, tum.* Tendrils of strength and sovereignty unfurled. *Tuuuum, Tuuuum.* Relief washed over me while he played, but eventually, the song ended. Jordi replaced the drum on the wall and returned to his mat.

"Gracias," I whispered.

It waited until Jordi had settled back down, well hidden under his blanket, then suddenly—Retribution.

"Who do you think you are, calling in a serenade?" The looming shadow of imminent punishment flooded my mind. I hissed in its direction, fed up with this interminable, redundant journey. Enough. *Shhheeeeee.* I hissed again, flicked my tongue, then clenched my jaws.

Clenched jaw. Flicked tongue. A flicker of a thought—"I do have sort of a square jaw… and a pointy chin… and slightly almond-shaped eyes too." I inhaled sharply in horror. "Oh no. Am I Lizard?

I lurched forward, bucket lodged between my knees. With my right hand, I gathered my dreadlocks and moved them back, away from the bucket. But the hand stayed there and lifted my head by pulling on my hair.

"You will submit. You will admire me."

"I will not," I hissed between my teeth. A wave of vomit followed the claim.

It pulled my hair further forward. "You will submit. You will bow in my presence."

"I will never. I'd rather die," I spat. Another wave.

My hand pushed my head almost into the bucket. And I remembered I'd been there before. I'd been drowned by the hand of a master. I had been a slave—chained, trafficked, whipped, discarded. I'd been… "You will submit. You will worship me and the ground I walk on."

The upheaval was complete.

"You're welcome to get out now," I answered in a full, stern voice. And it did—wave after wave. And with each wave, random images flashed in my mind. Archetypes, past

466

lives, ancestral memories—I couldn't tell. Any child who had stood up to the adult lost in senseless violence. Any leader who had a Dream in a violent world. Any prisoner of war, unflinching in the face of a firing squad. Any heart awakening to the truth of their own codependency. Even that firefly that escaped the tongue of the gecko.

I was all of those. *I* was the incompatible field. And the Lizard had to go.

Still shaking, I fell back onto my mat and smiled. Yes. I was that which resists and cannot be subjugated, though I might stray sometimes and get caught in webs. In the end, I was that, and as such, I loved myself.

The yellow and teal angular shapes faded. In their place, a poem floated to my tongue—a poem I'd memorized in my youth for no particular reason, simply because I felt drawn to it. I was surprised I still remembered it.

> *"Out of the night that covers me,*
> *Black as the pit from pole to pole,*
> *I thank whatever Gods may be*
> *For my unconquerable soul..."*

Each line spread through my being like a soothing balm. It was done.

When the poem ended, I whispered, "Gracias Ayahuasca. Gracias Abuelita curandera, Thank you."

A neutral voice emerged, calm and even, like a hand smoothing rumpled sheets. "I have removed the excess Lizard from you. Be mindful not to invite it back. Oh, and that lizard tattoo on your back—it's no longer your ally. You're attracting the wrong kind of energy with it. Cover it. Replace it with a peach and crimson hibiscus, so you may connect more deeply with your Flower-self."

And with that final order, I was finally set free. Only my toes continued moving by themselves. Up and down, and up and down.

৪০ · ৫৪

Around 8 a.m., the same day

Lillian began to stir. I had been sitting quietly on my mat for a while, wrapped in my blanket, arms around my knees. The journey was over, but as with any such strong medicine, the journey is only 20% of the healing. Now began the real work. What did it all mean? What were Lizards? Who or what did I need to remove from my life, besides Joe?

Jordi walked up the steps with bananas and slices of watermelon. He dropped them by the altar, sat on his mat, and invited me to breakfast with a smile.

"How did it go?" he asked.

I hesitated before answering and caught myself scanning him. He was tall and slender, but he moved fluidly and had a round posture, more like a water dragon. His jaw was soft and his cheeks and temples carved by deep smiling wrinkles. I relaxed, fairly certain that Jordi, at least, was not Lizard.

"Ppphew. Wow. This was a very different person than the Aya I met before." I pointed to the bottle on the altar.

Jordi smiled. "It's the same you drank before. Same brew, same batch, same bottle."

My eyes grew wide and my jaw dropped. Jordi laughed.

"Yes, La Abuela can take many forms. You released a lot last night. She must have helped you clear an old burden."

"And what about you?" He turned to Lillian.

She stretched her back and opened her arms toward the ceiling. "So wonderful!" She then turned toward me. "It didn't feel like a motherly love, as you described. It was just me, remembering my worth, finding myself perfect with my imperfections, and landing with this deep knowing that I am beautiful, smart, powerful, and deserve to be seen and respected."

"So, she *is* Lizard; the Lizard field was compatible with her," I thought. I felt a slight rise of nausea in my throat, but she continued, "Thank you so much, Maya, for crossing my path, for coming here with me, and for being a friend and sister, even though we just met yesterday." She then placed her hands together and bowed to me, then turned to Jordi, and bowed to him.

That, on the other hand, was not Lizard behavior as I understood it.

I scratched my head. What exactly defined a Lizard? Could a Lizard evolve to act differently than their original blueprint of seeking self-centered power and attention? Could there be "Good Lizards?"

On the drive back to town, I noticed that despite Lillian's sincere gratitude, I sat on the edge of my seat, arm entirely out of the car, as if trying to be as far away from her as possible.

"Tell me more about this lizard. I'm curious."

I had already shared too much. I shifted uncomfortably in my seat. "Well, as far as I understand, the guy I was obsessing over until yesterday is Lizard, and my seeking his love so desperately makes me Care Bear. My dad is probably too sovereign to be a Care Bear, but my mother is definitely Lizard. And…" I stopped abruptly and gasped.

"What is it?" Lillian asked, a note of genuine concern in her voice.

I pressed my lips thin and brought my hands to block them, refusing to speak the realization out loud.

"You alright?" Lillian insisted.

"Just by DNA, that means I'm half-Lizard and half-Care Bear. Lillian… that's why my feet move by themselves. It's remnant Lizard tail energy. You know how when a lizard's tail is cut off it keeps moving anyway? My feet do that!"

And as Lillian looked down my legs under the dashboard, even held in place by the straps of my flip-flops, my feet moved up and down, up and down, entirely on their own.

Puerto Viejo, Costa Rica - days and months following the Lizard Session

Joe

Two weeks later, my new tattoo had already healed—the decade-old lizard now hidden, its tail dissolved into the crimson center and its head morphed into the flower's stigma. I reached back and rubbed ointment on the flower. Then I opened the slender essence of my future-self bottle and dabbed the aroma generously on my hair, heart, and both temples. I looked into my own eyes in the mirror and smiled.

"Alright, New Self. Last step. Let's do it!"

I didn't need to send Joe a message to arrange the return of his headlamp. It was mid-afternoon. I knew exactly where to find him.

I parked my bicycle in front of the bar and spotted him exactly where I knew he'd be. He hadn't seen me yet, so I had time to check in. My heart was beating fast—I hadn't seen Joe since the night before the Lizards—but I felt resolute and solid. I began walking in his direction.

His eyes lifted and caught my approaching figure. He smiled. But as I got closer, my stomach began churning, and a wave of nausea surged to my throat. It tasted like lizards, like the taste of the purge I had left in the white bucket. I slowed down my stride and swallowed a few times. Suddenly, my diaphragm convulsed with a series of gags.

Joe stood up, concern obvious in his eyes.

"Maya, are you alright?"

"Wow! She really did it this time. I can't even approach him," I thought. I told him a partial truth: "I've been sick with COVID. I'm leaving your headlamp here, on this chair, in case I'm still contagious. Okay?"

"Yes. For sure. Take care of yourself. And let's hang out when you feel better."

470

Months went by. He didn't message me; I didn't message him. Occasionally, I'd glimpse him riding his motorcycle or sitting outside the bar, though he never noticed me. Each time, my throat tightened with that lingering taste of lizards.

"He doesn't deserve *this* strong of a reaction, Aya," I told La Abuela in my head. But she was firm: "It's not for him; it's for you."

It wasn't until May of the next year, only days before I left Puerto Viejo, that Aya lifted the spell that had kept me invisible, and Joe noticed me again.

"Maya! You're still in town!" His hands rose with surprise. "I haven't seen you in so long, I thought you were gone."

"Well, I wasn't gone, but I am leaving in a few days, back to the U.S."

"Oh, I'm glad I caught you then. I've missed you. Do you want to get dinner tonight?"

I paused to check. The nausea was gone, no longer needed. I didn't need to avoid him. And neither did I crave his company. But I was still a curious cat—what would it be like to sit across from Joe, now that the excess Lizard had been cleared from me?

The steaming plates of Pad Thai arrived at the same time as Joe's news.

"Oh wow. Valeria's moving here to be with you? That's wonderful!"

He gave a half-smile and glanced away.

"Is it not wonderful?" I asked.

He shrugged. "It's complicated. I've got a roommate now."

I raised an eyebrow. "Why is that a problem?"

"She's a *room*mate, not a flatmate."

"Aaah Ah. But... didn't you tell Valeria that if she moved to Puerto, you'd be with her?"

"I said I'd date her, yes. But we're not in a relationship."

There it was—that same line again. It tasted like lizards. Luckily, the Pad Thai was sufficiently spicy and aromatic to cover the taste.

"Does she know you're sleeping with your roommate?"

He shifted in his seat, lowering his eyes while reaching for his napkin. "Well, hopefully, I'll be gone before she gets here. That job I applied for in the States might come through. Then there will be no drama."

No drama.

My heart filled, not with disgust, anger, or love, not even compassion, but a quiet sadness.

In his life movie, he was a charming, ethical lover, plagued by dramatic women. And we were friends. In mine, he was a small lizard, exhausting himself with unconscious push-ups.

And neither were fully wrong.

As soon as I had left our twisted dance, another Care Bear had stepped in. And so it would continue for him, I imagined, until his almond-shaped eyes opened to the truth—if that was even his path. As Aya had said, it was not my job to fix him or anyone else.

But I could protect the little Sister, the next Care Bear in line.

As soon as I returned home, I sent Valeria a message.

"Hola amiga. I know you must be excited about your move and being with Joe, but it might not be what you think. I trust you'll follow your heart. I just fear if you come, it'll get broken."

She answered right away:

"Oh Maya… my heart is already broken. That's why I'm coming—to finish the lesson, so I never call in this story again."

I nodded. Yes. I understood. I had been there. She was on her own sacred mission for the collective, for the sisterhood.

As I closed my phone that day, a sense of finality washed over me—not just about Joe, but about a whole chapter of my life.

I never saw Joe again, and neither did Valeria once she flew back home to Argentina after a couple of months in Puerto Viejo.

Lillian

And Lillian, you ask?
She didn't fly home three days after Ayahuasca. While I was getting a tattoo, she was at the clinic, discovering she had COVID and couldn't board her flight. So she quarantined on a towel on the beach for a week. And since I'd been exposed, I quarantined with her.

I don't believe it was a random twist of fate. It felt like a gift, a necessary pause—likely woven by La Abuela herself—to let the medicine settle deeper and for our friendship to bloom.

I still can't tell you if Lillian was Lizard or not. But over those slow days—floating in the river, sunning on the sand, sharing our life stories—I learned something important: if Lillian was Lizard, then she embodied what an evolved, fully realized Lizard could be. Quietly strong. Proud, but uplifting. Rooted in an unshakable sense of worth that needed no external validation.

And just in case I really was half-Lizard… that gave me hope.

Lizards

It took months before I stopped glaring at the lizards on my wall like they were spies from another realm. Each time one dropped into its little push-ups, my feet would recoil, and I'd hiss, "I see you there. I respect you, but will not bow."

Isabel, one of my dearest friends, laughed as my feet recoiled when one darted under my chair. "You're ridiculous. Look at them—they're so playful and fun!"

She was right, of course. It was unfair of me to hold the jungle's cold-blooded wall-crawlers accountable for an archetype in my psyche. They were just spirited housemates, sun-drunk and busy with bugs, doing their age-old dance of stillness and sudden motion.

I would never ink their kind on my skin again—but we've made our peace, the lizards and I.

Marco

One more thing happened in the aftermath of my Lizard journey. I met a man.

Two weeks after the Lizard session, Marco stepped onto the dancing platform at Katuk. Our eyes locked. We didn't speak, didn't need to; our bodies found a rhythm, gliding together, lost in the dance and jungle heat.

He stayed in Puerto Viejo for two days. We swam to Cocles Island, ate ice cream as it melted down our fingers, laughed until our cheeks hurt, and discussed the mysteries of the universe until the first light of dawn.

When I spoke, he leaned in. If it rained, he pulled me close under the center part of the umbrella.

And when it was time for him to leave, he didn't linger. He left as suddenly as he had appeared, back to his life in Spain, leaving behind neither ache nor longing—only deep mutual respect, fondness, and joyous gratitude.

The day Marco left was the day I returned Joe's headlamp. That same night, my feet finally found stillness, no longer wagging like a lizard's tail. Thank Goodness that was over; the lizard feet always gave me the creeps.

474

I smiled to myself at the perfection of it all. Marco wasn't meant to stay; he was a reminder, a glimpse. Not of who I'd meet next, but of who I'd finally become.

Chapter 31
Mapacho, Moccachino, and the Mystery

We stared at each other, the grandmother Turtle-Whale and I.

Don't do it.

I felt her say it in the sly wink of her eye and the crookedness of her smile. The waves crashed at my feet, punctuating her warning.

Cocles Beach was wild that day. Giant waves hurled themselves at her shore; red flags snapped in the wind; lifeguards paced and whistled at anyone who dared to enter the sea's fury farther than waist deep. This was the domain of surfers, not swimmers. Not today.

But Ayahuasca had given me a task, and this was my last chance. If I hesitated even for a moment, the lifeguards would catch me. I'd have to out-swim the first breaks faster than they could reach the end of the beach.

I dropped my sarong onto the sand, shaking my head at the absurdity—the insanity, the sheer recklessness—of what I was about to do. And before I could come to my senses, I plunged headlong into the crashing waves and began the swim.

℘ · ℭ

Six months prior
Puerto Viejo, Costa Rica - November 2022

"This is for you." Sydney held out a tall slender glass jar with the reverence reserved for sacred medicines. Inside, seven paper cylinders nestled against each other. I didn't know what they were, but Sydney had just returned from the Amazon jungle of Peru, from a ten-day ceremony with Ayahuasca. I knew that whatever this jar contained was precious. I received it with both hands and brought it to my heart.

"Thank you. What is it?"

She smiled, closed her eyes, and rolled her shoulders.

"Mapacho!" The word was soft on her tongue. Mapacho—the name of a lover, friend, or beloved teacher.

I opened the jar. Mapacho had a rich, musky, earthy aroma.

"*Who* is he then?"

"He's Tobacco, the Sacred Masculine of the plant world. I got this Mapacho from the Maestro. It was rolled with prayers and ícaros by the Shipibo people of the Sacred Valley. And it's for you. During my ceremony, Ayahuasca told me to gift this to you."

I carefully placed the jar on the shelf in my small apartment, among the other treasures that filled my life with meaning: rose oil, sandalwood, and the essential oil blend that held the essence of my future self. Even with the lid closed, I felt his presence. Just having him on the shelf made me feel calmer.

I still had a week before my next Ayahuasca ceremony, but had no doubt Mapacho hadn't come to me randomly. This is how reality unfolded in the world of Ayahuasca—a world where time folded on itself, and every moment, past, present, and future was connected like threads in a mandala-web waiting to be revealed.

Within a week of ceremony, I expected any event or gift to relate to the theme of the upcoming journey.

The day after I received Mapacho, Isabel arrived in Puerto Viejo.

Isabel had been one of my greatest loves—not romantically, but that one special friend whose radiance had brightened my life.

For fifteen years, her grace and elegance had fascinated me. She moved through the world like a star ballerina, poised and deliberate, high heels clicking on the pavement. Perfect hair, flawless makeup—she embodied society's ideal of a woman, turning heads wherever we went. Even if she applied makeup to my face and dressed me in her clothes, in her wake, I was invisible—a wild weed in the shadow of a cultivated rose. But I understood; she was the queen, and I too was watching her.

We spoke every day when apart and had endless conversations on her sofa or in coffee shops when together. We carried each other through heartbreaks, moves, and money troubles. We were the definition of best friends—until one particular change broke us.

The year was 2015, when I published my first book. I suspected my endless talks about it had pushed her away—I was so captivated by my own journey—but when I asked, she only replied that she needed space. She vanished overnight. I sent flowers, even pleaded, but she was gone, and I walked on alone.

For seven years, we evolved apart. I roamed through deserts and mountains, until I landed, following Jaguar, barefoot in the Costa Rican jungle. She planted strong roots in the city, becoming a successful restaurant owner with the help and guidance of her husband.

Then one day, out of the blue, she reconnected:

"Hi, Melissa. Would you like to travel to Egypt with me? I want to hold ceremonies in the temples of Isis and Hathor, but I don't want to go alone. I can't think of anyone else I'd rather go with than you."

My heart leaped, but anger quickly followed. Did she think she could just reappear after breaking my heart like nothing happened, and expect me to drop everything and follow her to Egypt? I guess she did.

I hesitated for a few days. I wanted to be heard, acknowledged, validated, but to her, there was no drama. She had needed space; now she didn't.

The truth was, I had missed her, and she was back. Why be resentful? After all, didn't all the cells in the body replace themselves completely every seven years?

"Alright, Isabel, let's start new," I told her. "But I'm a chocolate maker now. I make enough to live, but not enough for Egypt, as wonderful as those ceremonies sound. Would you come to Puerto Viejo and sit with Ayahuasca with me instead?"

A week before the ceremony, Isabel stepped out of her private taxi, her stylish Birkenstocks landing on the dirt road in front of her Airbnb, and we hugged for the first time in our current versions.

That night, as we shared a meal by the beach, she sank into her chair, shoulders drooped and arms crossed.

"I'm tired, Melissa. Not just from the flight, but in general. Life feels so heavy these days, and I don't even know why. I have a great life, a great business, a great husband..." She trailed off, her gaze lost in the waves.

I nodded, but in my mind, I saw a different story.

Ayahuasca had called her, just like it had called Lillian. Egypt, my finances, our reunion—these were all threads woven specifically to bring her here, to the ceremony. Aya didn't call randomly. If Isabel was ready to rise beyond her burdens, answers would come, and perhaps, much more.

As for me, I couldn't deny the call. Every day, for weeks, as I sat cross-legged on the beach in meditation, the image of the Grandmother Vine had appeared at the forefront of my mind, vivid and insistent.

Of course, I would answer her call, even though I couldn't shake the memory of the last time we met. The journey with the Lizard still made me shudder.

༄ · ༄

Bribri, Costa Rica - November 2022

Jordi led the way through the jungle to the platform, and Isabel, Aniel, and I followed. Isabel held her dress up with both hands and walked carefully, eyes on the trail to avoid ants, rocks, and roots. But Aniel and I looked up at the vibrant flowers on each side of the trail. Our nimble feet were well-adapted to jungle walking.

Aniel and I had been close friends since we first met dancing at Katuk, a year prior, and we'd since partnered in hosting weekly Cacao Dances—I served the cacao; he led the dances.

"Isabel, this is Aniel, one of my dearest friends here." I introduced him to Isabel when she joined us for her first cacao circle. Aniel unfolded his long legs and stood, his presence as gentle as it was towering. Without hesitation, he wrapped Isabel in an embrace, holding her with a warmth and sincerity that would have felt out of place in her northern city. I watched as her shoulders relaxed, the tension she carried slowly melting away. When they finally parted, she looked up at him with a smile.

"You have such a comforting, peaceful energy." Tears gathered in the corners of her eyes. She added softly, "Thank you. I needed that."

Aniel had heard the call of Ayahuasca for years, but fear and lack of funds had held him back, until that day.

"You know, Maya," he said after the dance, "I've always been too scared to go to Aya, but I'd feel safe if I was with you. I think I want to go this week. I just don't know how to pay for it."

I jumped for joy. "Yes! You're coming. And don't worry about the money. If La Abuela is calling you, the path is already cleared." He smiled and embraced me even tighter than he had Isabel.

"Oh! I'd love to have that man's peaceful energy with us for the ceremony," Isabel had said, clapping her hands in delight. "I'll cover the cost."

Isabel's generosity seemed so effortless, so natural, in that moment. With a hand on my heart, I thanked her, then sent Aniel the good news: he was coming!

And so it was that I stepped onto the jungle platform with two of my closest friends, excited for an intimate sitting. Except… a woman was already there.

"Hi, guys! I'm Jenny!" Her high-pitched accent was unmistakably American—as American as her pink hooded pajamas. Aniel and Isabel walked to her mat, which she had placed in the center of the room—right in front of the altar. They smiled and shook her hand.

"Hey. Nice to meet you." I faked a smile, nodded in her direction, and dropped my bag on the mat farthest from hers. The arrangement worked well anyway, as it left the best mat—the one I called the "Queen's Mat"—for Isabel, and the longest mat, right next to mine and separating me from the pink-pajamaed lady, for Aniel.

"I'm so glad to meet you guys. Are you as nervous as I am?" She was a chatty one and immediately launched into her whole life story, pulling Isabel into a rapid monologue about how she ended up on this platform, with us.

I sat on my mat, completely ignoring her, and mindfully arranged my tokens of protection before me. I placed a Mapacho cigarette in the center, then two crystals (a black tourmaline and a clear quartz), a jaguar tooth, and a stick of Palo Santo with a lighter.

"Going to Ayahuasca without Mapacho would be like going to battle without your sword," a male friend had once told me. I had given him one of Sydney's Mapachos, and in return, he had gifted me the jaguar tooth for protection. I then had thought, "Why would I need a sword to meet Mama Aya, the kindest, most loving of Pachamama's master plants?" But that was before the Lizards.

I placed the second Mapacho at the corner of my mat, deliberately creating an energetic barrier between me and Jenny, who was still talking.

What was it about her? The way she spoke, the neediness in her voice... I glanced at Mapacho, seeking his grounding. I had come with a sword, and now my impatience was flaring up. Aya had taught me that, in the end, everyone and everything on the platform was part of the journey. My chest tightened. What if Jenny was here to mirror an aspect of myself I didn't want to see, some deep shadow I'd have to face?

"Hola, qué tal." Marc, the fire keeper for the night, stepped onto the platform, and with one bright smile, instantly dissolved my anxious thoughts. He dropped his rolled mat and blanket right next to mine in one easy motion. His curly brown hair and tan poncho reminded me of a poster of Clint Eastwood that had graced the wall of my room as a teenager. All that was missing was the cigarette. With long, calm strides, he crossed the space between our mats, embracing each one in his quiet strength.

"If I don't use it during the ceremony," I decided, "I'll gift Marc the second Mapacho in the morning." I smiled, imagining the character complete, until Jenny's high-pitched voice cut through my daydream and curled the corner of my lip.

℘ · ℭ

"Isabel," Jordi called. She crawled on all fours to the altar and received the chalice. I couldn't read her expression—whether she was curious or nervous—but sent her love and courage in my mind, in case she needed either. Jenny was next. She drank from her chalice with much grimacing. Then Aniel, who glanced at me several times before drinking the medicine in one gulp. Finally, it was my turn. I held the chalice to my heart and silently prayed.

"Ayahuasca, Abuelita… I come to you with fear in my heart today, but I will not show it for the sake of Isabel and Aniel. I trust, as always, that you know what I need. I stand before you humbled by your power, but as you have shown me my own resilience and courage, I also stand before you ready. Whatever journey you wish to grant me, even if it is as dark as my darkest shadows, I will go where you lead me. I will receive what you teach me. I just ask, if it is at all possible, that my friends meet you softly and gently. And I thank you in advance."

And with a straight back, head held high despite a wildly beating heart, I drank the medicine in one gulp.

Jordi wiped the chalice and set it back on the altar, then blew out the candle. One by one, we lay down, bathed in the chorus of frogs and crickets and the fire's faint glow, flickering under Marc's reverent care. And for about an hour, we rested and waited.

"I'm cold. I'm so cold. Oh my God. I'm so cold. So cold." Jenny's trembling voice tore through the peaceful night. I lifted my head to see what was happening with her. She had sat up and bundled herself in her blanket. Her pink hood was cinched tightly around her face, leaving only her

483

eyes visible in the fire glow. They darted frantically between us, pleading.

"Help me. Help me. I'm so cold," she whimpered.

A familiar pull of duty began lifting my shoulders, urging me to get up, to help, to ease her suffering. It was instinctive; rescuer was in my blood. But, no—not tonight. I lay back down, stiff against my mat. How cold-hearted was I that I didn't want to help this girl who was so cold, so cold, so cold? Her whimpering grated on my nerves even as it amused me. She was so dramatic, dramatic, dramatic. The ugly truth, right there: I was not compassionate—I only felt compelled to help from a sense of duty, to fulfill some unspoken role I had assigned myself.

Suddenly, the edges of the platform blurred and, right before my eyes, invisible claws shredded reality, leaving gaps through which darkness poured in. My breath caught. Oh, my. It had begun, and it was dark. I wasn't fully under the medicine's spell yet, but I feared where we were headed.

I braced myself on my mat and took a deep breath. "Okay, Abuelita. I trust you. Show me my shadows, my blind corners, whatever I need to see." I didn't think I had a choice, but I'd learned that welcoming the lessons eased the journey.

"I'm so cold..." Jenny's whimpers cut through even the blackness.

"She's not your concern, Child." Aya's words floated calmly into my mind, carried on black waves, thick as velvet. "Let the Masculine respond."

Just then, in perfect synchrony, Jordi and Marc crossed the platform to Jenny's aid. Jordi gathered several blankets while Marc's steady hand and warm smile soothed the trembling damsel. I watched them from my mat, and a warmth filled my heart—thank God for men! Man, the protector, the rescuer, honor-bound to rescue damsels in distress, even the irritating ones.

But just as quickly, the warmth faded, absorbed into an inconvenient thought. Why did her neediness bother me so much? Was it because I saw myself in her? Hadn't I needed men to see me, love me, return my calls to feel loved? The blackness thickened. It wasn't just dark—it was alive and pulsing.

"Aya… why is my journey dark?" I pulled the blanket snug to my chin, hiding from the night's chill and the dread of what she might answer.

"Don't fear the dark." Aya's words now curled like smoke through the shadows in my thoughts, almost sensual. "Black is the color of Mystery. And Mystery is the sexiest thing in the world. Mystery is the Feminine Principle herself."

The Feminine Principle? What did she mean? I was born female, but there was nothing mysterious about that—and truthfully, I was more wildling than woman. My idea of femininity looked more like Isabel. I moved my hand through the air, mimicking her elegance, and opened my eyes to see the flowers my fingers created. My nails were rimmed with dirt, and probably chocolate too. But in watching the fluid turns of my wrists and fingers, I found grace in the movements.

With each twirl of my hand, the blackness swirled closer, until it was inside me. My spine slowly lengthened, my body began to sway, my hips circled in slow seductive arcs.

Was this what it felt like to be Woman, Priestess, Queen? There was a power in those undulations unlike anything I'd ever felt. I could only catch a glimpse of it, though, a small taste at the edge of my consciousness. This Mystery felt primal and magnetic—a force that could pull worlds into its orbit simply by undulating.

I imagined this was how Isabel must have felt when she entered a room, commanding the attention of every male within sight. Isabel—maybe I was perceiving the Feminine Principle because she was here, in the flesh, on the platform.

"Ugh... Aaargh..." Isabel's raw, guttural purge interrupted my musings, instantly clearing the Mystery from my mind. But I smiled—this friendship meant more to me than any fleeting glimpse of some mysterious Feminine Principle.

I watched her, head bowed over the white bucket. With each retch, I imagined she was releasing the sorrow and grief that had weighed her down. I inhaled deeply and quietly blew a Breath of Love and Courage in her direction, the way Aya had taught me.

My breath traveled toward her, and in its wake, pulled away the blackness. Warm beige and bright white now filled my field. Beige, like the gratitude for our reborn friendship, and white, like the boundless, unconditional love I felt for her. And this love kept growing until my heart was so unbearably full that I feared it might burst.

Finally, Isabel lifted her head and our eyes met. I smiled, but her face revealed no emotion. She simply brushed hair off her face and collapsed back onto her mat.

Now everything was white, a shimmering haze of love and tenderness—gentle, soft, yet expansive. This was the opposite of the centripetal swirling blackness I'd tasted moments prior. Were Mystery and Love two sides of the same Feminine Principle? I couldn't hold either, yet their combined sweetness intrigued me. My body relaxed into the mat, breath steady, smiling with certainty: If this was the exploration at hand, this journey would be pleasant after all.

"It's time, Child." Aya's voice cut in, as though she'd been waiting for this exact moment, when Mystery and Love had finally settled into my being. "It's time to welcome Mapacho now."

I opened my eyes, feeling the subtle shift of the medicine deepening. I wasn't swimming yet. I could still sit and stand without much effort. I picked up the Mapacho cigarette in front of my mat and the lighter. I cradled both against my heart as I walked to the edge of the platform.

Aniel sat on the steps, arms wrapped around his folded knees and head bowed in the opening between them.

He seemed to be buzzing. "Bzzz bzzz perdonamos bzz bzz santificado bbzz…"

I silently sat beside him, leaned on my elbow on the tallest step, and slowly brought the flame to Mapacho. The light flickered. A warm bitterness enveloped my tongue. I opened my mouth and let the smoke escape. It rose toward the stars, creating phrases and poems with each expanding swirl. Mapacho was too powerful to be inhaled; just a few puffs were enough for his cool strength to descend into my body and ease my mind. I settled in his embrace, feeling like myself—content, assured, and calm.

"Aniel?" He looked up, eyes red, tears still rolling down his cheeks. I smiled and handed him Mapacho. The buzz I'd heard, I now understood, was a prayer. He'd been scared, but he was safe now, as we sat together. "Here. Share this with me."

He pulled on Mapacho, then also relaxed back on an elbow. He took a few draws and handed me back the cigarette. We smoked half of it in this way, passing it back and forth, as we'd always done, across all lifetimes.

The next day, when we recalled that moment, Aniel said he'd been scared that Aya would dredge up some ancestral traumas he'd have to face on his own, but when I handed him the cigarette, he felt my love for him, and Aya's love too, through me. And he knew, there was nothing to fear. And we laughed also. How natural it had felt to share that cigarette, even though in this life, neither of us smoked.

As Mapacho filled my being, the swirling colors of Ayahuasca faded, yielding to the earthy, grounding hues of tobacco. Brown, mocha, burgundy, amber, caramel, honey, all flowing and swaying. His spirit wrapped around my heart like a sheath of grounded wisdom and protective love. I leaned into the feeling, giving myself over to him. I felt Aya still by his side, two wise and ancient energies, distinct but equal. They knew each other… I'd even venture to say they loved each other, beyond just mutual respect.

Aniel stood up and placed a hand on my shoulder. Mapacho had calmed him. I understood he was returning to his mat. We looked at each other and smiled.

I sighed contentedly. What a gift Aniel was. A true soul brother.

"Correction," Aya interrupted. "He's a soul *sister*, experiencing a male lifetime."

I turned as Aniel stepped back onto the platform, and my eyes followed his fluid movements to his mat. A soul sister. Yes. It felt right. And I… of course—that made so much sense: I was a masculine soul, experiencing a female lifetime.

I descended the steps and sat on a round boulder by the sacred fire, feet planted on the ground, elbows resting on my knees, and two fingers reverently holding Mapacho. Marc had gone up to the platform; I had the fire to myself. Even just sitting, I felt taller, broader, physically stronger. This was me. The ease, the solidity, the strength. It was who I knew myself to be, at the core.

"If I've been mostly man," I asked Mapacho, "have I been a good man?"

A silky dark mahogany smoke curled around my mind as Mapacho explored my depths for an answer. And, as vividly as if the memories belonged to this lifetime, I remembered.

My hands proudly held ivory daggers slick with the blood of my enemy. The metallic taste of blood filled my mouth. Had I truly needed to kill the whole family? Screams and tragedy echoed around me. Was it my nature to pillage and rape? I felt no remorse. I had sought immortality through brave deeds and only acted as I believed right. I stood sovereign among my brothers. Some fought by my side, some died to protect me, others fell at my hand, their blood tempering both my sword and stature.

Another time, another life, I stood in darkness, shoulder to shoulder with every able man in our village—knives, bows, arrows, fists ready—my heart pounding with fear. The forest before us rumbled with the cries and wildness of lawless attackers. It didn't matter if I saw dawn, as long as our loved ones were safe.

Then, the scene shifted again. The soft touch of a woman caressed my skin. The fighting was over. Her wet, white cloth cleaned my wounds just as her love mended my heart. Her kind eyes, the way she smiled, washed away the blood and horror I'd seen. Women put their lives in our hands, and in return, gave ours purpose and sanctuary. How strong they were!

I opened my eyes to the current reality, to the fire before me, my cleansing, warming friend. With the flames and the jungle as my witnesses, I bowed to all women, my feminine self included, with gratitude. Then I bowed to Mapacho's last embers, glowing between my fingers, for the gift of these insights.

I picked up a stick and tended the fire. I'd always tended the fire. Alone under the stars on long nights of watch. But also with my tribe, when we gathered and danced around the flames, smoke mixing with laughter. And sometimes, when a woman had come to me, offering herself in the fire's glow. I'd taken her into my arms and worshiped her, lost in her warm skin enlivened by the fire, her wild hair silver in the moonlight.

Oh, how I loved my inner masculine, the way these tobacco browns anchored me in such a familiar stance, and this Master Teacher, Mapacho, leading the way. We, men, had come so far. Valor wasn't gained in battle anymore; it lived in facing ourselves, holding ourselves to the highest integrity. The bravest among us took on the hardest fights, the ones no one saw, making amends for our ancestors' legacy. Somewhere along the way, we had broken and lost the trust of women. Without their sanctuary, their magic, and guidance, many of us drifted, rudderless.

If I were given a chance to be a man again, I'd do it right. I'd study with Oak and Mapacho, and learn from Master Plants how to love well, protect when needed, and respect in all ways. I'd temper my impulses and serve as much as I lead.

I smiled… And I'd grow a massive beard.

I pinched the last of the smoldering Mapacho for just a few more puffs, a few more moments immersed in my own sacred masculine essence, but it was already fading.

"Don't be sad, Child." It was Aya's voice in my mind. "Your masculine essence is always available to you. But in this here and now, you have chosen the path of the Feminine, to embody its fullness. There is a depth of power here, a wellspring of magic you have only begun to explore. Male, female, light, dark—humans exist on a continuum so they may look into each other's eyes and find themselves in contrast. To understand the whole, you must also live as a woman."

I stood up, snapped a branch over my knee, and fed the fire. My body was smaller and softer now, my hands free of a warrior's calluses. Did I want to be a woman? To embody the Mystery? Not really. Not in that moment. I much preferred to embody Strength and Presence. But then I remembered. Through my masculine eyes, I had felt a woman's power— her grace, resilience, dignity, and unyielding resolve to love.

Hadn't her gentle touch melted my armor? Hadn't the slow sway of her hips pulled my whole world into hers? What if Aya was right and this petite form of mine held a depth of power I had yet to discover?

"Not only that," Aya teased, "as a woman, you get to attract a true mate and bask in the Masculine's love in physical form. You get to sit back and receive for once. Let the Masculine give, Child. Watch how it fills not just your heart, but also all those spaces in your life you didn't even know were empty."

I moved closer to the fire, hands open to its warmth. "I hear you, Aya, and it sounds wonderful, but I've made poor choices lately, and I'm not sure I trust myself to recognize a true mate."

"You made no mistake. Every choice brought you what you needed to heal and learn. Your path has been purposeful."

"But they weren't 'true mates,' so how would I even know if one appeared?" I thought back to the new moon ceremony on Playa Negra with Samantha, when I'd stated my intent. I didn't want just a mate; I wanted the Beloved, someone with whom I could create a new reality, instead of endlessly dismantling old ones.

"You'll know him by his essence. He'll feel like you in your masculine form." Aya's voice now floated lightly. She sounded amused. "Of course, he'll still be human, with his quirks, flaws, and shadows, and you two will need to communicate and compromise," she insisted on both words, her tone suggesting we, humans, do too little of both, then continued, "but he will be unmistakable to your heart"

True mate, the Beloved—I smiled, then chuckled, shaking my head. Honestly, it was easier for me to imagine being Tree than meeting this mate.

But just as I dismissively shook my head, the jungle and fire seemed to blur, and from the dance of Mapacho's browns, a lighter shade emerged—Mocha mixed with steamed milk, playful, younger, yet still unmistakably masculine. He reminded me of the mate I'd met when I was Tree but with an extra spark of mischief. This was a lover, an adventurer, a trickster even.

I felt him smile; he recognized me. And I recognized him; he was the one I'd been calling in. And in that moment, I had to admit I'd actually met him before.

It began in 2012, on the banks of the sacred Ganges in Rishikesh, India. I found myself pulled into a dimly lit room, heavy with the scent of fennel and cardamom. An old man with a weathered turban sat across from me, his eyes gleaming like polished stones softened by years of wisdom. He held my little finger gently, tracing the lines in my hands as though he were deciphering an ancient script.

I couldn't say why I stepped into his shop that day. I didn't believe in palm reading any more than in astrology or psychics. But the sign outside had made me chuckle: "Retired Math Teacher. Now Reading Palms. Come in, Know Your Future." It was the promise of equations turned mystical that had drawn me in.

"Your blood pressure," his voice was thick with an accent that sang each word, "will trouble you when you're older. Too low. You must walk, beta—long walks, like medicine."

Long walks, check. The Pacific Crest Trail was already on my horizon. Then, his face lit up, as if he'd uncovered a hidden treasure in my palm. He leaned closer, eyes darting between the deep crease on my hand and the astrological chart on his screen.

"You will have two life partners," he said. "The first you already met, when you were twenty-six." I nodded. Yes, that was Jack. "The second, you will meet in September this year."

His head tilted back and forth in that distinctly Indian gesture, neither a nod nor a shake, suspended between certainty and doubt. "But you," he sighed with a mix of fondness and frustration, "you can be very difficult, beta. Very stubborn. You'll need to wear red coral. A ring is best. It will protect your union, cool your temper."

"Red coral. Okay." I smiled. This man had met me less than five minutes prior, yet seemed to know a great deal about me. "And this life partner… could you tell me more about him?"

The old man lowered his voice, his eyes narrowing as if unveiling a secret. "This man," he began slowly, "he will be—"

But just then, the curtain parted, and two women stepped inside. Their crisp British accents sliced through the air like a guillotine, severing the flow of revelations.

"Hello, could we get a reading?" one of them asked.

The old man blinked, the trance broken. He folded the paper with my notes and pressed it into my hand. "Remember, beta," he said, his voice gentle. "Long walks. Like medicine. Good day now."

On September 1st, I woke up near the shores of Olallie Lake, a scenic section of the Pacific Crest Trail. I walked thirty miles that day. I napped in a meadow of alpine flowers under Mt. Jefferson's watchful eye, washed my socks in a river, ate pretzel M&Ms and tuna packets, crossed forested patches, and tiptoed across volcanic rock fields. And so it was for all of September. Oh, yes, I was in love—in love with this trail and its stunning views. But, still, on September 30th, I reached Canada and the PCT's northern terminus, tired, happy, and still absolutely single. I wasn't surprised, just a little disappointed.

But Isabel wasn't ready to give up on prophecies so easily. The moment I got off the trail, she whisked me to her favorite psychic. "Oh, you'll meet the love of your life this year. Very soon!" I raised an eyebrow. It'd better be soon; Mr. September was already late.

Then the numerologist, a month later: "Love is imminent. In fact, the chart indicates he's… already here?"

The big, imminent love of 2012. Yet every time I asked for details about the man himself, the session ended or was interrupted. "It seems this information is shielded," the psychic had said. Why? Why could I not know about this mate?

It would have been easy to mock fortune tellers and disbelieve, but the truth was, he *was* indeed already here. Whether his energy entered my field or I imagined it because of all the predictions, I began to feel him.

Some days, his presence was so palpable, I half-expected to turn a corner and crash into him. I felt his essence linger in the produce aisle of grocery stores, where our hands could have brushed reaching for the same avocado, or at any empty table of any sidewalk café where he could have just left. I held my breath, wore my best clothes, shaved my legs, rehearsed our initial greeting. I was ready for first contact. I knew this energy was him—exciting, mischievous, and so full of life.

But September was over, October came and went, and every month after that for the next ten years. I grew jaded. If I felt him, I shrugged. What was the point of getting my heart rate up? I met and loved others, but mostly I enjoyed my solitude, and eventually, he dissolved from my thoughts, like the last wisp of smoke of a fire that never truly caught.

And now, here he was, standing alongside Mapacho. And Ayahuasca knew him too. It wasn't my imagination or the wistful projection of a lonely heart. It was *him*—the same energy I'd felt before, except more real and vibrant than ever. I didn't know what to say. My eyes teared up. Until this moment, I hadn't realized how much I'd missed him, how deeply his absence had armored my heart. I sighed, relieved. Finally, I could love again.

Now that he was with me, I no longer needed the fire, so I climbed back to the platform and settled onto my mat. I cocooned us in my warm blanket—both my tired physical body and his vivacious mocha-colored energy. This Mochaccino, he already had me, and I began to slip into a flow of rapturous, romantic bliss.

"Ahem!" Aya cut in. "Mmm-mmm. Not too fast, Child." She was right. Where was my pride? I was swooning far too easily. I straightened up in my mind, hands on my hips in a stance I imagined would make my Caribbean Mama proud.

With a mock frown, I tapped my foot under the blanket and recomposed myself.

"Here you are. I see you," I told him in my mind, arching an eyebrow. "Where have you been for the past ten years?"

His essence wrapped me fully, and my intoxicated heart swayed in his flow. "I've been watching you from the spirit realm, savoring every twist and turn of your wild life, and you—you are amazing." He paused, letting the memory of ten years of my adventures linger. "I've seen your doubts about me, your pleas, your impatience, even your stubborn denial that I exist. 'Fine!' you say, 'I'll just stay single. The Catmobile and I, we don't need anyone else.' But deep down, you knew I'd show up. You've been waiting for me, calling me. Oh, yes, I was there on Playa Negra, the last time you called."

His spirit was so full of joy, so casual. If he had had a body, he probably would have reclined on an elbow, eyes fixed on mine, unapologetic.

"But why so long?"

"I wanted to get you to this point." The blurred impression of a man shimmered in my mind, his fists tight and feet stomping in place. "Come on, come on!" he teased. "I wanted us to crave each other, a thirst so deep that when we finally meet in the physical, we'll cry in gratitude and never let go. Like finding a water cache after crossing the desert on foot." He winked in my mind, knowingly.

I softened, but only slightly. "But, did it have to take *ten years*?" I asked once more, my tone gentler this time.

He was so real that I could have sworn, as he leaned in, the scent of mocha and tobacco wafted across the platform. "Time doesn't exist, my love. You and I? We play across lifetimes. Ten years is a blink. Can you feel this delirious thirst driving us near mad? If we'd met right away, we'd have missed this. The fire, the passion, the… exquisite agony. This is what makes love exceptional."

His words wrapped around me like pure love, and finally, I couldn't hide my smile.

I wanted to ask, "So, are you going to finally show up in my physical world now that we've officially met?"

But Aya stepped forward again. "Not so fast, Child. Remember, you're the Mystery. You're the prize, the object to covet. Let him be slightly thirstier than you."

I let Mama's sass seep into me and turned back to Mochaccino in my mind.

"You know what? You've made me wait too long, so it's your turn now. You wait for me."

His love for me pulsed through my own heart. To be a love match, I also had to be a worthy opponent.

"Oh! I see. And what exactly am I waiting for?"

"For my time visiting with my best friend to be over. And who knows, maybe longer. Time doesn't exist, remember? I'll call you when I'm ready."

His deep laugh filled my mind. "And how exactly will you call me?"

"I don't know yet... you just wait and be ready."

A crackling from the fire pulled me back to the jungle, to this reality. I lifted my head and scanned the platform. Bundled shapes breathed slowly, softly. Everyone was asleep, even Jordi.

Down by the fire, Marc sat on the same boulder I'd occupied hours earlier, when I'd been fully in my masculine. With the same long branch, he tended the embers, keeping the fire alive.

There he was, another Sacred Masculine fully embodied, his presence anchoring the night, promising peace for the whole tribe. I touched my hand to my heart and bowed slightly in gratitude. A gesture he wouldn't see, but it was for him, and all like him— the guardian protectors, so noble, patient, and humble. It's a special kind of strength, one that holds space without claiming it.

As I was still bowed, relishing the vision of the fire keeper, a mosquito buzzed near my ear. My hand automatically lifted to brush it off, but I stopped mid-movement. Never before had I noticed the range of tones and harmonies in a mosquito's buzz. It rose and fell like the delicate hum of a violin's highest string. I listened closer, fascinated, delighted. I wished it would keep buzzing.

"When you're in love, even a mosquito's buzz becomes a sweet lullaby." There was a hint of teasing in Aya's tone, and I giggled.

"It's true," I said aloud with a wide smile, and I let myself fall back, surrendered, onto the mat. I turned away from the fire, finding Mochaccino still here, waiting for me.

We stayed like this, Mochaccino and I, for hours. We stared into each other's eyes, even though he had no eyes, and held each other tightly, even though he had no arms. I was a flower, he had stars in his eyes, and our love flowed between us like a living, breathing thing.

But at the first light of dawn, his energy began to thin, as I knew it would.

With a loving nod in my direction, Mapacho, the silent guardian, placed his hand on my Mochaccino.

"Hey, don't forget to call me," he teased as the two of them faded into the hazy light of dawn. Two peaceful warriors, the Maestro and his apprentice, slipping beyond the horizon of my conscious mind, back to their own path and higher purpose.

The cool air of the jungle caressed my face, the songbirds' trills and chirps and the call of howler monkeys filled the air. In this liminal space at the edge of physical reality, only La Abuela remained, sitting comfortably inside my heart, a feeling of contentment about her.

I took a deep breath, savoring the last traces of Mochaccino's essence, then turned inward to Aya.

"Aya, he's right. How exactly *will* I call him?"

I expected she would guide me to conduct a sacred ceremony to conjure up love magic from the depth of my Divine Feminine Mystery. But instead, she said,

"You'll have to swim to Cocles Island, climb the sharp cliffs to the very top, and there, you must call him, as loud as you can, 'Ven!' (come!)"

I opened my eyes, brow furrowed, speechless for an instant—what had she just said?

"I have to swim to the island and yell 'Ven?'" I repeated. "*Ven?* So my love speaks Spanish?"

She didn't answer. Still no hint about him. As for swimming to the island, the waves had been wild for weeks.

"But, Aya, I can't swim to the island. It's too dangerous."

"Then I guess you don't meet your mate," she said flatly. I laughed, hesitantly. She was joking, right?

"Listen, Child," she continued, her tone gentle but firm. "For the next three weeks, while Isabel is in town, you will not write your book, you will not make chocolate. You will just watch her. Open your mind and take in her every move."

I smiled. Yes, it made sense. Isabel embodied the Feminine like no other. If I called in a mate, then I'd better prepare for his arrival, and what better teacher than my own best friend?

80 · 03

"Jordi, Aya said I have to swim to Cocles Island. But with these waves, how am I supposed to do that?"

Jordi burst into a bright laugh as he continued folding his blanket.

"Ah, that Abuela—she's clever. But you know, she doesn't always tell the truth. She's not here to give you the answers. She's here to push you, to make you think, to see how far you'll go to figure things out for yourself." He shifted his weight, his gaze steady on me.

"And sometimes," he continued, "what you think is her voice is your own thoughts, disguising themselves as her. You must sit with it. Ask yourself, 'Does this feel true? Or is it a story my mind is telling me?'"

80 · 03

As we left the platform, we passed Marc and Jenny sitting side by side on a log by the now-extinguished fire.

"Yeah, I woke up like, 'Why do I have so many blankets on me?'" She laughed, glancing at Marc. "What? Was I cold or something?"

498

Marc chuckled, his laughter mingling with hers as they leaned toward each other.

"I guess she's not all that bad if she can laugh at herself," I thought. As for Marc, he felt different. In the sunlight, the silent guardian of the night was once again just a man, simply enjoying a lighthearted laugh.

I paused next to him and held out the second Mapacho with two hands.

When he finally turned toward me, his eyes lit up and he stood suddenly. "Is this Mapacho?" I nodded and lifted my hands toward him, offering my gift. He picked it up carefully, one hand on his heart in gratitude. "I haven't had one of these in so long. Thank you."

"You're welcome." I noticed he had taken his poncho off. The shirt he wore underneath had interlocking lines, brown, amber, and mocha. I smiled at the Guardian within him. Then I walked away, a bounce of joy in my step. I caught up to Jordi, Isabel, and Aniel on the path through the jungle. Aniel turned and smiled. He seemed as happy as I felt on this glorious morning. The trees swayed, the flowers shimmered, sunlight danced through the canopy. Birds sang, ants marched, and the world felt more alive than ever.

And I wondered: "Now what happens?"

℧ · ℭ

We drove in silence through the town of Bribri and back to the main road. I was eager to hear all about Isabel's journey, but I sensed her energy was contained, guarded even, so I waited until we had dropped off Aniel to ask her.

"So? How was it?"

"Oh, nothing too special. She left after I vomited."

"What do you mean, she left?" I didn't know Aya could leave once a journey had begun.

"I mean, she left." I caught a hint of annoyance in her voice. She kept her eyes on the road, her hands on the steering wheel, and continued in a reticent tone. "I saw a

499

green face that looked like a plant, but with a woman's features, and with green spiraling tendrils all around her. 'Surrender,' she kept saying. She was scaring me a little. After a while, I said, 'Alright, alright, I'm surrendering.' I felt her move around in my heart, and I didn't like that at all. Then, suddenly, I felt nauseated and vomited—a lot. After that, I lay back down and she said, 'Oh, I see, you're a daughter of Isis, so we're equals.' And then she left. I couldn't feel her in my body anymore. Maybe because I'm already part of the Isis Mystery School, she knew she wasn't my teacher."

"What happened after she left?"

"Nothing. I slept."

I looked to the passing jungle and pressed her no further. I hadn't thought it possible for Aya to just… leave. But, I was still new on the path of Ayahuasca, and Isabel was the first daughter of Isis I had brought to the jungle, so... was it possible that Isabel was so closed off that the medicine couldn't reach her? No. Impossible—Isabel had been on a spiritual path long before I was. Then it must have been true; she was Aya's equal.

My eyes opened wide in awe. Maybe that's why Aya had asked me to watch her; she was a Teacher.

I relaxed in the rental car's seat. Three weeks—I still had three whole weeks with Isabel to learn, learn, learn.

༄ · ༄

And so, per Aya's instructions, I watched Isabel's every move.

Before she arrived, I had envisioned showing her Costa Rica's untamed beauty—jumping in waterfalls, kayaking emerald rivers, hiking jungle paths in search of toucans and macaws, and strolling along white sand beaches. We would rent her a bicycle, and I would treat her to the best Caribbean barbecue on the beach—fish, rice and beans, cooked in a metal half-barrel by a Rastafarian with dreadlocks as long as mine.

But these plans were self-indulgent, ignoring her refined tastes. Isabel preferred the comforts of town—restaurant dining and boutique shopping.

I followed her as she glided into shops and restaurants with quiet assurance, back straight, a slight smile, expecting the world to meet her high standards. And it did. When we settled at a table, servers straightened their jackets. When she brushed fabrics with her fingers or inspected jewelry as though it were already hers, shopkeepers hurried to assist her.

She never left a boutique without making a purchase, handing over her card without a second thought, unfazed by the rising total.

"Do you wear them all?" I once asked. As a truck-dweller, I'd learned to keep only what was essential or cherished in my space. Hers was a new, fascinating way—perhaps a more abundant way—of living life.

"I like to have choices," she replied, as if it were the most natural thing.

Aya had also instructed me to pause both writing and chocolate-making to spend more time with Isabel. As my usual income dwindled to nearly nothing, I remained unconcerned, trusting in Aya's guidance.

Despite the growing contrast in our finances, I followed Isabel through boutiques and fine dining without hesitation. Whenever the bill came, she reached for it without a second thought, her hand as casual as if she were brushing sand from her arm. No mention of cost, no glance in my direction, just the unspoken understanding that although I lived in Puerto Viejo, she had access to a different side of my town.

And how excited I was to have her in my town; how eager I was to introduce her to my friends and my community. During this time, a curious shift happened.

While I'd always been well-regarded on the local scene, now it seemed the whole town exaggerated. "Maya!" Everywhere we went, I was met with affection, warm smiles, and open arms. Isabel stood by my side, composed as ever, while I proudly introduced her, "This is Isabel, my best friend." She met each person with kind, polite smiles and graceful nods, and they welcomed her because she was with me.

The thought crossed my mind that this was the first time in all the years we'd known each other that I received more attention than she did. I smiled, imagining she'd be happy for me that I had found a home where I fit so effortlessly.

I watched her, and I saw her regal poise, her feminine grace, her polite kindness, and showy elegance. Yet, I didn't see what some others saw.

Debbie, my neighbor and friend, watched Isabel leave, her gaze following the swish of the flowy dress out the door. She turned back to me, eyes rolling. "What a load of ego baloney," she said sharply.

I looked up at her, puzzled.

Debbie shook her head. Then, mimicking Isabel with exaggerated haughtiness, she said, "I'm a daughter of Isis. This ancient plant medicine has nothing to teach me."

"And what if she is? What if it's true?" I could believe it.

Debbie's eyes softened. "Oh, honey…" Her hand swept my space as if to gather it all up in one explanatory gesture. "This woman is not your friend. She holds nothing but contempt for you and the way you live."

I glanced around, following her hand as it circled the room, trying to see what she meant. What was wrong with my aquamarine apartment? Then my eyes drifted to the window, catching the last glimpse of Isabel's dress as she turned down the street. "I'm going back to my air-conditioned room for a nap," she had said.

That seemed reasonable for someone unaccustomed to the jungle's moist heat. She only had a week left before her flight. Of course, she wanted to rest before returning to her busy city life.

"If you don't believe me," Debbie said softly, "just watch her. Watch her closely."

"That's what I've been doing," I replied, a bit defensively. "Aya told me to watch her."

Debbie stood and looked me in the eyes. "Then watch even harder."

And Debbie was just the first. In the days that followed, my little community gathered around me like a protective shell. "She's lovely when you're not around, but she rolls her eyes every time you open your mouth," seemed to be the consensus.

On Isabel's penultimate day, only the sea seemed to hold her interest. She had grown increasingly morose, and I had assumed she missed her life and her husband. This hot, moist jungle wasn't for everyone.

We sat side by side, gazing out at the island. She remained silent, seemingly content. When she finally smiled, I saw an opportunity to enhance her experience, so I pointed toward the tail of the island.

"You know, the entrance to the island is actually at the tail end over there. Tourists always try to climb the face, but the real way in is from the back."

She exhaled a long, weary sigh, her eyes fixed on the waves.

"Do you ever just... stop talking?"

The weight of her words hung in the air between us. I did stop, right then. We sat in this heavy, oppressive silence until my heart refused to be silenced. Then I stood up.

"I'm going to walk along the beach."

"Alright. I'll see you later." Her voice was calmer but devoid of warmth.

"No, I don't think I'll come back this way. I'll see you tomorrow at eight to return your rental car."

I walked away without looking back. I wasn't sad or even offended. Perhaps she was right. Perhaps I did talk too much. Sure, she could've been gentler about it, but I understood. She was on vacation; she had come to rest; and I... well...

"What a lovely color," I'd said, pointing to the restaurant's ceiling, a warm shade of mochaccino brown. Her eyes had rolled, and not to admire the ceiling.

"Let's go by Cocles Beach, in front of the island," I'd suggested later. "I want to check on the waves." Her lips had thinned into a silent no. She was looking for gifts for her friends back home. We had kept shopping.

"Do you think Mochaccino could be from Spain? Maybe I'll learn to dance the Flamenco." That one had earned me a hard eye roll, the kind that said, "I can't believe you're still talking."

"He said he's been watching me from the spirit realm. What if he's not incarnated? What if we meet only after I die? Maybe that's why I need to swim to the island, to die." She had walked away.

She told her stories too. Accountants. Business expansions. The intricacies of paperwork to purchase a villa in the south of France. Plans stacked neatly as ledger books. I did listen, but I was also high on love, my heart and mind wrapped tightly with dreams of Mochaccino.

Yes, as they said, she rolled her eyes whenever I opened my mouth. But could I really blame her?

When I reached Cocles River, where the river meets the sea, I sat with my feet in the cool water.

I remembered that in 2015, when she first began to drift away, she frequently urged me to "get to the point" of my stories. And the truth was, sometimes I told stories for the pure pleasure of storytelling, for the rhythm and joy of words creating worlds.

Did I ever just… not talk? Yes. I loved silence as much as I loved stories. But not with her. With her, I always talked. Always.

Why? Why did I always talk when I was with her? Suddenly, I saw: I talked because I was unconsciously uncomfortable and I wished to fill the dead space between us, as though filling it could mend it. My mouth opened in shock at the realization.

Ayahuasca, in her wisdom, would've seen this, seen the depth of my love for Isabel, and that it wasn't returned. But she also would have known I wouldn't have believed it back then. So instead, she had asked me to watch her, to find the truth on my own.

"Maya!" Thankfully, a joyous voice released me from my heavy epiphanies. I turned to see Kitty approaching, feathers in her hat and a jaguar tooth pendant like mine resting on her heart. She settled beside me and launched into a story about a poison dart frog she'd just found perched on her bicycle handlebar. "Better not lick your handlebars until the next rain," I replied. We both laughed, the mood returning to Caribbean light and easy.

"Maya, Kitty!" Now it was Aniel approaching. He sat with us, three joyous pairs of feet soaking in the cool river.

"I just applied for architecture school in San Jose. It's scary, but I feel braver these days." He glanced in my direction and smiled knowingly.

"That is wonderful!" Kitty and I leaned toward him, bringing him into a group hug. We stayed like this for a moment, soaking in his presence while we still had him.

Isabel had been one of my greatest loves, but in that moment, in that embrace, I felt the glow of a deeper sense of belonging, of having finally found my tribe.

The next morning, Isabel picked me up at eight, as agreed. We drove to town in silence until I turned to her, the question forming as I spoke it:

"How do you think this month together will affect our friendship in the future?"

"That's a big topic, one for another time." She shrugged, but I caught a flicker of dismissal. "We're soul-mates. We'll always be friends."

That afternoon, I resumed making chocolate. Isabel joined me on my patio as I prepared labels for the upcoming batch. Out of the corner of my eye, I watched her pinch the hammock's edge between two fingers, hesitating before brushing off a stray bug. She sat down gingerly on the very edge, her knees pressed tightly together, her hands folded neatly in her lap, as if afraid to touch anything else. Her gaze flickered to my hands.

"Is now a better time for that big topic?" I wasn't going to let her go without some clarity. "What did you mean when you said we're soul-mates and will always be friends?"

She sighed and straightened. "You do realize you talk an awful lot, and always about yourself. Honestly, it's draining. I can only handle it in small doses. But that doesn't mean we're not friends."

In that instant, two things clicked. First, this was the first time Isabel had spoken up with such clarity about her feelings toward me. And in spite of the harshness, I felt proud of her. The second was the most surprising: I realized I didn't want to be like Isabel; I wanted to be more fully like myself.

Aya hadn't told me to watch her because she was superior in the ways of the Feminine, but to help me find my own grace in contrast, to realize I preferred myself wild, barefoot, and with dirt under my fingernails.

"Well, Isabel, the thing is, I love myself as I am, and I'm not willing to change to suit your preferences." My voice was steady. My heart felt calm.

Her eyes narrowed in exasperation. "But really, Melissa, you can't expect everyone to sit through your endless stories. People have their limits."

"My name is Maya."

She stood up abruptly. "Is that truly what it's come to?"
"Yes, it has."

Without another word, she turned around and walked away.

Those were the last words we spoke.

The next morning, a message from her appeared on my phone: "Thank you for everything. I appreciate you." I stared at the message. My fingers hovered over the keyboard, but everything had already been said. I placed the phone face down on the table and wished her well. in my mind. It was over, and I felt strangely… free.

℘ · ℅

Cocles Beach, Puerto Viejo - Late March to April 2023

The strum of the guitar in my headphones lifted my arm slowly in an arc above my head, fingers curling into flowers. The clapping began—sharp, passionate—awakening my legs and Gypsy blood. One foot tapped against the sand, deliberate and proud, before tracing a defiant spiral. My hips followed, swaying with purpose, but my gaze never left the island.

I danced the Flamenco for her, letting the beat enliven me, offering her the new moves I was learning each week. Oh, but that Turtle-Whale was not so easily seduced. Four months had passed since the night I had spent with Mochaccino, and one month since I started dancing in the sand facing her, but her little eye and content smile remained the only signs of appreciation she granted me. She still would not lower her waves to let me swim to her.

With the passing weeks, the pangs of longing for my mate had subsided. Now, I danced not for him, but to see what might happen if I did call from the top of the island, as Aya had instructed.

507

Then finally, on the morning of April 3rd, passage was granted. Before she could change her mind, I dropped my sarong on the sand, slipped my flip-flops on my hands, ran, and dove into the almost calm sea. I swam mindfully, eyes on the island for the entire crossing, silently thanking her in advance for allowing me to climb on her back.

I reached her tail, and treaded water, waiting for the smallest of waves before swimming closer to her sharp rocks. I gripped a spire, and when the next wave pushed me up, I climbed the rest like a determined crab.

I stood on her first level, looking to the summit. To reach it, I'd have to scale the steep wall to the second level, then bushwhack to the top. There could be snakes coiled in hiding, unseen holes between the rocks, wasps' nests, and no guarantee that the resident hawks and pelicans would tolerate my intrusion. But I had come this far, and the summit was within reach.

I sat on my flip-flops and took a deep breath. I absolutely believed that whatever, or whomever, I called in, would come, so I had to be crystal clear about my intent before I shouted "Ven!"

I imagined this man stepping into my life on the physical plane. What would it be like?…

Inconvenient, honestly.

The feeling surprised me, but it was accurate. Every minute spent with this man would be time not spent writing. My mind would float with romance and giggles rather than focus on stories, archetypes, and plot twists. And with the limited social time left, how would I honor all the friendships I had built here?

I decided to add a caveat. I would call in a mate but ask that he enter my life only after my book was published.

But after the book was published, I'd want to travel— first on a book tour, then to satisfy my soul's hunger for adventures. I'd want to climb mountains and walk long trails again, and both endeavors were best enjoyed alone, without the distraction of another human. So if I met him, he'd have to wait until I returned.

But what then? I'd probably want to move somewhere new and exotic—Peru, Turkey, back to India. If I had a mate, this decision, like all decisions, would have to be a "we" compromise. I didn't feel ready to abdicate the sole captainship of my life. Perhaps I had never been ready, calling him through the window while I locked and braced the door.

I sat on my flip-flops for about an hour, entranced by the shifting blues and greens of the sea, the passing fish below, and the graceful swoops of hawks and pelicans above. Then, sufficiently satisfied with this moment of peace and solitude, I stood back up.

I looked up at the summit again, but I didn't scale the sharp rocks.

I jumped back into the sea and swam to shore.

ℰ · ℭ

Cocles Beach, Puerto Viejo - May 2023

We stared at each other, the island and I.
Don't do it.
I felt her say it in the sly wink of her eye and the crookedness of her smile. The waves crashed at my feet, punctuating her warning.

It was one of those days with red flags flapping and lifeguards whistling. But it was also my last day. My going-away party was over. People had cried. My bags were packed, my chocolate machine on a lease-for-sale plan, my bicycle gifted to a friend, and my bus ticket purchased. I was headed to the States with no plan to return to Puerto Viejo.

This was my last chance.

This was *the* island Aya told me to climb. If I left Puerto Viejo without calling and changed my mind later, it would be too late. I wouldn't fly back just to climb an island.

The waves crashed, the red flags snapped, and my feet were already moving. Shaking my head at the absurdity—the insanity, the sheer recklessness of what I was about to do—I plunged headlong into the waves and began the swim.

The passage was rough. With each large swell, I swam uphill, pushing against the water, then downhill, where I lost sight of the island. I didn't think about death. I just kept my head above the liquid turmoil and swam.

When I reached a point even with the island's tail, I treaded water, swallowing salt with every wave, and counted the swells. Their rhythm wasn't consistent, but it seemed that roughly every five large swells, a smaller one might allow me to swim in.

I waited, counting. After the fifth one, I pushed as hard as I could and grabbed one of the spires, but the sea disapproved of my breaking her no-passage rule. Before I could secure my other hand, a behemoth wave crashed over my body, plucking me off the rock and tumbling me against jagged edges. Pain flared as the rocks scraped my leg. I lost track of the surface, rolled and kept under by each new wave. I only knew where the rock was from the pain. I kicked off, heart pounding, mind singularly focused on preemptive gratitude: *Thank you for keeping me alive.*

I returned to treading, and began counting again. After the fifth swell, I lunged for the rock, and before the sea could toss me again, I clawed the spire and raced up. A wave crashed below me. I was on the island. Blood dripped from a long gash on my thigh, the sharp sting promising a scar. I smiled—from now on, wherever I traveled from here, the island would travel with me, her mark etched into my flesh. And as for the sharks, I didn't have to worry about them yet, not until the way back.

I looked up and began scaling the face to the second level. I had no flip-flops this time, but the protruding rocks were just sharp enough to hurt, not enough to pierce calloused flesh. From there, the bushwhack began. There was no grace, no finesse in my movements. I parted branches, stepped forward, and pushed through. Spiderwebs wrapped around my face, wasps threatened to escort me off, but eventually, a faint path appeared. I wasn't the first to climb to the top—I never assumed I was. I rounded the last few feet through brambles and piles of fallen coconut leaves and emerged, unscathed.

At the very top of the island, a coconut tree jutted out before curving upward, creating a small, smooth platform at its base. It was just the right size for a visitor to stand, elevated, and take in the 360-degree view. I stepped onto the platform and wrapped my arms around the coconut tree.

I took a quick check of the azimuths to get my bearings. The sun rose over Playa Chiquita—so, east. The beach stretched south; Puerto Viejo town lay to the north; and... where would Spain be? Just in case.

I giggled at the thought. Calling in the direction of Spain felt ridiculous enough to match everything else I'd just done. I'd swum through waves, climbed an island, risked my life, and now here I was, holding onto a coconut tree.

I took a deep breath and straightened my back.

"Ven!" I said in a calm, confident, and welcoming voice, matching the call with an enticing Flamenco curl of my fingers. I would not yell; I would not respect a man who came when summoned by a yell.

"Here I am. I've made it to the top of the island. I invite you to come into my life. You know I have a book to finish, that I need a lot of space for my own adventures, and that apparently I'm slightly insane. If you exist, I believe these are the very things you'll admire and cherish about me. I've come this far. Now, it's your turn. Come find me, I'll be in the world living my best life… Oh, and you might find the door to my heart closed when you get here. If you are who I think you are, I trust you'll invent a secret knock."

I gave a little bow, and that was it.

I turned to each cardinal direction, my arms outstretched, thanking the grandmothers of the east, south, west, and north. I offered gratitude to Yemanja, Goddess of the Sea, and to any God dwelling in the beauty of the clouds above. "Please, grant me safe passage back."

I climbed down to the second level and, with one last glance at the horizon, leaped into the water..

Chapter 32
The End of the Line Chapter

Cahuita, Costa Rica - May 2023

I slowly climbed the stairs, letting my eyes adjust to the dim light. I'd never been in that house before and hadn't found a light switch at the bottom. I landed each step quietly until my eyes were even with the landing. There, a shape emerged from the darkness, eyes first, fixed on mine. A cat. A large, rounded-back, male-faced, orange cat, resting on tucked legs and paws, guarded the landing by lying in the middle of the top step.

"Hi, Kitty!" I extended a hand toward the soft fur between his ears to comfort myself as much as to greet him. But as my fingers neared, he shrank away from my touch. No hiss, no aggression. Just a firm, silent refusal. His body slid from the landing and slunk past me down the stairs, vanishing into the dark.

What did it mean?

It couldn't just mean I met a shy cat. Oh, no—not minutes away from meeting La Abuela, and this time, on a new platform, with two facilitators with whom I'd never sat Ayahuasca before.

I watched the cat disappear at the bottom of the stairs toward the kitchen. A lump rose in my throat. I turned back to find the bathroom. A light switch awaited me right there on the wall. I could have sworn it hadn't been there moments before.

Pay attention. Everything is important.

This was a real bathroom, not a pit toilet in the jungle. I couldn't even imagine finding my way through the house and up these stairs once the medicine had me. Best I took care of all worldly business while I still could.

On my way back down, I peeked through the kitchen door in search of the orange cat. I meant to sit with him before the ceremony and ask him, if he was willing to share, what had spooked him about my energy. I leaned through the doorway. Three cats huddled around a dish—none of them the orange cat. Their heads snapped up, ears twitching. I hadn't made a sound, yet all three bolted, slipping through the back door. A kitten darted from under the table and ran after them.

I didn't like this omen at all. I straightened, squared my shoulders, and took a deep, slow breath.

Could it have nothing to do with me—just a house filled with scaredy cats?

I stepped onto the large wooden platform. Candlelight flickered, casting warm, golden pools onto the wood. The air smelled of jungle earth and copal. My heart settled.

Five mats, dressed in crisp white sheets, lay evenly spaced around the altar, waiting for us. The other participants—no one I knew—were already arranging their blankets, pillows, and sacred objects, their movements hushed and reverent.

I walked softly by the altar, draped in a vibrant woven blanket. At its center, a tall glass bottle held the dark brew. Ayahuasca—her presence was palpable. Around her, jungle leaves, flowers, small spray bottles, and bundles of feathers sat ready for the ceremony. A bowl of copal incense smoldered, its sweet resinous smoke curling through the air.

Behind the altar, two large, elevated chairs awaited the Shipibo Maestro and Maestra from Peru.

But they wouldn't come today. And, honestly, I wouldn't have come, if they had.

"How many cats do you have?" I asked Alexandra as I dropped my bag by the last remaining mat, exactly in the center of the room. She brought both hands to her face, hiding her eyes, which made Rob, her partner, laugh.

"I'm a little ashamed to answer," she said in a soft singing accent. "We just keep finding the cats, and I can't not take them in."

Rob laughed again. "It's because of her big heart. I keep telling her, there is nothing wrong with having seven cats."

She turned to him with a smile, and he leaned in to kiss her.

Alexandra and Rob were the reason I'd come.

Although I knew there would be ícaros (sacred songs), drums, and a ceremony of the kind I'd once claimed I wanted no part in, La Abuela had been calling me through meditation for weeks. Yet whenever I asked Jordi, he replied it wasn't time for him to hold a ceremony. This had never happened before—was she calling or not? Then I remembered the Sun and Moon platform where I'd once sat for a cacao ceremony with all the potency of stronger sacred medicines. Alexandra and Rob, the facilitators, had immediately felt like family, and the feeling had been mutual.

And, of course—as always unfolds in the world of Ayahuasca—the moment I thought of them, they announced an upcoming ceremony.

If La Abuela was guiding me to sit in the Shipibo tradition, in which Alexandra and Rob had trained for decades with the Maestro and Maestra whose chairs presided over the ceremony—whether physically occupied or not— then I trusted Her.

Draped in a white robe and a colorful ceremonial neckpiece, Alexandra looked like an ancient priestess. She

515

stood in the center of the platform, smoking copal in one hand, a bundle of feathers in the other, and called us one by one into the cleansing smoke.

First was a French woman. From France. She didn't speak English. I did. I spoke both. I didn't want to speak French—not really—but it was her first time with Ayahuasca, and her darting eyes told me that a little translation might ease her brave yet trembling nerves.

Next, a man stepped forward, his fingers moving quickly over his phone. He held it up to Alexandra. She read it, typed a few words back, and nodded. He was deaf. He closed his eyes as the smoke curled around him. Alexandra tapped his shoulder when the smudging was done. He returned to his mat beside mine and smiled at me. A smile just right. I closed my eyes slowly in answer—*yes*, happy to journey beside you too.

I stood in the smoke next, but kept my eyes open.

I was leaving for the States in less than a week. My chocolate melanger was already in the hands of its new leaseholder. Only two things remained: this ceremony and a going-away party at Katuk. But energetically, I was already drifting between the jungle and my Catmobile in the Sedona desert, giddy, light, and untethered. I had come to say Thank You before leaving. I had sensed, or imagined, that was why La Abuela had called me this time—to say Goodbye.

And that is what I told our circle when my turn came to share my intent for this journey.

"I've come to celebrate who I've become, to thank La Abuela for all the gifts she's given me: growth, insights, support, and love. I feel like a chapter of my life is coming to a close. This is my last ceremony."

As I spoke the last words, a tear slipped down my cheek. I couldn't tell if it was for the goodbyes or in gratitude for standing here as this upgraded version of myself.

The woman to my left spoke next. Her striking green eyes burned against the amber-bronze of her skin. She straightened her back, lifted her high cheekbones and sharp jawline, and declared:

"My family fled our country because it was set to fire and blood. We lived in poverty, from one refugee camp to the next. My father left us when I was six years old. He just walked out of the camp, and we never heard from him again. All I remember of him was that he was a violent man. But we survived without him, my mother and I. We made it to Canada. We made it. And we thrived through hard work. But still, this *ancestry*—generations of violence and wars—lives in my cells. This is why I've come. I'm here to clear the trauma of my ancestral line."

She stopped abruptly. Caught in the potency of her words, we all held our breaths for a moment—even Andrew, who couldn't hear her.

"Wow," I thought. "It's her first time with Aya, and she's calling in a full clearing of her ancestral line?" *Ffffffffh.* I blew a Breath of Courage her way before I could catch myself. "Brave woman—she's in for a rough night."

"I'm here to open my throat," the last woman said softly.

She was petite and wrapped in a brown, green, and golden shawl arranged like a cone around her body. She looked like an Elemental, a spirit of the land. I'd never actually seen an Elemental before—just caught glimpses of Woodlings on the Pacific Northwest Trail. But here was one, fully embodied.

"I might sing during the ceremony if that's okay with everyone."

We all nodded eagerly—except Andrew. Her voice was naturally melodious even in speech. I couldn't wait to hear her sing.

And so we were locked in. After a round of Rapé, a sting of Sananga, and finally a cup of Ayahuasca each, we lay back on our mats to await the medicine.

517

A few gentle plucks of guitar strings brought my attention back from the jungle sounds to Alexandra and Rob, sitting at the foot of the Maestro's chair with their instruments.

Tum tum… tum tum… The heartbeat rhythm of the medicine drum joined the slow melody on the guitar. Rob began singing, his voice low, steady, calling. He was inviting La Abuela to our space, to ceremony.

Within a few chords, I felt a trembling in my chest, a wobbling of reality, a shift. She was already here. So fast. The ícaro must have called her.

I knew that the Shipibo shamans worked mostly with the Cielo (Sky Ayahuasca), whereas Jordi grew and brewed the Rojo (Red Ayahuasca), so I had never met this particular Abuela before. Perhaps this one just arrived faster? Ayahuasca caught this thought in my mind and instantly dissolved it. Then I simply knew—she liked the ícaro and had come because it called her.

When the ícaro ended, the body scan began, swift and all-encompassing. This Abuela didn't linger in details. Waves of tingles flowed from my toes to my fingertips and back again. I followed her, curious where she might stop, eager to guess the theme of the journey ahead.

She stopped in my heart and pressed. She pressed and squeezed it to the point of physical pain.

What was left in my heart that needed to be pressed out so hard?

Ana, the Elemental in the cone shawl, began singing. Her voice rose like waves, mingling nonsensical sounds into a language I once had known yet forgotten. For a moment, the familiar sounds held me in a trance. Sobs rose from Andrew's mat, syncing with the rhythm of the melody. Ana's song turned plaintive, like a mournful wail, an undulating chant of grief. He followed her. If she sang louder, he sobbed harder; if her voice softened, he sniffled and sighed.

Oh, this song was for him, for his journey.

I understood the directionality of her song. I was merely in the way of its flow from her to him. I could rest, this wasn't for me.

I returned to observing the ache in my heart. It rippled through my chest and constricted my breath. I couldn't inhale fully, not even enough to gasp. Yet I knew I was fine—this was just an echo through time of asthma attacks I once had as a child.

And suddenly I remembered, through the echo, the colors and shapes of the source scene, which I had not personally lived, yet which was etched in my cells. There was a man—my husband, I think. Suddenly a blow. A flash of red. I was thrown against kitchen drawers. White glare. More blows. My lungs collapsed. Had I died? I couldn't tell. He left the kitchen in a drunken shame. The scene was blurry. *I couldn't see.*

I couldn't see, especially lately. I had needed to get reading glasses. My mother couldn't see either—she had worn glasses her whole life. I had had asthma, and she had suffered from chronic bronchitis. Though I wasn't fully immersed in the medicine yet, these thoughts emerged like woven threads—but the pattern was too vast. I couldn't see it.

Ana's song ended. Andrew sighed and stopped sobbing.

Wait a minute—Andrew couldn't hear. He couldn't hear the song.

The threads linked and interlocked. The women in my family couldn't see because they could no longer witness the violence of the men. And the men in my family couldn't hear—they all lost their hearing at some point—because they could no longer bear the cries of the women.

My stomach lurched, and a gurgle rose through my center core. I sat up, nausea already flooding my throat as I reached for the bucket. But I couldn't force the purge. Instead, a force seemed to scrub every cell in my entire body, gathering anything dark, toxic, ancient, putrid, abandoned, forgotten, aching, unresolved, and in the end, not even mine, into a massive wave of nausea.

I looked up to locate Rob and Alexandra, just in case. A cat ran by and stopped on the French woman's mat. I watched her stroke his fur. He made himself comfortable. Another cat jumped from the garden onto the platform. I hoped for the same attention, but the cat arched his pathway, obviously avoiding me, and instead settled with Ana.

Why were the cats avoiding me?

Because I was Jaguar.

Perhaps I'd always been Jaguar, guiding myself forward like the oak pulls itself from the acorn.

My field of vision narrowed to just the bucket and the curtain of my dreadlocks—jungle vines tethered to Jaguar's spirit. There was strength in me, a primal power exactly in proportion to what was coming. If I faltered even an ounce, this process would consume me.

What process?

I felt Ayahuasca gently push me aside, although my physical body remained firmly planted above the bucket, held upright by one arm pressing on the platform. My double-jointed elbow bent and circled as my body began to shake.

In the shaking, another scene emerged. I was a little girl with wooden clogs—les sabots—the kind worn in small provincial French villages. I wore a blue dress and a white apron. What had I done? Maybe nothing. But the man—my father—lifted and shook me with such force that both my arms broke. That was why I was born with hyper-extending elbows, and my mother before me, and her mother before her.

This body here, in this life, held the telltale signs of traumas passed down from all previous generations. Embedded in my DNA was the echo of broken bones, broken hearts, crushed lungs, fear, death, and even declining eyesight.

Ana began singing again. I retched. Her voice flowed through me, each note pulling nausea upward. Her tone rose; a small wave of vomit left. Suddenly the world narrowed to nothing but that small puddle of black foamy bile at the bottom of the bucket.

There was a snake down my throat and center core, as thick as my calf and as slick as scaly silk. I had never known that snake was there. The doctor had come to remove it.

"It will be unpleasant," she said with a wordless matter-of-fact energy. "Please stay aside; you couldn't handle everything that's coming out."

She tugged on the snake, lifting my throat.

Thank you, Doctor. Thank you for removing the snake. I'm ready.

And it came out. My body shook, my elbow circled, and Jaguar's vines bound me like roots, keeping me steady as the snake, generation after generation, came out, released in vile bile into the bucket, which I could no longer see. Images flashed—broken bottles, cutting, blood, drunken men, shame, more drunkenness, cries, and back to the beginning, in endless cycles.

It was Ana's song. Her song was calling the snake out. I *hated* that unrelenting song, even though her voice was hauntingly beautiful.

"Stop it," I yelled between my teeth. Then I feared Ayahuasca might mistake my plea to be addressed to her. She'd find me disrespectful and perhaps leave before the snake was fully out. "Not you!" I cried out. "Thank you, thank you," I whispered into the bucket, then realized, no one could tell to whom I was speaking, human or medicine. And so Ana's song continued, and the purging with it.

I stood to the side as glimpses of lives I hadn't lived flashed by, like a movie playing in fast reverse—a movie I couldn't see, only perceive as flickering shadows and mixed colors reflected on the wall of my mind.

Further and further back through time, my mind traced violence like a thread, unraveling from the provincial French village through wars fought on horseback with swords, and

521

even further, to apes shrieking as they ran with bones. I stood to the side, lost in the flow, anchored only in gratitude, repeating, "Thank you, Doctor, thank you..." like a mantra.

Suddenly, a spray. The soothing pink scent of flowers. A hand caressed my hair. Alexandra.

"There is a lot of power in your dreads," she whispered, caressing my head like a caring mother. "I know," I nodded. Just then, my body shook with such force that the circling elbow gave out. I collapsed, but a hand caught me. A male hand—the Sacred Masculine—his fingers found mine, and I locked into this anchor in the storm.

Ana's song finally ended, but I kept going, further and further back in time through the rise and fall of primordial forests. The violence was not yet human, but it was still there—in the snapping of jaws, the chase, the fight for survival. It wasn't cruel. It wasn't personal. Not yet.

"Please, don't let go," I said to the hand holding me.

"I'm right here. I've got you," it said back.

But even the hand couldn't hold me anymore. I wasn't just exhausted—I was emptied, scrubbed raw where the snake had been pulled free.

Was it fully out?

My hollowed body gave out, and I collapsed onto the mat.

I swam. There was no up, no down, no sides. No platform, no body, no colors, no shapes. Nothing. I simply swam in the wobbly nothingness of the medicine.

And still, her tendrils reached deeper, sucking the marrow from my cells.

"How far, Abuela? How far up the ancestral line are we going? How much more are you clearing?"

My neck suddenly snapped back, and the image of the Archaeopteryx—the oldest bird fossil—flashed in my mind, its neck frozen in classic avian death pose. Oh, no. All the way to the beginning? Did I carry the violence of my ancestors since the dawn of time? A moan escaped my lips.

Tum tum… tum tum… A drum answered my moan. Alexandra's voice followed, steady and wonderfully warm. The melody was unhurried; it simply circled, wrapping around me like a vine, like the arms of a mother. It anchored me, spiraling me inward and down. My breath deepened, my body regained gravity, and I felt the mat beneath me. The gentle ícaro had brought me back to this reality.

As I regained awareness, I noticed my head was where I thought my feet had been. Somehow, I had collapsed one way and awakened another. I scanned my heart, my core—the snake was gone. Two mosquitoes buzzed by my face. I reached for the blanket with one hand and pulled it over my body, then realized my neck was still kinked back in avian death pose.

Gathering the thick mane of my dreadlocks in both hands, I realigned my neck to my spine. My body still swam, wrung out and trembling, but my mind had surfaced into clarity. I remembered only glimpses of what had flashed through—too many faces, too many lives. I understood the forgetting was part of the medicine. A kindness, really.

How far had we gone?

Archaeopteryx—the oldest bird fossil.

From earthbound to airborne. Violence was older than flight, but wings marked the first great escape—a leap into a new dimension of possibility. And there was something else…

Wait a minute. That image—why that one?

Even mid-surgery, La Abuela had slipped in her signature playfulness. The Archaeopteryx—so oddly specific, so brilliantly random. The first to fly, to escape to the skies… yet she kinked my neck to mimic its fossilized death pose. She was either hilarious or more profound than I could grasp.

I felt her smile curl through me, pleased I'd gotten her joke at last. I chuckled, then laughed, and her joy rippled throughout me as we laughed together.

And with that, everything settled.

Every muscle in my body, so tense during the purging, finally loosened, safe on the mat. Alexandra's voice remained, her song cradling me in a kind of reassurance I hadn't known I needed. There was no urgency, only the endless patience of a mother or sister bringing me back piece by piece.

How resilient women were. Through eons of violence, they still found in their hearts a place for songs, for bright colors, for dances. They gathered and supported each other.

The original women's circles, I suddenly realized, weren't full moon witch gatherings, but safe havens from violence. They were a reprieve, a place where wooden clogs could be dropped, and hands could knit, create, and heal unhindered. With patience and love, they healed themselves and each other. They even healed those whose hands caused them harm.

Alexandra's song shifted, now light and playful. The notes danced upward, lifting my thoughts and mood with them. Ha, but women's circles had evolved. No longer born from the need to escape and heal trauma, they now sprang from shared excitement, from the joy of co-creation. A gathering of new energy, a female vision for the future. The song rose even higher, when suddenly—

Cocorico. Cocorico. Cocorico.

It wasn't even dawn, yet the strangest rooster crow tore through the night, interrupting Alexandra's song. Everybody laughed, except for Andrew and me.

"Was that a rooster?" Alexandra whispered to Rob.

"It's the comic-relief rooster," Rob whispered back, and they both giggled.

I smiled. They had both been such powerful anchors of safety during my journey, I had almost forgotten they were also loving, giggly humans.

But that rooster? My smile faded. I didn't think he was funny at all. That had been in French too. Roosters universally crowed a sort of "Err-uh-err-uhhh-uhhhhh," which we transcribed in English as "Cock-a-doodle-doo" and in Spanish as "Ki-kiri-kikí," but this rooster had very clearly said, "Cocorico." This wasn't a random middle-of-the-night rooster crow; it was a message, for *me*.

Cocorico—the rallying cry of the Gaulois, the people of Gallus, the proud rooster, now known as the French.

"Why do you reject your French heritage so much?" my mother once asked me under her breath. Didn't I know? The French invented... practically everything that mattered—the metric system, the hot air balloons, the baguette, the croissant, bold wine, and sophisticated cheese. And the French language was the language of love and diplomacy. *Cocorico!*

"I was born in the US. Don't you remember?" A poor argument, but the only one I knew would close that discussion.

The truth was, I didn't want to be French, speak French, or eat French. I didn't drink wine, and I was gluten- and lactose-intolerant.

I rejected it all—every last bit of it.

Ayahuasca pulled the threads taut, revealing the truth— Oh! I *had* to reject it.

Cocorico wasn't just a rooster's cry. It was the voice of my lineage, calling me back. The French pride I had fought so fiercely wasn't just arrogance; it was the armor of a people who had survived. I had rejected it, not because France, its history, or its pride were wrong, but because to heal a story, you must first leave it. You have to break its gravity, rebel against its pull, and live outside its cycles before you can return with the tools to transform it. Rejection had been my shield, my cocoon, my protection while I gathered strength, wisdom, and allies.

Because I wasn't just born into this lineage—I *chose* it. And out of all who had volunteered, I had been chosen. To be the one who breaks the cycles, who clears the traumas, who says, "It stops here, with me."

I was an End of the Line Kid. One of the greatest honors for a soul.

Ayahuasca wove the threads even tighter, revealing new connections in old stories.

Beyond *Cocorico*—the national pride—was a more intimate pride, passed down through the women in my family, generation after generation.

My grandmother—my mother's mother—was born and raised in a small village in the French countryside, where shallow greetings kept the village quaint while trauma brewed behind closed doors. She married a foreigner—from the next village, five kilometers away. Unheard of. Then came the war and their move to the big city with my mother, who was just a child. The villagers gossiped, their feathers ruffled. My grandmother traded her wooden clogs for work shoes, found work as a cleaning lady, and lived into her late nineties with her head held high, shoulders back, and a straight spine.

My mother grew up in that city. At thirteen, with nothing but her own courage, she took a bus to the judiciary court and told the *Juge des enfants*—the children's judge—what her father had done. The judge came to their home, and the violence ended that day. At twenty-one, she boarded a ship with one small suitcase and her cat in a carry-case and sailed across the Atlantic to Martinique. She never again lived in France. She broke away—the first in her lineage to leave the country. She still walks in the world with her head held high.

And there I was, seven years old, body braced to remain upright in spite of the blows. I wouldn't cry—I wouldn't give her that satisfaction. Instead, eyes burning but dry, I asked, "Do you think you'll be done hitting me soon? 'Cause I've got some playing to do and I'd like to get back to it." She had cried that day, and I had run back to the woods. At twenty-one, I packed my suitcase and left the island, bound for the U.S., never to return.

There was the thread: courage and quiet defiance passed down like an heirloom, not just in choices of lifestyles, but in our very spines—straight, unyielding, proud. Each generation cleared as much trauma as possible and passed on the rest as pain, which in turn carved the strength and resilience to continue the clearing, like a relay race to the finish.

I had seen it before—this rigid posture, this cold protective shell that demanded respect and obedience, masking fragility with the force of dominance. Ayahuasca had shown it to me that night with the Lizard. That's right… I was part Lizard.

Another connection.

Lizard and Jaguar were woven from the same thread.

Lizard armored itself against the world, enduring without question, hardened by wounds it accepted as life, unaware they were part of a greater story. Until an End of the Line Kid cracked it open, and Jaguar stepped through. Jaguar, who walked through the darkness with eyes open, hunting its own shadows to alchemize them into fluid mastery, transmuting survival into personal power.

At last, all the threads came into view, revealing the full mandala of my life, woven with flawless intent.

Nothing—*nothing*—had been wasted.

The kind, safe husband—his love, a cocoon. A place to rest and incubate until the call of destiny grew too loud to ignore. The years of solitude—an alchemical fire. They stripped me down and called me home. In the silence of the desert, I remembered who I was. I found the allies who would walk beside me, and the teachers who would guide me. Every relationship arrived like clockwork, specifically to crack me open. Heartbreak, confusion—these were the steps to the threshold, designed to unearth the old seeds my mother had carried—had passed to me. Not out of malice, but out of trust. Trust that I would take the pattern to its end, burn it clean, and offer something new.

And thanks to Aya, I had.

All of us—we were a team, bound by a love older than blood and stronger than time.

And for the first time I could remember, I felt real love for my mother. Not just forgiveness, but love rooted in respect, understanding, and gratitude.

Scenes of our life together unfolded in my mind. Every moment, every action reframed itself in the light of this new understanding, the light of Love. Tears welled in my eyes and spilled over.

I saw myself—a relentless, wild child pushing every boundary she set. My defiance, rejection, and constant self-reinvention were not so different from hers. She had come so far from her roots, bravely walking toward our shared goal without even a guide. No Jaguar, Cacao, or sacred medicines had shown her the way. She had only her own strength, intellect, and unyielding will.

Ha! Except she did have one ally…

…as the images unfolded, I noticed that in every chapter of my mother's life, there was always a cat.

A sweet black minette was her childhood companion. That same minette crossed the Atlantic, witnessed my birth, then crossed the Pacific to New Caledonia. A ginger tabby purred on her lap as she read me bedtime stories in Houaïlou. A striped minette's green eyes glowed in the shadows as I crept back into the house after my teenage escapades. She'd be there for my mother when I got caught, pressing against her legs as the anger, the outrage, set in.

Wherever my mother was, she had a cat—supporting, anchoring, and comforting her in ways I had never before understood.

I opened my eyes and scanned the platform, spotting three of the seven cats—one with Ana, another with Andrew, and a third with the French woman. The petite cat curled against Andrew stared at me through half-closed lids.

I had no doubt she could see the images in my head. I just hoped she understood—my childhood dislike of cats had never been personal. It was part of a greater rejection plan. As an adult, I loved, respected, even admired them.

She slowly closed her eyes. A silent acknowledgment. And I felt forgiven.

The guitar's strings pulled my attention back to my body, deeply relaxed, melted onto the mat like a liquid cat in the sun.

The notes filled my ears, each with its own color, mingling into a radiant spectrum that shimmered on the screen of my mind. There was such joy in those colors; I closed my eyes to take in the spectacle.

Through the colors, an old-fashioned Rolodex appeared, spinning in my mind—*prrrrrrr*—each card someone I'd met, each face flashing in a blur. Friends, acquaintances, even memorable strangers. Thousands of faces, spinning—each one a distinct glint of the rainbow, carrying its own hue of memory, essence, or lesson.

Who were they?

"Here is one," Ayahuasca said in a cheery voice. The Rolodex slowed and landed on the scene of Isabel and me, in the middle of a heated argument on my patio six months prior.

"A powerful one, that one! She volunteered to dissolve Spanish aristocratic pride in her paternal lineage—refinement like a mask, elegance as currency, status a survival strategy. She learned that poise could outrun poverty, that dignity could be stitched into fabric. She's here to unravel that spell and step into true wealth. That's why you were to not work when she visited. There needed to be a sufficient gap in your financial means for the pattern to be activated. Such a perfect trigger-pair you two are. And… she's right, you know. You two *are* soul-mates… and you will be friends again."

My heart constricted at the memory of our last days together.

"I'm not interested in that friendship, honestly. I wish her well, but it wasn't very nourishing. And I don't miss her."

"Of course. She hasn't cleared it yet, and you two are connected energetically. When she does, you'll wake up one day, smile, and feel like calling her. There will be no need for apologies. You'll both just know it's done."

The Rolodex spun again—*prrrrrr*—and stopped on a scene of Jim and me sitting by a fire in the woods. We were on mushrooms that night, and I saw it—his darkness. It loomed around him, thick and impenetrable, but he seemed completely unaffected. He joked, tended the fire, and kept the night safe for my journey. I hadn't known what to make of it then.

Ayahuasca now applied her lens to the memory. Jim's original blueprint unraveled before me—lines converging, all bottlenecked in his heart.

"He's here to clear both his father's and mother's lines!?" I couldn't believe it. Clearing one line had felt like a Herculean task; I couldn't imagine clearing two.

"Oh, he's here to clear more than that," she said with a glint in her voice. "But Jim doesn't play by the rules—never did, not even in the Beyond." She paused, her tone softening into reverence. "He's chosen to live one life holding on to as many end of lines as possible, all wrapped tightly and hermetically sealed in his heart. None of it will be passed to his children. He'll take it all with him when he passes from this realm."

My jaw dropped. That was the darkness I had felt from the beginning—compressed end-of-the-line burdens he carried so that no one else would have to. He wasn't even conscious of his choice; he simply lived. I bowed inwardly. Respect.

I'd never tell him—he'd chosen not to know—but I knew I'd never see him the same way again.

"And what if the burden is too great?" I'd known another who drowned his with alcohol and cocaine. But stories didn't dissolve that way; they only waited. "What happens then, Aya?"

"If he's not an End of the Line Kid, the thread continues—to a child, a sibling, someone not yet born. But if he is… then it clears. One way or another. Even if it takes a lifetime. Even if it takes his very last breath. The threads weave differently for each soul. Remember, it's always a shared task and linear time is an illusion."

"Aya, why do I know so many End of the Line Kids?"

"Because this is the time of the Shift. The time when the world unbinds itself from the old stories—fear, power, walls built higher than hope. The Earth, as an organism, is ready to rise, to spiral back out into the light after it fully explored itself spiraling in. And you—you are the dismantlers, clearing space for new growth."

She paused, her tone softening, playful now. "And it's not so dire and heavy as it seems from the density of physical reality. I promise—there was joy in your choosing. You couldn't wait to get here and get in it, front row for the big collective awakening. The last generation to truly be righteously dramatic."

Ayahuasca's words rang true. Of course, I would have chosen to live on Earth during this epic shift. I was a Storyteller, and this was one of the best stories in all of Creation.

"So, what happens after the End of the Line Kids? When there's no more trauma to pass on—do humans simply stop having children?"

"No, no," she laughed. "Then come the Rainbow Kids— pure creators—and the New Earth they've already imagined."

As she spoke, an explosion of vivid colors burst into my mind. My other journeys each had their own tones and color palettes, but this… She laughed again. "Yes, you were getting much too attached to the color schemes of your journeys. Let's break that pattern."

Waves of rainbows surged through me—sparkling, dazzling, almost alive—and with them a peace so profound it felt as if I'd never again have a care in the world.

An image began to take shape—a road, a village, a town.

The New Earth—I felt it, I saw it. Peaceful yet vibrant, like a sigh of relief. Cities were grown, not built. Each home was an agreement with the land, shaped with reverence by conscious carpenters who asked the trees before felling them. The walls breathed, vines laced with light, and roofs dripped with gardens that filtered water, clean and abundant. Fields of food flourished in quiet kinship with the soil, tended with songs. Children, barefoot and wide-eyed, ran free or sat in mossy circles, listening to stories told by elders and trees.

Humans no longer ruled the world—they walked in harmony with it. Hunters offered prayers before they aimed. Cooks thanked the plants before slicing. Teachers passed on the wisdom once revealed by cacao, by silence, by the sea. We didn't tame nature; we learned to belong to it.

Life still ended, as it always had. Cats hunted mice. Hands brushed away mosquitoes. But there was no dominance, no distortion. Only the sacred exchange—the dance of life in balance, of instinct without cruelty, of ending as part of beginning.

And yes, there were still roosters.

One stood on a post beside a communal oven, watching the scene like a monk. He didn't crow—but everyone still knew when he had something to say.

And in this gentler place, we turned to joy—minds exploring, feet dancing, voices singing, hands creating. Not from need, but from wonder.

Tum tum… I had been so gleefully lost in the rainbow vision of the Earth to come, I almost forgot I was on a platform in a jungle, where two kind humans had carried our journeys with songs. The liquid notes of the guitar strings joined the drum into a slow, tender melody. I felt each string pull me back into this reality, and I fought it at first—I was just there, in a world I always suspected existed, with the wisest, kindest, and most powerful teacher plant.

Leave me here, please.

But each drumbeat anchored me further into my mat, my body, this physical reality. Alexandra's soft voice rose over the drum and guitar, singing our farewell and our gratitude for all that was purified and healed during the ceremony.

Gracias Abuelita. Gracias.

La Abuela responded to the ícaro, fading from my consciousness like smoke on the breeze.

And she was gone.

ဆ · ൯

Cocles Beach, Puerto Viejo - the next day

Under the dappled shade of an almond tree friend, I buried my feet in warm sand and gazed at the ocean. The waves danced, throwing themselves onto the sand with reckless abandon before bubbling back to the sea.

Oh, I too was bubbling.

It was done. The mission I chose before birth—the honor of clearing the line, breaking its cycles, and opening the path for the Rainbow Kids—was fulfilled. Gracias, Abuelita.

And not just for me. In the morning circle with Alexandra and Rob, as we all giddily plunged fingers into cups of dates and almonds, sharing our journeys, I turned to the woman with striking green eyes.

"I think I picked up your intent. Aya cleared my matrilineal ancestral line."

She laughed, shaking her head. "And I picked up yours. All night, I saw how far I've come, how brave I've been… I felt a kind of gentle self-love I'd never known before. And you—every time you purged into that bucket, I felt lighter. Somehow, I knew what your journey was about. It was as if you were clearing ancestral lines not just for yourself, but also lightening those of everyone who carries violence in their blood. That's what I felt."

Yes. The feeling of accomplishment was vast, like the whole Universe grinning. But I hadn't done it alone. The triumph wasn't just mine. It was my grandmother's, my mother's, Logan's, Joe's—the whole team. The love and gratitude I felt for each of them filled my heart beyond capacity. Then, for just a moment, my consciousness opened, tasting a force even greater than love and triumph.

Play!

It was an honor—not because the world was a dreadful place with ugly structures in need of dismantling, but because I got to play at *this* level of the Game. Because a game it was. All of it. Life, the Universe, God, Aya, Jaguar—all of it.

And suddenly I was back. Back in my body, back on the sand, back to this absurd, magnificent, ridiculous game.

I giggled. The waves seemed to get the joke—rise, crash, retreat, rise again. They had always known. They'd been playing the Game for eternity and never tired of it.

So what happened now? Did I win? Had I done everything I came here to do? I doubted I'd live long enough, in this plane of consciousness, to see the Rainbow Kids' New Earth take form. So what else was there? What could possibly be more intricate and exhilarating than walking the path of an End of the Line Kid?

My eyes drifted over the ocean until they stopped on Cocles Island.

I suppose I could die now.

Or…

I could swim to the island again, and this time actually climb to the top, call as Aya had instructed me, and see what the next level of the Game might be…

Chapter 33
Epilogue

Bribri, Costa Rica – May 2023 (written that morning)

"Mama Aya, you sound like me."

"I do," she replies in my voice.

"If you sound like me, how will I know if it's you or me speaking inside my head when I'm off traveling the world and I need your guidance?"

"Sometimes, it will be me. Sometimes it will be you. And you will not know which is which." I feel her tendrils in my heart, like a tickle. "Isn't it delightfully fun?"

I laugh out loud.

It's only four days after the End of the Line journey. She warned me, "Stay on the dieta; you're going right back in." Three days later, Jordi called. He was preparing to sit with La Abuela and a friend. Did I want to join them? Of course, I did. One more meeting with Mama Aya to say goodbye and thank her before flying away.

Now it's toward the end of the night and Aya is fading, but still I feel her arms, her loving motherly arms, wrapped around my curled body. On the platform with me are two men—two wonderful friends: Jordi and Yolanda's husband—and four dogs. I feel safe with them, and for once, I have the

Queen's Mat.

They've been asleep a while. How long? I don't know—a fraction of a tree breath. But I won't sleep. I refuse. This is my last night with Aya. I leave Costa Rica in two days. Final destination unknown as of the writing of this story. And so, I won't sleep. I want to be with her until the last moment possible.

Tonight she crowned me—not above anyone, but as Sovereign Queen of my own Queendom, as I am—dirty nails and adventures, mountain climbs and wild dances, quiet meditations and oh so many questions, and a little wisdom, too—that kind of queen. She prepared me for the journey ahead, showed me my strengths, and stripped away anything childish, petty, or unworthy of a queen. She was a focused, relentless Maestra. All that she stripped out of me now lies in the bucket, waiting to be returned to the Earth.

"What should we title this chapter? I was thinking *Queen Bee*."

"You won't write this chapter. *The End of the Line Chapter* is the last chapter. If you want to write another chapter, you'll have to write another book."

I nod under the cover. Yes. That makes sense. It's in the name.

"I will miss you, Aya."

"Nonsense, Child. How can you miss me? I'm everywhere. I'm in the sound of drops on the roof, the aroma of the earth. I'm in the waving leaf, the twisted juniper, the howl of Coyote, and yes, I'm in you, too."

"Wait. You, Ayahuasca, are everywhere? Am I speaking with the vine or with Pachamama? Or with God? Who am I actually speaking with?"

She smiles in my mind. "As I said before, you're not meant to understand everything."

For once, it feels sufficient.

537

As the night continues to slip gently toward dawn, Aya retreats, and I'm alone in my mind. My eyes drift over the jungle canopy, slowly waking with the sounds of the day crew.

Just as I'm about to drift into sleep, her presence suddenly floods me again, like a flash of love.

"You might be a queen, but you're still my child." In her full Caribbean sass and green and red flower dress, she squeezes me in her arms.

"Listen. You are brave, beautiful, and powerful." She kisses my forehead, like a blessing. "Now, go out in the world and represent me well."

And just as fast as she'd returned, she's gone again.

But I still smile. And I know—not as a thought but as a full-body truth:

This plant loves me.

Still now, as on the first night.

And forever forward, wherever I may go.

And I also know, that I am hers, so I whisper into the night,

"I pledge allegiance to the plants, and to Pachamama, the Earth Goddess for which they stand—one unified, conscious planet, with freedom, sovereignty and respect for all."

૪ · ૭

The first light grazes the canopy. Aya is gone, but I still feel her love in my heart. I don't know when or if I'll ever be on this platform again... and I still have so many questions.

If she's always with me, as she said, then I should be able to just ask.

I decide to test it.

"Aya, why do you help humans heal? Wouldn't it be simpler to let us fall, and let the plants take back the Earth?"

A chuckle in my mind, and an answer in my voice: "Oh Child... why do you write?"

I pause, hesitate. "I'm not sure *I* write, actually. It's more like writing happens through me. And I love how it feels so I continue doing it."

"Exactly. Then you understand."

AFTERWORDS

Ayahuasca, La Abuela

The journeys with Ayahuasca described in this book are not typical.

No Ayahuasca journey is—she builds upon the psyche, the stories, the archetypes already within us.

Ayahuasca is not a high, a trend, or a balm for loneliness.

She is an ancient, wise, and powerful Teacher.

Seeking her guidance should never be a decision to partake, nor a curiosity to satisfy, but an undeniable call from the medicine herself.

If and when she calls you, you'll know.

Cacao Music

"Ever since Costa Rica, I played nothing but what I called Cacao music—grounded earth songs with wooden flutes, drums, didgeridoos, and softly picked guitars to a background of jungle sounds. I could have sworn the beans tasted sweeter when I played them Cacao music." From Ch. 24 - *Cacaocito*

Deep gratitude to *Ayahuasca (Original Motion Picture Soundtrack)* and every live set of **Poranguí** recorded at *Sugarshack*—sacred rhythms that walked beside me through my becoming a chocolate maker and the writing of this book.

Floripondia

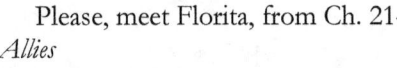

Please, meet Florita, from Ch. 21- *Allies*

https://www.instagram.com/ fungifloripondia/

Mushroom art, tattoos, illustrations, and eco-friendly merchandise.

Thank Yous:

Deep bows of gratitude to Jaron, Kuyoti, and Anthony for the wind beneath my publishing wings. Thank you for trusting my vision and financing my meticulous obsession.

Thank you to my Puerto Viejo tribe for your love and unending encouragement. Thank you for dancing on the platform by the sea, and for eating chocolate.

Thank you to Leah, Micah, Lily, Heather, Russ, and the whole gang at the Local Grocer in North Conway. You are the reliable, restful lily pad that lets my journeys unfold. You are family.

Thank you to the Yep Yeps in Dexter, to Jeannie in Pensacola, to Shannon in Los Angeles, to Zzenn in Sedona, and to Deborah in Bellingham for being a home when the Catmobile and I need one. And to everyone else who should be on this list—rest assured, you're in my heart (especially you, Pikachu).

Thank you to the Sedona Library for those large windows with views of red rocks. I chose you well as a publishing portal.

Thank you to Kyle and Hailey of Food for Bears in Conway, for your love, patience, enthusiasm, and throat tea—and for capturing the wild flow of my storytelling for the audiobook with such expert ears and tender hearts.

Thank you to Jordi. For everything. May you enjoy a well-deserved retirement.

Thank you to you, my reader, for coming along on this journey.

Truly, this book belongs to all of you.

MORE ADVENTURES BY MAYA WYLD:

CRAZY FREE
An Epic Spiritual Journey

Ten years before I met Jaguar, I lived an irreproachably comfortable and predictable life with Jack, my husband of ten years. The path to my dream future—to become a geophysics research professor—was clear and unobstructed. Then, one day, my soul slipped out and floated up.

At the time, I believed I was my physical self. Nothing about "me" could exist beyond it. A moment later, I was pulled back into my body—but not completely.

What had just happened? And who was this "I" that could float away? Was I going crazy?

There was only one way to find out: I dove into the Rabbit Hole.

I wrote *Crazy Free* to tell the truth about what I found down there, maybe so I'd believe it myself and never forget.

In my quest for self, I left everything I knew behind, walked from Mexico to Canada on the Pacific Crest Trail, kayaked the Yukon River, and explored the path of discipline in the Himalayan foothills. I loved so much it cracked me open. I made an off-grid home in the Catmobile and... you know the rest.

If *Once, When I Was Tree* is the bloom—*this* is the seed.

Before tree conversations, nomadic living, and plant medicines, there was the choice:

Surrender to the path of magic and unconventionality or shrink back into a world of debts, jobs, fears and fluorescent lights.

Pass it on
Leave a review
Tell your friends

Pachamama's Library of
Greater Goodness

ONCE, WHEN I WAS TREE – Wyld, M

Date   Read by

. The end .

www.ingramcontent.com/pod-product-compliance
Lightning Source LLC
Chambersburg PA
CBHW060401130626
46555CB00005B/1960